Beppi Crosariol

Anne Kingston's writing has appeared in *The Globe and Mail, Saturday Night, Toronto Life,* and the *Chicago Sun-Times Magazine.* She is a columnist for the *National Post,* where she writes on social and cultural issues.

www.picadorusa.com

Picador® is a U.S. registered trademark and is used by Farrar, Straus and Giroux
under license from Pan Books Limited.

For information on Picador Reading Group Guides, as well as ordering, please
contact Picador.
Phone: 646-307-5629
Fax: 212-253-9627
E-mail: readinggroupguides@picadorusa.com

Library of Congress Cataloging-in-Publication Data

Kingston, Anne, 1957–
    The meaning of wife / Anne Kingston.
        p. cm.
    Originally published: Toronto : HarperCollins, 2004.
    Includes bibliographical references and index.
    ISBN 0-312-42500-7
    EAN 978-0-312-42500-5
    1. Wives. 2. Women—Identity. 3. Women—Social conditions. I. Title.

    HQ759.K548 2005
    306.872'3—dc22   2004050621

First published in Canada by HarperCollins Publishers Ltd

First published in the United States by Farrar, Straus and Giroux

First Picador Edition: March 2006

10 9 8 7 6 5 4 3 2 1

Anne Kingston

The Meaning of Wit

Picador

Farrar, Straus and Giroux
New York

FOR KATIE, MADELINE, CLAIRE, AND SAM,
THE NEXT GENERATION OF WIVES

We live our lives through texts. They may be read or chanted, or experienced electronically, or come to us like the murmurings of our mothers, telling us what conventions demand. Whatever their form or medium, these stories have formed us all. They are what we must use to make new fictions, new narratives.

—Carolyn Heilbrun, *Writing a Woman's Life*

Contents

Prologue

Once upon a time, a gilded horse-drawn carriage passed through the palace gates accompanied by the hard clop-clop of hooves against cobblestones and the buoyant cheers of crowds lining the streets. Inside the carriage sat a bride, veiled, an impressionistic blur.

That is my first memory of July 29, 1981, the "Wedding of the Century" day, the day Prince Charles married Lady Diana Spencer. I had set my alarm for four and stumbled, like millions of others, bleary-eyed in front of the television. I had been drawn by a mysterious gravitational force. Free will had nothing to do with it.

My fascination with Diana was a dark secret. I chalked it up to a synaptic misfiring. That had to be it. Otherwise, it made no sense. I was only a year older than she, and living in my first apartment, as she had been. Even so, it felt as if decades, centuries, existed between us. Marriage was on my theoretical to-do list. I didn't realize then that I was among the first generation of women able to take such a laissez-faire attitude, able to see marriage as an option, like choosing a sunroof on a new car. A few friends from university had wed, an impulse I couldn't yet relate to. Marrying meant settling, as in down.

Nor did I need princely rescue. I harbored no seed-pearl or diamond-tiara fantasies. White was not my color. Princesses, even manufactured ones, weren't part of my landscape. Even so, fairy tales, even manufactured ones, can exert a narcotic effect. And, as a processed princess, Diana was central-casting perfect. She was young, barely past girlhood, while her groom was thirty-two. She was lovely, fair of hair and disposition. Her lineage was aristocratic enough. She worked in a kindergarten. Her maternal instinct was much lauded, a crucial detail, given the breeding duties required of her. Adding immensely to Diana's suitability was the fact she showed no signs of ambition for a career beyond wife. Not that anyone saw Diana becoming a wife. She was being transformed into a princess. There would be no palace drudgery for her, so we believed.

Diana was treated as a rare archeological find—a nineteen-year-old virgin excavated in 1980s London. Adding a medieval touch, one of her less discreet relatives revealed that Queen Elizabeth's gynecologist had examined the future princess to ensure her hymen was intact. Such creepy, retrograde details were overlooked, however, so focused were we on a fantasy custom-ordered for the modern female audience. Diana's was the ultimate before-after makeover—from unknown to celebrity, from pudgy teenager to sylphlike princess-to-be, from single girl to princess. But the makeover worked two ways. Diana brought to the prince and the royal family the illusion of youthful vigor.

More important, she gave the British economy a boost. Citizens, desiring a piece of the royal romance, queued up to purchase crockery and other mementos adorned with the images of the prince and future princess. Young women, entranced by Diana's story, imitated her clothing and haircut. After the engagement was announced, cheap knockoffs of her ring—an eighteen-carat sapphire surrounded by diamonds— sold out. One New York City jeweler reported that half his customers chose similar settings in the days after the wedding.

I remember feeling slightly horrified by my giddy excitement as Diana stepped out of her carriage at St. Paul's Cathedral. This was the big moment. Not the nuptials, but the dress reveal. The bride was swaddled in écru silk taffeta adorned with thousands of pearls and sequins and boasting a twenty-five-foot court train. She presented as the ultimate confectionery, a human meringue. Inexpensive versions of the gown would be available in stores a week later so commoners could purchase a polyester version of the fantasy.

An overhead camera provided an aerial view—Diana's slow procession down the aisle with her father, her train a long sliver of white against the bloody red of the carpet. Despite the pageantry, the ceremony was like all weddings—archaic yet common: the handing-off of the bride from father to husband; the "I do's" of eternal fealty; the couple exiting the church, newly conjoined.

After a joyous ride through the streets of London, the Prince and Princess of Wales stood together on the balcony of Buckingham Palace. The crowd called for them to kiss. They did, a quick peck, to the delight of their subjects. Were this a true fairy tale, the story would have ended there. Nice and neat. Happily ever after. Fade to black. Production credits.

But as we know, the camera kept on rolling. Charles and Diana's wedding imagery became fractured, confused. In the next reel, the princess transmogrifies into a tragic heroine. Her veil becomes her shroud, her gilded carriage a cage. The bridal costume that so resembled an elaborate pastry can now be seen as an ominous reminder of how she would become consumed by the role. She was the quintessential product. Years later, the *Vanity Fair* editor Graydon Carter, commenting on Diana's commercial viability, said, "When she was alive, Diana sold."

The horse-drawn carriage that transported her to her marriage morphed into a black Mercedes careering through a Parisian tunnel on the night of her death. The doting father who sat beside her on her wedding day was replaced by a louche playboy at her life's end. Diana might have freed herself from the shackles of her marriage, but to the end she was always the passenger.

We know so much more now than we did then. We know now that the alleged Wedding of the Century was an arranged marriage fraught with feudal overtones. As the future king, Charles, who had put off marrying, needed a wife to sit beside him as queen and, more important, to provide heirs, preferably male, to the throne. So blinded were we by the mythical romance of it all that we couldn't see this was not a love match, even if the bride believed it so. We didn't see that Diana had been slotted into her position like someone sent from personnel. For a time, she did her job well, producing two sons, "an heir and a spare." But then she made a fatal mistake: she didn't understand that her role, like all roles, had a script. And then, once she did understand, she chose to defy the narrative, for which she would dearly pay.

Most of all, we couldn't possibly have foreseen on that morning that Diana's life would mirror, in cartoonish proportion, a trajectory traveled by many women of her generation—enchantment to fairy-tale wedding, to motherhood, followed by disenchantment, adultery, betrayal, revenge, and divorce. And that she would experience renewal as a single-woman heroine, one who spoke in clichés of her marriage being a cage from which she had been freed. What was left unspoken was the fact that had she never been Charles's wife, no one would have been listening.

Diana's tragic tale encapsulates the confusion surrounding the modern wife. We see that wife, as we saw Diana, in uncertain terms—real yet iconic, a heroine yet a tragic figure. She represents past and present, fact and fiction. Most of all, she is a mystery. Which makes her definition ripe for manipulation, the perfect battleground for the insidious battle now being waged over female identity.

The Meaning of Wife

Chapter 1

The Wife Gap

Wife. Four letters. One syllable. Simple, or so it seems. Yet this common word has become one of the most complex signifiers in the English language, weighted by past definitions, blurred by personal biases. The associations it elicits are bipolar in their scope: by the beginning of the twenty-first century, wife was variously presented as the source of female damnation or salvation, enchantment or disenchantment, captivity or rescue. Take your pick. Evidence can be marshaled to support either case. The truth exists in neither.

At one extreme, the role of wife is perceived as a straitjacket, one an increasing number of women refuse to don, as reflected in a marriage rate that has been declining, with the occasional uptick, in North America for the past one hundred years. By 2004, unmarried women were the fastest-growing demographic. A thirty-year-old woman was three times more likely to be single than she was in the 1970s; the more money a woman earned, the more likely she was to delay or even forgo matrimony. A much-reported 1999 study from the National Marriage Project at Rutgers University found that high school girls were more accepting of cohabitation and children born out of wedlock than they had been in two decades. While they expressed a desire to marry, they voiced declining confidence that their marriages could last a lifetime.

This was not unrealistic. The nuclear family—husband, wife, 2.5 kids—had detonated, comprising only one-quarter of family formations in North America. Increasingly, women were giving birth to or adopting children without husbands or permanent partners. Single women professionals in their late thirties or forties came to represent 30 percent of people adopting Chinese babies nationwide in the United States, according to New Jersey–based Chinese Children Adoption International. Mainstream publications appeared to cheer them on. "Who Needs a Husband?" proclaimed a *Time* cover story in August 2000.

It was never a better time for women to be unmarried, or so we were told. Single women were the "new yuppies," according to one report. As *People* magazine put it: "Given so many choices [single women] don't have to settle and are willing to give up the old-fashioned romantic fantasy of being with a man in favor of the fantasy of independence." Certainly, tucking into a single serving of Lean Cuisine while watching reruns of *Sex and the City* was preferable to being a wife, according to the deluge of studies that reported how much more men benefit from marriage emotionally and financially than women and how men are far quicker to remarry after divorce or being widowed.

Media reports presented marriage as a dark domicile for women, dangerous and often sexless. Wifely victims of abuse and murder both proven and alleged achieved first-name status—Nicole, Laci, and, of course, Diana. The Australian sociologist Susan Maushart pilloried the role of the modern wife in *Wifework: What Marriage Really Means for Women,* published in 2002: "Becoming a wife will erode your mental health, reduce your leisure, decimate your libido, and increase the odds that you will be physically assaulted or murdered in your own home," she writes. Given such a scathing indictment, it would be reasonable to assume that Maushart had avoided the role as assiduously as she would salmonella poisoning. But no. She married twice, to divorce twice, and argued that the institution of marriage remains the best context available in which to raise children.

Within popular culture, wife is a ready term of derision, a sneer. On an episode of the television program *Will & Grace* that aired in 2001, Will, the gay central character, tells his straight female best friend,

Grace, who has been nagging him, to "stop being a wife." Grace, of course, is insulted. "That's the nastiest thing you've ever said to me," she responds. The number-one Nielsen-rated domestic sitcom *Everybody Loves Raymond* conveyed the same message during an episode in which Raymond attempts to placate his wife after he criticizes her cooking. "You're a good wife," he tells her. She looks at him, horrified. "Don't you ever, ever call me that again," she says, as the laugh track swells.

The characteristics associated with the traditional good wife—servitude, subordination, self-sacrifice, summarized in the pejorative *doormat*—were discordant with the qualities of independence, "self-realization," and ambition glorified by the culture. Successful single women scoffed at the wifely role. "The moment I want to get married and have children is when I am tired of being Elizabeth Hurley," the actress confessed in an interview in 2000. Yet she did manage to remain Elizabeth Hurley even after giving birth to a son two years later, though there was no husband or male companion in sight.

The actress Lara Flynn Boyle invoked imagery from the 1950s when she was asked if she was "wife material" in a 2001 *Vanity Fair* interview. " 'I would like to have a wife,' she responded. 'Who wouldn't. Let's see, what does a wife encompass exactly,' she asks, surveying the ladies brunching around us. 'A housemate. Maybe a pool boy. Does laundry. Misses out on all the fun. Doesn't sound too great, does it?' "

We need only look at two of the most dominant female cultural influences during the 1990s—the entrepreneur Martha Stewart and the media mogul Oprah Winfrey, both of whom are so famous that we know them by their first names—to see the disconnect between power and wife. Neither are married. Stewart divorced her husband in 1989 and never remarried. Winfrey, whose daily talk show serves up a virtual Greek chorus of the travails of modern wifedom, has never assumed the role. The talk-show host, one of the world's richest women, explained her decision not to marry her longtime companion, Stedman Graham, on *The Tonight Show with Jay Leno* in February 2003: "I'm allowed a great deal of freedom in this relationship now," she said, "and I think that if I married—as good as Stedman is—I think that his expectations of what I should be would change. I really do. 'Cause I think he's pretty old-fashioned in that respect, you know, that a 'wife' ought to be home sometimes, and I'm not ready for that right now. I feel if I had the role of wife, I would become someone else. I would then start behaving like a wife."

Given the perceived limitations of the role of wife, it isn't surprising that divorce is presented as a form of female liberation. Women initiate divorce two times out of three, goes the oft-quoted statistic, and they are less likely to remarry than men. Only in leaving marriages, women are told, and shown in books and movies, could they truly "find themselves." This message is not new. It was conveyed more than a hundred years ago by Nora Helmer, the wife who leaves a suffocating marriage in Henrik Ibsen's once-shocking 1879 play, *A Doll's House*: "I must try and educate myself—you are not the man to help me in that," Nora tells her husband, Torvald. "I must do that for myself."

Nora's words continue to resonate. Dr. Christine Northrup echoed the sentiment during an appearance on *Oprah* in 2001. The medical doctor, on a book tour for *The Wisdom of Menopause*, told the primarily female audience that menopause is a "time of opportunity and growth." It was during her own menopause, she confided, that she realized her marriage wasn't fulfilling. So she divorced and experienced a glorious rebirth. She spoke of "sleeping better, dreaming more, being happier and more creative." Weeks later, a cartoon in *The New Yorker* magazine parodied the buzz surrounding Northrup's book. Two ladies sit at lunch. The caption below them reads: "I was on hormone replacement for two years before I realized that what I really needed was Steve replacement." The jest was calculated to draw knowing laughter from women. Husband put-downs had replaced the now politically incorrect "Take my wife, please" humor of the 1950s and '60s. Women who meted out revenge on their cruel mates were cheered. Women who killed or maimed the bastards were lauded as heroines. The movies and books that told their stories could be counted on to draw large and appreciative female audiences.

Against this landscape of virulent antipathy toward the role of wife—a wifelash of sorts—a countervailing sentiment took root during the 1990s. Call it wifelust, as the traditional stay-at-home wife became the subject of a romantic revival. At a time when women were earning

57 percent of bachelor degrees, young women were being bombarded with husband-snaring advice so heavy-handed that Jane Austen would have found it offensive. At a time of confused gender roles, dating advice that harked back to the 1950s flourished. Books like the phenomenally successful *The Rules: Time-Tested Secrets for Capturing the Heart of Mr. Right* advised women to play hard to get. Young women were also counseled to hang on to their virginity as if it were a negotiating tool, and to marry young, before their "best-before" dates expired.

Princely fairy-tale rescue was presented as a primal female desire, as Cinderella emerged as a female role model. When Carolyn Bessette walked down the aisle to marry John F. Kennedy, Jr., "the world's most eligible bachelor," in 1996, *New York* magazine dubbed her "Instant Princess." Oleg Cassini, who designed clothing for Jacqueline Kennedy, announced, "As soon as she married a Kennedy, that immediately elevated her to the rank of top Cinderella."

Famous brides like Bessette were lauded as the epitome of female success. To employ the lexicon of the rash of "reality" dating programs that came to air in the late 1990s, they were "winners." And we couldn't keep our eyes off them. Brides were front and center as an unprecedented wedding mania enveloped the culture. Diana's extravagant, doomed fairy-tale wedding would, ironically, provide the template. At a time when nearly half of marriages ended in divorce, the middle classes hedged their bets by investing in ceremonies that put sixteenth-century papal investitures to shame.

The newfound fascination with the wedding in the 1990s heralded another cultural shift for female identity. The "dress for success" mantra directed at women in the 1980s was replaced with the instruction that women should "marry for success." As if on cue, John T. Molloy, author of the '80s best seller *Dress for Success*, which told women to replace frills and pastels with "power" suiting, came out with *Why Men Marry Some Women and Not Others* in 2003. The how-to manual promised "fascinating research that can land you the husband of your dreams" and offered advice on "Dressing to Be a Wife, Not a One-Night Stand."

Molloy's timing was propitious. Becoming a full-time wife was pre-

sented as the antidote to the female career frustration routinely documented in the press. Typical of the sensibility was an article that ran in
Elle Canada in 2001 advising young women to take low-paying jobs in
"glamorous industries" such as public relations or at auction houses
because "marrying well is the best labour-saving device—and ritzy
jobs can pave the way." Wives toiling in the workforce were beckoned
back into the home by the siren song of domesticity. As one female
social commentator wrote, "Staying at home in the 1990s has, for many
educated women, become what getting an MBA was in the 1980s: a mark
of achievement and status." In 1998, *The New York Times* proclaimed
the stay-at-home wife a "contemporary status symbol." In 2000, *Cosmopolitan* magazine reported that young women, dubbed "housewife
wannabes," longed to quit work. By 2004, the message was overt. "The
Case for Staying Home" blasted the cover of *Time*'s March 22 issue.
Inside, a bold-faced pull-quote proclaimed a 3 percent drop in the
number of mothers with children under three in the workplace since
1997. Of course, this is hardly an "exodus," especially during a recession
when more than two million jobs were lost. Hidden in smaller print was
that fact that 72 percent of mothers with children under eighteen
remain in the workforce.

A new wave of panic prose aimed at single women flooded the market, from the fictional Bridget Jones, fretting about her thighs and her
fear of "dying alone and being found three weeks later half-eaten by an
Alsatian," to books with titles like *Why There Are No Good Men Left: The
Romantic Plight of the New Single*. In an echo of the message given
Victorian women, the twenty-first-century woman was told that having
a career would interfere with her femininity and her fertility. The ever-
ticking biological clock was discussed so frequently that one assumed it
was an actual part of the female anatomy, a uterus-shaped hourglass.

A wife industry emerged, one that smothered women with advice,
instruction, invective. Young unmarried women were deluged with
mixed messages: on one hand, they were told they were having too
much fun and would pay for it later; they were told that single equated
with misery; that they should marry young, give up a career if they
wanted a career; that they should fight for government policies and

workplace changes if they wanted to combine wife and mother. But basically the books all gave the same depressing advice: compromise, settle, tone yourself down, and do it sooner rather than later.

The alternating currents of wifelash and wifelust, as discordant as they might appear, are inextricably linked, finely syncopated. What they represent is a conflict some forty years in the making, one that revolves around continuing attempts to dictate female identity through the definition of *wife*.

Before we review how this conflict came to be, let's look at the shifting meaning of the word *wife*, one that serves as a kind of female Rorschach test. Utter it to a dozen women, wives and non-wives, and you'll receive a dozen different responses. You'll hear a few stories of contentment ("Being a wife has given my life its fullest meaning"). You'll hear tales of calcified resentment ("If I had it to do again, I would never have married"). You'll hear utterances of hope ("Getting married would make my life complete"). There will be accounts that will break your heart ("I was beaten for over a decade before I left him"). You'll be greeted with a blank stare ("I don't see myself as a wife; I see myself as a mother"). You'll hear bitter grotesqueries best suited to a daytime talk show ("After I found out he was screwing my sister, I fucked his best friend in our bed"). And you'll hear stories from women who harbor no illusions about marriage ("I was looking for Mr. Right but settled for Mr. Good Enough").

But the meaning of wife transcends personal experience. It's a cultural concept that fibrillates through a broader landscape. There you will find "good" wives, "bad" wives, fictional wives, real wives, historical wives, mythic wives. Note that wives tend to be qualified by adjectives. That's because they've always been judged according to a paradigm, an unwritten script we all know by heart. More on that later. For now, let's just observe the scene. There's Diana, of course, along with June Cleaver and Hillary Rodham or Hillary Clinton or Hillary Rodham Clinton, depending on the era in which you're observing her. We will see the biblical Eve, Adam's subservient wife, in conflict with

Lilith, who, according to Hebrew folklore, was Adam's rebellious first wife. There's Medea, Cherie Booth Blair, Isabella Beeton, Yoko Ono, and Sylvia Plath. And don't forget the Simpsons—Mrs. Wallis, Marge, and Jessica. And Margaret Trudeau, the ex-wife of former Canadian prime minister Pierre Trudeau, who famously ran off with the Rolling Stones. On this landscape, one will also witness Lady Macbeth, Nicole Brown Simpson, serial wife Elizabeth Taylor, Elena Ceausescu, Eva Perón, Madonna, and Virginia Woolf (along with all her characters and her devoted husband, Leonard, who was known to be her "wife"). There are all six wives of Henry VIII, the unfortunate Anne Boleyn and Catherine Howard minus their heads. Plus an ever-changing parade of celebrities whose prominent love affairs and marriages we watch with voyeuristic thrill, waiting for the inevitable denouement.

We see the mythic Penelope spinning, waiting for Odysseus to return, Emma Bovary fatally seeking romance, Anna Karenina throwing herself in front of that train, Madama Butterfly in her tragic final aria as she kills herself after being replaced by a more socially acceptable wife. There's the overpowering silence of the attic-bound Bertha Rochester in *Jane Eyre*, the brilliant Isabel Archer in *Portrait of a Lady* who is resigned to an unhappy marriage, and, of course, Lucy Ricardo cowering in front of her husband, Ricky, who's telling her she has "some 'splainin' to do."

In an exalted position is Jacqueline Bouvier Kennedy, with her mahogany bubble of hair, standing stoic on that gray November day in 1963, her pink Chanel suit stained with her slain husband's blood. Less conspicuous, though no less a heroine to some women, is Lorena Bobbitt, also smeared with her spouse's blood after she severed his penis with a kitchen knife. But wait, further confusing the wife optics, there are two Jackies. First, the first-lady widow Jacqueline, but also Jackie O, the ultimate trophy wife as the tan, pampered spouse of Greek shipping magnate Aristotle Onassis. (Of course, we can't forget that the wife landscape wouldn't exist without men, who are there too, if less visible. And these men include centuries of legislators, statesmen, as well as famous and infamous husbands.) All in all, a surreal scene.

An enterprising type could invent a parlor game in which one links famous wives who share the same name. Take Nora. Three influential Noras come to mind—four, if you want to include Nora Barnacle, James Joyce's wife and muse. The most famous is Nora from *A Doll's House.* Then there is Nora Charles, the happily married socialite played by Myrna Loy in the *Thin Man* movies of the 1930s and '40s. That Nora is my wife heroine, a sharp cookie who teams up with her husband to solve murder mysteries and who is always ready with a dry martini and an astringent quip. Better known to the modern audience is Nora Ephron, author of the 1983 novel *Heartburn,* a scathing, thinly veiled account of her failed marriage to the journalist Carl Bernstein. This Nora is a pioneer of the wife-revenge genre that entertained us during the latter decades of the twentieth century. See, it's simple. Yet so freighted with subtext.

If you look up the word *wife* in *The Oxford English Dictionary,* you'll come across clues into the meaning but little illumination. *Wife* is a noun, a passive quantity, eager to conform to adjectival construction, be it as a faculty wife, a military wife, a political wife, or a housewife. The word *husband* is far more flexible, functioning as either a noun or a verb. *To husband* can mean "to till the ground, to tend trees and plants, to manage as a husbandman or to cultivate." *To husband* also means "to save," an association that takes on an ironic meaning, given the current obsession with the prince-rescue fantasy. *Husbandable,* fittingly, has commercial connotations, meaning "capable of being economically used." But *husband* hasn't historically taken on adjectives; terms like *military husband* or *faculty husband* do not readily trip off the tongue.

The role of wife has always defined a woman in the way husband does not define a man. It is a full-time job encompassing homemaker, hostess, cheerleader, mother, chauffeur, Jill-of-all-trades. The first reference to wife in the Bible, in Genesis 2:18, makes clear her supportive function: "And the Lord God said, it is not good that the man should be alone; I will make him an help meet for him." And for centuries, the *help-meet,* later *helpmate,* is what a wife represented, at least publicly; she was the domestic backup and emotional support required so her husband could go out and make a living.

But the wife had been untethered from her conventional moorings by the turn of the twenty-first century. By then, more than 70 percent of married women in Western countries worked outside the home. No longer was the wife legally defined by or economically dependent on her husband. No longer was wife necessarily a lifetime role. No longer were women expected to be virgins when they walked down the aisle. Nor were they legally required to take their husbands' names. Wife was not necessarily synonymous with mother. And for the first time in history, a wife did not have to acquiesce to the sexual demands of her husband without recourse to legal reprisal.

The freeing of the wife from her traditional restraints (restraints, it should be noted, many women successfully ignored) came as the result of the slow dismantling in Western culture of a universal and fundamental notion that had long defined the marital relation: coverture, the common law that dictated that a wife's identity be legally subsumed by her husband's. Under coverture, a married couple would literally become "one," a conceit still swooned over in romance novels. Its terms are spelled out in Sir William Blackstone's 1753 *Commentaries on the Laws of England*: "By marriage, the husband and wife are one person in law: that is, the very being or legal existence of the woman is suspended during the marriage, or at least is incorporated and consolidated into that of the husband; under whose wing, protection, and cover, she performs everything; and is therefore called in our law—in French a *femme-covert* ... it is said to be a covert-baron, or under the protection and influence of her husband, her baron, or lord, and her condition during her marriage is called her coverture."

For centuries, the role of wife served as the ultimate female control mechanism. She was property, transferred between male caretakers. Relations between a husband and wife were seen to be reciprocal rather than equal. It was the husband's responsibility to support his family; in return, the wife was expected to act as a companion, housekeeper, and mother. Wives ran family businesses, set the domestic agenda, and provided emotional ballast for their families, it is true. Under laws that stretched into the twentieth century, however, they were treated as unreasoning infants. Publicly, their voices were rarely heard, their stories seldom told. Only a husband could sue or be sued, draft wills, make contracts, or buy and sell property, even property that had originally belonged to his wife. A husband, but not a wife, could seek damages for the loss of consortium—meaning services, affection, and companionship—resulting from injuries to the spouse. If a wife committed a criminal act in her husband's presence, it was assumed to be under his direction. In that wives and husbands were viewed as one legal unit, they could not conspire against each other or steal each other's property. And just as a wife was her husband's property, so were any children born to the union, no matter who the biological father was.

The historian Lawrence Stone defined the situation of married women in England well into the nineteenth century as "the nearest approximation in free society to a slave. Her person, her property both real and personal, her earnings, and her children all passed on marriage into the absolute control of her husband." In *Democracy in America*, published in 1840, the Frenchman Alexis de Tocqueville expressed shock at the limited rights of the American wife: "In America, the independence of women is irrevocably lost in the bounds of matrimony: if an unmarried woman is less constrained there than elsewhere, a wife is subjected to stricter obligations."

Coverture was the focus of feminist ire for centuries. In *Declaration of the Rights of Woman and Citizen*, written in 1791, the French feminist Olympe de Gouges discussed the need for wives to have the right to divorce and to control property in a marriage. In 1853, the feminist Elizabeth Cady Stanton, who was married, wrote to Susan B. Anthony, who wasn't: "I feel that this whole question of woman's rights turns on the point of the marriage relation," she said in reference to wives' lack of autonomy over their bodies. When the suffragist Lucy Stone married Henry Blackwell in 1855, the couple declared that their agreement to marry in no way implied sanction of the then-present laws of marriage that "refuse to recognize the wife as an independent, rational being." Stone was doubly militant in being the first American woman to refuse to take her husband's name.

Coverture reflected the view that women were weaker vessels, put on Earth to serve their husbands and to bear children. Women were excluded from public life, unable to vote, own property, hold public office, or sit on a jury. But the role of the wife shifted with the Industrial Revolution, as women proved useful factory workers. Married women were allowed to be joint guardians with their husbands of children following divorce. In rare cases, they were given sole custody. By the end of the nineteenth century, women had achieved the right to property in marital breakdown, and many jurisdictions allowed wives control over their incomes. Laws changed, giving women access to higher education and the vote. Consistent with the fact that marital rights echo citizen rights, women were also allowed increased autonomy within marriage.

Still, the role of wife remained emblematic of female oppression. In *The Second Sex*, the groundbreaking feminist tract published in 1949, Simone de Beauvoir, who never married, made the extreme claim that marriage rendered women "parasitic": "Marriage is the destiny traditionally offered to women by society," she writes. "Far from freeing the matron, her occupation makes her dependent upon husband and children; she is justified through them; but in their lives she is only an inessential intermediary.... However respected she may be, she is subordinate, secondary, parasitic." It isn't until the institution of marriage is obliterated, she believed, that inequality between the sexes would end: "When we abolish the slavery of half of humanity, together with the whole system of hypocrisy it implies, then the 'division' of humanity will reveal its genuine significance and the human couple will find its true form." The message so inspired some women that they broke free of unhappy marriages. Years later, Norman Mailer admitted that after the first of his many wives read *The Second Sex*, she promptly divorced him.

The wife as political prisoner became an audience-grabbing motif of twentieth-century feminism, one that dovetailed neatly with political unrest, the civil rights movement, and a shifting economy. Betty Friedan's monumental treatise, *The Feminine Mystique*, published in 1963, resonated with millions in its claim that educated women were being held captive in their own homes: "In the past sixty years we have come full circle and the American housewife is once again trapped in a squirrel cage. If the cage is now a modern plateglass-and-broadloom ranch house or a convenient modern apartment, the situation is no less painful than when her grandmother sat over an embroidery hoop in her gilt-and-plush parlor and muttered angrily about women's rights. Is she trapped simply by the enormous demands of her role as modern housewife: wife, mistress, mother, nurse, consumer, cook, chauffeur, expert on interior decoration, child care, appliance repair, furniture refinishing, nutrition, and educator?"

Even though Friedan acknowledged that most women would marry and that, when raising a family, dependence was a necessary fact of life, a wife chasm began within the feminist movement. Being "pro-woman" by default translated into being "anti-wife." The National Organization for Women, founded in 1966 by Friedan with others, sought to eliminate wifely distinction from the vernacular in its proposal that the salutation *Ms.* be used to describe all women, whether married or not. It made sense: men were not categorized according to their marital status, so why should women be?

During the 1970s, the feminist journalist Gloria Steinem was elevated to role model when she vowed she would never marry. "I serve a purpose by being happily unmarried," she once said. "If everyone were married, it wouldn't be a choice." Steinem had little good to say about the institution, comparing it at various times to "a fascist dictatorship," "a slave plantation," "a prison," and an institution that rendered a woman "a semi-non person." She made famous the line "A woman needs a man like a fish needs a bicycle," a catchy conceit that became the smug slogan for a generation.

Steinem readily admitted that becoming a wife held little allure for her at the time. She graduated from Smith College magna cum laude in 1956 and was briefly engaged before she broke it off. "It didn't take courage not to want the picture of marriage that had been painted for us," she once said. "Once you got married, you could make no other choices; that was it. You took his name, his credit rating, his social identity. I have no idea why I resisted when so many other women who felt the same way did not. Maybe it's because I didn't go to school until I was 12, so I missed a little bit of social conditioning."

Though it was never said explicitly, marrying was seen to be a violation of the sisterhood. In *The Female Eunuch,* published to enthusiastic response in 1970, Germaine Greer echoed Beauvoir, claiming that "if women are to effect a significant amelioration in their condition it seems obvious that they must refuse to marry."

Meanwhile, that definition of wife was changing radically in the 1970s and '80s, to the point that diehard traditionalists would rightly wonder what the point of marriage was. No longer did women need their husbands' permission for access to credit or to start up a business. "Head and master" laws, which gave a husband control over any income brought into the household, were phased out. A man was no longer allowed to govern his wife physically. Husbands could be charged with raping their wives. Women were given the right to retain their own names after marriage and to maintain a separate home. Women who stayed at home minding families received a more equitable percentage of family assets upon the dissolution of marriage.

Wives entered the workforce in record numbers during these decades, spurred by stagnating real wages, a shift to an information-service-based economy, and the availability of the birth control pill as much as, if not more than, feminist treatises. Yet feminism provided a compelling ideology that both explained and animated the societal shift. And forty years later, it gets the credit, or the blame, for redefining the social role of women, depending on who's doing the talking.

This is where the story of wife becomes complicated, where the catch-22 of modern wifedom takes root. And that's because the majority of women become wives, for at least some part of their lives. But most of these women also work outside the home, which has resulted in a wife deficit within the home. Indeed, following the wifely exodus into the marketplace in the 1970s, demand for the kind of domestic services and support traditionally provided by the homemaker grew to the point that women themselves routinely complained that they needed domestic backup. This female rallying call was first voiced in the satiric essay "Why I Want a Wife" by Judy Syfers, which was published in the first mass-circulation issue of *Ms.* magazine in 1972. The magazine's cover image conveyed the modern wife's burden: a pregnant woman is shown

THE WIFE GAP   15

with eight arms extended, echoing the eight-armed Hindu goddess warrior, Durga. In each of her eight hands are the various accoutrements of modern wifedom: a frying pan, a clock, a duster, a typewriter, a steering wheel, an iron, a telephone, and a mirror. Syfers's conceit was a clever one: the modern wife needed her own wife. There was only one niggling detail: where would this fresh new wife supply come from?

Most women, when marrying, don't see themselves saddled with mops and babies. Some do, as is their imperative. But the social needs that have always governed marriage have shifted: Western women today marry of free will, spurred by personal desire. No longer is the institution perceived as a "sacred obligation," as the U.S. Supreme Court defined it in the late nineteenth century. By 1965, that judiciary described marriage vaguely, as an "association of two individuals." The reciprocal legal covenant that once bonded couples has been replaced by a far more demanding tyranny—the expectation that marriage provides happiness and self-fulfillment. Love, not legislation, is the new exacting master.

Couples marry not only for security and to raise a family but for romance, a grand adventure, that ephemeral happily-ever-after. Practical reasons for marriage did not even figure into respondents' answers to a Virginia Slims/Roper Starch Opinion Poll conducted in 2000 that asked, "What makes a good marriage?" Both women and men rated "respect for each other" at the top of the list. "Being in love" was second, followed by "sexual fidelity," "communication about feeling," and "keeping romance alive." "Financial security" ranked far lower on the list for both men and women, with only 59 percent of both groups claiming that it contributed to a stable, happy union.

Women want to become wives for a host of reasons unique to them. But there is a more basic reason. Like the word *husband, wife* is a word without synonym. It confers a unique status: there can be only one sanctioned wife for a man in Western culture, at least at a time. Even the wife-denigrating Simone de Beauvoir was not exempt from the word's primacy. In many letters to her lover, the writer Nelson Algren, written while she was working on *The Second Sex,* she referred to him as her husband and herself as his wife: "My beloved husband," she once wrote.

"You must write to me often, my beloved friend and lover, my dearest husband; for we must not feel apart from each other.... We have not parted and we'll never part. I am your wife for ever." Clearly the writer was seeking emotional resonance, the Hallmark moment that only a sanctioned marital relationship provides.

Unsurprisingly, Beauvoir had a difficult time admitting such vulnerability: "I am humiliated by being such an adoring wife, finding nothing to disagree with," she wrote Algren another time. "If it's true that men despise women who worship them, then I am on the wrong track. How come you get to be the big crocodile and I am just the little frog?"

(Algren was not Beauvoir's only foray into "wifely" behavior. Biographers later discovered that her lifelong seemingly egalitarian relationship with the philosopher Jean-Paul Sartre included regular bouts of subjugation. Beauvoir stooped when they were together to permit the shorter Sartre to feel taller. She bought him leather-bound books in which to write, while using cheap children's exercise paper for her own work. When near death in 1980, Sartre acknowledged the sacrifices she made, telling her, "You are a good wife.")

The singularity of the word *wife*—like that of *husband*—confers the comforting illusion of permanence, of being the One. This we witnessed in the slight—and temporary—spike in engagements and marriages after September 11, 2001. It explains why Raymond Carver married the poet Tess Gallagher, with whom he had lived for years, in a quickie Reno ceremony in 1988, when he learned he had only months to live. One of his last poems, "Cherish," describes watching her after their wedding as he savors her intractable position in his life: "Saying it then, against / what comes: *wife*, while I can, while my breath, each hurried petal / can still find her."

Even Gloria Steinem—poster-person for single life—married. On September 6, 2000, she wed David Bale, a man she had known a mere ten months, in a Cherokee ceremony officiated by a female justice of the peace. Unsurprisingly, the sixty-six-year-old feminist shunned the standard bridal fanfare—there was no white satin dress, no white dove release, no giving away of the bride, no gift registry at Restoration Hardware. The bride wore blue jeans.

The media treated Steinem's marriage not as a historical milestone but as an amusing news brightener, a millennial practical joke. "It was as if the Grand Mufti had renounced Islam," reported Britain's *Telegraph*. *Esquire* referred to Steinem's marriage in its "Dubious Achievements 2000" issue, declaring, "Turns out a fish does need a bicycle."

In interviews after the wedding, Steinem talked up the unique status that marriage conferred. "For us, we wanted a way of saying that we were committed to each other," she told *Time* magazine. "If we'd been younger, perhaps we would have had a child or done something else to say that we are committed together." She suggested that "what seemed conformist at 26—getting married—seems rebellious at 66." Being a wife no longer entailed subjugation, she claimed. "If I had got married when I was supposed to get married, I would have lost all my civil rights," she told Dave Tianen of *The Milwaukee Journal*. "It is possible now to make an equal marriage."

But before we stamp a politically correct Good Housekeeping seal of approval on the role (Steinem was, after all, the older, the more powerful and famous of the couple), consider the fact that the word *wife* was not once uttered during the ceremony. Steinem and Bale referred to themselves as *partners*, a gender-neutral term that implied theirs would be an egalitarian union, absent of the legacy of ownership, domestic servitude, or submission.

Indeed, it was Bale who cheerfully admitted to being the less dominant partner, as revealed in an interview the couple gave to Barbara Walters on *20/20* shortly after their wedding in which he joked that he occasionally introduced himself as "Mr. Gloria Steinem." (Tragically, the union would be short-lived; Bale died of a brain lymphoma in December 2003.)

The semantic jest, along with Steinem's refusal to refer to herself as a wife, is telling of the fact that despite legislative changes, the role of wife continues to be freighted with retrograde associations, as if the shadows and echoes of the past loom and reverberate through a wife script that has not been rewritten to accommodate the new modern wife.

This script is not taught, at least not explicitly. Western brides are no longer handed primers on the eve of their weddings with quaint, pedantic titles such as *The Lady's New Year's Gift, Maxims for Married*

Ladies, or *The Young Lady's Friend.* Women are not routinely subject to the explicit wife training that greeted female immigrants to Quebec in the seventeenth century. That said, wife schools do exist. The USO arm of the U.S. military runs a ten-day tutorial in Seoul, Korea, to train Korean women engaged to marry American soldiers and businessmen in the customs, behavioral requirements, and legal rights of the American wife. Similarly, faculty wives' clubs and parliamentary spousal groups offer gentle suasion in terms of how to play the role.

And that role comes with unspoken rules. We use the term *wife material* as shorthand to describe women suited to the role. These are not women who throw back Jägermeister shots or table dance on the first date. They are agreeable, devoted, hardworking; they do not want to draw attention to themselves. They follow instruction. And wife instruction is plentiful, delivered covertly via television programming, movies, magazine articles chronicling women's stunted professional advancement, advice books that lecture women on how to capture a husband, how to keep their marriages "hot," and, finally, how to emerge triumphant from divorce. This tacit script is also apparent in the current, unceasing wave of chick-lit entertainment, as well as in the growth industries that induce women to become brides and to embrace domesticity.

This unwritten code is most evident if we look back to the landscape where wives are celebrated and/or vilified. Exhibit A is Hillary Rodham Clinton, America's ur-wife during the 1990s, the decade in which the standoff between wifelash and wifelust began. The former first lady, like many women, believed that she could write her own script after marriage. She sparked her first wife-related furor during a *60 Minutes* interview she gave with her husband during the 1992 presidential campaign. That was the one in which she made the famous proclamation "I'm not sitting here as some little woman standing by my man like Tammy Wynette." Evidently, she was oblivious to the irony that (a) she was there, standing, or rather sitting, by her man and that (b) Tammy Wynette had married five times.

Rodham Clinton's attempts to present herself as an autonomous spouse who had a voice in government policy were met with sneering condescension by a parochial press and her husband's political ene-mies. Other first ladies had been involved in dictating policy in the past, but they were not as public about it. In 1914, Edith Wilson lobbied quietly for the Alley Dwelling bill of 1914 to demolish slums and build new housing with federal money. Eleanor Roosevelt stoked contro-versy when she pressed a resistant secretary of war to integrate the officer corps and fought for anti-lynching laws and workers' rights. Nancy Reagan, too, was believed to be a power behind the throne, which was rendered palatable because she stared adoringly at her hus-band in public. But a first lady who dared present herself as an equal was seen to be unnatural, even a freak. This we saw reflected in an image of Rodham Clinton that ran in the satiric magazine *Spy* in 1995 showing her as an androgyne—female on top, male below. Even in the 1990s, thirty years after the publication of *The Feminine Mystique*, decades after legislative changes had freed the wife, political wives, those highly visible public role models, were expected to remain sub-missive, secondary.

Hillary Rodham Clinton would prove adept at dipping in and out of the script when it was politically expedient to do so. She kept her maiden name after marriage (adding and subtracting Clinton over the years) but sacrificed her own career advancement by moving with her new husband to Arkansas so he could pursue his political ambitions. She participated in policy decisions but also willingly played the domesticated wife when required. Who remembers flinching in embarrassment as Rodham Clinton participated in a silly chocolate-chip-cookie bake-off with Barbara Bush during the 1996 presidential campaign? She won (rolled oats were her secret ingredient). Less suc-cessful were her forays into political policy. After her plans for health-care reform fizzled, Rodham Clinton was reduced to churning out conventional first lady feel-good books—*It Takes a Village, Dear Socks, Dear Buddy: Kids' Letters to the First Pets*, and *An Invitation to the White House*, a glossy tome one might have expected from Jacqueline Kennedy. She fussed with her appearance, particularly her hair, which became a political metaphor, as the public debated the semiotics of her bangs and the wisdom of her hairbands.

It wasn't until Rodham Clinton stood by her man during his adultery scandal starring Monica Lewinsky, however, that her approval ratings soared. It was predictable. Finally, she resembled a familiar wife model—bowed, subservient, humiliated. No longer was Rodham Clinton the manic, dangerous career gal like the one played by Glenn Close in *Fatal Attraction,* an entertaining piece of fluff that would be elevated to a much-cited benchmark of millennial gender politics. She had morphed into the sympathetic, devoted stay-at-home wife played by Anne Archer, who defends her home from external threat and welcomes her philandering husband back to the hearth.

Even so, Rodham Clinton's defense of her husband created unease. The public didn't want to be reminded that modern marriages are often calculated partnerships requiring unfathomable compromise. Hers was a no-win scenario: where once she was criticized for being too independent, she was later ridiculed for not being independent enough. It was the same conundrum experienced by another political wife, Cherie Booth Blair, who is married to the British prime minister, Tony Blair. In 2001, Booth Blair stoked controversy when she chose to take a leave from her practice as a prominent human rights lawyer to travel with her husband. Germaine Greer, worked into a self-righteous lather, said in an interview that Booth Blair was like a "concubine." She went on to say that the prime minister's wife is "an intelligent woman doing an important job. I don't want to see her coming around being a wife."

But Rodham Clinton also illustrates the complex, hidden power of wife. She exploited hard-won wife leverage to become a U.S. senator, to secure an $8-million advance for her autobiography, and to position herself for a possible run for the U.S. presidency. Any such campaign will be problematic, of course, just as it has been for other women with such lofty aspirations. And that stems from another lingering legacy of the wife script: the false assumption that wives, and by extension women, cannot be dominant; by definition they're beta, never alpha, that quality required in a leader. George W. Bush made this clear in a comment he made while he was governor of Texas. Praising his wife, Laura, while clearly taking a jab at Hillary Clinton, he said, "I have the best wife for the line of work that I'm in. She doesn't try to steal the limelight."

The fact that power and wife are antithetical concepts extends more broadly to how women are perceived in the public realm. Pat Schroeder, the former congresswoman from Colorado who dropped out from a run at the presidency in 1988, once described the White House as "a big tree house with a sign reading NO WOMEN ALLOWED." So entrenched is the notion of the exclusionary "boys' club" (which, more accurately, should be called the "husbands' club") that there is rarely public questioning of why more women don't run for top office. The author Erica Jong pinpointed the problem indirectly in a column that ran on the op-ed page of *The New York Times* in 2001. "What do American women want in a president?" she asked. "The same thing we want in a husband. Someday we might have a woman candidate, but until then, women want someone masculine but not so masculine that we can't control him." It is a stunning assertion, one that links masculinity to husband to public leadership. There is no room for wives, and by extension women, in that equation.

Jong's comment reflects the entrenched definition of wife as beta. And this is true even when the role is being played by a man, as it increasingly is. In *Hello, He Lied*, the producer Lynda Rosen Obst observes that in Hollywood, "wife" is the name given to the "nonpro," or a nonplayer, member of a couple: "When one spouse is a nonpro, he or she is definitely the wife, whatever the gender," she writes. "Doctor-husbands of lady agents are routinely ignored at dinner parties (unless they are plastic surgeons)...." To return to another definition in *The Oxford English Dictionary*, it's worth noting that the word *wife* is used to describe "the passive member of a homosexual partnership."

Though that is shifting, social discomfort prevails when the female wife is the more powerful member of the union. "Mr. Sharon Stone" was the sneering title accorded Phil Bronstein, a San Francisco newspaper executive, when he married the actress in 1998. Such a mindset takes us back to the 1950s, and the Cold War, when the wife holding the upper hand was registered as unnatural, even un-American. One psychological profile of Communist behavior read by both President Eisenhower and FBI chief J. Edgar Hoover during this period explained that "the tendency seems to be that in Communist marriages the wife is the more dominant partner." When the notorious Communist sympathizers Julius and Ethel Rosenberg were executed in 1953 for espionage, they were described thus: "Julius is the slave and his wife, Ethel, the master."

Even though Ozzie and Harriet have been replaced by Ozzy and Sharon Osbourne, the 1950s housewife embodied by television icons Harriet Nelson, Donna Reed, and June Cleaver continues to dominate wifely imagery. Here we should pause to consider that the roles of these fictional women were the creations of male scriptwriters, which, as we will see, meant that they mirrored the roles played by actual women for centuries.

Depicting the modern wife is a confusing prospect, one captured on the cover of the June 1990 issue of *Esquire* magazine, which was devoted to "The Secret Life of the American Wife." The image depicted the multiple roles played by the modern Western wife. A photograph of a woman was bisected into quarters: she was a career woman in a dress-for-success business suit; she was a lover in lingerie; she was a domestic worker attired in an apron; she was a mother, as indicated by a super-imposed graphic of her reproductive system.

The image drew fire. "How dare a woman be depicted as a side of cattle in a butcher shop?" letter writers fumed. Yet it reflected brilliantly the fragmented reality of the wifely role. The first cover mock-up for this book, in fact, featured an anonymous woman eerily resembling a 1950s sitcom wife. I rejected it, though no more contemporary image readily leaped to mind. Similarly, the British book jacket for Susan Maushart's *Wifework*, published in 2002, features a retro 1950s photograph of a housewife ironing. The image reflects a great big vacuum—a wife gap, if you will—that exists in the culture. On one side of this gap, the wife remains freeze-dried in a mythical 1950s and early 1960s, the point at which the twentieth-century feminist movement mourned her as being enslaved. On the other side of the chasm, the role of wife is breezily assumed to be a free-form improvisation, like Twyla Thwarp's choreography or an extended Ornette Coleman saxophone solo.

Within this wife gap exists an obvious, though unacknowledged, social conundrum. Women have been freed from the legal shackles traditionally associated with the role of wife. Yet that traditional wife has not been unshackled from our social, economic, and political infrastructures, a fact that affects all women, married or not. Meanwhile, June Cleaver has been left by the roadside, her important, if invisible, social and economic contributions marginalized.

Certainly we're aware women are being held back by something. We've been deluged by books, magazine articles, academic papers, and talk-show pundits offering the latest theory on why women aren't jetting to the top of corporations or political parties, why marriages have become war zones, why relationships between men and women had become so fraught. Solutions are tossed out with abandon. Women are told to "dress for success," to get on the "mommy track," to get off the "mommy track," to become more aggressive, to become less aggressive, to not marry or have children if we want to succeed, and, finally, just to throw in the towel and make wife a career.

Bookstores are filled with volumes of wife-related advice. We are held in the thrall of both fictional and real-wife stories, be they happy or sad, though we prefer the grisly ones. Yet the complex role the wife plays in the jigsaw puzzle of female identity is rarely examined. Not that this should surprise us. The wife has always been a supporting role, never the main act.

Vacuums tend to be filled. The wife gap is no exception. As we will see, it has been infiltrated by political agendas, corporate imperatives, and commercial forces that use the meaning of wife to exercise an insidious control. Despite legislative changes, the role of wife continues to be used as a female control mechanism. Where coverture shackled wives to husbands in centuries past, that shackling today takes a myriad of forms. As such, the meaning of wife doesn't simply influence married women. It has implications for both fourteen-year-old girls and forty-one-year-old divorcées, in that it influences perceptions of what it means to be a woman, even women's choice of career.

The wife gap is an abstraction, but its consequences affect the day-to-day lives of women. As the poet Jill Bialosky observes in an essay published in *The Bitch in the House*: "I had wanted to get married, but I realized now that I had never wanted to be a 'wife.'" A similar confusion is expressed by Peggy Orenstein in *Flux*, published in 2000. Orenstein writes that she "fiercely resisted the idea of being a 'wife'" when she married. Yet she also acknowledged that she easily "slipped into the role, especially when it seems, at least in the short term, to benefit me." In the first years of her marriage, she followed the old-fashioned husband-as-breadwinner script with a modern twist: she regarded her own earnings as belonging to her while her husband's earnings were to be shared by the two of them.

Women in the twenty-first century may go out into the workplace to become the men they once wanted to marry—another classic Steinemism—yet they remain influenced by the pull of a script assumed to have been abandoned in the 1950s. When Oprah Winfrey expressed concern on *The Tonight Show* about becoming "someone else" were she to marry, someone who will "start behaving like a wife," the audience understood she wasn't talking about behaving like a wife who was a Supreme Court judge or an astronaut or even Hillary Rodham Clinton. She was speaking of devolving into a June Cleaver clone dutifully dusting the living room, making the Beaver's lunch, and then preparing a jellied salad to take to the church social.

Vestiges of the old script continue to shadow women who have never even heard the word *coverture*. Studies reveal, for instance, that young women expect their husbands to be the primary breadwinners, even when wives work outside the home. Another report indicates that three-quarters of female college students believe that the employment of their future husbands should take precedence and that women are more likely to relocate for a spouse's career than men.

This shouldn't surprise us. For all the legislative change that redefined married women's status, for all the social shifting that reshaped women's place in society, for all the dreary droning on about gender, this perplexing juncture we find ourselves in stems in good part from the fact that the old-script wife, that meta-beta Wife, remains institutionally entrenched. No one has bothered to liberate her. So there she sits, like Mrs. Rochester in the attic, ignored but ever-present.

In *The Feminine Mystique*, Betty Friedan predicted that once enough women entered the workforce, necessary social changes such as government-sponsored "professionally run nurseries" would follow. That didn't happen. Rather, women learned to joke, with increasing bitterness, about needing wives of their own. On cue, a Wife micro-economy emerged. Occasionally its goods and services are sold at a premium, as is the case with catering, decorating, and therapy. More commonly, however, it employs a new underclass paid consistently with the negligible value traditionally placed on wife labor.

The presence of the institutional Wife is felt in other ways. Consider the ongoing media fascination with the "trend," one not backed by statistics, that wives and mothers are fleeing the workplace, tired of bashing their heads against the mythical glass ceiling (clearly not realizing that it is the entrenched Wife who's pushing her down). This has given birth to yet another wave of feminist backlash in which feminists of the '60s and '70s are routinely blamed for underplaying the satisfactions of domesticity and family. More grieviously, they are taking the heat for enslaving women in the new Wife economy, most famously in Caitlin Flanagan's much-raked-over article in the March 2004 issue of *The Atlantic Monthly, Dispatches from the Nanny Wars: How Serfdom Saved the Women's Movement*. In that, Flanagan defined "wife work" as "shit work."

Not surprisingly, feminism has become a convenient scapegoat for social dissent. The "women's movement," which never was a singular "movement" at all, is readily blamed for the anger and frustration over how women's roles have —and, more to the point, have not— evolved. But before we heap on more blame, remember that feminism initiatives of the 1960s and '70s didn't come with guarantees. More to the point, the "movement" suffered from its own wife gap. This is apparent in the June 29, 1998, issue of *Time*, the one that famously asked "Is Feminism Dead?" The accompanying article argued that the women's movement had "devolved into the silly" between the 1970s and the 1990s, using as evidence the contrast between the ditzy single character Ally McBeal and the level-headed single character Mary Richards from *The Mary Tyler Moore Show.*

Let's leave aside for a moment the foolishness of basing a critique of modern feminism on the behavior of television characters, even though the approach echoes the common, incorrect reflex to reduce the movement to the behavior of upper-middle-class women in the workforce. And let's not waste time blaming Ally McBeal's creator, David E. Kelley, for undermining hundreds of years of feminism. Like all network-television savants, he was merely adapting cultural currents—or in this case, cultural static—into mass-market fare.

The cover of that issue pictured the faces of feminist leaders Susan B. Anthony, Betty Friedan, and Gloria Steinem, along with Ally McBeal. None was a wife. Nineteenth-century suffragist Anthony never married. "I never felt I could give up my life of freedom to become a man's housekeeper," she once said. Friedan had been a wife, a miserable one. She divorced in 1969, six years after *The Feminine Mystique* was published, and never remarried. Later she would claim that her husband had beaten her. Yet she would also go on to admit that she exaggerated housewives' unhappiness in her landmark book. In her memoir *Life So Far*, published in 2000, Freidan wrote that she was "ashamed" she had denied the truth that "as a suburban wife and mother, I had many happy hours with my kids, my husband, my friends and neighbors..."

Obviously it was more effective, and incendiary, to present the wife as straight-out imprisoned victim. Which leaves us some forty years later trying to untangle grey from black and white as we cut through increasingly polarized meanings of wife that pit woman against woman and threaten to take us back to a time before women's rights could be taken for granted. Again, this isn't surprising. Every culture, every era, reshapes the wife to suit its purposes. Ours is no different. This will become apparent as we venture into the wife gap. There, the first apparition to greet us will be the bride—a commercialized, anesthetized creature awaiting her magical transformation.

Chapter 2

The Heart of Whiteness

So where did this frothy white bridal tsunami come from? At a time when fewer women are marrying, cookie-cutter, white-satin brides are everywhere—shilling for advertisers, tempting viewers as the stars of pristine bridal pornography, and, most insidiously, deployed to promote marriage by a newly entrenched wedding industrial complex.

The bride's emergence as the twenty-first century's most potent consumer icon—one that can be counted on to elicit a Pavlovian triggering of female desire—might appear at odds with the confusion over the meaning of wife. It isn't. Wedding mania is a direct response to the wife gap, capitalism's way of filling the void. If the modern wife is an enigma, the modern bride is a no-brainer. She's pure fairy tale, transmitting hope, purity, and primal desire. Within the marketplace, her ephemeral status only ramps up her appeal: with a shelf life of less than a day, she's ever fresh. Becoming a one-day bride, rather than a lifetime wife, is presented by marketers as the ultimate female fantasy, yet another one-size-fits-all fiction. Robin Ward, a brand director with the cosmetics conglomerate Estée Lauder, explained the efficacy of the figure to *Fortune* magazine in 1998: "When you think about it—a bride—it's timeless, it's positive in every woman's life, in every country of the world, and that's true whether it's this year or 30 years from now."

So potent is the bride's consumer allure that women in full bridal regalia are being enlisted to sell products with no direct relationship to the wedding. They appear in ads for Tylenol, Foster's beer, Kellogg's cereal, Häagen-Dazs ice cream, Coca-Cola, Seagram's coolers, Metropolitan Life insurance, Winston cigarettes, Pepsi, Buick, Dockers clothing, Nokia cell phones, Toblerone chocolate bars, even for the Canadian Cheese Marketing Board. As an advertising focus, the bride is a natural: she's the star of any scene, an apparition the viewer can't ignore, an ivory slash on the landscape, the female erection. She offers advertisers a ready-made narrative, an opportunity to riff on entrenched wifely stereotypes, as in a television commercial for Foster's beer in which the bride dunks her head devotedly underwater to retrieve a beer for her new husband. Or a print ad for Winston cigarettes that suggests a young bride is after her much older groom's money.

Most ads featuring brides are targeted at women. Some cleverly acknowledge the ambivalence many women feel about becoming a wife while capitalizing on the potent emotions stirred by the transient role that transforms her into one. A television spot for Kellogg's presents a bride and groom at the altar. The bride is distracted, eyeing an EXIT sign on the wall. A voiceover intones, "Life is filled with decisions. With Kellogg's NutriGrain cereal, you don't have to decide. It's delicious and nutritious." Finally, the bride speaks. "I don't know," she says, a response clearly directed at the groom, not the cereal.

Most often the bride is featured in serene isolation, implying that the ideal wedding tableau is a solo female fantasy. This too is useful from an advertising perspective. The bride alone, no groom in sight, communicates a flawless ideal separate from the messy, complicated, often prosaic reality of marriage. A self-satisfied solo bride spooning ice cream into her mouth appeared in a print ad for Häagen-Dazs that ran in 2001. "They can start without you," reads the copy. The pitch is brilliant, combining the seductive appeal of the bride with luscious dairy fat substituting for the groom. It's a telling snapshot of the romantic perception of contemporary marriage—an institution that promises both intimacy and total self-indulgence.

The modern bride's success as advertising icon stems from the visceral response she elicits, a reaction that transcends any calculated marketing machinations. She's as palatable as the foamy whipped cream she resembles. As such, the bride's new role as pitch woman is a logical evolution of her historical role as the ultimate packaged good. The word *bridal* itself is derived from the Old English *brideale*, or "wedding feast" (though one can't ignore the associations with "bridle," being controlled by a "groom"). In eighteenth-century England, the notion of devouring the bride was taken to extreme, terrifying lengths, as wedding guests pawed away at her in the belief that her garments possessed mythical properties. Two centuries later, the notion of consuming the bride, symbolically at least, continues with the wedding cake. As the social anthropologist Margaret Visser points out, "The cake stands tall, white, archaic and decorated, pyramidal like the veiled bride herself, and dominating the proceedings; it is a version of the bride, and the piercing of it dramatizes her rite of passage." The food writer Jeffrey Steingarten is more explicit. "The modern wedding cake," he concludes, "is a bride you can put in your mouth."

The edible appeal of the bride plays brilliantly in the mass marketplace. She is the star of a pageant we know by heart but that still gets to us every time. It's axiomatic: a story that ends with a wedding ends happily. And who doesn't love a happy ending? It's neat, processed, easily digestible, actively defiant of life's final act.

We saw in the 1990s, however, the introduction of a new, perverse genre of bridal entertainment, one that placed the lacy bride at the center of a voyeuristic peep show. At a time when marriage itself was in turmoil, lacking ballast, the perfectly scripted wedding offered a powerful catharsis. When Larry King asked Oprah Winfrey in a September 2001 interview why she wasn't married, the woman with her finger firmly on the pulse of the contemporary female psyche put it succinctly: "America doesn't care if I'm happily married. They want a wedding.... They want some doves to fly. They want a pretty Oscar de la Renta gown...."

And Oprah would provide her loyal public with just that on February 28, 2003. That was the last day of February sweeps, the period in which programmers pull out all the stops to increase audience numbers because viewership is being gauged to determine advertising rates. So the talk-show queen mounted the ultimate spectacle, serving up the "Oprah Fantasy Wedding." The program featured a couple renewing their vows in the "wedding of their dreams," which included a lavish ceremony officiated by the spiritualist Marianne Williamson, an $8,000 "fairy-tale" wedding gown, and a reception "fit for royalty."

Garry Marshall, who directed *Pretty Woman*, along with the television programs *Happy Days, Mork and Mindy,* and *Laverne and Shirley,* confirms the appeal of the wedding. "When your ratings went down, you turned it into a wedding. We got Fonzie married, we got Richie married, we got Mork married. We almost got Laverne married. We got Shirley married. When you leave it out, they ask you about it. I know when I did 'Pretty Woman,' a lot of the comments were: 'Why didn't you go one more scene? Why didn't you have the wedding?'"

When Marshall was directing *Pretty Woman* in the late 1980s, however, brides had defected from movie screens. From the 1960s to the 1990s, North American cinema experienced a bridal deficit. Consistent with the spirit of wifelash, the prevailing bridal cinematic trope was bridal liberation—from Dustin Hoffman sweeping Katharine Ross away in the classic final scene of the 1967 movie *The Graduate* to the last scene of the 1980 film *Private Benjamin* in which Goldie Hawn's character flees her second marriage at the altar. (To see the rogue bride as a modern cinematic trope, however, is incorrect. Defecting brides date back to *It Happened One Night* in 1934 and *The Philadelphia Story* in 1940.)

By the turn of the twenty-first century, though, there appeared to be a voracious appetite for the reassuring sight of the bride, as the word *wedding* or *bride* in a movie title provided assurance of box-office success. Moviegoers flocked to *Muriel's Wedding, The Wedding Banquet, Four Weddings and a Funeral, My Best Friend's Wedding, The Wedding Singer, The Wedding Planner, The Wedding Dress, Monsoon Wedding, American Wedding, Father of the Bride, Father of the Bride II. Mamma Mia,* the hit play about the planning of a wedding, shrewdly featured a glowing bride in its advertising. *My Big Fat Greek Wedding* proved to be the blockbuster sleeper movie of 2002, taking in more than $250 million at the box office in its first year.

Over-the-top celebrity nuptials costing millions and exuding garish bad taste were avidly observed—Céline Dion and her manager husband, René Angelil, who staged both an extravagant fairy-tale ceremony and a tacky *Arabian Nights*–themed Vegas renewal of vows, come to mind. Viewers thronged in front of their televisions to watch Jennifer Lopez make public the details of her engagement to Ben Affleck in an interview with Diane Sawyer. Lopez gushed about Affleck's serving up a parade of romantic clichés—carpeting the ground with rose petals, presenting her with an opulent 6.1-carat pink diamond, and serenading her with her own CD. (None of which, we know, wound up cementing their relationship.)

Even the courtship and weddings of civilians were transformed into popular entertainment on programs such as The Learning Channel's hit *A Wedding Story*. The "Vows" feature of *The New York Times* Sunday "Style" section—jokingly known by its huge female audience as "mergers and acquisitions" or "salt in the wound"—became a weekly must-read following its 1991 debut. The accompanying engagement announcements, wryly referred to by the same audience as the women's sports pages—filled with photographs of smug, smiling lookalike couples who see only happiness before them—are parsed with scholarly intent by readers for indications of future discontent. *The New York Observer*'s popular "Countdown to Bliss" engagement column is similarly perused for the salient indicators of modern love—the number of carats of the diamond and the lengths to which couples would go to stage weddings that reflected their "unique" individuality. In August 2002, for example, readers learned that one compulsive mother of the bride took an hour of calligraphy once a week for months to ensure that place cards at the reception would be perfect for the brief moment guests glanced at them.

Bridal lust spans every medium. In the late 1990s, when general magazine revenues were in decline, we saw an upsurge in bridal publications exuding a shiny, robotic automation and weighing as much as small-town telephone directories. The February 2001 issue of *Bride's* set a Guinness World Record as the largest consumer magazine ever published, at 1,286 pages and 4.9 pounds. In 2001, the Canadian magazine *Wedding Bells* boldly launched an edition in the saturated U.S. market. *Martha Stewart*

Weddings, a quarterly with a subscription base of more than 650,000, was published not four but five times in 2003. Non-bridal titles such as *Vogue* presented special bridal issues, knowing them to be magnets for advertisers. In August 2003, the Canadian gay magazine *Fab* published its first "bridal issue," the second largest in its history, to commemorate the legalization of same-sex marriage in the province of Ontario. No audience was left unexploited. Even women who had been married once, twice, even three times were offered hope with *Bride Again:* "the only magazine for encore brides." Women who bought these publications often did so guiltily, dismissing them as "female porn." But the promise of the perfect wedding proved irresistible. Women willingly suspended disbelief, compartmentalizing the wedding from the marriage.

It wasn't until the evening of February 15, 2000, however, that the carnivorous lust for bridal imagery fully registered. That night, more than twenty-two million people, most of them women in a post–Valentine's Day funk, tuned in to watch the Fox network's *Who Wants to Marry a Millionaire?,* a two-hour bridal bonanza conceived as an undisguised pander to the sweeps. The premise was a vulgar, commercialized update of the Cinderella tale filtered through a beauty-pageant format. Fifty eager-to-marry women gathered on the stage of the Las Vegas Hilton to compete to become the bride of a millionaire they had never met. As a bonus, the winner took home an Isuzu Trooper and a $35,000 three-carat engagement ring.

More than one thousand women sent in videotaped biographies. Fifty, ranging in age from nineteen to forty-three, were chosen. Fewer than one hundred men vied to be the groom. That dubious honor went to forty-two-year-old Rick Rockwell, a motivational speaker/stand-up comic who told program organizers he had amassed his money in real estate. The final five contestants donned white wedding gowns and answered questions tailored to convey how well they would adapt to "wifely" responsibilities, including what they would do if they found a woman's name and phone number in their new husband's pocket, and whether they wanted to have children. Rockwell selected Darva Conger, a thirty-four-year-old emergency room nurse. A judge performed the wedding ceremony before the couple left on a two-week Caribbean honeymoon from which they returned on the brink of divorce, all temporary illusion shattered.

Predictably, critics lambasted the program for depicting marriage as a commercial transaction, which, of course, had once been its purpose. Patricia Ireland, then the president of the National Organization for Women, denounced the show as "nothing more than legalized prostitution," the same claim some feminists had once made about marriage itself. But their protests went unheeded. The crassly mercantile fairy-tale premise attracted a demographic gold mine: one-third of all women under thirty-five watching television that evening tuned in. It provided a clear snapshot not only of what women craved as escapist entertainment but also of audience priorities; the same night only three million people watched the Republican presidential candidates' debate on CNN.

Such success prompted television network executives, who share with three-year-olds a delight in repetitive behavior, to devise a slate of similar programs presenting young women as eager to marry. And so it began, as record numbers of viewers tuned in to watch *The Bachelor, The Bachelorette, Joe Millionaire, Married by America, Race to the Altar,* and *Bachelorettes in Alaska,* which presented a group of women so eager to wed that they put on wedding gowns in a frigid climate to snare a husband. In the ultimate media-generated daisy chain, the ABC television network paid the couple who became engaged on its dating show *The Bachelorette* $1 million to air their lavish wedding during the November 2003 sweeps.

This bridal deluge in movies, on television shows, and in advertising during the 1990s did not spring forth spontaneously. It was underwritten and reinforced by a burgeoning wedding industrial complex, a machine fueled by the profit motive and lubricated by myth. This complex includes not only the wedding industry as we know it—the magazines, books, retailers, Web sites, jewelers, dress manufacturers, wedding-show organizers, and purveyors of goods and services presented as indispensable to the modern wedding. It also comprises a web of ancillary enterprises that stoke wedding romance as a revenue-generating strategy—from bridal TV porn to more subtle marketing tie-ins such as a promotional contest sponsored by *Us Weekly* in July 2003 in which a lucky reader would win the $7,000 "I do" dress of Elle Woods's dreams from the film *Legally Blonde 2*.

The bride, that pretty, anodyne, consumer icon, is employed as the complex's hooker. She is the top girl in the stable, one who can be counted on to lure not men but women. The bride's deployment makes sense. Given the confused and negative emotions summoned by the concept of wife, employing wifely imagery (to the extent it even exists) to seduce women into becoming brides would be a disaster. Brides, on the other hand, can sell anything, as we've seen, even the muddled prospect of wifehood.

In tapping into the most elemental of human hopes and desires, the wedding complex employs a doublespeak that would have George Orwell shaking his head. Eternal love is represented by goods that are consumed, products that are rented, and services as disposable as a Bic pen; waste symbolizes permanence; conformity is sold as individuality; and the ideal can be purchased.

If ever an industry was actively designed to create tenuous marriages based on unrealistic expectations, it would look just like the wedding industrial complex. The focus is exclusively on the wedding; marriage is the afterthought, the residue. The complex's prefabricated script presents the perfect wedding as providing the necessary structural underpinning for the perfect marriage. Miss a step, forget the embossed matchbooks or forgo the butterfly release, and your marriage is imperiled. Or so goes the unwritten message. And the unspoken rule is that the more money you spend, the happier you'll be, not only on your wedding day but also in your marriage.

The wedding industrial complex trains its attention on the future bride, pelting her with commercially motivated rules and regulations. These tell women that they can achieve self-expression and satisfaction as brides—and by extension later as wives—if they're willing to follow a script that cleverly and insidiously reduces them to unreasoning infants. It is an eerie echo of coverture. Except the difference now, an ominous one, is that the bride is not only the consumed but also the consumer.

. . .

The supreme entry point to the wedding industrial complex, into its dark heart of whiteness, is through a glass doorway on the southeast corner of Madison Avenue and Seventy-seventh Street in New York City. This is the portal to the flagship Vera Wang shop, or, as it's unofficially known, bridal mecca. Here, the term "ivory strapless silk-faced organza with a skirt of hand-appliquéd concentric pinwheels of silk tulle" elicits a shiver of anticipation, of primal female longing. Even on a chilly day in November, a cluster of women is gathered outside, their noses longingly pressed against the window. They're seeking a glimpse of the magic that has made Wang the unofficial godmother of the modern fairy-tale wedding. So ubiquitous has this bridal iconography become that even women with no intention of marrying know who Wang is, just as they know what Tiffany's "classic six-prong" engagement ring setting looks like.

It was in the late 1980s, while shopping for her own wedding dress at age thirty-eight, that Wang realized that "bridal" was an untapped fashion category. She was appalled by the selection of trashy polyester satin dresses adorned with sparkles and frills. Designers had abandoned the bride as a lost cause. Wang, a design director at Ralph Lauren who had also worked as an editor at *Vogue*, knew that fashion-minded women like herself were marrying. And they wanted show-stopping elegance. They wanted chic minimalist lines. They wanted to show off a gym-toned body. They wanted *wow*.

In 1990, Wang set up her bridal business and transformed the bridal dress into a fashion statement, an item that could cost as much as a Mercedes-Benz. In short order she became designer of choice for socialites, actresses, and models, a success that inspired other high-end designers—Richard Tyler, Carolina Herrera, Dior, Badgley Mischka, and Givenchy among them—to enter the bridal market. By the mid-1990s, that business was booming, with shrewd businessmen entering the fray, such as Richard Branson with his Virgin Bride Superstores. By 2003, Wang's privately run enterprise was estimated to be worth some $100 million in sales, and her dresses were sold around the world. So transcendent was her name recognition that she extended the Vera Wang brand to evening wear, perfume, eyeglasses, and housewares.

As I pass through the door, I suffer a flashback to that heady mix of glee and horror I felt watching Diana's wedding almost two decades earlier. In the pale-wood-paneled reception area, women in their twenties with fashionably poker-straight long hair thumb through *Vera Wang on Weddings,* a glossy best seller that serves up the modern bridal ethos. It presents the bride as a vessel able to assume a multiplicity of roles: there's the "Traditionalist," the "Modernist," the "Sensualist," the "Romantic," even the "Goth" bride. Wang understands that even though the modern bride longs to don the conformist white bridal uniform, she wants that uniform to reflect her individuality. Hence, her references to a military bride in full dress, the pregnant bride in her third trimester, and the lesbian bride.

Upstairs, the scene looks like backstage at *Swan Lake*: a frenzy of white silk, satin, lace, and froth. It is impossible to survey it all and not feel a sugary rush: the dresses are so luscious and creamy that you want to eat them. A half-dozen prospective brides are peppered throughout the space, each quivering with her own unique joy. They stand on round platforms before mirrors, inspecting their reflection as attendants fuss, arranging the trains. Most of the women here are under thirty-five. About one out of ten is marrying for the second time. Often women will bring their entire bridal party, or they will shop with their mothers for the first time since they were girls.

It's possible to run forty-one half-hour appointments a day through the salon, though the bride-to-be never feels that she's on a conveyer belt. Wang has tiered her pricing into five categories, just as car manufacturers do, so women can buy into the Vera Wang fantasy at various price points. A custom Vera Wang dress costs upward of $60,000; at the lowest end, there's the "Classic" line, which runs $2,000 to $3,000. But money is never discussed at the outset lest the illusion be marred. "These girls are a princess for a day," sales manager Lucy Wu explains. She points to the pearls and Swarovski crystal trimming on one dress. "It's like fairy dust," she murmurs.

The modern bride as a fairy-tale heroine is the primary myth that stokes the wedding industrial complex. As Wang told *The Los Angeles Times*: "I think it's every fantasy we've ever had rolled into one. I mean, it's from the time that we're little, there is Cinderella, Sleeping Beauty. There is all of that in all of us. And no matter how we are as business-women or liberated women.... There is in all of us also a romantic side, a sensual side, a passionate side. I think I've shifted the looks of weddings from being sort of dumb and—what is the word?—frilly, to having women think about weddings in general."

Casting the modern wedding as mythical fairy tale is a brilliant calculation. Recognizing that many independent women might rightly bristle at its extravagant, irrational edicts, the wedding complex has recast the bride as fulfilling her unconscious dream as a child, one who believes in fairy tales and who needs to be told what to do. An ad for Keepsake Jewelry that ran in bridal and women's magazines in 2001 exposes the mandate. It features a black-and-white photograph of a winsome blond girl, her front baby teeth missing, wearing a bridal veil. Seated beside her is a dark-haired boy dressed in a bow tie and top hat. A photograph of a giant diamond ring is superimposed on the image. "This is the ring she's dreamed about since she was 5 years old," the copy reads. "This is the ring she envisioned as a child dressing up. Playing at romance. The ring that began as a dream and is now a reality. The ring she will one day pass down to the children in her future."

So adorable is the imagery that it's easy to overlook the ad's questionable claims. First is the implication that a five-year-old "playing at romance" is capable of mature reasoning capabilities, that she could possibly understand the sexual desire that underlies romantic impulse. More preposterous is the notion that the dress-up fantasies of a little girl should entice a woman into one of the most crucial decisions she will make. No one would force a woman to commit to the career choices she divines for herself at age five. (Ballerina? Astronaut?) Yet it is acceptable, even encouraged, that the lacy, gossamer wedding fantasies of a five-year-old should be realized when she matures.

The notion that a Vera Wang strapless dress, a sit-down dinner for 150 in a Napa Valley vineyard followed by a white-dove release is imagery hardwired into a child's unconscious is, of course, ridiculous. Yet even intelligent women cleave to it. In her book *Bitch*, Elizabeth Wurtzel writes of the inescapable seduction of becoming a bride: "... despite perfunctory City Hall possibilities, every little girl grows up wanting a wedding at the Waldorf, the persistence of puff cloud dreams of a white dress and a train down the aisle is so deep-seated that my guess is—no exaggeration—it would be easier to eliminate racism or end poverty, to cure illiteracy or oust Fidel Castro than it would be to make girls stop wanting to be brides."

In *Something New: Reflections on the Beginnings of a Marriage*, published in 2000, *Self* magazine columnist Amanda Beesley writes, "I was eight years old and already I had begun to write the rules for my dream wedding ceremony." Beesley chose not to analyze why this was the case, though she did acknowledge that the bridal impulse was probably socially conditioned: "Blame it on society, the media, fashion, whatever: some of the most untraditional women turn old-fashioned when it comes to weddings."

Becoming a bride translates into being a consumer. Indeed, luring the future bride is seen by retailers as a pivotal branding opportunity. "If you can hook this consumer when she is in this life stage, you will fundamentally brand her for life," said *Bride's* publisher Deborah Fine in 1999. Nina Lawrence, who succeeded Fine at *Bride's*, portrayed the future bride as a giddy capitalist agent in her 2001 comment "Once a young woman gets a ring on her left hand, she is essentially on a spending spree."

From a marketer's perspective, promoting bridal desires as primal, unconscious impulses over which women have no control is a masterstroke, taking wedding planning out of the realm of practicality into irrational fantasy where budgets do not exist. How else could couples justify spending more on their wedding than the down payment for a house? The "wedding she's always wanted" proviso invites limitless spending in pursuit of perfection. What better justification than that her inner child made her do it?

The little-girl bridal fantasy is invoked whenever an irrational decision needs to be made, which is frequently. *Modern Bride* magazine used it to justify the purchase of a new dress in a roundtable in its April/May 2001 issue. One woman, admitting she was on a tight budget, asked about renting a gown rather than buying one to save money. The moderator shot it down: "Many financial decisions have to do with how you thought about your wedding when you were a little girl," she scolded. "If you've always had dreams about buying your dress with your mother standing by weeping, you are not going to be very happy in a rented gown." What the commentator didn't mention was that bridal magazines depend on dress manufacturers as their major advertisers; accordingly, most magazines don't carry advertising from bridal gown rentals or discounters. (Note, however, that this rule doesn't apply to grooms' clothing. "Forever never looked so good," reads the copy for Gingiss men's formal wear that ran in bridal magazines in 2001. The company, ironically, rents out clothing, which means "forever" is a temporary loan.)

Adult, educated women put up with the childhood regression imperative as part of the bridal role, one that encourages the bride to suspend reason and enter into marriage in a fuguelike state. The actress Alexandra Wentworth, writing in *Vogue,* captured the delusion that accompanied the prospect of becoming a bride: "The minute my boyfriend slipped that Tiffany engagement ring onto my finger, all I could think about was the dress. My concern was never, 'Is he the one?' but 'What the hell am I going to wear?' As we toasted with glasses of Cristal champagne, my mind raced with nightmare visions of satin bows, cheesy veils, and hideous silk flowers. Being an actress, I'm used to dressing up and playing a part. And here I was about to play the role of a lifetime."

Not only is the modern bride expected to adopt an artificial persona, but she is told her wedding day will be the high point of her life, rendering any other accomplishment secondary. As the famed makeup artist Bobbi Brown explained to one future bride during "wedding week" on the *Martha Stewart Living* television show in May 2001, becoming a bride is "your one day to be onstage, to be the center of attention."

But that claim too is another industry myth. As Wang's success makes clear, the dress, not the bride, is the star. So much so that a bride's relationship with her gown is now construed as the primary relationship underlying the wedding. "In my experience, brides have two great loves: their husbands and their wedding gowns (and not necessarily in that order)," wrote Jerry Shiner, the owner of a Toronto bridal gown preservation service, in a letter to the editor in Toronto's *Globe and Mail* newspaper. "The story of how they found their gown is often more romantic than how they found their man."

The dress, according to industry edict, must be white. White is the color of before. It's the hue of snow before the imprint, of clouds before the storm, of paper before the scribble. White is full of fresh hope, of endless possibilities. It is an abstraction, the refraction of all color. Which is fitting for an item occasionally purchased by women who don't even have a groom in mind. At the annual wedding gown sale in the basement of Boston's discount store Filene's, an event that rivals the bull run at Pamplona for risk of being trampled, many women who are single and unattached show up looking for a gown.

While it might seem as if women routinely spend thousands of dollars on their bridal dresses, the average price for a wedding dress in North America is closer to $800. But no matter how much a woman spends on her wedding dress, be it a sari, a cocktail frock, or a white-lace extravaganza, it's usually exponentially more than she would spend on a dress for any other occasion.

Such irrational expenditure for an item worn once is presented as simply another facet of the bridal "dream," as the introduction to *Vera Wang on Weddings* makes clear: "For most women a wedding gown represents far more than just a dress. It is also the embodiment of a dream, perhaps one she has nurtured since childhood. In this fantasy of idealized happiness, the groom represents perfection and the face of all human possibility. The instant a woman becomes engaged, however, all that energy and passion get transferred to her dress. What follows can be something akin to madness."

The "madness," the disconnect from reality, that besets the bride is not limited to her dress. It extends to cleaving to the myth of "tradition" that underlies the modern wedding. As Wang told *The New York Times* in 1998, young female celebrities, who serve as role models for young women, want "traditional" weddings: "I keep expecting the Hollywood weddings to be hipper, modern and offbeat, and they end up with weddings that are the most traditional," she said.

This notion of tradition, it should be noted, dates all the way back to 1987. That was the year Martha Stewart published *Weddings,* a glossy 370-page production that promoted lavish nuptials as a style statement for the middle classes, a way to express individuality as well as social status. *Weddings* chronicled more than forty elaborate nuptials, each with a distinctive theme that reflected the interests and exquisite tastes of the bride and groom—one at a ranch in Texas, another in Central Park, another on a yacht. Stewart transformed the wedding into a sumptuous party, one in which a couple incidentally happen to vow eternal allegiance. *The New York Times Book Review* gushed that *Weddings* was "a fifty-dollar, five-pound ode to perfect … a wedding voyeur's dream." The book became a publishing phenomenon.

In the introduction, Stewart forges a new link between individuality and a fabricated notion of traditionalism that justified inordinate attention and expenditure: "The wedding is a microcosm of the dreams and facts of American life," she observes. "What other event results in the single-minded attention of whole families for as much as a year; an expenditure often greater than that allotted for education; transformation of character from nonchalant libertine to concerned traditionalist; the suspension of all reality in the moment the bride, swathed with lace and net, floats down the aisle?"

The question was rhetorical, for the belief that an overproduced, lavish wedding was traditional for anyone other than royalty or the wealthy is false. The photograph of Stewart on her wedding day in 1960 on the back jacket of the book offered a more realistic glimpse of the so-called traditional wedding for the average couple thirty years earlier. There she is, wearing a simple, scoop-necked white dress made by her mother, a short veil, a string of pearls, and a pillbox hat. The book's fulsome homage to her husband, Andy, was also somewhat contrived in that the newly minted arbiter of the stylish nuptial was about to go through a protracted, messy divorce, a fact that would have marred the book's extensive publicity and enthusiastic reception.

The embrace of tradition was a masterstroke in that it filled a void. By the late 1980s, when the book was published, there was no clear script for weddings or, more to the point, for marriage. Stewart's notion of tradition coupled with the need for the "suspension of all reality" became convenient nostrums for the wedding industrial complex. In this context, tradition had nothing to do with heritage or even history; it was a fashion conceit contrived to provide the illusion of stability, to fill a gap with an illusory past.

Advertisers recognized that the notion of tradition might not be readily embraced by the modern bride, so they goaded her along. An advertisement for Waterford crystal, for example, presents a young woman in casual clothing, laughing at herself as she models a bridal veil in front of a mirror. The copy reads, "No, being the traditional bride doesn't feel like you, but neither does buying crystal stemware, but that's just part of the fun, isn't it?" The ad primes the bride as role player, having "fun" by spending irrationally on crystal stemware she will likely rarely use.

Women who would otherwise have nothing to do with archaic ritual, such as having their fathers give them away and pledging to obey their husbands, bought into tradition as an important element of their weddings. Tradition became a fashionable catch-all. It could refer to something as superficial as wearing a white wedding dress featuring boning. Or it could induce people who do not practice any religion to insist on a religious service for their weddings. According to *Modern Bride*, 87 percent of couples wed in a religious ceremony, while other studies suggest that only 38 percent of Americans attend religious services weekly.

The industry's celebration of tradition as a fashion construct also paved the way for a renewed acceptance of other traditions harking back to coverture. Many of these, such as a man asking his future wife's father for his daughter's hand, were presented as charming, if retrograde, gestures, even in cases where the couple owned property and had children together.

Tradition was celebrated for tradition's sake, as a trend, with little thought given to the broader implications. We saw this in the much-heralded "trend" in the late 1990s that saw women rushing to assume their husbands' names. "Name Droppers: More Brides Are Saying 'I Do' to Taking Their Husbands' Names," announced *Bride's* magazine in 1996. "Name Change Revival," trumpeted *The Globe and Mail* in 1998.

That women taking their husbands' names was a headline-generating issue seemed odd at a time when even political wives such as Cherie Booth Blair retained their maiden names professionally. There was also the fact that there is no registry of name change in North America, so tracking any trend in this area is next to impossible and invariably relies on anecdotal evidence. A 1994 study published in *American Demographics* claimed that 90 percent of American women adopted their husbands' names. (Of the rest, 5 percent hyphenated their names; 2 percent kept their maiden names and about 3 percent chose other alternatives such as using their maiden names professionally and their married names personally, or keeping their maiden names as second names.) According to a *Bride's* magazine survey of six thousand readers in 1996, 87 percent of wives-to-be planned to take their husbands' names—up 14 percent from 1992. "It's the younger brides that take their husbands' names easily," explained *Bride's* editor Millie Bratten. "They say everything from 'it's traditional' to 'it's part of his heritage and I want to be part of his heritage.'"

Other studies indicate that the higher the woman's social status or income, the less likely she is to take her husband's name. A study between 1980 and 2001, which extrapolated "normalized" figures derived from *New York Times* wedding announcements, Harvard alumnae records, and Massachusetts birth records revealed that fewer than 10 percent of women kept their own names in 1980, when the paper began reporting surname information, to a "sharp increase" to about 20 percent in 1985. By 2001, 35 percent of women said they would retain their own names. But the percentage of thirty-something college-educated women keeping their names actually dropped from 27 to 19 percent between 1990 and 2000. A decrease occurred even among women thirty-five to thirty-nine with established careers, normally the group most likely to be "keepers."

Claudia Goldin, a professor of economics at Harvard University and one of the authors of the study, concludes that a trend to take a husband's name represents a return to tradition. Yet if one truly wanted to look to tradition, one could consider feudal days, when the family name after marriage was that of the family with more social clout, no matter whether it was the man's or the woman's. By the nineteenth century, however, it was assumed that a woman would change her name to her husband's, consistent with the property-transferral aspect of marriage. In 1879, when the feminist Lucy Stone informed the Massachusetts court that there was no law requiring her to change her name, they drafted one.

The legal imperative telling women what to do on marriage has been replaced by social censure in which the issue of name change is a way of judging women, and their commitment to the marriage. Many women who take their husbands' names in the twenty-first century define themselves as feminists. They defend their choice to assume another name as representing more an act of free will than keeping the name they were born with. Other women reduce the matter to cosmetic preference, saying they prefer their husbands' names. I even heard a woman assert that taking her husband's name put her more on "equal footing" with him in that they now share the same name.

The much-trumpeted name-change revival is yet another sign of the fragility of marriage, one in which it remains the woman's job to provide ballast. Judith Newton, a professor at the University of California, explains it in terms of young women seeking stability through nomenclature: "I see desire on the part of young women in their twenties not to be divorced like their parents. They want to emphasize connection rather than individuality."

Most women who do change their names do so voluntarily, not because their husbands demand it. Laurie Scheuble, a Penn State sociology professor who has studied the name phenomenon with her husband, David Johnson, claims there's no link between a wife's name and marital happiness or unhappiness. She says women make their decision to change their name because "it's what's done."

One woman quoted in the *Globe and Mail* story on the trend to take a husband's name spoke in terms of family integrity: "We wanted people to see us as a couple, as a family, and this was an easy way to do that. The woman-as-property argument didn't enter into our discussion, because that's not the way we treat each other." Even so, she did admit that if she had had an established career, she would not have done it.

But if creating a single-family unit is the goal, why not adopt the wife's name? That choice remains so rare that when it does happen it is treated as front-page news, as was the case when New York lawyers David Soskin and Brande Stellings wed in 1998. *The New York Times* wedding announcement made clear that "Mr. Soskin will take Ms. Stellings's surname." The groom claimed his friends said he was crazy.

Equally uncommon are couples who create a new name, such as the University of Michigan graduate students Laura Aberbach and Barry Martin. After becoming engaged in 1991, the couple coined the name Arbreton, a composite of all their parents' surnames. The problem they encountered, however, was that Michigan law required men, but not women, to face a court hearing in order to change their names after marriage, a clear vestige of coverture. To avoid having to go through that process, Martin changed his name to Arbreton before the ceremony. The technicality is a reminder that for all the claims that one's name is an expression of self, it remains tethered to a social order, which in turn tethers us.

For a more comprehensive lesson in bridal branding and the corporate imperative that stokes the wedding industrial complex, one must travel thousand of miles south of Wang's Madison Avenue boutique to Lake Buena Vista, Florida. Welcome to Disney World. After you arrive, you must travel north on Floridian Way, past Seven Seas Drive, past Magnolia/Palm Drive, past faultless green fairways, then turn right through curlicue ivory-colored iron gates that have the words *Disney Wedding Pavilion* emblazoned on them. Don't be put off by the barren expanse of parking lot, or the antiseptic, soulless feel of the place. This is simulated romance central, the epicenter of Disney's copyrighted "Fairy Tale Wedding" program. Appropriately, the entire operation is built on former swampland.

Six to eight weddings take place every day, on average, throughout the twenty-seven-thousand-acre Disney World Resort. A couple can marry at a "New England yacht club," a "Polynesian resort," in front of the "Eiffel Tower" at the Epcot theme park, or on a copy set of *The*

Wizard of Oz. Or they can have a "Hollywood grand-style wedding" at the MGM Studios theme park, featuring a motorcade down "Sunset Boulevard," spotlights, screaming fans, paparazzi, and a walk down the red carpet. Most couples choose to wed at the nondenominational Wedding Pavilion, which sits on a tiny island, over a picturesque bridge, surrounded by the man-made Seven Seas Lagoon. The Wedding Pavilion, like everything else at Disney World, is retrofitted, a pastiche. Built in 1995, four years after the wedding program began, the structure is pseudo-Victorian. Every square inch has been calculated to exude pretty romance; it's no accident that Cinderella's castle, miles away at Fantasyland, is perfectly framed through the pastel-stained-glass window behind the altar.

The 2,500 or so weddings that take place at Disney World every year may pale beside the 120,000 in Las Vegas or the 2.6 million marriages that took place in North America in the year 2000. And certainly the overt commercialization of the scene would send a shudder down Martha Stewart's spine. But there is a strange kind of honesty here, in that Disney, the exemplar in merchandising sugary illusion, sells the purest high-octane rendition of the modern fairy-tale wedding, the most extreme version of its commercialized happily-ever-after iconography.

The edict for the Disney wedding program came in the late 1980s from the CEO, Michael Eisner, who saw the potential to cash in on Disney's growing stature as America's most popular honeymoon destination and on the fairy-tale imagery on which the company is based. The September 1991 launch of the program dovetailed with the Christmas 1991 release of *Father of the Bride,* a remake of the 1951 film starring Spencer Tracy and Elizabeth Taylor. Steve Martin reprised the Tracy role, that of a hapless man trying to cope with the prospective loss of his twenty-two-year-old daughter, who was presented, predictably, as a little girl, specifically Daddy's little girl. But true to Disney's new wedding mandate, the remake focuses more on Martin's trauma dealing with the excessive costs and aggravation involved in planning the perfect $250-a-head wedding. In the end, of course, all the inconvenience and financial sacrifice are seen to be worth it.

At Franck's Bridal Studio, a faithful re-creation of the froufrou salon operated by the manic wedding planner played by Martin Short in the movie, Disney couples are offered one-stop shopping for everything from concept to ceremony to Disney Honeymoon Packages. The only things you can't buy here are the wedding costumes. Once couples have met with a Disney sales manager to set a budget and sign a contract, they're turned over to a wedding-event manager, or, as they're called at Disney, a "fairy godmother" or "fairy godfather." At Disney, couples purchase as much of the fairy tale as they can afford. (This amount can be extended, however, via Disney's tie-in with American Express's Special Purchase Account. The account, which has no pre-set spending limit, gives the bride and groom "the freedom to have the wedding of your dreams," according to an Amex brochure.)

The perfect-wedding details do add up. Goods and services used in a wedding are sold at a premium, as if to reflect the transcendent nature of the occasion. On theknot.com wedding Web site, a "Promises Grace Unity Candle" sells for $29.95, whereas a similar ordinary candle could be purchased elsewhere for less than $10. At Disney, a knife to cut the wedding cake costs $25. Some might wonder why a bridal couple would need a special knife when any knife can cut a cake. That would indicate a lack of understanding of the ethos of the wedding industrial complex, which dictates perfection; all must be new and sanitized despite the lip service given to tradition.

At Disney, there seems no end to the optional add-ons. Fireworks begin at $3,000. A wedding cake topped with a white chocolate copy of Cinderella's castle starts at $900. A release of forty white doves will set a couple back $250. (These are not actual doves, but "Disney doves," meaning white homing pigeons on loan from Cinderella's castle, where they perform in the stage show.)

The program's defining motif is Cinderella. Her glass coach is its logo, an image etched on a broad selection of Disney wedding accessories, from cake cutters to champagne flutes. A Disney bride can arrive in Cinderella's glass coach with a costumed driver and footmen pulled by four dappled gray ponies, the use of which costs $2,500. A trumpeter will announce the bride's arrival. The major-domo from

Cinderella will deliver the rings down the aisle in Cinderella's glass slipper. At Disney they like to say that Disney is the one place where the modern bride's "Cinderella dreams can come true." (But though every bride may dream of becoming Cinderella, at least in the mind of marketers, brides married at Disney are not allowed to actually dress up as Cinderella. There is only one Cinderella at Disney World, and she is on the payroll.)

Obviously all women do not want to be Cinderella on their wedding day; most, one presumes, want to be themselves. But the "Cinderella dream" is the inescapable, animating metaphor of the wedding industry. As Lori Weil, national sales director of Bridal Givenchy, told the Associated Press, "Everybody wants to be Cinderella for a night."

Cinderella, a case study in one-night transformation, is a brilliant bridal role model if you're trying to get women to part with their money and their identities. The tale of the motherless char girl rescued by a nameless prince with whom she lives happily ever after has enduring appeal, across time and nations. It's been told in over three hundred variations, the first of which can be traced back to China in AD 850. The enduring allure of the Cinderella story has been dissected endlessly. Its resonance has been linked to the fact it taps into a child's primal fears— of the death of one's mother, the Freudian worry that one's father's love will be transferred to an evil new wife. Its appeal to grown women is far more complicated to parse.

The desire for rescue has been presented as hitting a primitive female nerve. Even Gloria Steinem admitted in her 1992 book, *Revolution from Within: A Book of Self-Esteem,* that her lack of confidence led her into "rescue" fantasies, which she exorcised by dating wealthy men.

In 1950, Walt Disney Studios copyrighted the Cinderella tale with the release of its animated movie based on the most famous version, by the French poet Charles Perrault. Writing in the late seventeenth century, Perrault sanitized many of the grisly elements found in the earlier Brothers Grimm rendition, such as doves pecking out Cinderella's evil stepsisters' eyes and the sisters hacking off their heels and toes in order to squeeze their feet into the glass slipper. He also introduced enchanting details such as Cinderella's fairy godmother and the coach that threatens to turn into a pumpkin if Cinderella is not home by midnight. Disney followed *Cinderella* with the successful release of *Sleeping Beauty* in 1959. But between the 1960s and 1990s, the fairy tale fell on hard times. Feminists decried what came to be known as the "Cinderella myth," blaming it for encouraging a female rescue fantasy that made women dependent on men and marriage. In 1981, Colette Dowling created a stir with the best seller *The Cinderella Complex: Women's Hidden Fear of Independence,* which argued that women's socially conditioned fear of independence—reinforced by the Cinderella story—was holding them back. Rather than go out and fend for themselves, they waited for something or someone external to change their lives.

Before fairy tales like *Cinderella* had been sanitized for the American marketplace, however, they were anti-marriage screeds. Most of them were indictments of marriage told by women, and hardly the happily-ever-after tales on which a wedding industry could be formed. The first "fairy tales," in fact, were told by disgruntled wives, passing on their knowledge to younger women. This was long before the Brothers Grimm, before Giambattista Basile, Hans Christian Andersen, and Charles Perrault—the men associated with the genre—came on the scene. And these stories were in no way endorsements of female servitude and transformation. Rather, the imaginative, often gruesome, tales were seditious indictments of female powerlessness and the dissatisfactions of marriage. They also reflected women's fears concerning childbirth, then the greatest killer of women. Recounting such stories was one of the only ways that women, who possessed no political rights, could surreptitiously rebel against social constraints.

Aristocratic women, frustrated by the strictures of marriage, brought the literary fairy tale to popularity in seventeenth-century France. Love and marriage in these often dark tales are not presented as a Utopian paradise. Responding to the common practices of arranged and forced marriages so typical of their class, these women expressed their frustrations and yearning for freedom to govern their own lives according to love, not social hierarchy or wealth.

But those were hardly the kinds of tales desired at the French court of Versailles, for which Perrault wrote his *Cinderella.* His audience at the court was looking for simplistic, feel-good, moralistic narrative. In this regard they were not unlike Western movie audiences in the 1990s, a decade that saw a "Cinderella simplex" replace the "Cinderella complex" of the 1980s. Rather than being seen as a symbol of female dependency, Cinderella was lauded as a heroine. This new archetype was presented, fittingly, on the cusp of the decade in the blockbuster *Pretty Woman,* which was produced by the Touchstone-Disney division. In it, Julia Roberts plays Vivian Ward, a Sunset Strip hooker; her prince, played by Richard Gere, is a corporate takeover specialist who arrives not on a white charger but in a red Ferrari. He hires her for a week, puts her up in his plush Beverly Hills hotel suite, and sends her off on a Rodeo Drive shopping spree that transforms her into a woman who fits into Los Angeles society. At the end of their week together, Roberts's character has been transformed; she recognizes the moral error of her ways, refuses his payment for sex, and decides to give up prostitution and return to school. Gere's character comes after her in a white stretch limousine. The movie ends with Gere and Roberts on a fire escape. "So what happens after he climbed up the tower and rescued her?" he asks. To which she responds, "She rescues him right back." The politically correct notion of shared rescue excused the film's retrograde premise. *The New York Times* gushingly described the movie as the "first post-feminist fairy tale." They were right on that point. What other fairy tale begins, "Once upon a time, there was a hooker who patrolled the Sunset Strip"?

In possession of a winning formula, Hollywood squeezed the trope dry. The 1998 movie *Ever After: A Cinderella Story,* set in sixteenth-century France and starring Drew Barrymore and Anjelica Huston, was billed as a "feminist fairy tale" because the central character was educated. So entrenched became the Cinderella myth that the *New York Post* billed the August 2001 funeral of the young R&B singer Aaliyah glowingly as a "Cinderella Funeral for a Music Princess." Even a Cinderella burial, it seemed, was acceptable fodder for female fantasy.

Cinderella is useful to the wedding industrial complex for several reasons. One, she represents the ideal consumer demographic: the upwardly mobile woman. She also reflects typical bridal anxieties:

the threat of the clock running out before the illusion is broken; the bewitching disguise required to seduce the prospective husband; the notion that the right man will provide the happily-ever-after ending.

Most of all, though, Cinderella's transformation echoes the commercial edict that the modern bride sublimate herself in the role. A cover line on the *Canadian Bride* Summer 2001 issue sums up the mentality that reigns: "Knockout Body—60 Days to a Sleek New You." The bride is expected to become a "new" version of herself, whether it be by losing weight, having cosmetic dental surgery, or undergoing laser eye surgery because a woman in glasses doesn't fit with the imagery of bridal perfection. The pressure is intense, as reflected in the slogan in an ad for Crest White Strips that ran in bridal magazines: "a day to remember, a smile they'll never forget...." The wedding consultant Deborah McCoy told *Canadian Bride* that over 80 percent of her clients vow to "lose 10, 20 pounds or more." To do so they often resort to such drastic measures as weight-loss pills and even plastic surgery. One bride who went on an eight-hundred-calorie-a-day starvation diet to lose twenty-five pounds was celebrated in *Wedding Bells* magazine. "When you're growing up, you envision looking glamorous and gorgeous on your wedding day," she explained. "No one pictures carrying extra poundage."

The excuse of childish fantasies was again invoked: "This is her 15 minutes of fame, the day that she has been dreaming of for years," says Gilda Carle, author of *Don't Bet on the Prince! How to Have the Man You Want by Betting on Yourself.* "She is willing to put herself through just about anything to achieve the image of her dreams." Again and again women's desire to transform themselves for marriage is presented as stemming from internal, rather than external, forces. "It's not the man who wants them to change," Carle says. "A man asks a woman to marry him because he loves her as she is. Anything that she tries to change about her body is a change that's coming from her own insecurity."

And of course marketers cultivate the future bride's insecurity, as reflected in a print ad for Weight Watchers in 2002 that showed a picture of a woman with a wedding dress: "Want to lose 20 pounds before my wedding. Want that wedding dress in a 10 and not a 14. Want my husband to see me walk down the aisle and go 'Wow.' Want to join Weight Watchers today."

The overriding conceit is one of conformity, one evident at its most full-blown at Disney World. At Disney, as in the world outside, couples create their own romantic fiction by borrowing from mass-market entertainment. Most often they make their "personal" statement by appropriating Disney imagery. A fog-shrouded copy of the forest entrance from Disney's 1991 box-office hit *Beauty and the Beast,* for example, is frequently requested, as are details from Disney's *Aladdin.* There is no room for irony in the Magic Kingdom. A couple will not pause to reflect before asking for imagery or music from a doomed love story such as *Titanic,* though couples married outside Disney don't either. Or they'll stage their nuptials with a glittering *Wizard of Oz* theme, the bride wearing ruby-red slippers, unconcerned that Oz is a facade.

Disney's success as a wedding destination is dwarfed by the dominant role it plays in the secondary romance industry that serves as a crucial adjunct to the wedding industrial complex. This informal industry comprises corporations such as De Beers, Mattel, and Harlequin Books, each of which supports the notion of eternal love and the fairy-tale wedding within the broader cultural arena.

Disney provides an excellent case study of how bridal lust is fueled. Through its ownership of the ABC television network, it promotes such fare as "Wedding Week" on the *Regis and Kelly* program. There are also audience-drawing contests such as a "Happily Ever After: Love in Times Square Contest," which aired on *Good Morning America* in June 2001, showing the winning couple exchanging their vows surrounded by fairy-tale imagery, including a horse-drawn carriage. Disney also orchestrates multi-media-sponsored tie-ins, such as one in May 2000 when Disney-owned ABC Daytime and ABC.com teamed up with WeddingChannel.com to join the Web sites with the ABC soap opera *All My Children,* in which viewers selected which Vera Wang dress a character would wear to her wedding, with the dress later given away as a prize.

More subtle is the manner in which Disney promotes a scripted bridal fantasy to the next generation of brides, the ones who would be "dreaming" of their wedding day. The primary conduit for this is fairy-tale movies such as *The Little Mermaid, Beauty and the Beast,* and *Pochahontas.* But Disney also sells the dream via its licensing relationship with Mattel, famed as the marketer of Barbie. In 1998, in a masterstroke of marketing synergy, Mattel asked Vera Wang to create a Vera Wang Bridal Barbie. The following year, the company issued a $500 Millennium Bride Barbie, a limited run of ten thousand dolls attired in a silver strapless gown "trimmed with radiant faux diamonds," faux diamond solitaire earrings, and a faux silver diamond tiara with a cascading veil.

Mattel's Princess Bride Barbie, a doll launched in 1999, embodies the expectation of bridal transformation. When it is in "princess" mode, the doll wears a blue velvet bodice. In "bridal" mode, the bodice is removed to reveal an all-white, glittering gown. She also carries a plastic silver "mirror," which, when held at one angle, offers a reflection of herself; when tilted down, it reflects the image of Prince Ken, her groom, who, appropriately, is sold separately.

In October 2000, Mattel issued a *Barbie as Princess Bride* CD-ROM based on the Princess Bride Barbie. According to Mattel's marketing, the CD-ROM "lets girls ages four and up help Princess Bride Barbie discover true love, then create the ultimate fairy tale wedding." In the game, girls explore the "enchanted" world of Princess Bride Barbie and "bring the fairy tale to life" by playing games and activities such as sorting the wedding invitations, mixing up a "magical" wedding cake, designing the "perfect" wedding dress, conducting the orchestra, and helping Prince Ken sail his ship back to the kingdom.

Disney's wedding script for little girls is child's play, however, next to the cunning marketing of the diamond under the aegis of De Beers, the monopoly responsible for transforming a common, overmined gem into a symbol of eternal love. It was De Beers that created the desire for that engagement ring that began as a "dream" in the slumbering mind of a little girl in the ad for Keepsake Jewelry. Like so many of the assertions that underlie the wedding industrial complex, that one too is a myth. The "dream" of the diamond engagement ring did not belong to a little girl but to a middle-aged South African businessman named Harry Oppenheimer who was motivated not by love but by love of profit.

Oppenheimer was the son of Sir Ernest Oppenheimer, the powerful South African businessman who took control of De Beers Consolidated Mines in 1929. De Beers was founded in 1871 by Sir Cecil Rhodes as a way of regulating the huge diamond deposit unearthed in South Africa in the 1860s, one that amounted to 90 percent of the world's diamond supply. That discovery instantly reduced the value of a gem that had been rare, and thus precious, since antiquity. Scooping diamonds out by the ton rendered them little more than bits of pressurized carbon that had their greatest value in industrial applications.

The British financiers who had organized the South African mines were not prepared to see their investment disappear, so they created De Beers to control supply and pricing of the gem. While other commodities such as gold, wheat, and pork bellies fluctuated wildly in price, De Beers' strict supply-demand policies ensured that the price of diamonds rose each year following the Depression. If demand slumped, De Beers stockpiled. Or it bought up new mines, froze out challengers, and mopped up excess supply.

Manipulating supply was meaningless without stimulating consumer demand. And the most effective way to do this, decided the men who ran De Beers, was to create a market for diamond engagement rings in North America. With that in mind, Harry Oppenheimer traveled from Johannesburg to New York in 1938 to meet with Gerald Lauck, the president of the then-thriving advertising firm N. W. Ayre. Ayre was given the task of making diamonds "an inseparable part of courtship and married life" in North America. The idea was to instill the notion that diamonds possessed an emotional value that far exceeded their market worth. Additionally, buying a diamond had to be seen as a lifetime proposition; that way, no one would try to resell it.

Ayre's first gambit was to link diamonds with movie stars, a practice that continues to this day. It also set up the Diamond Information Center, a De Beers marketing arm that tells people what to look for when buying a diamond. The center would become the official source of industry "trends" as it predictably reported the unflagging popularity of diamonds, such as one study released in 2002 that claimed 84 percent of all U.S. brides had celebrated their engagement with a diamond engagement ring. In 1948, the Ayre copywriter Frances Gerety, a woman who never married, came up with the slogan "A Diamond Is Forever," a line that brilliantly linked diamonds to eternal romance while allowing consumers to hope that their diamonds would never depreciate in value—which is not the case, as anyone who has ever tried to sell a diamond can attest. The fact that the line represented wishful thinking didn't deter *Advertising Age* from proclaiming it the greatest advertising slogan of the twentieth century.

The diamond engagement ring was sold as "a psychological necessity" without which a marriage proposal shouldn't be taken seriously. The message extended to Japan, where centuries of arranged marriages precluded the need for romantic symbols. In 1967, De Beers began using Western imagery to sell the diamond as a visible sign of progressive, luxurious, Western values: by the 1990s, more than 70 percent of Japanese brides wore diamonds.

De Beers was fastidious in always presenting diamonds in a favorable context, going so far as to demand that magazines not place its ads with "adjacencies to hard news or anti-love-romance theme." It hosted celebrity auctions and engineered product placements on television programs. In 1997, the company persuaded *Baywatch*, then the most popular television program in the world, to devote an entire episode to a story about the purchase of a diamond engagement ring.

De Beers also put a value on the future wife directly linked to her husband's earning potential. That arrived with its edict that an engagement ring should cost two months of her future husband's salary. The size of the diamond, went the marketing message, represented the depth of love, as illustrated in one De Beers ad: "You can't look at Jane and tell me she's not worth two months' salary. Just look at her. So I wanted to get her the biggest diamond I could afford. One that other men could see without getting too close."

The value of the ring was a flexible standard, however, based on what the market would bear. In Europe, men were asked to shell out the equivalent of one month's salary; in Japan, brides were assigned a higher price tag by De Beers as men were expected to spend three months' salary on their future wives.

De Beers' marketing also influenced the engagement dynamic. In promoting the "surprise" proposal, the company perpetuated the notion that women play a passive role in the marriage decision. As Ayre's internal memos made clear, this strategy was calculated to benefit diamond merchants. Its research revealed that if women are asked to pick out their engagement ring, they pick a less expensive ring than their fiancé does. The De Beers Web site even offers a link titled "Engagement Proposal Ideas," gambits included to make the diamond a "game piece during a game of Monopoly," an unintentional irony given De Beers' stature as a monolith.

We continue to remain tethered to De Beers' dictum that the man propose, even when that proposal has been wrung from him as a result of "The Ultimatum," that marry-me-or-walk edict that underlies many engagements. Even then, the surprise is a crucial part of the mix. One poll conducted by theknot.com Web site revealed an overwhelming 70 percent of women said they didn't expect their proposal when it happened.

It's worth noting that as the wedding industrial complex became more entrenched, the lavish engagement ring became a more celebrated cog in the machine. Media reports of non-celebrity engagements routinely include detailed descriptions of the ring, down to the number of carats. The insinuation is obvious: the bigger the diamond, the greater the love. Or, more cynically, the greater the bride-to-be's accomplishment. The engagement ring was even elevated to a cinematic plot point in the 2002 movie *Sweet Home Alabama.* Female audiences swooned as a young man had the legendary Tiffany open its flagship New York store after-hours so his wife-to-be could pick whichever ring she wanted.

Within De Beers, however, no one deludes themselves about the gem's financial value. As Nicky Oppenheimer, De Beers' chairman and the son of Harry, told a British reporter in 1999, "...diamonds are intrinsically worthless, except for the deep psychological need they fill." But while diamonds may be intrinsically worthless, they are so psychologically valuable they have been capable of financing civil wars on the

African continent. According to reports, diamonds—the bigger the better—were traded by African militants to buy guns and underwrite mass killing and mutilation in the Congo, Sierra Leone, and Angola. Gems sold this way became known as "blood diamonds" or, more politely, "conflict diamonds."

De Beers said that none of its diamonds fell into that category. But the taint surrounding blood diamonds, combined with accusations of price fixing against De Beers and increased competition from new suppliers during the 1990s, proved too much. In 1994, the U.S. Justice Department laid price-fixing charges, which prevented De Beers from selling diamonds into the country directly. In 1999, the company announced that it was ending its control supply system and would use Diamond Trading Company as its brand name. It began identifying products with a "forevermark" logo to avoid any confusion with blood diamonds. In 2004, De Beers SA pleaded guilty to the price-fixing charge and paid a $10 million fine, which paved the way to do business again in the United States.

Public airing of De Beer's questionable practices didn't affect demand. In February 2004, the company announced sales of $5.5 billion. Only a few voices dared suggest that the romance of the stone had been compromised. Susan Emerling, writing for *Salon*, greeted the news of De Beers' strategy with a cynical eye: "From now on, you'll know if that big rock your fiancé has just put on your finger was dug out of the ground by brutalized children or waddled out of a war zone in a smuggler's rectum."

Not that women caught up in bridal dementia cared. In 2003, the writer Molly Jong-Fast, the daughter of novelist Erica Jong, was profiled in *The New York Observer*'s "Countdown to Bliss" column. She admitted that before she became engaged she and her fiancé had been sensitive to the politics of diamonds: "We were like, 'No diamonds!' she said. 'Little children on the Ivory Coast lose their hands for diamonds!' But then all of a sudden, Grandma Rose's ring came into the picture, and we were like, 'What little children?'"

The comment signaled the paradoxical position of the modern bride. Just when she no longer has concerns about being consumed legally by the act of marriage, she runs the risk of being subsumed by a huge, white, shimmering, artificial engine driven by commercial forces that dictates her behavior and redefines her identity. Coverture has been replaced by commercial forces that work to reinforce conformity and make women subservient to events spinning beyond their control.

Women, and they are many, who reject the fantasy bridal construct can't completely avoid the white-lace vortex. Kate Cohen, author of *A Walk Down the Aisle: Notes on a Modern Wedding,* writes that she made every effort to reject wedding-industry pressures, spending less than $350 on a dress and doing the cooking for the reception herself. Yet she was unable to escape it entirely: "Until the summer before my wedding, I didn't buy a hair dryer or a razor and Adam had vowed not to marry me if I wore any makeup, but in an effort to look more beautiful, more bridal, more like the way I felt I was supposed to look on my wedding day, I did do something I never dreamed I would do. I joined Gold's Gym."

It's common for women to complain about losing control over one of the most important days of their lives. Helen, a twenty-one-year-old student, speaks of being overwhelmed by the process: "If I'd had my way, it would have been really small and simple, and that was what we initially intended. I just felt caught up in this big thing that I didn't have any control over, and people just kept pressing me to do this or that. I was under a lot of stress." "I felt like I was hemorrhaging money," says Shawna Snukst, twenty-nine, whose September 2000 wedding ended up costing more than $50,000. "Everything was so completely overpriced. I was appalled."

Planning the perfect wedding is even capable of transforming an intelligent, rational woman into a monster commonly known as "Bridezilla." On the frugalbride.com Web site, the newly engaged April Pickering Torresan writes of driving to a convenience store to buy all the bridal magazines she could get her hands on. "It was the Unleashing of BRIDE-zilla," she wrote. "There was no turning back. I became completely obsessed with weddings and not just my wedding either. ALL weddings." *The New York Times* dubbed such women "aesthetic-fixated" brides. As they are, given their obsession over the width of the petals in the flowers of their bouquet, or how photo-genic the officiant.

The Bridezilla phenomenon has become so ingrained that even bridal magazines—the very publications that encourage obsessive attention to detail—have had to acknowledge it. *Modern Bride*'s April/May 2001 issue featured a questionnaire titled "Is Your Wedding Taking Over Your Life?" At one end of the scoring was the "Hesitant Honey," who was advised that "if you don't start calling the shots, you may end up with a wedding that has nothing to do with your personal-ity and taste." At the other extreme was the "Frantic Femme," who was counseled, "To help you get a grip, remember that your wedding is only for seven hours of your life, and your marriage is for a lifetime." Such concern was not unlike a drug dealer expressing worry that his customers might end up addicted.

The drug addiction analogy is not that far-fetched. The fixation on wedding ritual is a narcotic, a shot of morphine that inures participants from focusing on the marriage, the point of the ritual. The wedding is always presented as the last scene of the fairy tale, never the first scene of the marriage. No one would want to emulate Charles and Diana's marriage. Yet demand for their regal wedding imagery remains insa-tiable, so much so that in November 2002, the former New York mayor Rudy Giuliani gave his future wife, Judith Nathan, a sapphire-diamond engagement ring similar to the one Charles gave Diana.

The "fantasy" white wedding has become so disconnected from mar-riage that even people who shun wedlock want in on the ritual. In *Unmarried to Each Other,* Dorian Solot and Marshall Miller, founders of the Alternatives to Marriage Project (which defines itself as "a national nonprofit organization advocating for equality and fairness for unmar-ried people, including people who choose not to marry, cannot marry, or live together before marriage") buy into the commercial extrava-ganza of the perfect wedding. "There's no reason you can't wear the white dress, walk down the aisle, exchange I do's and rings, and dance the Electric Slide all night long," they write.

There is another way to interpret the insanity surrounding the mod-ern wedding—and the bride's place in it. And that is the fact that it

echoes the irrational underpinnings of modern marriage. When shopping for a mate, we look for nothing less than the One, a romantic construct lifted from Plato's *Symposium,* which posits that we are all sliced in
two, "like a flatfish," before birth and destined to search out our perfect
matching halves. It is not uncommon for women to announce they knew
they had met their future husbands after knowing them mere minutes.
The New York Times' "Vows" column of March 10, 2002, describes one
bride who says she knew she had found her future mate after exchanging
only a few e-mails: "She hadn't felt the touch of his hand, hadn't heard
his voice or even seen his face, but some time around their third e-mail
exchange Kirsti Karina Scutt decided that Edmund Everett Edwards
was the man she was going to marry." The bride holds a master's degree
and is therefore capable of rational thought. Yet when a friend showed
her Edwards's photograph before she actually met him, Scutt became
giddy. "That's my husband," she said. And just over three years after
their first e-mail exchange in the fall of 1998, they were wed.

Becoming a wife is presented as being grounded in desire, not practical considerations, though there is no doubt these play a role. Ask
people why they marry and the reasons invariably veer to the self-
referential—because they're ready to settle down, because they want
someone to grow old with, because they've found their soul mate. As
the journalist Lynn Darling once wrote, "I married the man I married
because I liked his version of myself better than my own." As a rationale, it's more compelling than that of a woman I know who realized she
wanted to marry a man when she saw him cup a ladybug in his hands
and then release it outdoors. She's now divorced.

Women raised in divorced families—one-quarter of all brides by
2003—are particularly bereft of a script for marriage. The actress
Jennifer Aniston, the child of divorced parents, expressed the sentiment of many in an interview in *Vanity Fair* magazine: "I didn't have
a fantasy of what marriage would be like. I had no idea. I didn't grow
up surrounded by any form of marriage." She knew only that she
wanted her marriage "to be based in love—not money, not security....
Just finding someone who was your best friend, who you could grow
with and share the passage of time—and that's what I found." Her

wedding to Brad Pitt in 2000 was fittingly an elaborate event, complete with fireworks, estimated to cost more than $1 million.

While bridal transformation is key to the modern bridal script, the one word rarely mentioned by wedding magazines is the one that describes what the bride will actually be transformed into: *wife*. Thumbing through thousands of glossy wedding magazines yields less than half a dozen references to the word *wife*. When it does appear, it reinforces the notion that a wife is the caretaker of her husband's behavior. *Modern Bride* reminded new wives that it's their job to restrict their groom's drinking at the wedding, lest he get drunk: "If you're worried that your sweetie might not resist imbibing, just remind him what can happen in bed to a man who's been over served—maybe that will keep him on the up and up."

But even though the word isn't used, the bride is reflexively cast in a familiar "wifely" role—as the organizer, the social facilitator, the family peacemaker, the custodian of the couple's sex life. Most pronounced is the association made between wife and domesticity. We see this in advertising suggesting that the bride is marrying not the groom but a household appliance. This conceit dates back to ads that ran during World War II. One for the Proctor Dual automatic toaster in 1942 shows a picture of a uniformed airman kissing his bride. In the foreground sit two pieces of perfectly browned bread and the copy "Love, honor ... and crisper toast. Here's a husband whose toast will be just the way he wants it."

Likewise, General Electric advertised a refrigerator with an illustration of a bridegroom in tuxedo and top hat carrying his bride with the slogan "The one you've always wanted." It's not clear if the reference is to the refrigerator or the groom. But the bride's broad smile suggests she can't wait to engage in wifely duties, be they defrosting the refrigerator or having sex. A T-Fal ad that ran in 2001 echoes the theme. It features a photograph of a man and woman in a dreamy trance. The copy compares the pots and pans to the man: "Like the perfect husband—clever and attractive." An ad for KitchenAid appliances that appeared in the *Martha Stewart Weddings* Summer 2001 issue featured a pile of white wedding gifts festooned with bows and ribbons, which resembles a bride. The copy reads, "Underneath the fancy ribbons and bows, I patiently wait. Hard-working, strong and intelligent. I am the perfect choice for a lifetime of happiness." Whether it's the bride or a prominently placed automatic mixer that's doing the talking isn't certain.

Some advertising, recognizing the fact that this is the twenty-first century, addresses the fact that the modern husband might occasionally take on household duty. An ad for Hoover vacuum cleaners shows bride and groom figurines on top of a wedding cake with the groom pushing a tiny Hoover. Of course, the ad is targeted at women. And what better way to sell the drudgery of housework to a bride than to suggest it might be done by her groom?

Unsurprisingly, the profound rift between being a bride and becoming a wife is the source of cognitive dissonance for many women. Writer Allison Glock expressed the schism in *Elle* magazine in 2000: "Once you're married, life is defined by the Before and After, the gap widening as each day passes, the single you either fading gracefully like a pressed flower or growing weedlike into some unbearable specter of youth and vitality and breasts that pointed north."

The message is clear: marriage is an unnatural reverse metamorphosis in which the bride is the butterfly, the wife the lowly caterpillar. Even Vera Wang, who became rich selling the chimera of fairy dust, downplays her identity as a wife. When asked by an interviewer, Wang listed her role as a wife behind that of being a career woman and mother. "First of all, I'd define myself as a businesswoman," she told *Town & Country* magazine. "Then mother. And I say this after busi-nesswoman because the financial responsibilities are so overwhelming in my mind I regard my own security, and that of my family, as very much interwoven with my business.... My third role is wife. My hus-band says he's left to last, but I enjoy my married life. I try not to bring work home."

The disconnect between bride and wife is not new. In *The Future of Marriage*, published in 1972, the sociologist Jessie Bernard introduced the term "a shock theory of marriage" to explain the phenomenon: "marriage introduces such profound discontinuity to the lives of women as to constitute emotional health hazards." Bernard blamed this shock on "the end of the romantic idealization that terminates the honeymoon." This, she writes, is known in research literature as "disenchantment." This dislocation, according to Bernard, was the result of several factors—lack of privacy, no longer being on best behavior, and also "when the wife ceases to be the catered-to and becomes the caterer-to."

By the 1990s, the decade of the full-blown fairy-tale wedding, the notion that women experienced a crisis at marriage was entrenched. In *Marriage Shock: The Transformation of Women into Wives*, published in 1997, author Dalma Heyn interviewed hundreds of young wives, all of whom said they experienced dislocation after marriage and altered their behavior to conform to a traditional wifely script. They also found themselves monitoring their husband's behavior in a way they never did before marriage, such as noticing how many drinks he had. They would even feel guilty when they bought new clothing for themselves. Their husbands hadn't asked for these changes; in some cases, they didn't even like the more demure persona their wives were adopting.

Easing women through marriage shock became rich fodder for even more bridal self-help books, which served as an antidote to the wedding industrial complex. Marg Stark, author of *What No One Tells the Bride,* says she wrote the book to help other brides through the "identity crisis" she experienced after her wedding.

"During the engagement and first years of marriage, I worried that I was not as blissed out as everyone expected me to be. I feared married life would subsume the independent, feisty woman I had become when I was single. As much as I loved my fiancé/husband, I was not prepared for the profound identity crisis my engagement ring brought on. An incredible newlywed code of silence inhibited me and my newly married friends from talking about our fears and adjustments."

She counsels women not to fall into the trap of the illusory perfect wife, "that they need not kill themselves trying to be Martha Stewart by day, sexpot by night. Your husband fell in love with you, not with the ideal you have of the 'perfect wife.' The more you relax, the more you fall in love with him rather than with your fairy tale, the happier you will be."

Of course, many women don't want any part of the fairy tale, which has created yet another marketing opportunity. Web sites such as indiebride.com, a "site for the independent bride," emerged, in which women could vent their concerns about changing their names, and read articles about how to call off the wedding, or with titles like "Do Wives Get a Bum Deal?"

One woman who defied the wedding industrial complex entirely, ironically, was Alexis Stewart, daughter of Martha. When Alexis married in October 1997, her wedding was not prominently splashed in her mother's flawless *Martha Stewart Weddings*. Instead, it was relegated to "Remembering," a one-page feature on the back page. In the piece, Stewart admitted that she started her own "secret plan" for her daughter's wedding when Alexis was ten years old. She planted a row of apple trees along a path, anticipating that by the time her daughter was old enough to marry, they would form a natural canopy through which she could walk with her groom. But her daughter did not share her mother's notion of bridal perfection. Instead, she wed in a civil service at New York City Hall, wearing a gray flannel pantsuit, and she rejected her mother's offer to throw her a big, splashy party.

Her mother chose not to embrace her daughter's alternative script for the modern bride, one that is active, defiant, and unwilling to conform to unwritten rules. She expressed only sadness and disappointment. "It was not the wedding I dreamed about for Alexis," she wrote. One can only wonder, Why not, if that was the wedding her daughter wanted for herself? Alas, even a grey-flannel wedding cannot ensure marital happiness, as eventually Alexis Stewart divorced.

The gulf between mother and daughter, between consumer impulse and heartfelt need to connect, captured perfectly the dilemma facing the woman on the threshold of becoming a wife in the early years of the twenty-first century. As we will see, it is a dilemma that becomes more pronounced when that bride is transformed into wife.

Chapter 3

Mystique Chic

The emergence of the "traditional" bride dovetailed perfectly with another pseudo-retro boom taking root during the 1990s. Increasingly, housework—an endeavor reviled for decades as drudgery, as the source of women's psychiatric problems, as the very root of female oppression—was presented as both fashionable and, even more perversely, a surefire route to female satisfaction.

Call it mystique chic. Call it the ultimate backlash to *The Feminine Mystique.* Whatever its title, cleaning toilets and mopping floors became the focus of Downy-soft-core porn targeted at women. *British Vogue* added a housekeeping column peppered with tips from celebrities. *Canadian House & Home* proclaimed "the luxe laundry room" a "hot trend" for 2003. Lavender-scented water for ironing became the perfect, if unused, gift for time-strapped professional women. Britain's Channel 4 broadcast a seven-part makeover series with the guilt-inducing title "How Clean Is Your House?" A bevy of businesses popped up selling high-end cleaning products—lemon-verbena dishwashing liquid and the like—to time-strapped women who savored the idea of owning them, if not actually using them. As evidence of how cosmetic this new lust to clean was, the U.S. retailer Nordstrom sold Caldrea-Green Tea-Patchouli dish-soap liquid at its makeup counters.

Housekeeping books vaulted to the top of best-seller lists. Cheryl Mendelson's *Home Comforts: The Art & Science of Keeping House* became the unexpected blockbuster of the late 1990s. Weighing in at more than three pounds and more than eight hundred pages in length, the book was celebrated as a lyrical ode to the joys of making beds with hospital corners and eliminating dust mites. It wasn't an isolated event. *Talking Dirty with the Queen of Clean,* a spot-removal guide, sat atop *The New York Times* "Advice and How-To" best-seller list for most of 2001.

The "talking dirty" double entendre was calculated to play off the fact that this new housekeeping was actually being sold to women as an erotic experience. In *Domestic Bliss: How to Live,* published in 2002, single, childless author Rita Konig advised women to regard housecleaning as a sexual opportunity: "Do the housework in your underwear—it's much easier and boys will love it, especially if you are in your highest heels," she writes. The British magazine *Red* cut to the chase on its July 2000 cover: "So is housework the new sex?" it asked. The improbable answer was yes. Erotica is, after all, fueled by fantasy. And fantasy is precisely what the new mystique chic is—an illusory refuge from the drudgery of the corporate workplace, a nostalgia for a way of life many women born after 1960 had never known, which made it the most potent form of nostalgia possible.

The new domestic arbiters were nothing like the prissy scolds of old. No, they were gorgeous overachievers such as the voluptuous, cashmere-encased Nigella Lawson, the well-born British television chef and cookbook author known as "the domestic goddess." In addition to writing best-selling cookbooks and hosting a cooking show from the sleek kitchen of her London home, she also found time to be the food editor for *British Vogue,* write for *The Times,* and contribute social commentary to *The Observer.* In 2001, she beat out Harry Potter author J. K. Rowling for the British Book Award author of the year for *How to Be a Domestic Goddess,* a cookbook that turned the lost art of baking into a fashionable pastime for the millennial gal. In 2002, she introduced a line of Nigellaware home products. The following year, she married the British advertising megamogul Charles Saatchi.

The mystique that came to surround housework during the 1990s wasn't simply a fashion statement; it was a political statement, one intended to lure women into a world every bit as mythic as that inhabited by the enslaved housewife of *The Feminine Mystique*. It was high concept, focused on the elevation of "the domestic arts," once the only outlet for female self-expression. Fittingly, its grand arbiter, Martha Stewart, had never even been a stay-at-home wife. Stewart, a hardcore careerist, had worked as a model, a stockbroker, a caterer, a best-selling author, and a mass-media entrepreneur. Her CV made her the perfect Type A proxy for an audience composed of women who arrived home exhausted from work to confront equally fatigued husbands, resentful children, meals that needed to be prepared, laundry that had to be washed, and home-work that needed to be reviewed. Stewart provided anesthetized relief from their workaday grind: listening to her dulcet tones and detailed instructions on how to candy flowers or fashion a Valentine's wreath out of red pistachios conferred the kind of blissed-out calm usually associated with tranquilizers. Few of her viewers had any intention of curing their own salmon or gilding quail eggs for Christmas tree decorations. We tuned in for a comforting parallel reality played out at Stewart's showcase home, Turkey Hill, the Graceland of good taste. Hers was a controlled, genteel universe in which time was so expansive that tinting sugar cubes pastel colors seemed a logical way to fill it.

For some women, however, Stewart's manic perfectionism became the source of frustration, even fury. They resented her guilt-inducing, impossible-to-achieve standards. Despising Martha became a way of focusing fury arising from a broad swath of modern frustrations induced by the high standards and commercial imperatives she represented.

But if one looked more closely at the source of Stewart's appeal, it could be seen as rooted not in domesticity at all, but in a desire for her hermetically pure, flawless domestic landscape uncluttered by a husband or children. When relatives were needed to fill out a happy-family tableau for her holiday specials, they were imported, then shipped out again. As she became increasingly iconic, she took to telling assistants, "Remember, I'm not Martha Stewart the person, I'm Martha Stewart the lifestyle." She was like the fictional Betty Crocker or the "perfect" creations depicted decades earlier in Ira Levin's 1972 novella, *The Stepford*

Wives. Her publicly traded company, Martha Stewart Living Omnimedia, of which she was chairman and chief executive until criminal
charges forced her to step down in 2003, brought in annual revenues of
hundreds of millions. Her staff numbered more than six hundred.

In the 1990s, during her ascent, Stewart was not unlike the bride standing alone in her perfect wedding dress—unreal, unsullied, filled with
endless possibility. Her wildly successful magazine, *Martha Stewart Living,* which launched in 1990, led the onslaught of home-centric publications that echoed bridal magazines in their depictions of an idealized,
unachievable life form. "Shelter" periodicals represented both a backlash and an antidote to the flurry of publications directed at the "self-
actualized" working woman that emerged during the late 1970s and '80s.
These magazines, with "me"-centric titles such as *Self, Working Woman,*
and *Playgirl,* celebrated hard-bodied, striving women eager to follow
male convention. By the end of the 1980s, however, women were ready
for the softer contours found in publications such as *Victoria,* the magazine of "romantic living," which began publishing in 1987. By 2003 *Victoria's* circulation of close to one million readers exceeded those of
Architectural Digest, House & Garden, or *House Beautiful.*

Victoria taps into a larger domestic revival that romanticizes the Victorian home, or, more specifically, its surfaces as measured in its gracious depictions of wicker, herb gardens, and English drawing rooms
festooned with spiced orange pomanders at Christmas. Women reading
Victoria don't dwell on the fact that during the years in which Queen
Victoria reigned, 1837 to 1901, wives were the legal appendages of their
husbands. Or that during the Victorian era, physicians routinely warned
women that their reproductive organs suffered when they left home to
pursue a university education. Nor did they reflect on the fact that in
order to reclaim a time of seeming domestic nirvana we have to cast
back nearly 150 years. *Victoria's* readers want nothing more than a temporary escape into the cozy damask womb the magazine provides, a
place devoid of ringing cell phones, disruptive televisions, or computers
that offer their children twenty-four-hour access to pornography.

The spectre of such cosseted comfort also underlined the success of
Cheryl Mendelson's *Home Comforts,* a book that answered questions

many women were too domestically inept to ask: the temperature at which to keep a refrigerator (above 32°F, under 40°F), the shelf life of bleach (no longer than a few months), how to roll socks (three options, with diagrams), even how to wash your hands properly (lather and rub for as long as it takes to hum "Yankee Doodle Dandy").

No matter that the volume was destined to sit gathering its own dust after its novelty wore off. It provided a seductive glimpse into a universe of comfort and order. Like many other women, I took a copy to bed with me as if it were an escapist mystery novel. And it was, given its forays into such exotic territory as the proper lumen ratings for light bulbs.

What made *Home Comforts'* message resonate was not merely its barrage of household tips. Its highly politicized subtext, one that echoed Ralph Waldo Emerson's essay "Domestic Life," written in 1840, rang true to readers at the end of the twentieth century. Like Emerson, Mendelson presents the home as the crucial bridge between the personal and the public. As she puts it, it's "housekeeping that makes your home alive, that turns it into a small society in its own right, a vital place with its own ways and rhythms...." Without such order and routine, Mendelson notes, domestic chaos is bound to reign: children are more likely to be plonked in front of the VCR or computer and less likely to learn to play a musical instrument or even read a book; meals eaten on the run lacking nutritional value contribute to childhood and adult obesity; and ignorance of basic household sanitation can lead to serious health consequences. Mendelson's proposed solution to such domestic malaise is to return to a Victorian mentality: "My own experience," she writes, "convinces me that there is still no other way to make a good home than to have attitudes toward home and domesticity modeled on those of [a] traditional woman."

It was an intriguing conclusion, even if Mendelson's own example contradicted it. For it's unlikely her opus would have been taken as seriously without her impressive professional credentials, which include a Ph.D. in philosophy and a Harvard law degree. Tellingly, the book's jacket assigns value to Mendelson's accomplishments in this order: "philosopher, lawyer, sometime professor, and a homemaker, wife and mother."

The message of the domestic revival was clear: all is not well inside the modern home. Chaos lurks under the unkempt surfaces; the modern family is in disarray, lacking cohesion, order, contentment. The automatic reflex was to return to a mythical time when the wife was happily housebound and her work valued. This was evident in the reissue in 2000 of the classic Victorian housekeeping manual, *Mrs. Beeton's Book of Household Management,* which was first published in 1861. Obviously, most women living in the twenty-first century don't require Beeton's advice on the best way to kill a turtle, or the need to stock the household pantry with opium, or even on how to boil and carve a calf's head. What the 1,112-page manual did offer, however, was entry into a realm in which the role of wife was clear-cut: her sphere was the "private," her husband's the "public." It was a model that worked on a very practical level, assuming the need for female professional satisfaction was not part of the equation.

Like Martha Stewart, Beeton was not ever a full-time housewife. She was a domestically disinclined twenty-three-year-old mother and working journalist when she began writing her manifesto in 1857, one targeted to an emergent class of working women who were equally unschooled in the domestic arts. Nonetheless, she presented the housewife as the architect of a household's happiness: "I have always thought that there is no more fruitful source of family discontent than a housewife's badly cooked dinners and untidy ways," she writes. During Beeton's time—an era when women were denied citizens' rights—the wife's power within the home was absolute, at least in theory. "A wife," Beeton writes, "is the first and last, the Alpha and Omega in the government of her establishment; and ... it is by her conduct that its whole internal policy is regulated."

Beeton would never witness the book's enduring success. She died in 1865 within days of giving birth to her fourth child. Her husband, Samuel, said to be bereft after his wife's death, was shrewd enough to recognize the growing cachet of her name and thus did not announce her passing immediately. The book would be republished every few years and her name would be trademarked and attached to a range of books, goods, and foods.

.   .   .

More than a hundred years later, when North Americans were spending less time on domestic tasks than ever before and when fertility rates
were dropping to all-time lows, romanticizing the housewife and
housekeeping took on a strange logic. Supply-demand imbalances had
rendered the housewife a luxury, leading *The Sunday Times* of London
to proclaim in 1996 that "being a full-time mother, once an unacceptable option for any self-respecting feminist, is becoming not only
acceptable but also, perhaps, even a source of envy." In November 1998
The New York Times Magazine echoed that sentiment, naming the
housewife a "contemporary status symbol," along with the Viking
range, a "networked secretary," and a key to the best beach in California. She was, the magazine gushed, "the ultimate trophy, reflecting
prosperity and proving to the children the assurance that they are, in
fact, the center of the universe." The magazine would repeat the message in 2003, in a cover story titled "The Opt Out Revolution," which
chronicled professional women who chose to stay at home with their
children as a social trend.

This new housewife species was hardly the enslaved creature Betty
Friedan sought to liberate in *The Feminine Mystique.* The twenty-first-
century housewife—more commonly known as a "stay-at-home mom"
or, more odiously, a "soccer mom," a yummy-mummy—sent the message that homemaking was not a form of enslavement but of fulfillment.
The housewife's contented visage also reemerged in commercials, like
one for chocolate granola bars in which a woman enthuses, "Being
a mom gives me all the satisfaction I need."

Stepford wives were back in style, this time not as objects of derision
but of envy. When Levin's novella was published in 1972, it was intended
as a satiric gloss on men's fear of encroaching feminism. The story is
told from the point of view of Joanna Eberhart, an ambitious, free-
spirited photographer who moves reluctantly from New York to the
fictitious New England town of Stepford with her husband and two
children. Once settled into leafy suburbia, Joanna witnesses with dread
the metamorphosis of intelligent women around her into blank-faced

drones boasting Barbie-doll-proportion figures that even swivel, like the doll, at the waist. To her horror, she discovers that these domestic robots have been created by the husbands of Stepford, who formed a secret club after Betty Friedan came to town to address a new local chapter of the National Organization for Women. Their goal was to replace their newly ambitious wives with sexually compliant facsimiles focused only on keeping the house spotless and pleasing them. The perfect wife in this context is an artificial construct—flawlessly coifed, sexually willing, endlessly agreeable. As a male character in William Goldman's popular 1975 movie adaptation promised, "She'll cook, she'll clean, she'll be like one of those robots in Disneyland."

By 2002, the term *Stepford wife* had been recast as a fashion statement. Magazine editors used the term "very Stepford wife" to describe the September 2002 fall shows in New York, which were filled with pastel colors, fruit prints, and exaggerated hourglass silhouettes. In reporting on the collections, *The New York Times* made reference to the polarized fashion options presented to modern women: "In the last few years, designers and photographers have remained as enthralled by the notion of a sexually avaricious, post-feminist she-male as they have by the idea of the cosseted young matron in stultifying domestic circumstance."

The conflict between the stereotypical "post-feminist she-male" and the "cosseted young matron" wasn't one that simply played out on fashion runways. It infiltrated the culture, as became evident in the announcement in early 2003 that *The Stepford Wives* was being remade, starring Nicole Kidman, one of Hollywood's most bankable stars. A significant social shift had transpired between the two movie adaptations: in the early 1970s, the domesticated, compliant wife was held up as a male fantasy; some thirty years later, becoming that wife was pronounced a female fantasy, one offering not servitude but liberation. The powerful allure of the Stepford-wife prototype was revealed in a much-publicized survey that ran in the June 2000 issue of *Cosmopolitan* announcing that many young women were "housewife wannabes." That the study appeared in *Cosmopolitan* at all was itself a significant social indicator: when Helen Gurley Brown took over that magazine as editor in 1965, it targeted the newly independent single working woman. A generation later, it revealed that young women "honestly aspire to the domestic life" even before they have children. According to the survey, 68 percent of three thousand married and single women between eighteen and thirty-four said "they'd ditch work if they could afford to." The *Cosmopolitan* article made mention of another poll of eight hundred young women that found that two out of three would rather stay at home than struggle up the corporate ladder.

The housewife wannabe survey quickly assumed the cultural currency of the famous—and famously debunked—statistic that women had as great a chance of marrying over forty as being killed in a terrorist attack. As the *New York Times* columnist Maureen Dowd wrote shortly after the survey was released, "Five years ago, you would often hear high-powered women fantasize that they would love a Wife, somebody to do the shopping, cooking, carpooling, so they could focus on work. Now the fantasy is more retro: They just want to be that Wife."

The lure of domesticity was attributed to a much-debated litany of causes. There was the argument, vociferously voiced by conservatives, that it reflected the inevitable backlash to the unfulfilled promise of late-twentieth-century feminism, which advocated that women find an identity beyond cooking and cleaning. It was presented as the response to women's frustration that advancement and access to top-level positions had not materialized as quickly as expected. Women were fed up with the unrealistic Superwoman construct that had emerged in the wake of feminism, one they knew to be mythic yet still felt compelled to emulate.

Domestic chic emerged, like the wedding industrial complex, as a consequence of the wife gap. As wives left the home in record numbers in the last decades of the twentieth century, there was no back-and-fill mechanism, no new alternative script. As a result, even the most egalitarian couples found themselves falling into a traditional groove after the birth of children, even though both held down demanding jobs. The true impact wasn't felt until the 1990s, after a generation had passed and the progress for women that had been expected had not happened.

But rather than attempting to cope with the fundamental systemic problems that were created by the homemaker leaving the home, it was easier to look back in time, to once again present much-maligned domesticity as a desirable, status-filled occupation. The problem with sending women back into the home is obvious: it's not an option for many married women whose minimum-wage jobs are not a glorious route to self-actualization but rather a means of putting food on the table. And let's not forget that the majority of women say they don't want to leave their jobs even when presented with the choice. (A survey undertaken by the research group Catalyst in 2002, for instance, revealed that 67 percent of women in dual-career marriages would continue working whether or not they needed the money.) But dealing with such structural problems is complex. Why bother when one can recycle the happy housewife once again as a feminine ideal?

The romanticization of domesticity evident in the 1990s is not a new development. Rather, it's the latest riff on a theme that ran through the twentieth century like the bass line of a Robert Johnson blues song. Modern working wives are but the latest examples in a long continuum of frustrated working wives. Yet somehow we have come to regard their "balancing" problem as unique to them, a fact evident in the thundering ovations accorded Allison Pearson's *I Don't Know How She Does It: The Life of Kate Reddy, Working Mother*. The novel, the sensation of the fall 2002 publishing season, provides a witty account of the trials faced by a sleep-deprived, perpetually frantic, guilt-plagued thirty-five-year-old hedge-fund manager and mother of two. Pearson's rendering of Kate Reddy's life drew gasps from working mothers—those who found the time to read it—who were amazed the author was able to glimpse into the dilemmas they faced in their own lives.

On the surface, Kate Reddy appears to have it all—a kind, attentive husband, sweet children, a high-powered, high-paying job, Armani suits. Yet in her endless scramble to keep it together, she is left with little in the way of personal fulfillment, which intangible working women have been told they are entitled to. Like many real women, the character has been conditioned to see a woman's life in terms of an either-or equation. As she puts it, "So before I was really old enough to under-stand what being a woman meant, I already understood that the world of women was divided in two: there were proper mothers, self-sacrificing bakers of apple pies and well-scrubbed invigilators of the washtub, and there were the other sort." The fact that Kate Reddy is the "other sort" fills her with self-doubt and self-loathing. She writes end-less self-improvement lists, frets about her children loving their nanny more than her, faces sexism on the job, avoids sex with her husband, and contemplates having an affair with a colleague. Eventually, she throws in the towel and quits her job. "Do I believe in equality between the sexes? I'm not sure ... they could give you good jobs and maternity leave, but until they programmed a man to notice you were out of toilet paper the project was doomed. Women carry the puzzle of family life in their heads, they just do."

Kate's plight resonated with a wide, well-heeled audience in part because it contained a message women had been conditioned into hearing—that combining a high-powered career and motherhood is impossible, even for smart, rich, energetic, and hyperorganized women.

But here's the thing: Kate Reddy's conundrum is hardly a modern one. More than a hundred years earlier, the few wives who had profes-sional ambitions were similarly frustrated. In the late nineteenth cen-tury, the aspiring writer Charlotte Perkins Gilman was prompted to visit Dr. S. Weir Mitchell, anxious over her inability to balance new motherhood with her desire to have a career. The doctor, a leading neu-rologist, maintained that a "nervous woman needed to learn that domesticity was the cure and not the cause of her disease." He told Gilman that relief could by found by immersing herself in domestic life and prescribed complete bed rest, overfeeding, mandatory naps, daily massage, and no "outside stimulation." It was a regimen similar to that now experienced by Wagyu cattle before they are transformed into $100-a-pound Kobe beef. After a month in Mitchell's sanitarium, Gilman returned home with the prescription to "live as domestic a life as possible." Gilman tried to follow the advice until it drove her to the brink of insanity, an experience recounted in her classic 1892 short story, "The Yellow Wallpaper."

The writer was not alone in her worry that domesticity would stifle her creative ambition. Between 1880 and 1913, as women gained access to higher education, the marriage rate reached its lowest point in American history and the birth rate fell. Even though the vast majority of women saw marriage as necessary salvation, a burgeoning group of educated young women was concerned that the obligations of marriage would interfere with serious work.

We now see that advances made by women during the first decades of the twentieth century were met with a firm push back into the house. Scare tactics were employed freely. One Canadian federal government report issued in 1910 concluded: "Where the mother works, the baby dies."

Educated women were counseled to rethink the pleasures and satisfaction of domesticity. Lilly Frazer's *First Aid to the Servantless*, published in 1913, was typical of the propaganda: "We shall hear less of breakdowns and neurasthenia and of rest cures ..." she promised. "Simple pleasures will in time be revived and artificiality may be doomed; the higher a woman's education, the better housewife she will be."

In 1921, the year after women got the vote in the United States, the first attempt to remove them from the federal civil service was made. To pander to female ambition, household manuals emphasized the "professional" status of the housewife as they equated scrubbing floors and dusting with "science." "Home-making" was cast as a creative, fulfilling activity that the housewife could enjoy once the drudgery of housework was completed, something that would show her family how much she cared. "Home-making is housekeeping plus," wrote Lillian Gilbreth in *The Homemaker and Her Job*, published in 1927 and chockablock with faith in psychology and progress. "The plus is the act, the individual variation, the creative work," she wrote. "The housekeeping is the science ... the necessary activities that must be carried out in order that one may have time for the rest." (Here we must note that like so many domestic arbiters who preceded and followed her, Gilbreth was a stunning overachiever who was not defined by her housekeeping prowess. She was an industrial designer, left to raise her eleven surviving children and maintain her husband's consulting business after his death.)

Of course, the housewife also served an economic purpose by staying in the home. As the person in charge of goods and services consumed by the family, she was capitalism's secret agent. Accordingly, advertisers and manufacturers targeted wives as the "chief purchasing agents" for their families, a development that would establish the premise that women are "born to shop." By the early 1930s, when 44 percent of women in the North American labor force were white-collar workers, legislation literally forced the wife back into the home. Most school systems in the U.S. and Canada decreed that women quit teaching when they married, a federal law repealed in 1937 in the U.S., though some states restricted women's employment in government until the 1950s.

World War II gave many housewives their first sanctioned taste of work outside the home as they were encouraged to fill positions vacated by enlisted men. By war's end, when their efforts were no longer required, these women were summoned back to domestic life. In 1943, *The New York Times* announced that "real women" would be happy to go back home once the war ended. "Real women," however, disagreed. A U.S. government survey of women in war-related jobs in 1944–45 revealed that three-quarters expected to stay in the workforce after the war. And half the women who called themselves housewives before the war said they intended to keep working. The American government had other plans, however, as it indicated in a radio ad that ran in 1944:

"How do you like your job, Mrs. Stoner?" an announcer asks.

"I love it," Mrs. Stoner replies.

"How about after the war?" the announcer asks. "Are you going to keep working?"

"I should say not," she answers. "When my husband comes back, I'm going to be busy at home."

"Good for you."

One might ask why Mrs. Stoner would be any more "busy" at home after the war, when during it she had held down a job as well as taken care of the home. But the comment reflected the emotional component that tethered wives to domesticity. And this imbued housework with meaning that elevated it from what it really was—a series of tasks that anyone could perform. As wife's work, housework was not simply chores that needed to be done; it was elevated to a gesture of love and support. Thus began the guilt-pride seesaw that women experienced over housework, one quickly capitalized on by advertisers. After the war, Adel Precision Products Corporation, a heavy-machinery manufacturer, ran ads with a young child asking, "Mother, when will you stay home, again?"

Once more, "anti-wife" hiring policies were institutionalized. It wasn't until 1955, for instance, that restrictions on married women in the Canadian federal public service were removed. Putting the wife in her proper place was evident in a speech given by the U.S. president Harry Truman in 1948 to commemorate the one-hundred-year anniversary of the first women's conference held at Seneca Falls, New York. The U.S. Women's Bureau, which hosted the conference, titled Truman's address "The American Woman, Her Changing Role: Worker, Homemaker, Citizen." When the president gave the address, he shifted the order so that "Homemaker" came first, "Worker" last.

Efforts to keep wives housebound by engaging their attention with contests, the latest mod-cons, and elaborate recipes proved fruitless, though, as the number of women in the workforce swelled again during the 1950s. Young women aspired to something beyond the home. Years before she married Jack Kennedy in 1953, Jackie Bouvier wrote in her graduation yearbook that she would "never be a housewife." (How ironic, then, that she would become meta-housewife to a nation, the perfect hostess presiding over a White House she transformed from a dowdy office block into a splendid, antique-filled public space. That legacy would create a role model for future first ladies, one that had little to do with the kind of public service espoused by Eleanor Roosevelt but rather one steeped in fabric swatches, paint chips, and china patterns. Jackie Kennedy may not have influenced U.S. policy directly, as Edith Wilson and Hillary Clinton were accused of doing, but the implications of her legacy are indeed political and had profound social implications.) Appropriately, Lucy Ricardo, the most prominent wife in the popular culture of the 1950s, was a desperately frustrated homemaker, forever scheming to get out of the house and achieve her own celebrity.

The emergence of the suburbs provided yet another excuse to keep the housewife housebound. A now famous June 1960 *Time* cover story described the suburban housewife thusly: "the thread that weaves between family and community—the keeper of the suburban dream.... With children on her mind and under her foot, she is breakfast getter ('You can't have ice cream for breakfast because I say you can't'), laundress, housecleaner, dishwasher, shopper, gardener, encyclopedia, arbitrator of children's disputes, policeman ('Tommy, didn't your mother ever tell you that it's not nice to go into people's houses and open their refrigerators?')."

Betty Friedan, who lived in suburban New York but worked as a journalist, quoted the *Time* article extensively in *The Feminine Mystique,* references that presented the suburban housewife as continually agitated and insecure, masking the torpor of her life with superficial concerns: "If she is not pregnant, she wonders if she is. She takes her peanut-butter sandwich lunch while standing, thinks she looks a fright, watches her weight (periodically), jabbers over the short-distance telephone with the next-door neighbor. She keeps the checkbook, frets for the day that her husband's net raise will top the flood of monthly bills (it never will)—a tide that never seems to rise as high in the city as it does in the suburbs. She wonders if her husband will send her flowers (on no special occasion), shoos the children next door to play at the neighbor's house for a change, paints her face for her husband's return before she wrestles with dinner. Spotted through her day are blessed moments of relief or dark thoughts of escape."

The fact that Friedan's manifesto hit a collective nerve when it was published in 1963 could have been predicted. Housework had already been blamed for driving women to tranquilizers—an updated version of Gilman's sleep cure—or even the brink of insanity, as reflected in the title of Peg Bracken's 1962 best seller, *I Hate To Housekeep: When and How to Housekeep Without Losing Your Mind.* But while *The Feminine Mystique* is credited with propelling wives into the labor force, a destination many wives had been trying to infiltrate for decades, other

developments made it possible. Foremost was the invention of the birth
control pill, available in both the United States and Canada in 1960. By
allowing women to control their reproductive capacity, the Pill allowed
women to sidestep the either-or choice of career or motherhood. It
even made it possible for them to delay or forgo marriage if they so
desired, making wife an elective role for the first time in history.

Given the Pill's momentous impact on the definition of wife, it is
appropriate that the impetus for its development came from two
women employing their wife leverage: the famed birth control advocate Margaret Sanger and the philanthropist Katherine McCormick.
Sanger and McCormick are often overlooked in discussions of the Pill's
invention. That invariably focuses on the men who "fathered" it—the
research scientist Goody Pincus, the chemist Carl Djerassi, and the
obstetrician John Rock. But it was "mothered" as well, by two iconoclastic wives. McCormick, born in 1875, was one of the first women to
earn a degree in science from the Massachusetts Institute of Technology. After graduating, she married Stanley McCormick, the founder of
International Harvester Company. Her husband was diagnosed with
schizophrenia shortly after they married, which led to her decision to
remain childless. McCormick and Sanger met in 1917. McCormick
assisted Sanger by helping to smuggle diaphragms from Europe for her
birth control clinic in New York City. By that time, Sanger was known
as the controversial pioneer of the twentieth-century birth control
movement. In 1922, after divorcing her first husband, the former nurse
married oil magnate James Noah H. Slee, with whom she had an "open"
marriage long before the term was coined. In 1951, the seventy-five-
year-old McCormick joined forces with seventy-one-year-old Sanger,
employing their husbands' vast fortunes to shepherd into being that
"magic" pill Sanger had spoken of for decades.

The playwright and politician Clare Booth Luce had it right when
she proclaimed the Pill the lynchpin to female emancipation: "Modern
woman is at last free as a man is free, to dispose of her own body, to earn
her living, to pursue the improvement of her mind, to try a successful
career." A 2000 study by Claudia Goldin, professor of economics at
Harvard University, and Lawrence F. Katz, contends the birth control

pill is more responsible for women's ascent in the workforce than abortion reform, affirmative action, or even feminism: "The pill lowered the cost to unmarried women of pursuing careers," they write. "Before the pill, young women in college had to factor in the cost to their social life and their prospects for marriage."

But the Pill was not the only driving force. A shrinking economy also made the dual-income household an economic necessity for many families. So much so that in 1974, the number of married women with jobs in North America exceeded those working within the home for the first time, and the uneasy dichotomy between women who "worked outside the home" and those who "worked within the home" began. Movies focusing on the housewife—*Who's Afraid of Virginia Woolf?*, *The Stepford Wives*, *Montenegro*, *The Graduate*, *Up the Sandbox*, *Diary of a Mad Housewife*, and *A Women Under the Influence*—depicted the species as a repressed, unhappy anachronism. She no longer served as a useful target for advertisers. Instead, marketers sought to appeal to the newly independent working woman who picked up the check with her Amex card and smugly told the world she used L'Oreal hair color "because I'm worth it."

Books written about housekeeping during the 1960s and '70s treated the subject as a sociological investigation rather than a how-to. Their messages were dire. Ann Oakley's influential book *The Sociology of Housework*, published in 1976, argued that women's responsibility to do housework kept them subservient to men. "Miles are walked in exchange for a feeling of perpetual defeat," Oakley writes. An equally bleak picture was painted by the Canadian journalist Penney Kome in *Somebody Has to Do It: Whose Work Is Housework?*, published in 1982, which documented the dollar value and personal costs of unpaid work in the home.

The one housekeeping how-to book that resonated with a large female audience during the 1970s would end up becoming the source of much female angst. This was Shirley Conran's 1975 book *Superwoman*, intended as a tongue-in-cheek, guilt-free guide to "effortless housekeeping," as reflected in the epigram on its first page: "Life is too short to stuff a mushroom." The *Superwoman* title was meant to be ironic, as Conran, herself a divorced wife and struggling mother, made clear at the outset: "This book is to help you do the work you don't like as fast as possible, leaving you time for the work that you enjoy." As the author explained later, "It was more 'Down with Superwoman,' a liberation from the shackles of housework." Women could handle both home and career, Conran claimed, as long as they didn't adhere to the standards of housekeeping previous generations had regarded as the norm. Shortcuts, such as Scotch-taping a drooping hem, were recommended. As for visits from one's mother-in-law, Conran advised: "Never mind scrubbing and polishing, just fill a huge vase with flowers and push a strong gin and tonic into her hand."

What had been intended as an aid to the time-strapped working wife and mother quickly backfired, becoming ammunition used against her. Marketers, intuitively sniffing a desirable yet impossible-to-achieve consumer role model, appropriated the Superwoman as an advertising staple. She made her debut in the late 1970s in a television spot for Enjoli, "the eight-hour perfume for the 24-hour woman." Switching outfits from a cocktail dress, a business suit, and casual clothing, the "24-hour" Enjoli Superwoman pranced about singing that she could "bring home the bacon, fry it up in a pan and never, never let you forget you're a man."

The Superwoman icon, we can see now, reinforced the most insidious aspect of the wife gap. And that was the fact that married women who worked outside the home continued to play the housewife within it. A foreshadowing of this was evident in the Enjoli commercial when a male voiceover, clearly the husband, intoned, "I'll cook dinner for the kids tonight," as if he was doing her a special favor, which of course he was.

The ongoing unequal distribution of domestic labor in households in which both partners hold down full-time jobs has been documented by study after study since the 1970s. The numbers vary and have shifted somewhat as men assume more household responsibilities. Even so, the underlying message remains constant: working wives remain the primary domestic custodians.

In *Second Shift: Working Parents and the Revolution at Home,* a study of fifty mostly middle-class, two-career couples published in 1989, the sociologist Arlie Russell Hochschild found that wives typically came home to another work shift, in which they did 75 percent of the household tasks. A 1995 study at the University of Maryland revealed that women did an average of 17.5 hours of housework each week, while men did only 10 hours. In her "2000 National Survey of Families and Households Working Paper" Lina Guzman studied data on working couples with children at home, concluding that "wives in the sample spend a [monthly] average of 39.35 hours on housework compared to an average of 19.52 hours spent by husbands."

A television commercial for Pour-a-Quiche that ran in the 1990s unwittingly conveyed the domestic double standard. The ad, intended to market the product as a practical solution for harried two-career couples, begins with a shot of a husband and wife driving home together from work. In the next scene, the wife is presented as a domestic solo operative, cooking and serving dinner to her husband and children.

That the modern wife remains a domestic servant is blithely assumed in textbooks used in North American universities. *Sociology of Marriage & the Family: Gender, Love and Property* asserts that "wives still do the bulk of the cooking and cleaning, as men acquire a 'domestic servant' following marriage." Wives also contribute more "emotional labor" to the marriage. And while that is changing, it is changing "very slowly," according to Scott Coltrane, chairman of the sociology department at the University of California, Riverside, and co-author of the textbook.

In such a landscape, it shouldn't be surprising that women continue to express confusion about their domestic identity following marriage. Lynn, a woman I interviewed who runs a Wall Street recruiting firm and earns more than her architect husband, says that before she was married in 1999 at age thirty-two, she and her future husband went out to eat dinner or ordered in during the week. They still do. Soon after their wedding, however, she questioned whether her behavior was "wifely enough." "I actually wondered whether I should start making dinner for him," she says. "I was appalled that I reacted that way. But it was as if some voice from deep inside was telling me that's what I should be doing now that I was a wife."

Susan Maushart, a twice-married, twice-divorced mother of

three in Perth, Australia, and a senior research associate at Curtin University, expresses a similar sentiment in *Wifework,* claiming that after marriage women reflexively feel the responsibility to take over most of the housework as well as the more subtle, "emotional care-taking" ("from organizing His underwear drawer to arranging His social life"). "The moment a man gets married, his domestic work-load almost disappears," she told an interviewer. "He immediately gets about 70 per cent less cleaning, 50 per cent less cooking and 90 per cent less laundry.... And these days you're at pains to deny that you're doing it, because apart from being exhausted by it, you're ashamed of yourself."

Anthropologists waded into the debate, blaming the inequitable breakdown of labor in the two-career home to physiology. In *Why Men Don't Iron: The Fascinating and Unalterable Differences Between Men and Women,* by a married couple, Anne and Bill Moir, published in 1998 and later made into a television series in Britain, the discrepancy in the amount of housework men and women do is chalked up to gender differences in chemical makeup: "Men are neurologically primed to find household routine difficult," they write. "Women, on the other hand, are hormonally primed, finding it less stressful than men do." But if household routine is "difficult" for men, perhaps it's because they have never been forced to learn that it is, in fact, the very opposite of difficult; it is the unending repetition that makes it oppressive.

Husbandly avoidance of housekeeping was made glaringly apparent in a Statistics Canada study released in August 2003. It revealed that the spouse with the greater economic clout dictates who cleans the house. Yet when the woman is the primary breadwinner, it isn't the man who cleans. Rather, outside help, usually in the form of a "cleaning woman," is brought in. Families in which women earn 75 percent of the house-hold income, the study found, are more than twice as likely to bring in domestic help than households in which the wife contributes less than 25 percent of the income. Yet when the man is the primary breadwin-ner, the wife tends to do the household work, even when she also holds an outside job. The media looking for real-life examples of such cou-ples after the report was released had a difficult time finding women willing to discuss the issue. Many didn't want to embarrass husbands who are not the primary breadwinners.

Women expressed anger anywhere they could over the double duty they performed—in polls, on television, to one another. Their frustration was neatly summed up in a cartoon that ran in the September 18, 1999, issue of *The New Yorker*. One cavewoman complains to another about her husband, who sits at her feet, blissfully sketching stick figures: "I've had to be both hunter and gatherer now."

But while women laughed, nodding their heads ruefully in agreement, the fact remained that they continued to be both hunters and gatherers. But why? Certainly men are as capable as women of cleaning floors, of changing diapers, and of cooking dinner, despite the prevailing "women are from Venus, men from Mars" mindset that presents women as nesters by nature.

One point rarely made in the never-ending debate about housework is that women do it because they want to do it. What no one discusses, because it is so politically charged, is that governing the home can provide women with a psychological payoff, a domestic "power premium" of sorts that can be traced back to the nineteenth century and Isabella Beeton.

Such a domestic power premium was evident in media commentary following the February 2003 release of 2001 Statistics Canada census data that once again surprised no one in its declaration that women continue to spend more than twice as much time as men on domestic responsibilities. In a story that ran across the Canadian Press newswire, Sally Ritchie, a television producer in Toronto who does most of the housecleaning but shares child-raising duties with her husband, revealed the reflexive self-criticism of some women who have chosen not to control the homestead. Ritchie referred to herself "a freak" because she refuses to do "absolutely everything" around the house, as most married women she knows do.

Cynthia Pugh, who was interviewed by *The Globe and Mail* about the study's findings, said her husband does a little more than one-third of the housework (whether she works outside the home was never specified). Her comments made clear that she understands that she willingly perpetuates the unequal distribution of labor. "The odd thing is," she said, "the more he does to help, the harder I find it. The less I do around the house, the less I feel like Mom."

The wife in the house is reassuringly identifiable. "House" and "wife" is an easy, reflexive pairing. The wife outside the house doesn't conform, which makes her a ready target for derision. But the relationship between house and wife is more complex, as revealed in the 1990s, a decade in which women were once again pulled back into the home, as if the vacuum created by the wife gap had created a centrifugal suction.

The high-powered career wife who had been lauded in the 1980s for burnishing her husband's image, was, by the mid-1990s, presented as a professional burden to her husband. In 1994, the term "Hillary Wife" was coined by *The Wall Street Journal*, an influential publication among the business class. The reference, of course, was to then–first lady Hillary Clinton. The term was employed to describe women whose professional ambitions and lack of domestic inclination became liabilities for their husbands. The article, "A Career Wife Complicates the CEO's Life," noted with considerable dismay that many chairmen and presidents of large companies were no longer receiving the spousal support with business entertaining, shirt laundering, and child rearing that they had come to expect. Marriages in which both partners had demanding careers were depicted as unhappy juggling acts. Tellingly, the failure of one marriage profiled was blamed on the wife's busy schedule, not the husband's. As the article put it, "her high-powered job and frequent business travel left her little time to accompany him on corporate trips abroad."

The working wife and mother was presented as not only compromising her husband's happiness and career prospects. She was also seen as putting her children at risk. The simmering resentment toward women with demanding careers was evident in the coverage of the 1997 trial in the U.S. of the British au pair Louise Woodward in the murder of nine-month-old Matthew Eappen. Rather than focusing on the crime, the media placed the child's grief-stricken medical doctor mother, Deborah Eappen, under scrutiny, using her example to dredge up every backlash theory about working mothers devised since the turn of the century.

A *New York Times* article, "When Waaa Turns to Why," suggested that affluent women who worked were "selfish" and that their decision to work was a matter of pampered choice: "But for many other families, there may be more choice involved and thus more hand-wringing over what to say. Point to money as the reason why Mom has to leave and children can become fearful or too money-conscious. Talk about self-fulfillment, and she essentially comes off as selfish, putting herself ahead of them."

The line of reasoning perpetuated and reinforced the view that a wife's work is of less value than her husband's, no matter how much money she might earn. It also stoked the myth that women entered the workforce to supplement the family income for "niceties": "But rightly or wrongly, child experts and working mothers say, it is the mothers in two-paycheck homes who are usually perceived as having more of a choice about going to work."

Even though both of Matthew Eappen's parents were doctors, the wife's professional obligations, rather than the husband's, were presented as dispensable. Middle-class wives who had careers, *The New York Times* suggested, were even committing a form of adultery: "Although a second income helps pay the bills, working really is not about the money for some of these women, especially after higher tax rates and the cost of child care kick in. Instead, going to work becomes similar to an illicit pleasure, almost akin to sneaking off to have an affair."

The piece concluded that eventually most women couldn't deal with the "emotional baggage" of juggling home and work: "For others—and no one knows how many—the emotional baggage becomes too heavy to haul to the office, leading some to give up their jobs or cut back their hours, often relegating themselves to the so-called mommy track."

By 1997, the notion of the mommy track was well known. The term was introduced in a 1989 study published in *The Harvard Business Review* in which the author Felice N. Schwartz recommended that women working within corporations be classified in two categories: the "Career and Family" woman who needed to be slotted into lower-paying positions in return for a flexible schedule that allowed her to accommodate family needs, and the "Career Primary" woman who should be put on the fast track to the corporate boardroom. If women were going to thrive and advance within corporations while raising families, Schwartz argued, the corporate structure would have to offer more latitude. Her proposals were denounced as "dangerous" and "retrofeminist" because they could give corporations an excuse to further derail women's careers. What no one discussed was that the corporate structure, with its built-in assumption that male employees have wives, also worked against women in far more insidious ways.

By the late 1990s, we had become conditioned to hear stories of thwarted female advancement. Even Superwoman couldn't get ahead, as women who attempted to balance high-flying success and family were likened to the foolish mythical figure of Icarus who flew too close to the sun with his wax wings. In 1997, Nicola Horlick, a successful pension fund manager, became a nationwide symbol of scorn in Great Britain after she was suspended by her employer, Morgan Grenfell, over an alleged breach of contract. The bank claimed Horlick was in talks to join a competitor and was poaching her own colleagues, a move that would have been considered business as usual had one of her male colleagues been accused of it. What propelled Horlick into the media glare, however, was not her alleged misconduct as much as the fact that, at age thirty-five, she was able to handle her bank's £11 billion pension fund business, head a thirty-five-person team, earn a £1 million salary, and still be a wife and mother. *The Guardian* referred critically to "the delighted headlines yesterday that suggested the superheroine who soars above is to be grounded, brought down to earth where she belongs."

The barrage of bleak directives aimed at working wives continued with the dire warning that executives abandoned by their busy working wives were turning their assistants into an "office wife" to handle the domestic—and emotional—duties their real wives had abnegated. Being an office wife, explained *The Sunday Times* of London in 2001, is "exactly like being a normal wife, except for the sex." The leading "office wife," according to the article, is Anji Hunter, aide to the British prime minister, Tony Blair, whose lawyer wife, Cherie, was not around to organize his schedule. So it falls to Hunter to make sure Blair gets the brand of bottled water he likes, goes to the gym, and watches his diet.

The claim that men require an office wife to take care of them given that their real wives have gone AWOL reflects a new reality: forty years after the publication of *The Feminine Mystique*, the workplace has switched places with the homefront as the source of female frustration. By the turn of the twenty-first century, the corporation was presented as the prison for wives and mothers that the suburban home had once been. The residential plate-glass windows that required constant cleaning had been replaced by the glass ceiling, an abstract concept summoned to explain why women were not reaching top positions as readily as men. So intractable was this invisible barrier that it became reflex to picture office buildings outfitted with transparent ceilings after a given floor on which women could gaze upward longingly at Florsheim lace-ups and Gucci loafers. The glass ceiling is now pre-sumed to be a fixed architectural detail within the modern corporation, part of its design, which, in fact, it is. That so-called abstract glass ceil-ing is in fact a wife barrier, one that is firmly childproofed, but only if you are a woman.

Even though women make up more than half of the workforce, their representation in top positions in government, corporations, or univer-sities fails to come close to reflecting their educational accomplish-ments. Women who achieve top rank, like Condoleezza Rice, the most prominent woman in the administration of George W. Bush, are often single or childless. Of the chief executives of Fortune 500 companies in 2002, only six were women, a negligible 1.2 percent. Only 6 percent of the top jobs in Fortune 500 companies—meaning senior vice presi-dents and above—were held by women, and fewer than one in ten board seats of Fortune 500 companies were held by women. The repre-sentation in politics was only marginally better.

It has reached the point that women are treated as a separate—and unequal—species at the corporate level, a fact apparent in a report about female lawyers published in Toronto's *National Post* newspaper in Sep-tember 2003. Titled "At the Top of Their Game," the article listed Canada's top twenty-five female lawyers. Right away, the isolationism is apparent: not the "top twenty-five lawyers" but the top twenty-five female lawyers. The article revealed that although the country's law schools had been turning out roughly equal numbers of male and female graduates for more than a decade, the number of female lawyers in private practice hovers around 25 percent and that of female equity partners in big law firms averages only 20 percent. Once again, the work-balance equation was presented as the culprit. One lawyer, who has two children and whose husband is also a lawyer, conceded that if her husband was being honest, he would admit that her staying home would be easier for him than for her. But staying home wasn't an option for her: "I would turn into a monster because I wouldn't be fulfilled, I wouldn't be happy."

Just as in the previous century, the siren song of domesticity heard in the late 1990s and first years of the twenty-first century was invoked at a time of female professional advancement and visibility. More women than men were enrolled in professional schools for the first time in history. And while it is true women are not highly visible at top levels, they are making significant advances. "More Women Poised for Role as CEO," trumpeted *USA Today* in 1996. According to the research firm Catalyst, women holding "clout titles" increased from 7.3 percent in 2000 to 9.9 percent in 2002. (*Clout titles* defines positions that wield the most corporate influence and policy-making power, including chairman, chief executive officer, vice chairman, president, chief operating officer, senior executive vice president, and executive vice president.) In 2002, women represented 15.7 percent of corporate officers in America, up from 12.5 percent in 2000, and 8.7 percent in 1995. And for the first time, women were gaining ground in two new areas: chief financial officer and general counsel.

So why was it that the imagery surrounding the women intent on seeking a satisfying work life was increasingly bleak? The stereotype of the clawed, unbalanced career woman leaped onto the screen in the 1987 movie *Fatal Attraction,* in which Glenn Close played Alex Forrest, a predatory, unhinged woman hellbent on uprooting Michael Douglas's character, Dan Gallagher, from his idyllic family life and beautiful stay-at-home wife. The contrasts between the crazed careerist and loving housewife presented in the movie were so formulaic that they were laughable. Forrest's minimalist loft, bereft of any domestic warmth, stood in stark relief to the Gallaghers' cozy domicile. When Close's and Douglas's characters engage in their first frenzied sexual coupling in that arid loft, it's over a sink filled with dirty dishes. By movie's end, the family has retreated to the suburbs of New York, not far from where Betty Friedan once lived.

By 2001, the portrayal of women devoted to career was even more dire. While Alex Forrest had been given a sliver of a life separate from her career—albeit a neurotic one—the single female corporate climber embodied by Julie Styron in *The Business of Strangers* had none at all. Styron, a middle-aged vice president of a high-tech firm, played by Stockard Channing, lives a soulless, hermetic existence void of any meaningful human connection. She is first seen walking alone through an empty airport, her expensive stilettos click-clacking on the floor, her dress-for-success suit showing off her treadmill-toned body. She is divorced, childless, overmedicated, and struggling with hot flashes. As the movie begins, she's paranoid that she's about to be fired when her boss announces he's flying in to meet with her. To cope, she turns to Scotch, Zoloft, and a long-distance telephone therapy session with her psychiatrist. As it turns out, her boss appoints her chief executive. The victory is hollow, however, as revealed over the course of the movie, which deals with Julie's relationship with Paula Murphy, a woman in her twenties whom she just fired, played by Julia Stiles. Their conflict mirrors the divide between two generations—Julie's, which believes success in the workplace can offer the personal fulfillment that domesticity cannot, and Paula's, which has no intention of sacrificing itself on the corporate altar. At the movie's end, Paula jeers at what she sees as Julie's vacant life: "Your secretary is your best friend," she sneers. "That's pathetic." Julie is equally disdainful, predicting that Paula will end up marrying a "sensitive husband" she will eventually leave and come crawling back to make her coffee. It is a lose-lose scenario, with neither generation willing to listen to or learn from the other.

The character was emblematic of the way the alpha female was presented by both popular culture and the media. We saw it too in the treatment of Allison Schieffelin, a forty-year-old corporate bond trader in New York, who in 1998 charged her employer, Morgan

Stanley, with sex discrimination, alleging that was the reason the firm had not promoted her to the position of managing director. The press presented Schieffelin as a sad case—a broken marriage behind her and no children, because, as she put it, her brutal work schedule meant "I couldn't even handle a goldfish." Her identity was so wrapped up in her professional persona that when she was fired, she asked tearfully, "Couldn't I just keep my ID badge as a memento?" *The Chicago Tribune* summed up Schieffelin's alienated status in the title of a story about her: "From High-Flyer to Outcast." But Schieffelin would prevail. In an out-of-court settlement, the former bond trader received $12 million of a total $54 million, paid out by the investment banker.

As an antidote, services sprang up telling women the answer was to reclaim their femininity. One much-publicized example is Bully Broads, a monthly gathering held at the Growth and Leadership Center in Mountain View, California, in the heart of Silicon Valley, designed to tamp down women's aggressive instincts. The goal is for these women to become less intimidating, to let go of their need to control, to soften their edges by smiling more and lowering their voices, and not to fear appearing vulnerable. Participants are present under strict orders from their employers, who are paying $15,000 to wean them away from their controlling, bullying, aggressive ways. Intel, Lockheed Martin, Hewlett-Packard, and Sun Microsystems are among the many corporations that have signed up.

The no-win solution facing the ambitious careerist would, ironically, confront mystique chic's primary cheerleader, Martha Stewart. Her arrest and sentencing delighted many, as a sort of Marthenfreude took hold. She was portrayed as a woeful figure—lonely, an insomniac workaholic, "Little Miss Perfect" (according to *Us Weekly*). But the greatest irony was her sentencing—five months in prison, five months of house arrest at her grand Bedford, New York, compound, where she literary became, a la *The Feminine Mystique*, a prisoner of her own domestic perfection.

It was only fitting, then, that the new fonts of wisdom on this barren careerist landscape should be housewives. Affluent stay-at-home mothers were cast as heroines, in fiction and in fact. The message was transmitted in the film *One True Thing*, released in 1998, in which Meryl Streep portrays a saintly, if somewhat manic, homemaker skilled in selecting fabric swatches, constructing clever Halloween costumes, and making the perfect soufflé, even while battling terminal cancer and dealing with an adulterous husband and a grown daughter who doesn't appreciate her mother's sacrifices. The fact that Streep was playing a satisfied housewife during the era of mystique chic provided a nice gloss on shifting social mores. A generation earlier, she had been awarded an Oscar for her portrayal of a frustrated housewife who leaves her marriage in search of personal fulfillment in the 1979 film *Kramer vs. Kramer*.

The housewife as unappreciated martyr was also the theme of *Stepmom*, released the same year. In that movie, Susan Sarandon plays an affluent divorced suburban mother, who, until she too is afflicted with terminal cancer (clearly these martyrs are too good for this world), is always there to dispense Band-Aids, Rice Krispie squares, and loving comfort. Both films reinforced the by-then entrenched view that an irreconcilable rift exists for women between career and family—between the nurturing, sacrificing, patient qualities required to be a wife and mother and the ambitious, self-serving qualities seen to be valued in the workplace. In *One True Thing*, the conflict is between mother and journalist daughter, played by Renée Zellweger; in *Stepmom*, Sarandon's Supermom squares off against her ex-husband's future trophy wife, a successful photographer, played by Julia Roberts, so lacking in basic parenting skills that she forgets to pick up the children. Both Roberts's and Zellweger's characters eventually give up their work to become caregivers. Roberts's character quits her job when she realizes she can't pursue her career and also attend to the children's needs. Her boss criticizes her for choosing domesticity: "You've lost your edge, your focus, your dedication. It's very disappointing. You're making a career decision here."

Indeed, she was. And it was a decision young women were increasingly told they must make. In 1996, the London *Sunday Times* referred to "the impossible demands of home and career" faced by women. The working woman, it claimed, "longed to bid the power-suited 1980s stereotype—briefcase in one hand, baby in the other—goodbye." More women, it claimed, "dream of 'watching my kids become really successful' than of having a career." A survey published by the Canadian government suggested that "having children presents a formidable obstacle to women's advance up the managerial ladder," noting that only 55 percent of female executives in the government had children, while 97 percent of male executives did. Significantly, 20 percent of women without children said that not having children was part of their strategy for getting ahead.

"Does having a career kill your chances of having a kid?" asked *Fortune* magazine in January 2002. The question was rhetorical. According to the just-published *Creating a Life: Professional Women and the Quest for Children*, written by Sylvia Ann Hewlett, the answer was a resounding yes. Hewlett, an economist who teaches at Barnard College, New York, announced "an epidemic of childlessness" in corporate America. The higher a woman's position in a U.S. corporation, she claims, the less likely she is to have children: 49 percent of women who are forty and making $100,000 or more in corporate America are childless, versus only 19 percent of forty-year-old men in the same salary bracket, she writes. She also alleges that many women are victims of a "creeping non-choice": they delayed having children to further their careers only to discover they were no longer fertile.

There is another way of looking at the numbers, of course. Nearly half of women do manage to combine career and family. But that wasn't news worthy of the cover of *Time,* the *Oprah* show, or the other media outlets that leaped on the story. Hewlett's alarmist message was repeated far and wide: "When it comes to children, [women's] options seem a good deal worse than before," she writes. "Women can be playwrights, presidential candidates and CEOs, but increasingly, they cannot be mothers." This rule apparently did not extend to the author, herself a mother of five whose last child was born when she was fifty-one as the result of difficult in-vitro fertilization treatments. It didn't matter. Her timing was propitious, reflecting social discontent.

Hewlett's message was part of a larger backlash targeted at twentieth-century feminism. The proposed solution? A return to the

1950s. Caryl Rivers, a journalism professor at Boston University, captured the sentiment when discussing Hewlett's book: "The subliminal message is, 'Don't get too educated; don't get too successful or too ambitious.'"

What we should not lose sight of is that Hewlett's message is a recycling of one given working mothers since the nineteenth century: having a career risked a woman's fertility. As the British physician Arabella Kenealy put it more than a hundred years ago: "Every woman who uses her natural vitality in a profession or business or in study will bear feeble, rickety children."

One also had to ask whether there was a relationship between the siren song of domesticity targeted at women and more systemic shifts during the 1990s, specifically the declining fertility rate and epic corporate downsizing in North America. The first half of 2001 experienced the largest decline in employment in the United States since the 1991 recession. The service sector, where female positions dominate, was particularly hard hit, experiencing the first recorded drop in employment since 1958. Canada, too, experienced some of the largest layoffs in the country's history. In such a climate, it isn't surprising that the rare woman who reached the pinnacle of corporate life was told to go home again, literally. When Carly Fiorina, a wife and mother of grown daughters, was named CEO of the computer giant Hewlett-Packard in 1999, an appointment that made her the most powerful woman in corporate America, an Internet chat board frequented by HP employees featured one shrill posting headlined, "Back to the kitchen, Carly." When Fiorina later ran into corporate turbulence in 2001, a *New York Observer* article was equally hostile, declaring "Pack It in, Babe. You Stink."

Small wonder that according to surveys broadcast in the media, women were increasingly willing to do just that. Research from the London School of Economics released in 2000 revealed almost 25 percent of women were unhappy with their working lives, compared with 15 percent in the early 1990s. Women who left high-profile positions to return to the home were heralded as brave pioneers; statistically, these women represented a minuscule percentage of the female workforce, yet the "trend" of successful women dropping out was greeted as if it were a stampede across the Serengeti. "They Conquered, They Left" was the headline of a *New York Times* story in 2002, with the subhead: "Are powerful women more likely to be quitters than men?"

Yet the same names seemed to pop up in every story that illustrated the trend. When Brenda Barnes, president and chief executive officer of Pepsi-Cola North America, walked away from a $2 million annual salary in 1997 to spend more time with her three children, she became a poster girl for work-family balance. Oft quoted was her parting line that she "didn't want to miss another birthday party." In the political arena, Jane Swift, the acting governor of Massachusetts and the first elected U.S. politician to give birth while in office, left politics in early 2003. Swift's attempt to juggle parenting and politics had made her the subject of criticism and even financial censure when she was fined $1,250 by the state's Ethics Committee after it was discovered that members of her staff had babysat her infant daughter while Swift was lieutenant governor.

The high-profile female departures reflect the fact that corporate structures permit no middle ground for women, or for men, at the top. Slowing down isn't an option. "Goodbye Boss Lady, Hello Soccer Mom," a *BusinessWeek* cover story in 2002, examined the "low success rates of keeping top women in senior executive jobs." As the article framed it, the working mother is doomed: "Even programs such as telecommuting and flextime often fail. Taking advantage of such schemes is often tantamount to asking not to be promoted. Moreover, these strategies don't do enough to change career trajectories, still largely patterned after men's life cycles—with no allowances for breaks to raise kids."

One of the most high-profile lauded corporate defectors was Candice Carpenter, co-founder and CEO of the Internet site iVillage, which was established, ironically, to help women succeed in raising a family while having a successful career. In 2001, at age forty-nine, Carpenter married Peter Olson, chief executive officer of Random House, and announced she was exchanging the role of CEO for that of homemaker and wife and mother to their children from their previous marriages. She even changed her name to his. Her decision, unsurprisingly, received huge media play, as she was lauded a "born-again evangelist of power domesticity."

In interviews, the new Mrs. Olson admitted that her views on dependency had shifted. Like many women of her generation, she had been raised to believe that dependency equaled weakness. "I was raised to avoid the dependency thing at all costs," she told *The New York Times*. "And what I learned is that the only thing worse is independence. I was a poster child for it. Finally, I thought, 'What have I proven?'"

The new Mrs. Olson even admitted to having a blissful moment while washing her husband's socks, one that forced her to ponder the generational differences between her and her mother: "I realized my mother used to wash socks and think, 'Where did I go wrong?'" One difference between Olson and her mother, however, was that Olson did the laundry secure in the knowledge that she didn't have to. She holds a Harvard MBA; she has reinvented herself professionally several times and left the workforce buttressed by a $1.3 million severance package and a book contract. Olson makes clear that even in the top echelons, work within the directly "paid" labor force can be as much drudgery and as personally unsatisfying as working within the home. "Being a CEO is hell," she says.

When men dropped out from high-profile positions "for personal reasons" or to "devote more time to family," no one suggested they couldn't cut it. There were no covers proclaiming "Goodbye Boss Man, Hello Soccer Dad." Instead, it is generally presumed that they were pushed or exercising the luxury of their wealth. In 1990, Peter Lynch shocked the business community when he quit as head of Fidelity Investments' hugely successful Magellan Fund at the age of forty-six to spend more time with his wife and daughters. He claims he got "hundreds and hundreds" of letters from men commending him. He's now back at work, though in a lower-profile position. Likewise, Brian Swette, chief operating officer of the highly successful Internet auction site eBay, left his post in 2002 to spend more time with his children. "I see them at holidays and see them whenever I can, but it's impossible to do them justice and the job justice," he said. Even the Clinton administration labor secretary, Robert B. Reich, stepped down in 1997, claiming he found the work-family imbalance in his own life untenable. This is disquieting: if the person responsible for a nation's workplace policies can't cope, what hope is there for everyone else? Reich taught at universities, wrote a memoir that voiced his frustration with life in Washington, and unsuccessfully ran for governor of Massachusetts.

In such a climate, it seems logical that young women would regard wife as a career choice, even though it's an option that doesn't extend to men. Why be a lawyer, goes this line of reasoning, when you can marry one? Or even better, a famous, rich man who would sweep you away from the prosaic details of everyday life. Such imagery converges perfectly with that propagated by the wedding industrial complex.

A generation after the advancements of the women's movement, finding a wealthy mate was once again presented as a righteous pursuit for an educated young woman. In early 1998, a *New York Times* article extolled the benefits of "glamour jobs"—high-profile, low-paying positions in auction houses, at women's magazines, and at public relations companies—that put young women in the orbit of rich men to marry.

The piece read like a first draft by Edith Wharton. According to its author, Monique P. Yazigi, glamour jobs "are thought to be the only jobs worth having because of their opportunities for making the 'right' friends and for meeting a suitable (read wealthy) mate." The "unwritten age limit for glamour jobs is 35, by which time many women expect to be comfortably married." Well-educated women clamored for the positions, the newspaper claimed, while young men with similar backgrounds and aspirations go to work on Wall Street or into the professions. Nadine Johnson, a public relations agent, outlined the options: "If you were a talented young girl fresh out of college, where would you go—to a bank or financial institution, or *Vogue,* where you're part of a bigger picture? They're involved in the shiny world of beauty, fashion and show biz. They think they're going to meet someone amazing that is going to take them away on a white horse."

What we were seeing was the Superwoman being replaced by the equally mythical Superwife living the life of mystique chic. But as *Cosmopolitan*'s "Housewife Wanna-bes" survey made clear, young women did not equate being a housewife with the suburban torpor described in *The Feminine Mystique*. Rather, they had fantasies of a Martha Stewartesque domesticity, free of financial concerns or drudgery, featuring a Mercedes SUV, yoga classes, and plenty of time for self-expression. As one young woman put it, "I'd write in the afternoon and spend the rest of the day taking classes, going to the gym, or meeting with friends for coffee. In the evening I'd make incredible meals and finish the night having rockin' sex with my husband." Only a few women expressed concern that they might lose their identity (as opposed to gaining a new one). "Although I do dream of keeping house, I really wonder whether I'd feel like less of a person without something outside of the home to define who I am," said Deborah, a twenty-four-year-old editor.

Had the *Cosmopolitan* survey asked young men whether they would like to give up work, many would likely have answered the same way. But no one asks men, with the exception of those who have just won the lottery, if they would consider quitting work if they had another means of support coming in. Instead, young men were asked how they felt about their wives staying home. Of more than five hundred men polled, over 70 percent said they would be happy to have their spouse keep house, though more than two-thirds of them would prefer their spouse to stay home only after the first child was born.

A shift is clearly under way. U.S. Census figures released in 2002 revealed that for the first time in twenty-five years, a growing number of women at the peak of their careers were dropping out to stay home with their families. The rate of working mothers with children aged one or younger fell to 55 percent from a record high of 59 percent in 1998. The number marked the first significant decline since the Census Bureau developed the indicator in 1976, when the rate was 31 percent. The share of women who stayed in their jobs during their first pregnancy also slipped for the first time since 1961. Birthrates, too, were on the rise in the United States. By 2002, American women were having more children than at any other time in the past three decades—2.1 on average in a lifetime. For the first time since 1971, enough children were being born to offset deaths.

Whether women were returning to the home out of conscious choice or by default is not clear. One British survey revealed that six out of ten working women claimed they wished they could quit their jobs and said they feel pressured by the "domestic goddess" image to simultaneously hold down a job, care for families, and entertain friends. Three thousand British women eighteen to forty-five took part. Nearly 90 percent said they envied well-off women who do not have to work.

According to a survey published in 2001 by Update:Women, a British research firm, women were focused more on family and home than at any other time in the past two decades; in a study it conducted in the late 1990s, the percentage of working women who said career is "as important as being a wife and mother" plunged 23 percent from 1979. It went on to predict that the big family will replace a big income as a status symbol. As the researcher Laurie Ashcraft put it, women in their twenties were no longer as driven to succeed in the workplace as their mothers were: "It's show me the baby, not show me the money."

Rather than acknowledging that women were returning to the home for a raft of reasons—a true desire to be a wife and mother, for instance, or as the result of frustration—it was interpreted in some quarters as proof that feminism had served up a false bill of goods. A predictable target of the backlash was Betty Friedan, whose motives for writing *The Feminine Mystique* were questioned. One critical biography, Daniel Horowitz's *Betty Friedan and the Making of the Feminine Mystique: The American Left, the Cold War, and Modern Feminism,* accused her of misrepresenting herself as an average homebound housewife, deceiving readers by downplaying her education in order to connect with her audience; she was also accused of exaggerating the magnitude of women's unhappiness in order to please her publishers.

What the critics overlooked, however, was that even though Friedan was an unhappy wife when she wrote her groundbreaking treatise, she assumed that most women would marry and have children. As she wrote in an epilogue to the book, published in 1973: "I couldn't define 'liberation' for women in terms that denied the sexual and human reality of our need to love, and even sometimes, to depend upon, a man." But she also stressed that this would be possible only with policies that allow women to choose to have a family with the confidence of access to adequate child care. What she didn't anticipate was that women might actually *want* to stay home and raise children.

Unsurprisingly, for all the talk of "power domesticity" put forth by marketers and those who wanted women back in the home, thanks to the wife gap, the actual perception of the housewife has improved little since Friedan's day. The political correctness that advocated using the term *working outside the home* to define women with jobs so as not to offend those who "worked inside the home" didn't alter the fact that housewives' work was not taken as seriously as paid work.

Everyone has heard tales like one told by a woman I know who holds an MBA and gave up her job as a financial analyst to stay at home with her three sons in Toronto. She once attended a dinner party with her husband's colleagues. "I overheard a woman ask my husband what I did," she says. "And he said, 'Nothing, she stays at home.' I was crushed. Does he really believe that?"

Attempts to redefine the role of housewife tended to focus on super-ficialities such as nomenclature or the need to shift one's attitude. In *The Smart Woman's Guide to Staying at Home,* published in 2001, Melissa Hill, a former equities analyst in London, suggested that the housewife be referred to as "household manager," as if importing workplace ter-minology would elevate the role's status. In April 2003, the Canadian women's magazine *HQ* chose to revive the *Homemaker's* title it had aban-doned in the late 1990s. At that time, dropping *Homemaker's* was not unlike the shrewd image makeover undertaken by Kentucky Fried Chicken, which became KFC to avoid any unsavory "fried" association. By 2003, the tide had turned. As the *Homemaker's* editor told the *National Post* newspaper, "Being a homemaker is not a negative anymore." Yet the magazine couldn't disassociate from the having-it-all mantra. Its relaunch issue featured a story on Bonnie Fuller, then editor of *Us Weekly* magazine, with the title "Working Moms ... Can They Have It All? Bonnie Fuller on Balancing Work, Love and Children."

For all the accolades accorded this new homemaker, there existed no new script for women who chose to stay home. Instead, it was easier to look back in time for solutions. And these retrograde glances were served up by a flurry of best-selling books that counseled women to return to the same kind of idealized domesticity that, ironically, had given rise to the twentieth-century feminist movement in the first place.

Books written by women who had flourishing careers attempted to reassure women that they should be fulfilled by housework. In *What Our Mothers Didn't Tell Us*, a book published in 1999 that instructs women to marry and have children while in their twenties, Danielle Crittenden waxes romantic about 1950s suburban life: "For all of the scorn that has been leveled against the marriages of the 1950s, those of us who are too young to have experienced them can only read about them with a kind of awe and—dare I say it?—wistfulness. Compared to today's frantic two-career households, the suburban married life that seemed so stifling and unfulfilling a generation ago seems blissfully peaceful and affluent."

Meghan Cox Gurdon, writing in *The Women's Quarterly*, a conservative journal once edited by Crittenden, presents staying at home in the idyllic terms of a Procter & Gamble commercial: "The dark secret of housewifery is that it's fun and deeply gratifying," she writes, adding, "the housewives I know deal with the groceries and cooking and all the other drudgery and yet still manage to paint, write, play piano, ride horses, fiddle about on the Internet, and volunteer for charities and schools."

While she alludes to the domestic boredom often mentioned in Friedan's *The Feminine Mystique*, Cox Gurdon claims that women can transcend it if they set their minds to it: "I hadn't bargained on the boredom—or rather, what initially felt like boredom—of spending all day with small, volatile people who are not interested in foreign affairs and need a lot of feeding," she writes. But by the article's end, she has intellectualized the dull routines of housework much as Isabella Beeton did, only employing New Age terminology: "The point of being at home is the being, not the doing. It's like Zen. Outwardly, you perform mundane tasks. Inwardly, you are the heart of your family."

Mystique chic presented women with yet another unrealistic and unachievable standard, one that accorded status to the domestic role rather than the person in it. Arguably, the new Superwife faced even more daunting standards. The mythic Betty Crocker shilling cake mix had been replaced by a mythic Martha Stewart fortified by corporate backup. The pressure felt by women was so intense it manifested itself in a bizarre female affliction reported by British doctors as "Nigella Syndrome." The source was the multi-talented Nigella Lawson. After her husband died in March 2001 following a lengthy public battle with cancer, women turned to their physicians, ashamed because they weren't as capable of coping as Lawson. And they didn't have her onerous responsibilities—two children to raise, a television show, a book due at the publishers and a dying husband to tend to.

But mystique chic didn't only fuel female insecurity. It also created a new battle for moral superiority, not between men and women but between working mothers and mothers who stay home. The conflict was cogently captured in an article that ran in the August 2001 *Talk* magazine titled "My New Client." It was written by Amy Bookman, a former agent at Creative Artists Agency who gave up her demanding, high-paying career to stay at home and raise her newborn son. Bookman found the transition a shock, even with the assistance of a nanny. The first day of her new life, she writes, "I was off the team. Not only off the team but seemingly off the planet.... A little disorientation and depression were to be expected. But I never imagined how lonely my new life would seem."

She found herself alienated both from the friends she had once worked with as well as from other mothers, most of whom were ten to fifteen years younger than she. Quickly she learned that her new role had no currency among her former colleagues. When she provided her new occupation as "housewife and mother" for an industry event, she arrived to find the space beside her name blank. "Being a mother was not considered an occupation," she writes. "It was most certainly not a networkable job."

Bookman's conclusion that "any way you slice it, mothers today can't win ..." reflected the no-win equation confronting both career and stay-at-home mothers. "Who's the Better Mom?" blared the headline of the October 21, 2002, *New York* magazine. On its cover was a woman in a business suit next to a fit stay-at-home mom in workout gear. The article suggested both were equally frustrated: "Stay at home mothers are presented as wanting to have something that's a reflection of her as an individual—a label that says she's a capable, creative person who knows about more than just baby formula or after-school programs. The working mother wishes she had more free time to be available to her child."

There is a solution, of course. And that is for the working woman to have her own wife, whether in human form or in the guise of an infrastructure that substitutes for one. As countless surveys and anecdotal evidence make clear, the ascent of women with families to top positions was made possible by partners who stayed at home with the children or by domestic replacement in the form of hired help, an option not viable for many working women. Carly Fiorina of Hewlett-Packard had a male wife: her second husband, Frank Fiorina, retired from his executive position at AT&T when their conflicting job schedules kept the couple from seeing enough of each other. Of the 187 participants at *Fortune* magazine's Most Powerful Women in Business Summit in spring 2001, 30 percent had househusbands. And of the fifty women on the 2002 list, more than one-third had husbands at home either full- or part-time. In explaining how she "had it all" in an article in the Canadian magazine *HM,* Bonnie Fuller acknowledges that her architect husband works from home and is there to take the children to appointments and attend school events.

The need for a wife in the home was made clear, ironically, in the backstory to Allison Pearson's *I Don't Know How She Does It,* the novel lamenting the modern wife's no-win situation. At the novel's end, the protagonist drops out of the workforce, though it's apparent that her ambitions will not stay tamped down for long.

Pearson's homage to her husband, the *New Yorker* film critic Anthony Lane, in the book's acknowledgments reveals a more prosaic truth: in order to complete a book about a wife and working mother coping with the kind of pressures women had been facing for more than a century, Pearson herself needed domestic support. As she puts it, "While the fictional life of a harassed working mother was being created in our house, he loaded the washing machine, cooked dinner, read

Owl Babies three hundred times and even found time to write the odd film review." Ironically, Pearson's willingness to concede domestic space to her partner reveals a truth of juggling work and family, one never gleaned by her central character, who is given to uttering snappy one-liners like "Men need women more than women need men; isn't that the untold secret of the world?"

Whether men or women need the other more is mere scorekeeping. The issue facing women—and men—at the beginning of the twenty-first century is one of removing the stigma from the role of wife and recasting its value. A working woman raising a family requires wifely support. And she has to be able to relinquish domestic control without seeing it as a weakness or a failure. This won't happen until domestic work is stripped of the emotional meaning that has always tethered it to the wife. Cleaning a toilet isn't an act of love. It is a chore that needs to be done. And it doesn't need a wife to do it.

Yet it would be a mistake to dismiss the lure of domesticity as a plot hatched in the boardroom of Procter & Gamble to sell more detergent. It also represents a deeper percolating discontent within the culture—the fact that the home and its caretakers have been marginalized, with the result that social values and familial relationships have been eroded. Caring relationships have been replaced by a domestic services industry offering the services traditionally performed by the wife—everything from nanny agencies to baby masseurs to birthday party planners.

The housewife renaissance also reflects an inchoate yearning for the self-sacrifice and devotion of the traditional wife, a woman who would have been shocked by the concept of "having it all." What is needed early in the twenty-first century, it is clear, is the woman who wants to "give it all." The only problem is that that woman has left the building. And even the seductive siren song of a mythical domesticity won't bring her back.

Chapter 4

Sex and the Married Woman

The coy question posed by the British magazine *Red* in 2000—"So is housework the new sex?"—was more on target than anyone could have predicted. Soon after, it became apparent that wives were in the midst of a full-blown "sex crisis," one indirectly linked to the assertion that women were channeling all their erotic energy into domesticity. If housework is the new sex, it would follow, then, that sex, for many burned-out women, has become the new housework—a chore, something you have to do before you can get to something really pleasurable, like polishing the silver or ironing with lavender water.

This newfound carnal emergency was first manifest in reports that women were withholding sex from their husbands. Think of it as the modern-day version of the sex boycott in Aristophanes' *Lysistrata*. In that classic play, a group of Greek women, fed up with their husbands' war-mongering, stage a sex strike until their menfolk cave in and agree to a truce.

Oprah Winfrey declared the unofficial modern wife-sex boycott a "national epidemic" on her February 5, 2002, program. This new crisis, she said, was the result of "young wives who love their husbands but don't want to have sex with them." One such wife was Amy, a pretty woman in her thirties who hadn't had sex with her husband, Jeremy, in months. She claimed she both "loved" and "liked" her husband but said sex had become "dirty" for her after she became a mother. Amy also revealed that she was juggling an overwhelming list of responsibilities. She was the mother of two, a student, and also held a part-time job. "By the end of the day," she said, "I don't have any more to give." Her husband, she confessed, was "at the bottom of the pecking order."

Amy, like millions of other wives, was languishing in the wife gap, exhausted, overworked, stretched thin, resentful of her husband. Yet her lack of desire was explained as a personal sexual problem rather than the result of a broader social puzzle. And that was consistent with the emergent view of female sexuality, which was that it too was in dire crisis. According to a widely publicized study published in *The Journal of the American Medical Association* in February 1999, no less than 43 percent of American women suffer from some form of "sexual dysfunction." The National Health and Social Life Survey conducted by researchers at the University of Chicago and Robert Wood Johnson Medical School in Camden, New Jersey, was the first ever on the subject of female sexual satisfaction, a shocking fact in itself. According to its data, one-third of women said they regularly didn't want sex, 26 percent said they regularly didn't have orgasms, and 23 percent said sex was not pleasurable.

Should one bother to look at the study's methodology more closely, it's apparent that many of the women suffering from scary-sounding "sexual dysfunction" might have been plain old "tired." The seventeen hundred women interviewed, who ranged in age from eighteen to fifty-nine, were asked whether they had experienced at least one of seven so-called sexual difficulties for more than two months at some point during the previous year. These were loosely described and included social and psychological factors as well as medical problems such as lack of sexual desire, difficulty becoming aroused, inability to climax, pain during sex, anxiety over sexual performance, and not finding sex pleasurable. Any woman who answered yes to just one of these questions was lumped in the "dysfunctional" group. The fact that the majority of the women attributed their lack of sexual desire to stress and fatigue was glossed over. So too was the effect depression has on sex drive. By year 2000, women were twice as likely to report depression. They are also more likely than men to be prescribed antidepressants with some kind of libido-decreasing side effect.

"Having a Life: Work, Family, Fairness and Community in 2000," a study published by the Centre for Labour Research at Adelaide University in 2002, revealed similar findings. Working mothers, it found, were dismayed at the toll that juggling a job and family commitments took on their sex lives. "Women find they can't be a terrific worker, a wonderful mother and have great sex at night under the current arrangements," reported researcher Barbara Pocock. She concluded that the resentment some women harbored toward partners who did not share the domestic workload undermined their sex lives. "Anger and resentment are the enemy of intimacy," she said. "A proportion of women have husbands who have shifted but most thought the arrangement just wasn't fair."

The situation even extended to male "wives"—men who assumed responsibility tending the home while their mates went out to jobs. One househusband recounts his frustration in a 2003 book, *The Sex-Starved Marriage: A Couple's Guide to Boosting Their Marriage Libido,* by the therapist Michele Weiner-Davis: "My wife makes more money than I do, so we've agreed that her job comes first. She doesn't appreciate what I do to make our family run.... When my wife comes home, all she does is nag. Then she gets mad when I have no desire to kiss or hug her or even make love. I know our sex life stinks, but what can I say? I'm not into it."

It was hardly a surprise, then, when *Newsweek* published a cover story, "We're Not in the Mood," in June 2003, announcing the prevalence of sexless marriages. According to the article, between 15 percent and 20 percent of married couples have sexless marriages, defined as having sex fewer than ten times a year. The situation has become so entrenched, apparently, that even former U.S. labor secretary Robert Reich jokes in speeches about the pressures on working couples. "Have you heard of DINS?" he asks his audience. "It stands for dual income, no sex." Yet according to what people tell researchers, DINS is most likely an urban myth: working women appear to have sex just as often as their stay-at-home counterparts.

But the article reinforced the fact that, for many women, lack of a desire for sex is unrelated to hormonal deficiency or sexual dysfunction. Rather, it's the product of calcified resentment stemming from the domestic power premium: "For many couples, consciously or not, sex has become a weapon. A lot of women out there are mad. Working mothers, stay-at-home moms, even women without kids. They're mad that their husband couldn't find the babysitter's home number if his life depended on it. Mad that he would never think to pick up diapers or milk on his way home. Mad that he doesn't have to sing all the verses of 'The Wheels on the Bus' while trying to blow-dry his hair."

Withholding sex could be seen as the ultimate abnegation of the wife's role as a marriage's sexual custodian. Even into the twenty-first century, it remained the wife's job to crank up the erotic vibrancy, or, to employ a cliché favored by women's magazines, to keep the marriage "hot," as if it existed on the stovetop. Wives were even expected to be on marital duty while fantasizing about other men, as a cover line on the February 1999 issue of *Redbook* makes clear: "I Slept with Harrison Ford and My Husband Didn't Care—You Share the Sexy Dreams That Keep Your Marriage Hot!"

In the sexual arena, as in every other, wives have been—and continue to be—deluged with advice. In 1957, Maxine Davis primly encouraged wives to shoulder the burden of "sexual adaptation" in *The Sexual Responsibility of Women*. In *Total Woman*, published in 1974, Marabel Morgan famously advised wives to greet their husbands at the front door naked, wrapped in Saran like yesterday's leftovers. The unintentionally hilarious directive made the not-so-subtle link between wifely sexuality and domesticity, one also echoed in the suggestion that a woman dress up in a flirty French maid's uniform as a prelude to a steamy evening.

Even the Superwoman in the late 1970s Enjoli commercial included carnal caretaking as part of her domestic drill when she pranced around singing that she'd "never, never let you forget you're a man." It was the kind of onerous multitasking that made the fourth century B.C. orator Demosthenes' strict categorization of the wife's sexual role as procreator seem like a cakewalk. As he put it, "We have mistresses for our enjoyment, concubines to serve our person and wives for the bearing of legitimate offspring." By the end of the twentieth century, the wife was expected to be omnisexual—to stimulate, to serve, and to bear children.

Viewed from a historical perspective, expecting the wife to maintain the marriage's sizzle was like asking the incarcerated to tend the prison's grounds. The containment and control of female sexuality was one of the foundations of Western marriage. The institution provided a neat socially engineered box in which female desire was sanctioned. The marital bond was a way of legislating sexual behavior, of perpetuating a family's lineage in a no-muss, no-fuss format.

Providing sex, even when she didn't feel like it, was regarded as a nonnegotiable part of the wife's job description well into the second half of the twentieth century. This was yet another manifestation of coverture, of the fact that a bride's wedding vow provided an omnibus "yes" to any sexual advance a husband made. (Matthew Hale, the eighteenth-century British jurist, introduced the notion that a man cannot be charged with raping his wife. Hale, the last jurist to insist on persecuting witches by hanging, devised the concept of "spousal immunity" in 1736, writing, "But the husband cannot be guilty of a rape committed by himself upon his lawful wife, for by their mutual matrimonial consent and contract the wife hath given up herself in this kind unto the husband which she cannot retract.")

The wife's sexual role in the marriage was central to her spousal identity: "Intercourse with one's husband was the obligation of wives; it was part of what being a wife signified," pointed out the legal scholar Jill Elaine Hasday in 2000. Over the short course of one generation in the late twentieth century, however, that crucial aspect of what "being a wife signified" was eroded. Laws passed during the 1970s and '80s allowed women to charge their husbands with rape (though, as will be discussed later, coverture continues to shadow "marital rape" legislation). Women's widespread use of the birth control pill, legal access to abortion, entry to the workplace in record numbers, as well as their increased financial independence, shifted the perception of female sexuality. The moral censure adjudicating that "good" women preserved their virginity until they married diminished, given that the majority of women no

longer walk down the aisles virgins. Women who bear children out of
wedlock are no longer subject to social stigmatization; indeed, unmarried single-mother celebrities like Madonna, Calista Flockhart, and
Julianne Moore were lauded as trendsetters. (Both Madonna and
Moore are now married.) Marriage as a means of governing paternity
was also rendered obsolete: DNA evidence rather than a marriage
license now determines the legal father of a child.

The most significant shift affecting the perception of marital sex was
the positive fact that women finally felt entitled to their own sexual satisfaction, a notion radically at odds with more than a century of dutiful,
"close your eyes and think of England" wifely sex. The consequences
had a profound, often unsettling, effect on the marital sexual dynamic.
In the course of a generation, the wife, rather than the husband, was
perceived to be the one who determined sexual frequency. And here
a definite gap existed between the generations. One married friend of
mine in her early forties recalls telling her sixty-eight-year-old mother
that her husband pressed her to have sex in the morning, a time when
she tends to be distracted with getting the household up and running.
She told her mother she usually rebuffed his advances. "My mother was
shocked," she says. "She said, 'You should do it just to keep him happy.
It doesn't matter if you're not in the mood.'"

A television commercial that ran in 2000 for the Canadian department store Zellers attempted to convey the retailer's empathy with the
pressures of being a wife by playing off her reluctance to have sex. A
husband is shown praising his wife's shopping skills and rubbing her
shoulders suggestively—only to be rebuffed. "It's not gonna happen,"
she snaps, and walks off.

For all the sea changes in the legal and social definition of marital
sexuality, a mythical wife-sex script prevailed. Some young wives
report feeling an irrational sense of sexual duty following marriage,
not dissimilar to the sense of domestic duty reported by other young
wives. One twenty-six-year-old woman remembers the first time her
husband asked her to have anal sex, something she didn't want to do. "I
remember freaking out and feeling that I didn't know how to deal with
it," she told me. "I felt he was saying, You're my wife. You have to do

this. He didn't say it, but I felt it. I look back on it now and see that the problem was mine; I was not able to assert myself. I was still reeling from deciding to get married. I may have skewed it all in my own head. I probably would have reacted differently if it had been a boyfriend. But I felt that I was being put upon, even though we didn't end up doing it that time."

Not all wives are boycotting sex. Many are trying to rewrite the sexual script, in a modern update of their roles of sexual caretakers. And this brings us to a conference room in the Varscona Hotel in downtown Edmonton, Alberta, on a blustery November evening in 1999. Here twenty-one wives, ranging in age from twenty-eight to forty-two, have gathered. They all exude an affluent, toned glow, the result of regular yoga and spinning classes. Their clothing is expensive-casual—cashmere sweater sets, Theory trousers, Teenflo shirts. They know one another through their husbands, who are all members of Edmonton's Young Entrepreneurs Organization, a group of up-and-comers under forty. As such, they have much in common—coping with their husbands' absences, raising children, renovating houses. Most have taken their husbands' names. Many have given up careers to stay at home with their children. A few years ago, one of the wives came up with the idea to have a monthly girls' night out. In the past, the group had gone bowling, to movies, attended a cooking class. Indeed, tonight's instruction could be viewed as a variation on the culinary instruction their mothers took during the 1970s to learn how to make puff pastry or authentic Indian curry.

At the front of the room, the instructor, Lou Paget, unpacks a metal Halliburton valise filled with red satin bags containing rubber phalluses in an array of flesh tones. These Paget refers to as the "instructional product." The forty-five-year-old Paget has acquired celebrity status for her seminars teaching women about oral and manual sexual technique. She's a regular contributor to popular women's magazines as well as to *Playboy*'s "Advisor" column. Her sex guides are best sellers. She has been the subject of documentaries on the BBC and German television.

Paget is refined yet approachable, qualities that caused the media to dub her the "Martha Stewart of sex tips." Tall, with long strawberry blond hair, she possesses a thoroughbred quality; her clothing is impeccably tailored, her voice a well-calibrated purr, her delivery part anatomy lecture, part girlfriends' dish. "I don't like the term *blow job*," she jokes, invoking Catskills humor, drumroll now, "because blowing has nothing to do with it."

Some of the wives who attend Paget's seminar are there to defend turf. *GQ* magazine would refer to Paget's seminars as "a must-do on the list of every Hollywood missus who fights to keep her husband away from actual porn stars or, at the very least, transvestite hookers." *Vanity Fair* also ran an article covering one of her seminars, which intimated that both Mrs. Tom Hanks and Mrs. Steven Spielberg had received instruction. The article revealed that some wives saw mastering sexual technique as a way to benefit materially: one wife who approached Paget at a seminar asked her how big a ring she'd get for performing a certain act; it reported that Paget responded, "Quite honestly, fairly large." When recounting the story later, Paget confides that what the magazine didn't print is that the woman wanted to know about oral-anal sex. "She was really negative about it," Paget recalls. "And I'm thinking, Why the heck, babe, are you here? So she asked me, 'How big a ring will I get?' And I said, 'Pretty large,' and she said, 'Fine, I'll do it.'"

The mood at the seminar is apprehensive and giggly. Some women in the group had been uncomfortable about the subject matter and chose not to show up. As the women nibble on appetizers, sip wine, and catch up, Paget brings the session to order. Each picks the plastic model of a penis that she'll practice on for the rest of the night. "We have the six-inch, eight-inch, or the ever-so-popular five-inch executive model—also known as the Porsche driver," Paget says, as the group laughs.

Slowly, the mood thaws. The more practical women in the crowd select phalluses approximating the size of their husband's penises. Others in the all-white group joke about living a fantasy and pick out large black models. Each woman gingerly places a plastic penis on a dinner plate, the scrotum facing her. "Don't worry," Paget tells the group, "they've been washed in the dishwasher."

Paget can relate to the women's wariness. Born and raised in Calgary, Alberta, she came from a privileged WASP family that had been uncomfortable discussing sex. After her marriage failed, she decided to move from Calgary to Los Angeles and start fresh. Yet one of the unhappier aspects of her marriage—an uninspired sex life—gnawed at her, so she decided to do some research. When she did, she discovered most of the information directed at women was inadequate and vague, belonging to the "light a candle, put on a negligée, open a bottle of wine" school of sex tips.

Paget understood the potential power of wife sex, one that had been suppressed in a culture that continued to make jokes about the desexualized wife. (Q: "What's the difference between your wife and your job? A: After five years your job still sucks.") She had talked to many men who told her that their wives ceased to be sexual after marriage and that they felt they'd been sold a false bill of erotic goods. "They have sex two, three times a week before marriage, then their wives cut it back," she says. "That's not what they signed up for."

The wives who attend Paget's seminars know what she calls "the importance of maintenance, that psychological part of the relationship." It's not that these women are afraid of their husbands' leaving them, Paget points out, but rather that they have a commitment to the marital relationship and realize that sex is a major part of it.

Even so, Paget is aware of a sexual double standard, a legacy of the good girl/bad girl morality that once separated women who waited to be married to have sex and those who didn't. Some of the wives who attend Paget's seminars admit that they're nervous about telling their husbands just how sexually experienced they are; they're concerned it will brand them as promiscuous, a label at odds with the traditional script in which the "good" wife is synonymous with the chaste woman. "The most important thing for a lot of women is their reputations," Paget says. "They don't want to put that in jeopardy. For them to say that they know a lot of stuff—that's a tough one. If a man has a lot of experience, a woman is thankful."

This good girl/bad girl script continues to exist, if in a distilled form. The double standard by which women are judged according to how sexually active they are is but another manifestation of the wife gap: women are told that expressing their sexuality is a badge of independence, yet, when they do, they find themselves judged by 1950s standards. In yet another foray into the ever-expanding how-to-snag-Mr. Right market, the 1998 book *What Men Want: Three Professional Single Men Reveal What It Takes to Make a Man Yours*, the authors, Bradley Gerstman, Christopher Pizzo, and Rich Seldes, made the distinction between "good for now" girls and women with "wife potential." A woman willing to sleep with a man before the fifth date, they contend, doesn't have "wife potential."

Similarly, the female co-authors of the best seller *The Rules: Time-Tested Secrets for Capturing the Heart of Mr. Right* were adamant that women keep a man waiting for sex, and never, ever sleep with a man on the first date. As Ellen Fein and Sherrie Schneider put it, "If you play your cards right, you can have sex with him every night for the rest of your life when you're married." And they also tell women looking to lure a future husband that if they do sleep with a man before marriage, they mustn't be a drill sergeant, demanding he satisfy her.

Paget has been invited to speak to the group of young wives in Edmonton this wintry evening by Melissa Schulhof, a thirty-two-year-old mother of two, whose husband, Peter, works in real estate. Schulhof met her husband in 1985, when she was sixteen. He was six years older and would be her first and only boyfriend. In 1993, he proposed at the top of the Eiffel Tower. They married the following year. Schulhof attended a Paget seminar in Calgary at a girlfriend's bachelorette party earlier in the year. She was impressed and thought Paget would be perfect for the wives' group.

Over the next four hours, under Paget's tutelage, the women's heads bob up and down over the instructional product as she runs through various techniques. There's the "Ode to Brian," also known as the "Penis Samba," the "Basketweave," "the Tantric Cross," and an "Italian" method of fellatio that involves putting a condom on using only the mouth.

Paget also explains the differences between clitoral orgasm and G-spot orgasm, the erotic benefits of humming while administering oral sex, the etiquette of swallowing semen, and the effective use of a pearl necklace as a means of penile stimulation. At the end of the class, the women line up to buy signed copies of Paget's books.

A month later, at the Young Entrepreneurs' Christmas party, the women who had attended the seminar show up wearing pearl necklaces. It's an inside joke, a reminder of Paget's instruction. Husband after husband approaches Melissa Schulhof to thank her for bringing Paget's methodology into their lives.

Lou Paget's seminar on that cold November night can be viewed as representing a crossroads in terms of wifely sexuality. On one hand, it reflects the entrenched role of wife as sexual caretaker. But the young women sitting around tables sucking away on plastic phalluses are also iconoclasts of sorts, in that they're recasting the traditional associations of wifely sex—as obligatory vaginal intercourse, intended for the ordered procreation of the species.

Viewed thus, it could be seen as a bold bid to break from a script that sees marital sex as the antithesis of erotic. Having sex with your legal spouse isn't forbidden; it's bidden. It isn't illicit, it's licit. It isn't foreign; it isn't furtive; it doesn't pulsate with the anticipation of the new. The day-to-day contact and proximity of marriage was seen as inviting the death of the carnal urge. Ironically, the "companionate" marriage so vaunted in the culture—the "he's my best friend" tribute gushed by new brides—seemed a recipe for bedroom disappointment. In one *USA Today* survey, both men and women wrote in to say that sex ends with marriage—or with the birth of a baby. One woman joked that her sex life after marriage is so dull that her waterbed "is like the Dead Sea."

Wives enthusiastically administering blow jobs to their husbands can also be seen as part of the latest installment in the story of the wax and wane of the wifely libido, a narrative that possesses all the twists and turns of a P. D. James mystery. If you look to the Bible, you'll find no shortage of sexually avaricious women or sexually satisfied wives. In Paul's First Epistle to the Corinthians 7:3–4, the marital sexual bond is presented as reciprocal: "Let the husband render unto his wife due benevolence; and likewise also the wife to the husband. The wife hath not power over her own body but the husband: and likewise also the husband hath not power over his own body but the wife."

The Greeks believed men and women had equal capacity for sexual pleasure; they also falsely postulated that a woman must experience orgasm in order to conceive. Depictions of the wife in the eleventh century showed them to have healthy libidos. In 1068, a group of Norman women demanded that William the Conqueror release their husbands from military service so that the men could satisfy their wives' sexual needs. Medieval literature, too, is rife with women possessing sexual appetites that are as, if not more, voracious than their husbands', Chaucer's Wife of Bath being a primary example.

In Christine de Pisan's lyric poem "In Praise of Marriage," a rare historical account of marital sexuality from a wife's point of view, believed to have been written at the turn of the fifteenth century, she writes: "Prince, he drives me crazy with desire / When he tells me he's entirely mine / He will make me swoon with sweetness / Certainly the dear man loves me well." Even the Puritans, those famous sexual prudes, advocated shared sexual satisfaction as a key to a lasting marriage. William Whateley's wifely conduct book, *A Bride's Bush*, published in 1623, stressed mutuality as the ideal, as "mutual dalliances for pleasure's sake" were encouraged between a married couple.

The female libido was short-circuited publicly in the nineteenth century as the quintessential "goodness" of a wife became tied to her sexual purity. Christian doctrine was interpreted to admonish that sex was strictly for procreation. As such, the act was part of a job description, a matter of work rather than play or pleasure, with performance measured in the delivery of children.

But here is the catch-22: while marriage sanctioned female sexuality, women were seen to undergo a sexual muting when they became wives. A classic example can be found in Thomas Hardy's nineteenth-century novel *Far from the Madding Crowd*, in which an elderly man's passion for a woman is quelled once she is "ticketed as my lawful wife." He solves the problem by removing her wedding ring, calling her by her maiden name, and fantasizing that they are not married.

In *Babbitt*, Sinclair Lewis's indictment of middle-class American society published in 1922, wife Myra Babbitt is described as "sexless as an anemic nun. She was a good woman, a kind woman, a diligent woman, but no one, save perhaps Tinka, her ten-year-old, was at all interested in her or entirely aware that she was alive." Sex in the Babbitt household after twenty-three years of marriage was banal at best. "She passed from feeble disgust at their closer relations into what promised to be ardent affection, but it drooped into bored routine."

Even in the wake of 1960s feminism, wife muting prevailed. As *The Washington Post* put it in 1970, "It is only young unmarried girls who are allowed to be entirely female ... as soon as they are married they are expected to mute their sexuality somewhat, and when they become mothers this neutralization is carried even further." This isn't surprising. The wife gap meant the wives were silent wallflowers during the sexual revolution of the 1960s and '70s, decades when the sexiest thing about having a wife was that you could swap her. Radical feminists went so far as to suggest that all sexual relationships within marriage are a form of legalized rape or legalized prostitution. Catherine McKinnon, America's foremost feminist legal scholar, held that all heterosexual sex should be considered rape unless explicit verbal consent can be proved. As a position, it was destined to alienate women, most of whom didn't want to live in a world that presumed all sex is forced and all men are guilty. Men, after all, are our brothers, our fathers, our lovers, our husbands.

When the wife was acknowledged in a sexual context after the 1960s, she was invariably portrayed as frustrated by the confines of marriage. The literary icon of the era, Isadora Wing, the young married heroine of Erica Jong's *Fear of Flying*, headed out on an orgasmic Grail Quest via a series of ultimately pointless "zipless fucks" that eventually brought her back, defeated, to her husband. Couples looking to increase marital sexual vibrancy were counseled to "open" their marriages, to eliminate the restraints of monogamy, to experiment with adultery in tandem.

The daughters of these women, girls raised in the 1970s and '80s, however, had a radically different sexual perspective; they had, as studies like to put it, been "masculinized." What that meant was that young women were behaving more like men—or, more precisely, that they were behaving contrary to the role for which women traditionally had been socialized. The author Nancy Friday, who has chronicled young women's sexual fantasies for several decades, referred to twentysomethings as "a new race of women" in her 1991 book *Women on Top*. Unlike the women she interviewed for *My Secret Garden*, which was published in 1973, young women of the '90s were not weighed down by guilt about their sexual fantasies and discussed them with relish.

A 1994 University of Chicago National Health and Social Life Survey claimed the behavior of young women accounted for the greatest sexual changes in the American population. Like men, the study reported, young women were seen to exhibit unpredictable patterns of sexual experimentation, cohabiting and breaking up with many sexual partners. While the average age of sexual initiation for girls has traditionally been several years behind that of boys, among the youngest generation surveyed (those born in the late 1960s and early '70s), both genders began their sexual experimentation at an average age of 17.5 years. This conclusion was echoed in "The American Freshman: Thirty-Five-Year Trends," a summary of attitudes from 1966 to 2001, published by UCLA. It noted "a gender convergence" in values as women's and men's educational and career aspirations became nearly identical.

Still, the disconnect between lover and wife could not be shaken. Losing her sexual allure was a premarital concern of Marlen Cowpland, the glamorous trophy wife of the Canadian high-tech entrepreneur Michael Cowpland. Marlen, a voluptuous, flamboyant blonde who married Cowpland in 1992, was aware that becoming a wife could potentially compromise her sexual self-expression, as she told her husband's biographer: "When we got married I had just one condition," she said. "I was scared, because I thought, what if we get married and the excitement goes and he doesn't treat me as a lover anymore, he treats me as a wife? So we made an agreement, and that's one thing he never does—he never treats me as a wife. He introduces me as his wife, but he treats me as his lover."

In *Marriage Shock: The Transformation of Women into Wives*, published in 1997, the author Dalma Heyn writes of young women self-muting, of reflexively downplaying their sexuality in public, following marriage, even though their husbands didn't ask them to. One is a woman named Tracy, who before marrying her husband attended his office Christmas party in a cropped top and short black leather skirt and danced all night with his colleagues. The year they married, however, she "rejected a little sweater dress as too short, too sexy" and attended the party in a more conservative tweed business suit. At the party the following year, she didn't dance at all; instead, she watched the secretaries on the dance floor. "How lively and sexy they looked, so different from the wives!" she is quoted as saying.

Heyn also writes of young wives who clean up their "sexual résumés." One woman, Antonia, reports that before her marriage, she was able to speak openly about her sexual needs and past to her husband, Jonathan. After marriage, however, she became demure and he became possessive: "he was more uptight about my old boyfriends, and even my former husband, after we married," she says.

The wife as an object of sexual desire remained anomalous within the culture into the 1990s. So much so that when Carlsberg beer produced a television commercial presenting the wife as an erotic creature, it was intended to shock. In the fifteen-second spot that first aired in 1998, a man and woman stand in the doorway of a seedy hotel room, writhing in passion, their mouths on one another with the desperate purpose of strangers who have just met or of long-separated lovers. The moment is charged, illicit, anticipatory. A male voiceover then delivers a one-two punchline: "A friend of mine tried to tell me that the best sex I'd ever have would be with my wife. He was right." The screen flashes to a bottle of Carlsberg beer.

The approach was a fresh gambit, one with considerable marketing acumen behind it. The Carlsberg campaign was targeted at men and women aged thirty to forty, a desirable consumer demographic comprising people who had had their taste of sexual freedom and found it lacking. They were aging and sensitive to the risks of sexually transmitted diseases. Certainly, it's in the beer company's interest to elevate fidelity: the monogamous consumer is a brand-loyal consumer. Still, it's telling that the ad was staged in a hotel room, not the marital bedroom. It was removed from the domestic trappings believed to curb sexual desire.

Beer ads notwithstanding, the sexualized wife is a shock the culture isn't quite ready to absorb, even though countless men are turned on by their wives. It's only been within the last generation, after all, that the courts have made it possible for a wife to sue for "loss of consortium," meaning the legal right to the company, affection, and assistance of her husband, something men had been entitled to for centuries. What that means is that a wife's right to sexuality and the pleasure derived from it was considered equal to a husband's.

Part of the problem is that since the nineteenth century, successful wife sex—in terms of public discourse, at least—was linked to procreative vaginal intercourse. Its success was measured in terms of children, not orgasms. Even in this age, one considered to be so sexually enlightened, the association between vaginal intercourse and "legitimate" sexuality prevails. In *Tempted Women: The Passions, Perils, and Agonies of Female Infidelity*, published in 1994, Carol Botwin captured the sentiment by coining the term "Everything But" to describe how married women described affairs that did not include vaginal penetration. She quotes one woman: "My lover and I are good Christians and believe that only intercourse constitutes infidelity." The fact that vaginal intercourse was not engaged in by former president Bill Clinton in his notorious affair with Monica Lewinsky clearly justified, in his mind at least, his claim that "I did not have sexual relations with that woman."

The relationship between vaginal intercourse and marital sex had far-reaching consequences for female sexuality. The most obvious was that while vaginal intercourse is reliable when procreation is the goal, it's less dependable as the route to female sexual pleasure. As Dr. Jed Kaminetsky, a prominent New York City urologist who specializes in female sexuality, told *New York* magazine in 2001, "Most women don't assume they're going to have an orgasm when they have sex."

The same point was made nearly a hundred years before, in the earliest known study of women's sex lives in the U.S., which was conducted by the Stanford University professor Celia Duel Mosher and based on data compiled between 1892 and 1920. Many wives reported that they were routinely expected to submit to unwanted sex they didn't enjoy. This sad disclosure was echoed in Katharine Bement Davis's landmark 1929 study, "Factors in the Sex Life of Twenty-two Hundred Women." Davis, a social scientist, sent ten thousand letters to selected wives, asking them to answer and return an anonymous questionnaire about their sexual experiences. Women reported that they entered into marriage believing that their husbands had the right to control the terms of sexual intercourse. One woman reported, "My mother taught me what to expect. The necessity of yielding to her husband's demands had been a great cross in her own life."

Still, more than half the women surveyed reported that they came to enjoy sex as the marriage progressed, even though only one-third of women claimed that their sexual needs were as strong as their husbands'. The study also revealed that 7 percent of wives had experienced premarital sex, and that 40 percent of married women and 65 percent of single women admitted to practicing masturbation.

This latter point is significant. It showed that women were seeking and experiencing orgasms, though not necessarily with their husbands. Over a hundred years ago, we should be cheered to know, the sisters were doing it for themselves, frequently with the assistance of electromechanical vibrators, or the housewife's "little helper," as they were known long before tranquilizing pharmaceuticals held that honor.

The first electromechanical vibrator was invented in the early 1880s by the British physician Joseph Mortimer Granville. It was intended to allow doctors to administer "therapeutic massage" more easily to female patients. Therapeutic massage was the medical euphemism for genital stimulation, an age-old "remedy" for "hysteria"—that catch-all disease that mysteriously plagued women throughout the centuries.

The symptoms of female hysteria included sleeplessness, nervousness, and any other kind of female behavior that the male of the species might find baffling. Today, such behavioral tics are readily associated with general stress. But in the late nineteenth century, a time when marital sex was often unsatisfying for women and masturbation was discouraged or forbidden, female sexual frustration manifested itself though the more medically acceptable "hysteroneurasthenic" disorders. Women turned to doctors who stimulated them manually to orgasm, a "remedy" that was in no way considered improper, as it did not involve vaginal penetration and therefore did not violate the marital bond. Nor was the female patient's response ever referred to as an orgasm; rather, it was known by the more clinical "hysterical paroxysm."

Granville's invention was a boon to the medical establishment, as it allowed doctors a way to administer these "paroxysms" more efficiently, and therefore to see more patients. As Rachel P. Maines writes in *The Technology of Orgasm: Hysteria, the Vibrator and Women's Sexual Satisfaction,* "In effect, doctors inherited the task of producing orgasm in women because it was a job nobody else wanted."

As Maines documents, the first vibrators were enormous contraptions, steam-powered or controlled by foot pedals. With the advent of electricity and compact batteries, the devices became increasingly cheap and portable, which allowed women to buy them for themselves. The vibrator was the fifth household appliance to be electrified, after the sewing machine, fan, kettle, and toaster. (Electrifying the iron and vacuum cleaner was evidently a lower priority, as that didn't take place for another ten years.)

Between 1880 and 1930, personal vibrators were advertised as domestic aids in women's magazines. One ad that ran in *Women's Home Companion* in 1906 celebrated the vibrator's virtues in unambiguously sexual terms: "Penetrating, invigorating, all the pleasures of youth will throb within you." When marketed to men, vibrators were recommended as "gifts for women that would benefit the male givers by restoring bright eyes and pink cheeks to their female consorts." A 1918 Sears, Roebuck and Company Electrical Goods catalog featured an ad for a remarkably versatile vibrator (under "Aids That Every Woman Appreciates") that offered not only sexual stimulation but also domestic assistance, given its attachments for churning, mixing, beating, grinding, and operating a fan.

When vibrators were featured in the first pornographic films of the 1920s—including one with the amusing title *Widow's Delight*—and the relationship between the device and female sexual satisfaction was made explicit, the items were quickly pushed out of the public eye, not to resurface until the 1960s as sex toys that could be used jointly by men and women.

Still, the vibrator remained linked to the dissatisfied wife. In the play *Signs of Intelligent Life in the Universe,* written by Jane Wagner, Lily Tomlin jokes about the vibrator in domestic terms: ". . . think of it as a kind of Hamburger Helper for the boudoir. . . . Why, the *time* it saves alone is worth the price. / I'd rank it right up there with Minute Rice, / Reddi-wip and Pop-Tarts. . . . / Ladies, it can be a real help to the busy married woman who has a thousand chores and simply does not need the extra burden of trying to have an orgasm."

The portable vibrator rescued women from having to turn to doctors for relief from their so-called hysteroneurasthenic disorders. But it was also perceived as a threat to conventional male-female sexual roles. A woman with a vibrator is capable of taking control of her own satisfaction; she doesn't require a man to send her into "paroxysms" of ecstasy.

Just as legislation prevented wives from employment in government agencies during the previous century, lawmakers also attempted to control women's access to orgasm. As late as 1998, Alabama passed an addition to the obscenity statute of the state law that "makes it unlawful to produce, distribute or otherwise sell sexual devices that are marketed primarily for the stimulation of human genital organs." The penalty for selling a sex toy in the state, where neither Viagra nor masturbation is against the law, is a maximum $10,000 fine and up to a year of hard labor. The next year the American Civil Liberties Union challenged the law, arguing that it violated the constitutional right to privacy and personal autonomy, and was clearly aimed at women. The U.S. district court judge ruled in their favor, but the appellate court unanimously upheld the law, saying, in effect, that Alabama's "interest in public morality is a legitimate interest rationally served by the statute."

Until the sexual revolution of the 1970s, female sexual satisfaction was not discussed publicly, nor was it well documented. The Dutch physician Theodoor H. van de Velde was a rare early champion of wifely sexual pleasure in *Ideal Marriage,* written in 1926: "Every considerable erotic stimulation of their wives that does not terminate in orgasm, on the woman's part, represents an injury, and repeated injuries of this kind lead to permanent—or very obstinate—damage to both body and soul."

For the most part, however, the medical establishment ignored the female orgasm to the point that at the turn of the twenty-first century, we are just beginning to understand the role of hormones in female libido, or even of the purpose of those fifteen thousand pudendal nerve fibers that exist in a woman's pelvic area.

Female sexuality had been ignored by doctors for a simple reason: there was no perceived need to know. Why go to the trouble of splitting the atom, metaphorically speaking, without incentive or pressure to do so? The analogy is intentional. We are now beginning to recognize that the female body is a bomb waiting to detonate in terms of sexual response. In *Woman: An Intimate Geography*, Natalie Angier piquantly refers to the vagina as a "Rorschach with legs." The clitoris, she points out, is devoted purely to sexual pleasure, containing twice as many nerve endings as a penis. And in terms of sexual stamina, a woman is capable of experiencing fifty to one hundred orgasms in an hour, whereas three to four climaxes a night are considered Olympian for a man. Such a snapshot of female physiology is diametrically opposed to the cultural understanding that women have more delicate sexual urges than men. On this point, Angier quotes the primatologist Barbara Smuts asking the rhetorical question: "If female sexuality is muted compared to that of men, then why must men the world over go to such extreme lengths to control and constrain it?" The answer is obvious: the quest to uncover the physiological truth about female sexuality represents a Pandora's box, one that, once opened, would forever change the perception of women, and of wives.

But we didn't open that box. Instead, we saw the creation in the late 1990s of a burgeoning, highly profitable female orgasm industry, one that was an eerie echo of the doctors who controlled women's hysterical paroxysms a century earlier. Attending to the new female maladies of "sexual dysfunction," "hypo-active sexual desire disorder," and "female arousal disorder" is big business, driven by pharmaceutical conglomerates and a new crop of doctors who specialize in the recently invented disorders.

In fact, the drug industry was instrumental in diagnosing these new female "medical conditions." At a conference held in 1998 in Boston, eighteen of the nineteen medical practitioners who signed their names to a new definition of female sexual dysfunction had financial interests or other relationships with a total of twenty-two drug companies. And two of the authors of the 1994 National Health and Social Life Survey reporting high rates of female dysfunction later noted links to Pfizer, the manufacturer of Viagra.

Female Viagra is only one of many potential medical panaceas created to deal with the so-called problem. There are also Avlimil, an herbal concoction that promises to help women put sex back into sexless marriage; suppositories and creams that increase blood flow to female genitals; testosterone; the Peruvian maca root, which is credited with restoring female sex drive; as well as therapeutic devices, including, ironically, the vibrator.

Even the U.S. government jumped into the fray in May 2000 when the FDA approved the Eros system, a soft plastic suction cup placed over the clitoris and attached to a vacuum device to help women achieve orgasm. The Eros device, as well intended as it may be, reflects retrograde attitudes toward female sexuality. The contraption is available only by doctor's prescription, meaning that a woman must first be diagnosed as dysfunctional in some manner before she can shell out close to $400 for it. Then there's the matter of its name. Naming it after the Greek god of love reflects the entrenched association between female sexual response and emotional response. Which is not to say that emotions don't play a role in women's desire to have sex with their husbands, as the studies pointing to female frustration with their onerous workloads make clear. Even the medical establishment recognizes that a medicine cabinet filled with prescriptions for "female sexual arousal" is pointless if a woman is filled with anger, anxiety, and guilt. As one doctor remarked in *New York* magazine in 2001, "As sex therapists are fond of saying, no drug will cure a woman who hates her husband."

Attempts to eliminate the censors governing female sexuality have been met with criticism, even suppression. In the 1950s, the pioneering sex therapist Alfred Kinsey ignited controversy when he likened the

belief in consistent female orgasm through penetration alone to a conviction that the earth was flat. Kinsey claimed that 70 percent of all
women don't experience orgasm by penetration alone. The 1976 best-
seller *The Hite Report* was the first survey of female sexuality taken
entirely from women's point of view. It was also the first full-scale work
devoted to female orgasm, and it came to the contentious conclusion
that "the only orgasm the penis accomplishes is its own." Shere Hite
also reported that more women experienced orgasm through masturbation than intercourse, though they enjoyed intercourse. The book
was roundly criticized for its lack of scientific research and was banned
in nine countries.

Then, in what appeared the ultimate attempt to desexualize women,
research from the Kinsey Institute published in the June 2003 issue of
The Archives of Sexual Behavior chose to exclude orgasm as a measure of
female sexual satisfaction. According to that study, women were more
sexually satisfied than had been reported in the famous University of
Chicago study that proclaimed half of American women were "dysfunctional." But as the Kinsey Institute director, John Bancroft,
explains, the higher level of female satisfaction resulted from the fact
that the study approached female sexuality in a new way: it "emphasized the importance of non-physiological components of sexuality as
well as the general importance of mental health." In other words, it
didn't focus on arousal and orgasm, as most clinical sex satisfaction surveys have. And what it concluded was that women didn't need to have
an orgasm to be sexually satisfied.

The study, based on a random telephone survey of 853 women aged
between twenty and sixty-five who had been in a heterosexual relationship for at least six months, found that the best predictors of a woman's
sexual satisfaction are her general emotional well-being and her emotional relationship with her partner. From there, it went on to conclude
that emotional closeness to their partners could be as satisfying to
women as arousal and frequency of orgasm during sex.

It's an approach that can be viewed as both progressive and regressive. On one hand, it makes the important, often-overlooked acknowl-
edgment that male and female sexual responsiveness are different and

that emotional connections figure significantly in human sexual response. On the other, the study takes the ubiquitous "Men are from Mars, women are from Venus" mentality to an extreme, dismissing the fact that both men and women are hardwired to experience orgasm, and both have equal need for its pleasure and its salutary benefits, which range from relieving stress to boosting the immune system.

The study claimed that it's healthy for women not to want to have sex when they are tired. As Bancroft notes, the inhibition of female sexual desire can be "a healthy and functional response for women faced with stress, tiredness, or threatening behavior from their partners." Certainly that's good news for all those tired, stressed-out respondents in the University of Chicago study who've been walking around thinking they're sexually "dysfunctional." But being told that inhibited sexual desire resulting from stress and fatigue is "healthy and functional" doesn't go any distance in dealing with what is emerging as the true source of female sexual frustration.

Just as women were being lured back to a mythical domesticity during the 1990s, so too was there a romanticization of other wifely conventions, namely ceremonial rituals that once defined wifely sex. This was manifest most boldly in the renewed fascination with the virgin. Maidenhead mania ruled—from the freshly thonged, self-proclaimed "virgin" Britney Spears to the soap-scrubbed evangelism of the Southern Baptist Convention's "True Love Waits" campaign, which encourages both male and female teenagers and college students to sign abstinence pledges. On television, the central characters of both *Felicity* and *Buffy the Vampire Slayer* agonized about losing their virginity before both did, to their considerable regret. Even the U.S. government promoted virginity, as federal funding for abstinence-only sex education grew from $2 million annually in 1996 to $135 million in the proposed 2003 budget. One program with the catchy moniker "Marriage Before the Carriage" sponsored a contest in which the woman able to wax most eloquently on the virtues of forswearing childbirth for marriage would win a shiny red Jeep.

A power chastity movement emerged based on the belief that the sexual freedoms extolled not only by feminism but by society at large had been harmful for women. Wendy Shalit, a twenty-three-year-old philosophy graduate from Williams College in Willamstown, Massachusetts, created a media firestorm in 1999 with the publication of *A Return to Modesty: Discovering the Lost Virtue,* which celebrated a return to Victorian morality and modesty. Likewise, Danielle Crittenden's *What Our Mothers Didn't Tell Us: Why Happiness Eludes the Modern Woman* received widespread coverage for its contention that women should preserve themselves for marriage. Crittenden invokes the hoary dictum "Why buy the cow when she's giving away the milk for free?" before advising women to form a cartel in which they refuse men sex before marriage: "But if women *as a group* cease to be readily available—if they begin to demand commitment (and real commitment, as in marriage) in exchange for sex, market conditions will shift in favor of women." Not only does the comment take us back to a time in which a wife was a purchased commodity, her market currency tied to her sexual purity, but it also assumes that women, "as a group," share the same objectives in life, which, of course, they do not.

The Victorian edict that the bride bring her preserved virtue to the wedding, a gift veiled in white tulle for her new husband, also returned with a vengeance to the culture in a faux form. Retrofitting virginity, if only symbolically, was perceived as a way to differentiate married sex from the premarital sexual relationships most women engaged in. Even the feminist Naomi Wolf, who detailed the loss of her virginity at age sixteen in her book *Promiscuities,* wrote rapturously about the notion of reclaiming her virginity symbolically when she married in 1993. She wore a dress described as a "marked-down, beat-up yellowing gown" that looked like it "had been worn by someone who'd been sleeping in a forest." Yet, technically, it was white: "In white," she writes, "we retrieve our virginity, which symbolizes that sexual access to us is special again."

Much more drastic was the "trend" reported by popular women's magazines that saw a few women going to the extreme of having their hymens reconstructed. The procedure, a hymenoplasty or hymenorraphy, used to be restricted to cultures known to suppress women, where the consequences of not bleeding at first intercourse, or being a "non-virgin" bride, can be severe. In many Mediterranean and African cultures, the husband's family may take revenge through violent punishments and banishment of the non-virgin bride because she "shamed" them. Among the Yungar people of Australia, girls without hymens before marriage were starved, tortured, or even killed. In Muslim countries, the non-virgin bride may be killed by her brothers, uncles, or father. The perpetrators often escape prosecution owing to the customs that justify such murders.

A typical hymen-repair surgery involves suturing the remnants of the ruptured hymen together or attaching a flap of skin from the vaginal wall across the opening. In certain cases, where bloody sheets are a mandatory part of the wedding-night ritual, a gelatin capsule containing a bloodlike substance is inserted into the vagina. In China, where they often undergo hymen replacement in anticipation of marriage, they routinely purchase the "Jade Lady Membrane Man-Made Hymen," a do-it-yourself hymen-repair kit.

In Egypt, women are paying $100 to $600 for the operation. In Turkey, the price for hymenorraphy is estimated to be between $140 and $1,500. The June 8, 1996, issue of the British medical journal *The Lancet* cited an example of a woman who "managed to avoid sexual intercourse [with her new husband] for four months by pretending to be insane ... [while] she was saving up for the operation."

But the practice also spread to the West, where women do not fear reprisal if they aren't virgins. In 2001, *Marie Claire* magazine claimed that the majority of women who visit the Plastic Surgery Center in New York City for "reconstructive gynecology" are Latin American. One woman, "Sandra," was quoted saying that her fiancé would never have proposed if he had known she wasn't a virgin. He was too good a catch—successful, handsome, and Latin American—to risk losing. So she had her hymen replaced.

The Toronto plastic surgeon Robert Stubbs, who charges upward of $2,000 for the procedure, was quoted in *Maclean's* magazine as saying that while most of the few requests for hymenoplasty come from women from Muslim cultures, he had also operated on a Russian musician in her early forties who wanted her hymen restored as a symbolic gesture before her second marriage.

North American women not willing to take such drastic measures found nonsurgical ways of reclaiming their maidenheads. We saw the terms *revirgining* and *secondary virginity* surface in the media in 2002 to describe women who choose to forgo sex for weeks or months before their wedding night in order to make the experience more "meaning-ful." Revirgining was presented as just another chore on the bride's to-do list, a way of importing sexual spark to the honeymoon. The pre-wedding regimen of Nicole Ratliff, a twenty-four-year-old bride-to-be, was detailed in *The New York Times*: "She exercises with a personal trainer so her arms look buff in her strapless gown. She works on her tan to get rid of the swimsuit lines across her shoulders. She guzzles 124 ounces of water daily to hydrate her skin. And since July 26, three months before the day she will say, 'I do,' she has been abstaining from sex with her live-in fiancé, David Crawford, and plans to continue until after they are married." Like other women interviewed in the article, Ratliff associated being a virgin—even a "revirgined" virgin—with virtue, an echo of the nineteenth-century association of female virginity with a moral state as well as a husband's property right. The nearer she got to her wedding, Ratliff says, the guiltier she feel about straying from the values of her religious upbringing. Kim Burgess, a thirty-eight-year-old woman interviewed for the article, said she and her fiancé refrained from having sex for a month before marrying: "The holding out makes you feel that you've been a good girl," she says.

In North America, where few couples expect to produce blood-stained sheets on their wedding night, newlyweds still feel obliged to keep up the charade of the wedding-night "consummation," to "make it official," even if the couple is tired, stressed, or has had too much to drink at the reception. Paula, a friend of mine who married in 1996 at twenty-six and divorced two and a half years later, remembers sex on her wedding night as "a disaster." "We had thirty people up to our suite, and we partied until six in the morning," she explains. "Everyone was totally trashed. After they left, he insisted on having sex because, after all, it was our wedding night. It was as if our marriage would be jinxed if we didn't. It was bad, really bad." Another woman I know recalls sitting in the hotel room, exhausted after her wedding reception, looking at her husband warily and saying, "I guess we'd better do this."

Every woman is a singular narrative, unique in her love, her pleasure, and her desire. Still, the parade of advice treating all women as a singular entity continued unabated in a new spate of wife sex advice books. Recognizing that all was not right in the modern marital bedroom, some of these books looked back in time for an answer, recommending that marital harmony could be restored only if women surrendered to their husbands as they had a century ago. As Laura Doyle put it in the popular *The Surrendered Wife*, "The first rule for a great sex life is to be respectful and wear something sheer and lacy." In *The Sex-Starved Marriage: A Couple's Guide to Boosting Their Marriage Libido*, Michele Weiner-Davis recommends that wives submit to sexual activity even if they don't want to in order to foster emotional intimacy with their husbands. The author went so far as to invoke Stepford wife imagery to argue her case: the "Stepford wives of her mother's generation may have been robots in the home," she said, but adds: "The baby boomers were created in the late 1940s and 1950s. A lot of babies were made then." The argument fails to convince. First, it's quite possible that a lot of babies were born because women in the 1940s and 1950s didn't have access to reliable contraception; second, there is no reason to assume that a generation of boomers was not the product of Stepford robotic sex.

Taking another tack, a slew of books published in the late 1990s presented marital sex as the ultimate in erotic stimulation. As Lana L. Holstein, M.D., the author of *How to Have Magnificent Sex*, puts it, "Good sex is the last frontier for couples." In *The Case for Marriage: Why Married People Are Happier, Healthier, and Better Off Financially*, published in 2000, conservative social critics Linda J. Waite and Maggie Gallagher contend that among other benefits of marriage, married couples report the highest level of sexual satisfaction (couples merely living together have sex more often but, somewhat mysteriously, enjoy it less, they report).

As they present it, the comfort of commitment allows couples to more readily reach sexual nirvana. Nerve.com, a New York–based Internet magazine, published an issue devoted to married sex in 2001. It featured articles such as one from a man's perspective on making love to his pregnant wife and one by a nerve.com co-founder and confessed female serial cheater on getting engaged. Lorelei Sharkey, one of the magazine's editors, says she and her colleagues felt compelled to take on the topic in order to counter the "kind of sterile, family-values approach to it, that you make love within the sanctity of marriage and you don't get the hotter aspects of it. [We wanted to] embrace [marriage's] sexiness and explore how sexy true love and monogamy can be." Our generation, she says, is "more comfortable asserting themselves sexually and talking about what they want, about their fears, hesitations and desires, and what they want from life including from their partners and their marriages."

Concurrently, women were confronted with a spate of sex manuals championing the monogamous orgasm as the highest form of pleasure. Many of these focused on Chinese Taoism and Buddhist Tantra, ancient techniques said to be favored by rock star Sting and his wife, Trudie Styler, that require couples to spend hours exchanging "sexual energy."

Achieving multiple orgasms and spiritual oneness was the irresistible marketing pitch behind *The Multi-Orgasmic Couple: Sexual Secrets Every Couple Should Know,* by the married couple Mantak and Manee-wan Chia. More extreme and performance orientated was *Extended Massive Orgasm: How You Can Give and Receive Intense Sexual Pleasure,* by Vera and Steve Bodansky. The Bodanskys, both behavioral scientists, achieved a measure of fame for their seminars in which Steve Bodansky prods his wife into paroxysms of pleasure for hours on end. The image of a multi-orgasmic Vera Bodansky on public display, however, can be seen as little more than the sad continuation of the wife lying on a doctor's table more than a century ago, being massaged to orgasm as if she were a class project.

The actress Kim Cattrall jumped on the joy-of-married-sex bandwagon in 2002 with *Satisfaction: The Art of the Female Orgasm,* written with her then-husband, Mark Levinson. Given that Cattrall gained fame playing Samantha on *Sex and the City,* her writing a how-to book on female pleasure seemed like an obvious publishing gambit. The character of Samantha is a fortyish female orgasmatron, a woman who has been compared to a man in her need for fleeting, impersonal sexual conquests. Achieving orgasm is a breeze for her; in fact, an entire episode of the show was based on her anguish when she briefly lost the ability to have one.

But while Cattrall's fame as Samantha clearly got her the book deal and drew crowds during its publicity tour, the actress distanced herself from the unrealistic, intimidating standard the character presents. As Cattrall made clear, she was writing for the vast majority of women, who, as she saw it, are sexually dissatisfied. "We confirmed that the majority of women don't have good sex lives.... And most people don't admit that," she said in one interview. "And this isn't just this year or last year or the last few years, and it's not a few women. It's millions of women."

Cattrall writes in the introduction that one of the purposes of the book is to "debunk the myth that attractive women with sexy images have fabulous sex lives. The hype and glamour surrounding show business and people in it reinforce the fiction." She admits that her screen persona created a problem in her own sex life in that men expected her to be like the randy gym teacher she played in the 1982 movie *Porky's,* or the insatiable, skilled Samantha. "Sex wasn't fulfilling for me," she writes. "It certainly wasn't fulfilling for the men I was with." The forty-five-year-old actress confides that it wasn't until she met Levinson, husband number three, in 1998, that sex became pleasurable for her. (Sizzling sex, alas, was not enough to keep the marriage together; the couple separated in 2003.)

Cattrall's sexual vibrancy at age forty-five also flouted the socially entrenched belief that women past childbearing age were asexual and thus denatured. This too is a continuation of the longstanding link of "legitimate," wifely, female sexuality with procreation, and thus youth. Women who defined themselves foremost as wives and mothers were most afflicted by the perception. Sarah, the wife of a New York businessman, complained bitterly in *New York* magazine about losing her sexual allure: "Once you're past the age of being a sex object, you have no function," she lamented. "There's a kind of desperation. If he threw her over for you, he'll throw you over for the next one—unless you get one old enough to bury him." In a 1998 interview, Margaret Trudeau Kemper, who had once been married to the Canadian prime minister Pierre Trudeau, blamed her deteriorating mental health on menopause, noting, "I thought my usefulness was finished. After all, I believed my job on Earth was to procreate and be a pleasant sexual diversion for hardworking men."

The emphasis placed on the sexually viable wife heralded the acceptance of hormone replacement therapy, or HRT, in the 1960s. Originally, the idea of pumping menopausal women full of estrogen was promoted as a boon not to women but to men: it made an aging wife going through "the change," as menopause was then known, easier to be around. That's how the Manhattan gynecologist Robert Wilson presented it in his landmark book, *Feminine Forever: Menopause—The Loss of Womanhood and the Loss of Good Health*, published in 1966 and underwritten by the drug company Wyeth-Ayerst (now Wyeth).

Wilson writes of menopause as a "living decay" in which women descend into a "vapid, cow-like" state. Menopausal women who didn't take hormones, he argues, were "castrates." Supplemental estrogen, he insists, would magically transform these bovine crones into supple, more sexually viable and younger-looking wives and mothers. "Such women will be much more pleasant to live with and will not become dull and unattractive," he writes, words that predated the Stepford wife phenomenon by a decade.

Wilson went to the extreme length of suggesting that cranky women who didn't take hormones were even putting themselves at risk of being murdered by their husbands. The book tells the story of one husband, a member of the "Brooklyn underworld," who came to him threatening to kill his menopausal wife if her moods didn't improve. Wilson writes that he administered Premarin to the wife, ostensibly assuring her survival, though he does intimate that homicide might await other wives unwilling to take medication: "Outright murder may be a relatively rare consequence of menopause—though not as rare as most of us might suppose," he writes ominously.

Early films intended to educate doctors about hormone treatments preyed on the insecurities of an aging wife. *Physiologic and Emotional Basis of Menopause,* a 1972 film produced by the drug maker Ayerst, made the link between taking estrogen and keeping one's husband happy: "When a woman develops hot flashes, sweats, wrinkles on her face, she is quite concerned that she is losing her youth—that she may indeed be losing her husband." A woman in a nightgown, sitting in a plaid easy chair in front of a fireplace, laments her fate: "My boys are both gone and my husband is away a great deal with his work. The evenings bother me most. And I think we all give thought to the fact that our husbands might become interested in a younger woman, but I don't dwell on the subject."

Despite all the happy ads promising a chemical fountain of youth, HRT has always been associated with risk. In the 1970s, progesterone was added to the mix when researchers found that taking estrogen by itself increased the risk of uterine cancer. Even so, in 1975 and again in 1989, *The New England Journal of Medicine* ran stories linking HRT to increased incidences of cancer in women. In 2002, a national study on HRT concluded that the benefits of HRT are overshadowed by the risks of breast and ovarian cancers, heart attacks, strokes, and blood clots, and that these risks increase with time. The finding was hardly surprising. How could we believe that replacing a woman's hormones for decades was as safe as taking the gray out of her hair? What was more shocking is that millions of women in North America ingested synthetic hormones without any randomized, controlled clinical trial having taken place first.

Still, millions of women were willing to embark on HRT because they wanted to eliminate temporary hot flashes, mood swings, and memory loss, and trusted their doctors when they said it had the added benefit of reducing the risk of heart attack and osteoporosis. They also liked the extension of youth it seemed to provide. A new generation of women was unwilling to cease being sexual with menopause. The same generation that grew up with what Erica Jong referred to as the "zipless fuck" is now looking for the ageless version of the same thing.

The results were apparent in the August 2002 issue of *Vogue*. Titled "The Age Issue," the magazine showcased "stylesetters from 16 to 80+," women who are beautiful, vital, and eerily ageless. Showing us what our sixties can look like is the writer Barbara Amiel Black, wife of Lord Conrad Black, looking like no other sixty-one-year-old on Planet Earth. Lady Black candidly confesses to fretting occasionally about the traditional script that denies older women their sexuality, the one that says there's something untoward about being a bombshell later in life. "I know I shouldn't like sexy looks," she says. "But I'm not quite ready to play dead and play safe."

All the talk of female sexual dysfunction, oddly enough, didn't figure in the concurrent endless discussions of female adultery. That the two might be linked was not the subject of news magazine covers. And that's because wifely betrayal, as trendy as it might be, remains the subject of confusion in a culture not sure how to process it.

Historically, men's infidelities were to be expected, or at least more readily tolerated. Consider that just as there's no male equivalent for *slut*, there's no female equivalent of *cuckold*. Yet female adultery was not and is not a rare event. True, getting a handle on its prevalence is difficult, in part because statistics are notoriously unreliable, but also because many women don't discuss their affairs, even with their closest friends.

All indicators, however, point to increased incidences and increased husbandly vigilance. Much of this evidence is anecdotal, such as the reported spike in DNA paternity testing. There's also the fact that a $49.95 home-test infidelity kit, CheckMate, that tests for semen stains is doing monster business in North America and Europe, selling more than a thousand units a week. According to the product's marketing director, Brad Holmes, some 85 percent of its clients in the United States are men: "The stereotype of the dutiful wife married to the cheating husband is outdated," he says. "If anything, now it's the other way round. Women (who statistics have long maintained stray less than men) are cheating like crazy."

Academics were delving into the "paternal discrepancy phenomenon," a reference to children being fathered by men other than the
mother's public partner. One study conducted by British biologists
announced that roughly 9 percent of children fall into this category. A
medical researcher working on the genetics of breast cancer who gathered DNA from children and their parents discovered a 10 percent incidence of "paternal discrepancy" but didn't publish the finding because
she feared her funding would be jeopardized. A *Times* of London story
was more alarmist, claiming that "as many as one in seven children was
not sired by the man who believes he is their father" and that "mistrust
over paternity may be an overlooked factor in family breakdown."

Unsurprisingly, given the frustrations associated with domestic sex,
the office was proving to be ground zero for the affair, providing more
ammunition for the argument that women venturing into the workplace
is fraught with peril. A study conducted by *New Woman* magazine, which
claimed that 58 percent of seven thousand women readers confessed to
straying, found that most women meet their lovers at work. A Baltimore
psychologist, Shirley Glass, commented in 2003 that working long hours
together meant men and women might form emotional attachments
that led to sexual dalliances. As Glass presents it, work is an oasis from
domestic conflict: "The work relationship becomes so rich and the stuff
at home is pressurized and child-centered. People get involved insidiously without planning to betray." Liaisons born of the new infidelity
are seen to be much more disruptive—and much more likely to end in
divorce. "You can move away from just a sexual relationship but it's very
difficult to break an attachment," says the Rutgers University anthropologist Helen Fisher. "The betrayed partner can probably provide more
exciting sex but not a different kind of friendship."

"The double standard for adultery is disappearing," Fisher empha-
sizes. "It's been around for 5,000 years and it's changing in our lifetime.
It's quite striking. Men used to feel that they had the right. They don't
feel that anymore."

The climate was such that evolutionary behaviorists, those people
who deal with human hardwiring—the "our inner caveman can never
be wrong" theories—felt compelled to revisit female sexuality to

explain increased female infidelity. Out the window went the Darwin-
ian theory that men are hardwired for promiscuity, given their biological need to get out and sow those spermatozoa. And that women are
not; since we can bear only a limited number of children, and usually
end up taking care of those children, we have to be highly selective in
terms of who's granted access. No longer was it fashionable to argue
that security-craving wives were afraid to imperil their position by
cuckolding their mate. Instead, evolutionary psychologists were making the argument that women were not naturally monogamous. In *The
Dangerous Passion: Why Jealousy Is as Necessary as Love and Sex*, published
in 2000, David Buss argues that women stray for several reasons. At the
top of the list is to secure "mate insurance," a backup in case the regular
mate falls out of commission. Or women weary of a relationship can
use an affair to evaluate future husbands so they can "trade up." There's
also Buss's "orgasm" theory, which is not that women seek them
because they feel good but because they increase the odds of "sperm
retention" and thus conception. Apparently, in our endless quest for
quality genes, women are most likely to have adulterous sex when the
odds of conceiving are the highest.

No matter what their motivation, women looking beyond their
marriages for fulfillment became a recurrent trope in popular entertainment. On the popular television series *Dharma & Greg*, which
is now in syndication, it is wife Dharma, not husband Greg, who is
tempted to have an affair with her college professor. The episode, a
two-part cliffhanger—will she? won't she?—was screened during
sweeps week in February 2001. She didn't. In the 2002 season finale of
The Sopranos, frustrated wife Carmela Soprano explained the effect an
abstinent dalliance with another man had had on her: "I felt probably
like someone who was terminally ill, and somehow they manage to
forget it for a minute."

The wife who harbored adulterous desire is a prominent cinematic
theme, running through movies as diverse as *Chicago, The Good Girl, Far
from Heaven, Secretary, Lovely and Amazing, Unfaithful,* and *Y tu mamá
también.* Invariably, the married woman who strays is the object of sympathy rather than censure. No longer does she end up in front of a train

like Anna Karenina or dying a painful death by poison like Emma Bovary. Instead, an affair is seen as a marital tonic, a few days at the spa.

In the wildly successful *Bridges of Madison County*, which was first a book, later a movie starring Meryl Streep, the central character is a bored housewife and mother of two, who is revitalized after a four-day affair with a photographer. In the 2002 movie *Unfaithful*, one female character likens having an affair to a recreational diversion, "like taking a pottery class."

As any woman can attest, women stray for a long list of reasons— boredom, love, lust, revenge, the simple need for someone to touch her. And many of us are perfectly capable of compartmentalizing these dalliances, of having an affair without any intention of leaving the marriage. Still, the adage that women have sex to get love, men give love to get sex, though breaking down, prevails. The adulterous wife is presented as motivated by grand passion, whereas adulterous husbands are just screwing around. "When a man cheats, we assume it's all about a new naked body, but when a woman does it, we assume it's for love," wrote the novelist and social critic Katie Roiphe.

The double standard was glaringly apparent in the treatment of Charles's and Diana's affairs. While hers seemed justified, his seemed comic or disgusting or unmanly, depending on your point of view. Men and women have affairs for different reasons, the Manhattan urologist Dr. Robert Kolodny insists. "The greatest percentage of women are looking for an emotional rapport that is missing from their marriage, a relationship that gives them ego strokes. Men are looking for genital strokes." In *Sexual Arrangements*, the co-authors Janet Reibstein and Martin Richards write, "We believe men and women act differently in affairs even if they're having them now with more frequency."

In *The Erotic Silence of the American Wife*, published in 1992, author Dalma Heyn attempts to detonate some common myths about women and sex, such as the belief that women are monogamous by nature and that happily married women don't commit adultery. Her evidence was obtained through interviews with married women who had had affairs. She posits that having an affair is a way women attempt to reclaim the individuality they felt they had lost in marriage. She concludes that affairs could "empower" women and even strengthen their marriages. Few women she spoke to had regrets about their dalliances. It was a message many didn't want to hear. The author received menacing threats; when she appeared on *Larry King Live*, callers phoned in to denounce her.

Even when she is straying, the wife is often presented as doing it not for selfish, complex reasons but as a way to keep her marriage "hot." *Elle* magazine told readers that "an affair can be a sexual recharging." *Harper's Bazaar* suggested that marriages could actually be improved by affairs: "Because they get their fill of rapture elsewhere, these women are not apt to complain or nag or find fault with their husbands."

Alternatively, having an affair is presented as a way a woman could endure a hollow marriage. The lover of a married female character in Candace Bushnell's 2003 novel, *Trading Up*, is described this way: "He was a valve, an outlet that allowed her to blithely continue on with her marriage, allowing her to pretend there was nothing missing from her life."

As I was mulling over the mixed messages about female infidelity, I went to see *Crimes of the Heart*, a documentary about adultery by the Canadian filmmaker John Haslett Cuff. In it, women talk about the pleasures their affairs gave them and the risks they were willing to take to have them. Cuff also interviews his mother, a spirited, acerbic woman close to eighty years of age. She had repeatedly cheated during her marriage and is unrepentant about having done so. He asks his mother about her motivation. "Was it out of some kind of emotional need?" he asks. She looks at him as if he is daft. "An orgasm is always nice," she retorts.

The audience howled in appreciation of her candor. I laughed along with them, though her response resonated with me for hours. I couldn't help thinking of those women lying in their doctors' offices a century ago, waiting for pleasure to be administered. And that we haven't come very far in terms of enlightenment if an old woman's admitting that she went out to seek orgasms her husband couldn't supply was greeted with surprised laughter in a darkened theater in the spring of 2003.

Chapter 5

Love Hurts:
The Abused Wife as Icon

Any walking tour through the modern wife landscape has to pause at the address formerly known as 875 South Bundy Drive in the upscale Los Angeles neighborhood of Brentwood. It was there, on the evening of June 12, 1994, that Nicole Brown, the ex-wife of former football great O. J. Simpson, was found slain and blood-soaked. Her throat had been slashed so brutally that the glistening white of her larynx and cervical vertebral column were visible. Her friend Ronald Goldman was also discovered dead at the scene, his blood pooled and tracked across the terra-cotta tiles inside the meshed-wire gate, among the tropical shrubbery and fragrant bougainvillea. The address attracted so many ghoulish gawkers that the townhouse's next owner changed the number to 879 and renovated extensively, as if a new street number and finishes could exorcise the past or keep people away. But still they came.

In the months following the murders, the public hunger for details of the killing, and of Brown and Simpson's abusive relationship, was insatiable. In October, U.S. television news outlets fell into a frenzied auction for a surefire audience grabber—a videotape of the February 1985 nuptials of O. J. Simpson and Nicole Brown. As a bonus, the tape included footage of a giddy Brown getting decked out in her bridal finery. Bidding rose above $2 million before the syndicated tabloid pro-

gram *A Current Affair* walked away victorious. The program also paid
the murdered woman's father, Lou Brown, $162,500 to narrate the play-
by-play. From a return-on-investment point of view, it was money well
spent. The Simpson wedding video was a moth-to-flame audience
draw, tailor-made for November sweeps.

Grotesque voyeurism? Of course. Which meant it fit right in with
the theater of the abused wife that emerged in the latter decades of the
twentieth century, a sensational side effect of feminism's noble effort
to shine a light on a heretofore dark secret. The abused wife was the
ultimate victim—of her husband, but also of her misplaced love and
of her hurtful marriage. The Simpson wedding video fit neatly into
this dramatic construct. It provided the perfect fantasy counterpoint
to the horror show the marriage would become: the beatings; Nicole
Brown's panicked calls to 911; the divorce; the final horrible discovery
of the bodies.

The video also provided a reminder that Simpson and Brown had
once been husband and wife, conjoined in that romantic "oneness,"
wedded for better and for worse. Less than a decade later, an engrossed
public would learn just what that "worse" constituted for Brown when
photographs used as evidence at Simpson's criminal trial for her murder were circulated widely in the media. They showed Brown's face
bruised and battered by the man she'd wed in white on that sunny,
hopeful California day. The images read like a map of pain, brutal testimony of endurance in the name of what she believed to be love.

Though the photos were discomforting, they were not shocking or
even uncommon. Not by 1994. By then the iconography of wife abuse
had become so entrenched in the culture that it no longer horrified
many viewers; by then, the "domestic-abuse cycle" was as familiar as
the perma-press cycle on a washing machine. We understood that
domestic abuse begins with the promise of love. Then it descends into
darkness, into various forms of violation—hurtful words, hurled
objects, smacks, punches, kicks, even rape. Then those three magic
words—I love you—are uttered, and all is well before the violence
commences anew.

Brown followed this script to the letter. She met O. J. Simpson when she was eighteen, fresh out of high school. He was eleven years older, famous, powerful, charismatic. She left junior college to travel with him, forfeiting any plans for a career. The couple, who had two children together, presented as the perfect high-wattage pair. She was his second wife, a trophy with long blond hair, brand-new silicone breasts that he would later brag he "bought" for her, and a tanned, toned body. Unseen to almost all was the marriage's violent tenor. It was later learned that police were repeatedly called to their house. In one of those calls, Brown screamed, "He's going to kill me, he's going to kill me!"

Simpson would eventually be charged with battery, to which he pleaded no contest; he walked away from the charges, paying a small fine, performing community service according to his own schedule, and choosing his own therapist for counseling instead of joining the group sessions required of many defendants.

Eventually, Nicole Brown left. She didn't leave earlier, her sister Denise told the press, because she was afraid. More significantly, she stayed because "she was so in love with him." Even after the couple's 1992 divorce, they tried to make it work. A final attempt at reconciliation collapsed three weeks before her death. She had put her condominium up for rent, reportedly in an attempt to distance herself from her ex-husband even more.

But even women who leave, as Brown did, do not always escape. Some men, like O. J. Simpson, see possession of a wife stretching out beyond the bounds of matrimony, as if a marriage license offers an extended ownership warranty. This Brown knew. Investigators who found the now-famous photographs of her battered body in her safe-deposit box after her murder also found a note that read, "If anything happens to me, you know who did it."

The cycle of abuse has been played out by a multitude of women like Nicole Brown. Many of them also achieved a perverse sort of celebrity after their stories became public. Only six years before Nicole Brown became a household name, the shattered face of Hedda Nussbaum had stared out from the front pages of newspapers and magazines, yet another hideous mask of suffering. Nussbaum was a children's book editor who lived with her common-law husband of twelve years, Joel Steinberg, a corporate lawyer. News reports of the couple's life invariably mentioned that they lived in a brownstone once rented by Mark Twain in the "prettiest part of New York City's Greenwich Village," as if that charming detail might explain why Nussbaum endured the violence.

The story of Nussbaum's private purgatory came to light in 1988 during Steinberg's trial for the beating death of their six-year-old adopted daughter, Lisa. Neighbors had called the police to complain of the screams from the apartment. But no one could persuade Nussbaum to bring charges. When police came to the Steinberg-Nussbaum apartment on November 2, 1987, they encountered a scene of hideous squalor. Lisa was comatose as the result of repeated physical abuse and three-year-old Mitchell was tethered to a playpen, filthy, drinking sour milk. Two days later, Lisa died.

Nussbaum, the star witness for the prosecution, was held to be physically and mentally incapacitated on the night of her daughter's murder. Though she lived with Lisa when she was being abused, the fact that she too had been beaten was seen to mitigate her culpability. She was given full immunity in return for her testimony. During the trial, it was revealed that Steinberg had kicked his common-law wife, strangled her, beaten her, urinated on her, hung her in handcuffs from a chinning bar, lacerated a tear duct by poking his finger in the corner of her eye, broken her nose several times, and pulled out clumps of hair. He'd also taken the blowtorch the couple used for free-basing cocaine and scorched her with it. Steinberg was sentenced to twenty-five years in jail. Nussbaum received a year's sentence at a psychiatric center, after which she worked a series of menial jobs, sold Avon cosmetics, and worked for a law firm.

The understanding that marital abuse could render women incapable of reasoned behavior had been established long before Nussbaum took the witness stand. A decade earlier, Francine Hughes had been immortalized by the book and later the movie *The Burning Bed*. Hughes incinerated her abusive ex-husband, Mickey Hughes, in 1977 after dousing the bed he was sleeping in with gasoline and igniting it with a match. She had been divorced from the man for six years, but he refused to leave the marital home and continued to demand what he claimed were his "conjugal rights." She called police, but they refused to become involved. So she took matters into her own hands. At trial, she was acquitted on the grounds of temporary insanity. In the process, she was elevated to a heroine in the ongoing struggle for women's rights.

The Abused Wife Hall of Fame was a late-twentieth-century development, the result of the spotlight put on marital violence in the 1960s and '70s. Before then, battered wives were not a matter of public concern. This is not to say that women considered marital violence acceptable. In the early nineteenth century, the Women's Moral Reform Society rallied against alcohol as the primary cause of spousal battery, rape, and the use of prostitutes. Still, laws in most Western countries included allowances for a husband to "discipline" his wife, and judges often looked the other way when a husband beat or even killed his wife for being unfaithful.

When references to wife battery did occur in popular culture, they were often intended as a source of amusement. In the 1950s, Jackie Gleason drew laughs with his boorish "To the moon, Alice, to the moon" threats to his sharp-tongued television wife on *The Honeymooners*. Even the beloved domestic comedy *I Love Lucy* treated marital violence as a joke. In one episode, a group of women gathered in Lucy's living room for a meeting of the "Wednesday Afternoon Fine Arts League" end up gossiping about a "knock-down, drag-out" fight between a couple they all know. As her friend Ethel tries to bring the meeting to order, Lucy pipes up, asking, "Is it true Bill gave Dorothy a black eye?" The question is greeted with the swell of the laugh track.

During the 1960s, the first women came forth on television talk shows to discuss being beaten by their husbands. When they did, their identities were hidden behind disguises and aliases. Remaining faceless was necessary to prevent reprisals from their husbands. But the desire for anonymity also reflected a social stigma, the perception that a wife who was beaten, or "disciplined," had not been a good wife and therefore had justifiably provoked her husband.

The abused wife was embraced by the women's movement as a hidden victim requiring social support. She also served as a convenient symbol of women's subordinate, compromised role within the political battlefield of marriage. In the absence of more positive wife models in the wife gap, the abused wife became the most identifiable wife, one who would influence the perception of wives, even though, as far as we know, most are not abused.

Throughout the 1970s and '80s, battered wives emerged from the shadows into the klieg lights. A torrent of statistics confirmed that the home was a dangerous front line for women, and that becoming a wife put a woman's life at risk. The first epidemiological study of domestic violence in 1976 by the sociologists Murray Straus, Richard Gelles, and Susan Steinmetz reported that physical assault occurred in 28 percent of American homes. Before long, domestic abuse was commonly denounced as an "epidemic." Battery was said to be the leading cause of injury to American women, and one in three women who enters an emergency room has been abused. Additionally, it was reported that almost one-quarter of pregnant women seeking prenatal care have experienced domestic violence of some sort.

The Burning Bed, Faith McNulty's 1981 book chronicling Francine Hughes's case, quoted Dr. Alan Willoughby, a clinical psychologist, saying that extreme, abusive relationships such as the Hugheses' were common. "There are countless Mickeys and countless Francines," he said. "We must stop reacting to these cases as isolated and aberrant, but see them as a broad stream in our culture...."

Statistics served up the frequency of abuse in a numerical tidal wave. One study had a woman beaten every eighteen minutes in the United States, another had it at every twelve seconds. One much-quoted study reported that about one in four women will be attacked by her partner at some point in her life. The National Coalition Against Domestic Violence in the U.S. pegged the incidence of assault higher: it asserted that at least one incident of abuse will occur in two-thirds of all marriages. Another study estimated that one in three women would experience a severe or life-threatening act of violence by an intimate during her adult life. In *Rape in Marriage,* Diana Russell wrote that one in seven women is raped by her husband, and that "marital" rape is the most common form of rape.

Feminist activists militated for a change in the laws that gave husbands the right to physical governance of their wives. One of the first targets was the "marital rape exemption," a legal clause upheld in many countries that protected a man from prosecution for raping his wife. It wasn't the first time this legal precept had come under scrutiny. The need to remove the constraints of a husband's "conjugal rights" over his wife, in fact, had been the focus of the first organized women's rights movement meeting in 1848 at Seneca Falls, New York.

But more than one hundred years went by before action was taken. One case, the 1978 court action *Rideout vs. Rideout,* in the United States, was seen as pivotal in thrusting public attention on the issue. In that litigation, a supermarket checkout clerk, Greta Rideout, accused her husband, John, under a recently passed Oregon reform law, of raping her. It was the first time a man was charged with raping a wife who was living with him. John Rideout was acquitted, but the ensuing torrent of protest led to change. In 1982, a precedent was set in Canada when Ronald Kay Wood was convicted of raping his wife. In 1983, rape laws were broadened to sexual assault laws, and for the first time it became a criminal offense for a man to rape his wife, though the spousal rape exemption was not removed from the Canadian Criminal Code until 1995.

Immunity from marital-rape prosecution for British and Welsh husbands was removed in 1991, a measure that was greeted with outrage in some quarters. The British magazine *The Spectator* criticized the House of Lords, which passed the legislation, for bowing to "feminist orthodoxy."

Even so, spousal or marital rape continues to have a separate classification in many jurisdictions. The term itself is rife with the double standard that still governs the perception of violence in a marriage: *marital* is a modifier that makes that violation appear sanctioned, thus less injurious. The term *domestic abuse* is similarly insidious. Calling such brutality *domestic* places it firmly behind a metaphorical white picket fence. *Domestic* summons up images of a feral animal that has been tamed. By definition, domestic matters refer to the sanctuary of the home, a refuge that is private.

And despite many public service announcements, domestic abuse is seen to be a private matter; indeed, this perception is so entrenched that a soldier in the U.S. military can have a record of marital violence but still receive a "good conduct" commendation, a fact that came to light after four wives were murdered by their husbands at the Fort Bragg, North Carolina, military base in the summer of 2002.

The separate sphere accorded domesticity made law enforcement loath to become involved in battles between husbands and wives, even as laws changed. Again, it took an extreme, horrible incident to shift this sensibility. That was the case of Tracey Thurman, who would become yet another exalted member of the abused-wife pantheon. Thurman, the twenty-four-year-old mother of a three-year-old boy, successfully sued the city of Torrington, Connecticut, and its police department in 1985 for failing to adequately protect her from a violent attack by her estranged husband that left her partially paralyzed. Her lawsuit charged that between 1982 and 1983, Charles Thurman, or Buck, as he was more commonly known, repeatedly threatened her life and the life of their young son. When she called the police, she stated, they often ignored her complaints. When they did respond, they were of little or no help. Buck Thurman was arrested twice; the first time he was not prosecuted; the second time he received a suspended sentence and was issued a restraining order to stay away from his estranged wife.

On the day of the final attack, Buck Thurman arrived at the house where she was staying. Tracey Thurman called the police. One officer arrived, but while he was still in his car across the street, Buck Thurman dragged Tracey by her hair into the backyard and stabbed her thirteen times. At trial, the officer who had taken a bloody knife from Buck Thurman said he hadn't seen a body, even though he had heard a scream. He surmised that "for all he knew, the man might have stabbed a dog or a chicken."

Later, while the officer stood by, Buck Thurman, wearing heavy work boots, stomped on Tracey's head until her neck was broken, her spinal cord damaged, and her body numb. The police finally radioed for an ambulance and backup car, but even then they did not take Buck Thurman into custody. Five officers who arrived on the scene concentrated on getting Tracey Thurman into the ambulance. Finally, when

Thurman began climbing into the ambulance to attack her again, they wrestled him to the ground.

The case represented a significant precedent: it was the first time a U.S. federal judge permitted a wife to sue on grounds that she was afforded less police protection against her husband than she would have been if a stranger had threatened her. As such, it was a watershed moment: a state recognized that a wife was legally autonomous from her husband. The ruling resulted in Connecticut legislation called the Thurman Law, which requires police to respond to domestic violence as they would to any other crime. The legacy of the case continued into 1996, when the state legislature passed a law creating permanent restraining orders. The $2.3 million settlement received by Tracey Thurman compelled the insurance industry to press municipalities to provide training for police on domestic violence or risk losing their coverage.

An abused-wife infrastructure was created, comprising crisis centers, shelters, support groups, advocacy agencies, and government-funded programs. A burgeoning field of academic scholarship was devoted to study abused women. An entire month—October—was turned over to Domestic Violence Awareness. In 1998, Hedda Nussbaum joined this network when she appeared on the speakers' circuit, charging upward of $3,500 an hour to address college audiences on the subject of "relationship violence." In early 2003, Nussbaum began shopping around a book proposal based on her abused-wife status. Diana, the Princess of Wales, became an avid supporter of abused women's shelters and causes. She herself viewed her situation as that of an abused woman. "I have been battered, bruised and abused mentally by the system for 15 years … ," she wrote in a letter to her butler, Paul Burrell, published in his 2003 book, *A Royal Duty.*

The abused-wife infrastructure was built on the belief that if women could only leave their abusers—in other words, cease being wives—the problem would be solved. But the connective tissue that linked husbands and wives in abusive relationships proved far more difficult to sever. Despite the reflex to assume that all women in violent marriages were subjected to the same script, there is no typical abused wife. The community of battered women spans class, race, and geography. (Statistics show that abuse is far more prevalent in lower socioeconomic levels, but those are the cases we see. Studies also show that people in higher income brackets don't report as readily or have the resources to deal with it.) And, not surprisingly, the strategies and reactions of women who are abused vary significantly. A few initiate the violence, some participate in it, others do not.

Women who stay in abusive relationships do so for a variety of reasons, not simply because they are so victimized that they can't leave. The entrenched abused-wife script, however, did not see these women as in any way autonomous. It did not accept that for some women a potentially violent relationship may feel better than a life alone. Or that women who stay in abusive relationships value connection more than safety. Or that even in the face of physical pain and mental anguish, a woman might choose to be in a relationship that she cares about deeply, one that provides her with a sense of who she is in terms of family and community, and in which she is raising her children.

There is also the fact that some women recognize that leaving might be a more perilous choice. Like Nicole Brown, who called 911 but didn't want to prosecute, many abused women don't want their husbands arrested or put away, a fact that has resulted in police officers' being trained in victimless prosecution, or laying charges without the victim's consent.

Introducing the notion that women are in any way responsible for being beaten or mistreated might appear only to add to their violation, but to cast someone as victim doesn't always serve her best interests. Presenting her in the black-and-white terms of victim adheres to the text that portrays the wife as passive and subservient. It suggests that wives, and by extension women, do not possess independent agency—that they don't have tempers, don't initiate household fights, don't behave in a controlling manner, and aren't capable of harm. This view is reflected in the comment of a trial judge in the Francine Hughes case who said, "What kind of woman would burn up her husband?" (Later, he had to disqualify himself from presiding over the case.)

There is no question that men are bigger, stronger, and more prone to quick violence than women. And certainly a man can more readily physically hurt a woman than a woman can hurt a man. But, as the writer Patricia Pearson points out in her fascinating 1997 book *When She Was Bad: How and Why Women Get Away with Murder,* "girls and women were contributing their share to the cycle of rage, injury and pain," even though violence is universally considered to be "the province of the male." The truth is that not all women cower in fear in the face of domestic abuse. We too can become furious. We too can get drunk or high or fed up and lash out.

Unease with the idea that wives can occasionally be complicit in violence led to the suppression of discussion and data that back up the fact that women can play an active role in marital violence. Some studies dating from the early 1970s, for instance, suggest that women are as likely to initiate the violence and even to assault men. Often, though, these reports are not released, such as one from the Kentucky Commission on Violence Against Women in 1978 that found 38 percent of assaults were perpetrated by women. Another study by Carleton University in Ottawa, funded by the Canadian government, released only those findings that related to victimized women, not those that referred to men who were subject to violence by their spouses.

The subtraction of wives' wills from the cycle of domestic abuse is an unspoken truth, similar to the silence surrounding domestic violence decades earlier. But suggesting otherwise is fraught with potential problems. For one, it runs contrary to feminist doctrine, which sees wife assault as fitting neatly into patriarchal patterns of male oppression. There is also the concern that blaming women in any way may undermine the funding to or support for necessary services being offered to women.

As a result, it has become easier to present women who lash back severely against their abusers not as acting out of a reasonable self-defense but as passive creatures who have fallen into a robotic state in which they are unaccountable, like Hedda Nussbaum. It's the same sensibility that minimizes the influence of women who bully their husbands by referring to them as *nags,* which suggests irritating, trivial, and ineffectual, rather than *controlling,* the term used to describe men, which connotes an exercise of power.

When Francine Hughes was acquitted on the grounds of temporary insanity, the sentence disappointed many of her supporters who had hoped the jury would return an unequivocal not-guilty verdict, one that said that after having endured fourteen years of abusive beatings, she, on the night she bid her husband his fiery farewell, was perhaps experiencing the sanest moment of her unhappy life. After all, Hughes recognized she had committed a crime; once she'd lit the match, she drove to the police station and turned herself in.

A few years after Hughes's sentencing, "battered-woman syndrome" replaced temporary insanity as a defense for women accused of murdering abusive partners. Until then, a history of abuse was introduced in the courts to reduce a woman's sentence, not to mitigate it. The battered-woman syndrome furthered the view that women become so degraded and demoralized as the victims of unpredictable violence that they sink into a state of psychological paralysis, a sort of fugue state under which they are not legally accountable for their behavior.

The term *battered-woman syndrome* was coined by the Denver clinical psychologist Lenore E. Walker. Walker makes the relationship between marriage and battery explicit in her influential 1977 book, *The Battered Woman,* a study based on 120 women who had endured vicious relationships. "The marriage license in our society also seems to serve as a license to violence," Walker writes. She claims that as many as 50 percent of wives are battered. She presents abuse as a three-phase pattern: the tension-building phase; the explosion or acute-battering-incident phase; and the calm, loving-respite phase. Walker, who uses the term *wife* interchangeably with *woman,* expands the definition of battered women to include not only physical abuse but also verbal and psychological abuse, which blur the lines of what is and what isn't abusive behavior. By Walker's definition, a battered woman is "repeatedly subjected to any forceful physical or psychological behavior by a man in order to coerce her to do something he wants her to do without any concern for her rights." As she presents it, sex and battery are part of the same continuum: "Actually, (in the batterer's mind) the beginning of a man's 'right' to hurt a woman starts with his right to make love to her."

Walker asserts that women who are abused are programmed into a state of "learned helplessness," a phrase she lifted from the research of Dr. Martin Seligman, a University of Pennsylvania psychologist, who had given random electronic shocks to dogs confined in locked pens. Seligman discovered that in time the dogs stopped trying to escape and instead adopted strategies to make life less intolerable. Even when cage doors were left open, they did not attempt to flee. They had to be dragged to the open door before they finally escaped. The modern wife would be compared to these dogs.

In 1982, Walker testified in the first U.S. federal court trial in which the battered-spouse defense was used. The case arose in San Diego County, where Mary Louise Player, then thirty, was charged with fatally shooting her thirty-four-year-old Marine Corps sergeant husband, Joseph, following what both prosecution and defense acknowledged were eight years of beatings and sexual abuse. To counter the prosecution's claim that Player could have escaped from the house with her four children on the night of the fatal shooting, Walker testified that Player was convinced that her escape would have been short-lived. Player believed her husband would track her down and kill her and her young children. The defense was only partially successful. While the prosecution had sought a first-degree-murder verdict, Player was found guilty of the lesser charge of second-degree murder. Player was paroled from federal prison in December 1983 after serving only ten months of her three-year sentence.

Walker became an influential force in the domestic-abuse infrastructure, furthering the view that battered women are not accountable for their actions. Battered women had fresh vogue, which meant Walker was able to charge as much as $3,000 a day for her services. Courts did not always buy her argument. In 1990, for example, she testified for Peggy Sue Saiz, a woman who killed her husband in his sleep. The day before the murder, Saiz practiced target shooting; the day after, she had gone dancing. Jurors rejected her story and convicted her of first-degree murder. Walker also took the stand at the 1990 trial of the Menendez brothers, who killed their parents; their defense was that their parents' controlling, abusive ways had stripped them of their identities. Most shockingly, Walker was enlisted as an expert witness by O. J. Simpson's lawyers at his criminal trial, a move that amounted to the defense stealing a weapon from the prosecution's hands. Walker said at the time she would have appeared for the prosecution had they asked her. In the end, her testimony was not required.

Walker's psychological lingo sounded credible on the witness stand; it played to the notion of women as passive recipients of abusive male behaviour. Battered-woman syndrome also answered the standard prosecutor question of why women didn't leave a relationship when they or their children were threatened, and also justified murders that could not be justified as self-defense, such as those involving no threats or beatings at the precise moment of the crime or in which the spouse was asleep. What it didn't explain, however, was that if a woman had fallen into a state of "learned helplessness," like a shocked dog, how did she summon the aggression necessary to kill?

The battered-woman-syndrome defense was enshrined by a Supreme Court of Canada ruling in May 1990 involving the case of Angelique Lavallee, a Winnipeg woman who killed her common-law partner after four years of abuse. Lavallee pleaded not guilty; her lawyer argued that Lavallee suffered from the syndrome and had killed her partner in self-defense, even though she shot her abuser in the back of the head as he left the room. Lavallee was acquitted.

It is not surprising, then, that the abused-wife defense is frequently invoked when women kill their husbands, even in cases where abuse is difficult to detect. One such case, in which a wife who killed her husband walked free, took place before the Canadian courts in 1996. On December 8, 1995, before daybreak, Lillian Getkate took a rifle and shot two .223-calibre bullets into the neck and left shoulder of her husband, Maury, while he was sleeping in their bed. Both bullets entered and exited his body, killing him immediately. After the shooting, Getkate left the couple's small, white two-story house in Ottawa, taking their two children, a four-year-old boy and a nine-year-old girl. Just before 5 a.m. she called 911. When police arrived, they found the body. Getkate told police that before her husband was killed, she was sleeping with her daughter because the girl had had a nightmare. She said that she heard a person run out her front door after her husband was shot. Investigators found no signs of forced entry or struggle at the home. They also found hidden in the Getkate basement workshop a Ruger Mini-14 .223-calibre rifle. Elsewhere they came upon a pile of unpaid bills and a notepad in Lillian Getkate's writing: "pension: $2,100, back pay: two wks., vacation time: 12 days if Maury dies [and] pension: submit a claim for myself and kids." Two hours later, Lillian Getkate was charged with first-degree murder.

At trial, Lillian Getkate's lawyers used the battered-woman-syndrome defense; they argued that she had killed her emotional and sexual tormentor, a man caught up in weaponry and paramilitary training. Getkate testified that she was a victim of repeated assault by her husband, to whom she had been married eleven years. She said he routinely insulted, shoved, threatened, and grabbed her, dragged her by her hair, and raped her. She told the court that her husband had threatened to kill her. Once, she said, he forced her to have sex in a public parking lot. His words were that "I was his wife. It was my duty," she testified.

On the night of the murder, just before she shot him, they had had sex twice, once with her consent. The second time, she says, she was raped in the living room outside their daughter's bedroom. She said she feared for their children. She also told the court she had no recollection of killing her husband, that she had fallen into a "dissociative" state. When she went upstairs to their bedroom, she found him covered in blood, she said.

Her actions and testimony mystified everyone who knew the couple. Maury, a thirty-seven-year-old industrial psychologist, appeared to be a devoted family man. No one could recall his ever losing his temper. Lillian, who was thirty-five when she killed her husband, was a foot shorter and eighty pounds lighter. She was a Brownie leader and regular churchgoer.

Maury Getkate had an interest in martial arts that was depicted as sinister at trial. He taught his future wife to handle and shoot guns. In court, two diametrically opposed portraits of the couple's marriage emerged. Her defense argued that he hid his abusive tendencies. The Crown said she had fantasies of killing him and resented his devotion to his work. The jury also heard of the Getkates' financial woes. On the night of the murder, the Crown argued that Lillian Getkate became angry after he insulted her sexual performance.

The jury found her not guilty of second-degree murder but guilty of manslaughter. In other words, it didn't believe she had acted in self-defense. Lillian Getkate served eleven days in jail before she was given a conditional sentence to be served in the community. She was free. Her release prompted the Crown prosecutor Julianne Parfett to say that the decision to spare her jail sends a message that women can kill, claim they have been abused, fail to prove it, and remain free.

The battered-woman-syndrome defense is both positive and negative. On one hand, it is employed to defend women who live under heinous abusive circumstances and clearly feel they have no way out. Yet it also cleaves to the definition of wife according to coverture. Women who are beaten by their husbands and respond by lashing back—even by killing them—are perceived to be lacking free will. Bringing in the battered-woman syndrome denies that such behavior is reasonable. Rather, they are seen to be rendered temporarily psychotic.

If the courts have to free a woman who kills in self-defense, at least they don't have to concede that she is a reasonable person who has acted justifiably, as any man might, in order to save her life. On the contrary, thanks to the syndrome Walker mapped out, the court can see her as a special case: a bit unbalanced. Often, these women are presented as not even remembering what they did, like Rita Graveline of Luskville, Quebec, who was acquitted of killing her husband, Michael, in 1999. Specialists brought in at trial claimed that Graveline suffered from "non-insane dissociative automatim," a robotic state triggered by battered-woman syndrome. It was not a defense, it should be noted, often employed by men in similar circumstances.

Women who had acted desperately, courageously, even heroically to save their children were "let off" on the strength of expert testimony suggesting obliquely that they weren't quite right in the head. In 1992, in an article in *The New York Times*, Elizabeth Schneider, a law professor, pointed out that "many battered women lose custody of their children because judges see them as helpless, paralyzed victims who can't manage daily life. And if a woman seems too capable, too much in charge of her life to fit the victim image, she may not be believed."

The notion of the "good wife" features in many discussions of domestic abuse. One study, based on interviews with abusive men and published in 1988, revealed that 78 percent of abusive men justified their conduct in light of their wives' failure to fulfill the obligations of a "good wife." Even Nicole Brown spoke of the "good wife" in a letter that was never used in the trial. "I wanted so to be a good wife," she wrote. "But he never gave me a chance."

In 1989, Sara Thornton became Britain's most famous battered wife after she killed her husband, Malcolm, with a kitchen knife while he lay in a drunken haze. During the trial, her character came under attack, primarily because she didn't conform to good-wife conventions. In addition to accusations that she was promiscuous, it was introduced that she had had three abortions, had attempted suicide, and didn't wear underwear before her marriage. In 1990, she was convicted of murder and sentenced to life. The judge told Thornton that in the face of violence, she could have "walked out or gone upstairs." In 1991, Thornton wrote directly to the registrar of criminal appeals: "I am not mad, I am not bad, I was subjected to intolerable pressure, enhanced by a society that did not want to care. When my husband threatened to kill me, I cracked ... I am a modern woman and I ask for modern justice." She was freed after a retrial in 1996 after serving five and a half years.

The Guardian newspaper referred to Thorton as an "icon for battered women." By that time she was also the subject of a mini-industry. Her correspondence from prison with a journalist was published as *Love on the Wing: Letters of Hope from Prison.* She was the star of a Channel 4 special, *Provocation.* In 1996, the BBC aired a docu-drama entitled *Killing Me Softly.*

It is nothing new, of course, for someone who has killed to become a celebrity. Thornton, on the other hand, was someone the public could readily empathize with: an abused woman first and a killer second. The press was sympathetic; as *The Independent* newspaper said, "to find peace she is beginning to acquire martyr status."

To claim, as the BBC does, that the dramatization of Thornton's story "serves a wide public interest" is either to misrepresent her case or to suggest that such mental abnormalities are a female commonplace. *Killing Me Softly* also failed to note that the ultimate victim in the Thornton case was not Thornton but the alcoholic, sporadically violent, and now-dead Malcolm Thornton.

That husbands might even be justified in abusing—or even murdering—a wife who was not good was evident in the acceptance of the "nagging and shagging" defense used in British courts. In 1991, Singh Bisla strangled his "nagging" wife, Abnash, "to shut her up" after two hours of verbal abuse. Giving him an eighteen-month suspended sentence, the judge said, "You have suffered, through no fault of your own, a terrible existence for a very long time." In 1994, Roy Geech of Manchester was given a two-year suspended sentence after being found guilty of killing his wife of thirty years by stabbing her twenty-three times with a kitchen knife when he apparently discovered she was having an affair. "Your mind was so affected that your responsibility for what you did was very considerably diminished," said Judge Rhys Davies, Q.C. "You have not only been a man of good character but you are also a good man." In 1997, David Hampson got six years for manslaughter after beating his wife to death with a hammer and burying her body in the garden because she was said to have nagged him; his sentence was reduced to four years on appeal. At trial, the court heard that Hampson snapped after twelve years of constant criticism and "torrents of abuse." In the original sentence, Judge Allen said, "I have to bear in mind that society is concerned for human life and such killing cannot be tolerated, even accepting, as I do, that your wife behaved to you in a way which was calculated to impact on your mind." That same year, the High Court of Edinburgh allowed David Swinburne to walk free after stabbing his wife eleven times when she told him she was leaving him for another man.

· · ·

In all the justifications and explanations of domestic abuse, there is a notable void. And that is the failure to answer why it remains such a virulent, entrenched social problem. A 1998 Statistics Canada survey, for example, proclaimed that half of all Canadian women have experienced sexual or physical assault, as defined by the Criminal Code, by the age of sixteen. One rationale for the proliferation of domestic abuse (more positive reports of declining numbers were not played big) is that feminism itself, the movement that brought domestic abuse out of the closet in the 1960s and '70s, has created wives who were no longer willing to be subordinate to their husbands. The psychologist Robert Butterworth of Los Angeles, for one, has suggested that the trigger for much domestic abuse is husbands' anger at women leading independent lives within a marriage. "With the rise of the women's movement, roles changed dramatically," he told *The Guardian* in 2000. "Married men don't 'own' their wives any more. A lot of men would just love to wish away the women's movement but they can't. I think it's fascinating that so many American men today are marrying foreign brides who are much more passive in relationships."

The subjected, controlled wife is the antithesis of what modern women believe they should be. It is unsurprising, then, that many women who are subject to physical and emotional abuse in their marriages are unwilling to identify themselves as such. They don't want the world to know that the person they chose, the person whom they love, has treated them badly. In an interview with *The New York Times,* Denise Brown reflected this denial, refusing to admit that her sister was a battered woman. "I don't want people to think it was like that. I know Nicole. She was a very strong-willed person. If she was beaten up, she wouldn't have stayed with him." That statement presumes that Nicole Brown's only option if beaten was to leave. But beaten women, even strong-willed ones, often choose to stay.

And this is because the legal doctrine that allowed men the right to physical governance of their wives had been replaced in the latter years of the twentieth century with a romantic imperative that reinforced the relationship between passion and ownership. This was evident at the Simpson trial when Denise Brown testified that she had been with her sister and Simpson in a restaurant. Everyone had been drinking. "Suddenly he grabbed Nicole between the legs," she said. "He grabbed her crotch and kept his hand on it. He looked her in the eyes. His eyes were full of rage. And he said: 'Remember, honey, this belongs to me. To ME!'"

He was, of course, wrong. Her crotch did not belong to him. That he would presume it did, however, reflected the fact that possession, a relic of coverture, continues to pulse though the culture. Tellingly, the media covering the Simpson trial often referred to Brown as Simpson's wife, even though they were divorced. She was also frequently referred to as Nicole Brown Simpson, even though her credit cards revealed that she had changed her name back to Nicole Brown. But the notion of wife ownership ran deep. In the 2001 film *In the Bedroom,* a man who brutally murders a man his estranged wife has been involved with explains his actions: "He was doing my wife," he said, as if that fact would justify his violent behavior.

The ready acceptance of this excuse reflects the inextricable bond between passion and violence in mass-market entertainment. We sing along to the Beatles' catchy "Run for Your Life" played on oldies rock stations, in which Paul McCartney sings that he'd rather see his former girlfriend dead than see her with another man. We swoon when Rhett sweeps Scarlett up the grand staircase in Margaret Mitchell's *Gone With the Wind,* even knowing that the scene has been deconstructed as a thinly disguised rape.

Much has been made of that famous scene occurring late one night after the Civil War is over. Rhett Butler staggers home drunk, angry that he hasn't had sex with his wife in ages, seething with jealousy over her love for Ashley Wilkes. When he arrives, he swings Scarlett into his arms and takes her upstairs to the bedroom. In the novel, Scarlett is described as struggling and screaming, "wild with fear." Suddenly, on the landing, she surrenders to "a wild thrill ... arms that were too strong, lips too bruising ... for the first time in her life she had met someone ... who was bullying and breaking her." Cut to the morning after. Rhett is gone, but Scarlett lies in bed beside a rumpled pillow in the golden sunlight, her face flushed with the memory. "He had humbled her, hurt her, used her brutally through a wild mad night and she had gloried in it...."

The woman-wanting-to-be-vanquished scenario is the plot motivator of countless romance novels. He pursues. She resists. He overcomes. His sensuality is dangerous, aggressive, forceful. She is swept away. It is a formula that resonates with women. In the U.S. alone, twenty-five million women read an average of twenty romance novels each a year; 49 percent of all paperbacks sold are romance novels. The romance-novel formula, in fact, mirrors Lenore Walker's three phases of abuse—the tension-building phase; the explosion or acute battering incident; and the calm, loving respite. Substitute sex for battery, and it is the very pattern found in the classic *Gone With the Wind.*

Reading books with beguiling illustrations of Fabio on the cover can be seen as harmless diversion, an escape from the humdrum of the everyday, even from relationships that fall short of the fantasy ideal. Less benign is the fact that the overheated terminology of romance novels is often employed to minimize the gravity of brutal attacks by men on their wives and girlfriends. When a New York City cop dragged his ex-girlfriend out of police headquarters, where she worked, shot her four times, killing her, then killed himself, the *New York Post* headline blared: "Tragedy of a Lovesick Cop." The tragedy was his, the headline implied. He was the one who lost his woman. His crime was not pumping bullets into her body but rather loving too much. Likewise, when an unemployed man, rejected by the girlfriend who supported him, set fire to a crowded social club where she worked, and eighty-seven people died, *New York Newsday* reported: "Love Story Ends in Hate." When the heavyweight champ Mike Tyson beat up his ex-wife Robin Givens just days before he went to prison for raping another woman, reporters wrote zippy leads about "the Tyson-Givens love match." When a man murdered his wife and her boyfriend, *The Winnipeg Free Press* proclaimed, "Love Triangle Ends in Stabbing Death" on its front page. A man kidnaped his estranged wife, raped her, accused her of an imaginary affair, and choked her to death (all in front of the children), and a reporter wrote that he "made love to his wife," then strangled her when "overcome with jealous passion."

The erotic is tethered to a ballet of dominance and submission. The 1986 movie *9½ Weeks* is a classic crowd-pleasing example. That movie documented the short-lived sexual relationship between Elizabeth, a fragile, divorced gallery owner in New York, played by Kim Basinger, and John, a menacing, wealthy man who "sells money," played by Mickey Rourke. Slowly he draws her into high-drama impersonal sexual game-playing that frightens, thrills, and ultimately degrades her. He blindfolds her, eats food off her, threatens to spank her when she looks through his closets. She is presented as falling under his control, stealing a necklace from a store on his instruction. He dresses her in clothing of his choice. In a department store, he takes her to the bed section and commands her to get on a bed in front of a saleswoman. "Spread your legs for Daddy," he instructs. She complies. He sets her up with a female prostitute who taunts her, then turns to him for sex. In the end she finally leaves him, dazed and bewildered.

Such a male dominant–female subservient dynamic exists at the core of modern Western erotica. In his memoir, the comedian Richard Pryor writes of his marriage with the actress Jennifer Lee: "If you hit a woman she'll either run like a banshee in the opposite direction, or she's yours. The sting of violence is like voodoo. A hex. A black spell. You're possessed. Locked in a diabolic dance." Even O. J. Simpson was romanticized as a fictional character in the repeated references that compared him to Othello.

As was the case with Nicole Brown, "love" is the reason women stay in violent relationships even when they have the resources to leave. There is some logic in this, even if it isn't readily apparent. Love, rather than necessity, or even social expectation, has come to be the underlying motivation behind modern marriage, although other factors play as significant a role. The notion of the couple becoming "one," the legal construct of coverture, has been transformed into a romance-novel trope, the "you complete me" nostrum uttered by the Renée Zellweger character in the 1996 movie *Jerry Maguire*. Women didn't have to marry by the 1990s; they wanted to marry because they were in love, which, according to popular-culture renditions, is a feeling independent from behavior. In other words, a woman could be beaten but still assume she was loved.

The "you and me against the world" mentality that fuels romance novels and romantic movies even played a part in the Rideout rape story. Greta Rideout, heralded as a feminist heroine, reconciled with her husband briefly after he was acquitted of raping her. An interviewer who went to the couple's apartment during their reconciliation recounted that a hand-lettered sign on the wall proclaimed "Love can endure all things."

And the transformative power of love meant that people could change. One of the most frequently quoted biblical passages at weddings is an adaptation of I Corinthians 13, which, in a modern translation, states: "There is nothing love cannot face; there is no limit to its faith, its hope, and its endurance." In the words of the 1970 weepy blockbuster *Love Story*, "Love means never having to say you're sorry." Which is why so many women, like Nicole Brown, hold out hope.

Tellingly, interviews with abused wives are often peppered with the language of perfection associated with endless love. In 1995, Dorothy Joudrie, the sixty-year-old estranged wife of Calgary executive Earl Joudrie, was charged with attempted murder after pumping six bullets into her husband. Her lawyer successfully argued at trial that her action had been committed in a robotic trance that had resulted from being routinely abused during the first half of their thirty-seven-year marriage. Even though Earl Joudrie's physical abuse was seen to have ended eighteen years before he was shot, the rationale held up. Dorothy Joudrie spent time in a psychiatric hospital, after which she underwent counseling. In an interview after the trial, Joudrie explained that she regarded her marriage in the unrealistic terms of a fantasy: "I made everything look perfect," Joudrie said. "I would always put on a facade." Such a rationale is predictable from a woman of Dorothy Joudrie's generation who was raised believing the good wife didn't talk back.

What is less understandable is that young women raised in a seemingly more enlightened time, women who are not wives, are enduring abuse from their partners. "Dating abuse" involving teenage girls and their boyfriends emerged in the 1990s as a subcategory of domestic abuse. It even fostered the creation of a new acronym, IPV, which stands for "intimate partner violence." In her much-publicized book,

But I Love Him: Protecting Your Teenage Daughter from Controlling, Abusive Dating Relationships, the psychotherapist Jill Murray claims the majority of abusive relationships begin early, frequently in high school. "Many girls said they were confused about the signs of abuse and at first had considered their husband's or boyfriend's jealousy, possessiveness, control and isolating behavior very flattering," she writes. Murray adds to the grim statistics surrounding violence toward women by men whom they love, claiming that one in three girls is abused by her boyfriend, either physically or emotionally. She also contends that the number of girls who now abuse boys is vastly underreported.

In February 2002, Oprah Winfrey devoted a show to teen dating abuse. The television host claimed that "experts say teenage girls are being hit, shoved, slapped or verbally and emotionally abused in record numbers. Some are forced to have sex." One teenage girl named Christy admitted, "I think my biggest fear would be to lose him. I'd be devastated. The good in my relationship outweighs the bad through it all. Sometimes I'm shocked that I tolerate the things he does and that I let him do and say the things he does to me."

But it isn't only young girls who are accepting the unacceptable. In *Not to People Like Us: Hidden Abuse in Upscale Marriage,* the social worker Susan Weitzman documented what she called "upscale violence," cases of abuse among middle- and upper-class women. These are women who have a way out; they're educated, successful, and live in households where the combined income tops $100,000. "If my practice and research reflect anything, it's that upscale violence is out there in huge numbers," Weitzman says. The reason women stay in what she calls "well-appointed prisons," she concludes, is not that they're immobilized with fear but rather because they "idolize" their husbands and are "impressed with his charisma and socio-economic standing." They excuse their husbands' violence as bad temper. "Even women with Ph.D.s, M.D.s and their own money negate the power of what they can do on their own." Domestic abuse has thus become part of the romantic continuum, the dark side of the fairy tale.

The abused women brought into the spotlight to inform the public of a hidden issue remained there as fodder for dramatic spectacle, feeding into the culture's fascination with the relationship between violence and romance. In the 1950s, audiences didn't see Jackie Gleason belting his television wife. By the 1980s, however, viewing wives being beaten and raped became movie-of-the-week fodder, virtually guaranteed to garner high ratings. The kick-ass breakaway stories of abused wives— from Francine Hughes to the singer Tina Turner—were chronicled by popular books, documentaries, and movies. The violence in these movies was justified as representing the interests of women. Many networks followed the broadcast with phone numbers of social service agencies, hotlines, and counseling groups.

The story of the tumultuous Rideout marriage was dramatized in the 1980 made-for-television movie *Rape and Marriage: The Rideout Case*. In 1984, Farrah Fawcett played Francine Hughes in *The Burning Bed,* which won top ratings for the time period, and also garnered an Emmy nomination. Likewise, *A Cry for Help: The Tracey Thurman Story* drew a crowd when it was first broadcast in 1989, fourth in the Nielsen ratings for the week it played.

"Women in jeopardy" became a hot publishing genre, a reflection of the success of *I, Tina,* Tina Turner's memoir of her abusive relationship with her musician husband, Ike, later made into the popular 1993 movie *What's Love Got to Do With It.* "It's what's selling in Hollywood now," said Steve Delsohn, a book agent who headed the West Coast office of a New York–based literary group. "I must have gotten ten phone calls from agents looking for books about 'women in jeopardy,' which is the new buzz phrase. The whole trend is kind of grotesque."

Taking on the role of an abused wife with the moxie to leave became a rite of dramatic passage for a young actress, a surefire way to increase her credibility and her odds of winning an Emmy or Oscar. When Fawcett took on the role of Francine Hughes to shed her jiggly poster-girl image, the media gushed about how brave she was. Her hair was stringy, she wore baggy cotton dresses, and her makeup-free face was often bruised.

In 1987, Whoopi Goldberg received an Academy Award nomination for her portrayal of an abused wife in *The Color Purple.* Julia Roberts followed her breakout role as a hooker turned Cinderella in *Pretty Woman* with that of a Cinderella turned victim in the 1991 film *Sleeping with the Enemy.* She plays Laura Burney, a beautiful young wife in a marriage that looks from the outside to be idyllic. Her husband is a handsome, successful investment counselor; they live in a stunning glass-paneled house on Cape Cod; he calls her "princess." Behind the perfect facade lies the nightmare. This prince is endlessly controlling, berating her over the fact that the bathroom towels are not lined up properly; he tells her which dress to wear; he beats and bruises her in irrational jealous rages. To escape, Roberts's character fakes her death, moves to middle America, and starts a new life that includes a relationship with a sensitive drama teacher. Her husband tracks her down and threatens her. She ends up killing him in self-defense. The last shot of the film is the lingering image of her wedding band lying on the floor next to her husband's body. She is free at last.

On the heels of her phenomenal success in the light romantic comedy *The Wedding Planner* in 2001, Jennifer Lopez played an abused wife in the 2002 theatrical release *Enough,* another fairy-tale-turned-horror-story. In this version, a struggling waitress is swept off her feet by a rich, charming man and ends up physically and emotionally abused. When her attempts to escape with her young daughter are foiled, she sees no alternative but to train like a commando and kill him.

The iconography of domestic abuse had its photographer laureate in Donna Ferrato, who came to the subject while documenting a seemingly happy, sexually adventurous American couple for Japanese *Playboy* in 1981. One night, Ferrato, who was living with the couple during an assignment that took them to New York sex club Plato's Retreat, was awakened by noise. She grabbed her Leica and ran down the hall to find the couple arguing violently in the bathroom. She watched the husband strike the wife, oblivious to her presence. Ferrato crouched, snapped a few photographs, and then tried unsuccessfully to stop the blows. A year after the beating, Ferrato used the pictures to persuade the wife to carry through with her divorce. *Playboy* refused to publish the images, as did every other magazine Ferrato approached. This was, after all, 1981. The photographs were raw, neither reader- nor advertiser-friendly. Ferrato would go on to become a determined witness to marital violence, riding in police cars, visiting hospital emergency rooms, and living in women's shelters and prisons. She published two books, *In the Name of Love* and *Living with the Enemy*. She began winning awards, including one for her work in the 1993 Academy Award–winning documentary *Defending Our Lives*.

The deluge of battered-women imagery resulted in a battering ennui by the end of the decade. In 1989, the actress and filmmaker Lee Grant narrated and directed the documentary *Battered* for HBO. But she admits that when the idea was brought to her, "it had been worn, and shopworn, and done."

"I had seen some pretty good documentaries on the subject," she said. "I resisted. Then I saw two pieces. One was on the bride burners in India, women who were killed because their families didn't come up with their dowries. And the other was on the murders for honor in Brazil, where men shot their wives if dinner wasn't on the table, or if the wives enrolled in a course. When they were asked in court why they did it, they said, 'My honor was offended.'" Their self-righteousness appalled her. She changed her mind.

In 1977, the Canadian filmmaker Gail Singer directed *Loved, Honoured and Bruised,* the story of Jeannie Fox, a mother of five who was married for sixteen years and abused for fourteen. Eventually Fox gathered the courage to leave her home, a farm in rural Manitoba, with her children and seek refuge in a hostel for battered women in Winnipeg. After it was aired, Singer told me, she was shocked by the number of women she knew who approached her to tell her that it resonated with them, that they were in similar marriages.

Some twenty years later, the National Film Board of Canada, a government-funded agency, approached Singer to direct another film on violence against women. She was reluctant at first. She thought it had all been said. When she told people about her new project, they tended to roll their eyes in a been-there, done-that gesture. Recognizing the fatigue that had come to surround the subject, she gave the 1997 release *You Can't Beat a Woman* the wry subtitle "Another Film About Violence Against Women."

By the 1990s, the public no longer flinched at the sight of the abused wife. She had become a noble commodity, able to sell magazines, win awards, further careers, and even promote products such as tobacco. *People* magazine ran the cover story "Battered Beauties," featuring the flawless faces of well-known glamorous women who said they had been abused by their boyfriends or husbands. The list was long: Robin Givens and Mike Tyson, Madonna and Sean Penn, Stephanie Seymour and Axl Rose, Pamela Anderson Lee and Tommy Lee, Carrie Otis and Mickey Rourke.

In 1999, Philip Morris Company used one of Donna Ferrato's photographs as part of its national campaign against domestic violence. The cause was shrewdly selected, given the company's need to burnish its image at a time when its principal product, tobacco, was being excoriated as a social evil. It spent $2 million on domestic-violence programs nationally, a small fraction of the $60 million it spent on charity in 1999. That same year, it spent $108 million on advertising to tell the public about it, an expenditure that allowed the company to circumvent rules that prohibit cigarette companies from advertising.

The female faces in the Philip Morris campaign were not broken, crushed, or bruised like Nicole Brown's or Hedda Nussbaum's. They had been sanitized for commercial purposes. One print ad presented a young, beautiful doe-eyed Hispanic woman, her eyes gleaming, her face flawless. A television commercial showed another attractive woman, pregnant in the first scenes, then playing with a small child. In a voiceover she talks about her husband's violence during her pregnancy and how she had to find refuge in a shelter. The final scene shows the woman and child on a pristine beach; the Philip Morris name is flashed, along with a description of the company's generous support for programs against domestic violence.

In the ultimate capitalization on bridal lust, bride imagery was integrated into the iconography of wife abuse. So powerful was the lure of the fairy-tale bride, apparently, that she proved useful in directing public attention to the potential horrors that could befall a wife. But there existed another link between the bride and abused wife: both are depicted in mass media as existing in a fugue state. An ad for Help USA, a public service agency for abused women, that ran in women's magazines in 2001 featured a photograph of a bride in an elaborate veil, facing the altar. The copy reads: "I, Maria, promise to love and obey, to not talk back, to hide all of my bruises, and to live on the street once I fear for my life." It goes on: "Nobody plans to be a victim of domestic violence. Fortunately there's HELP USA."

In June 2002, the Mexican-born actress Salma Hayek donned a wedding gown to attend a protest march in Washington, D.C., that called on Congress to increase funds for domestic-violence prevention in the Latino community. She was inspired, she told the press, by the 1999 fatal shooting of the bride Gladys Ricart by her jealous ex-boyfriend in Ridgefield, N.J., as well as by the wedding dress worn by the former abuse victim Josie Ashton on her two-month walk from New York to Miami in the fall of 2001. Also present at the Washington protest were staff members of *Marie Claire* magazine, eerily attired in white bridal dresses donated by the bridal emporium Kleinfeld's as part of the cover story for the publication's October 2002 issue. In her speech at the Capitol, Hayek referred to "tradition," that mythical construct linked to the "perfect" fairy-tale wedding. "Sadly, domestic abuse has become almost a tradition in certain sectors of the Latino community," the actress said.

Sadly, the Latino community is not the only place the abused wife is viewed as a "tradition." The fact that husbands no longer have the right to physical or sexual possession of their wives under law, and increasing public sensitivity to domestic violence, should have heralded a new development in wifely self-possession, a new chapter in definition of the meaning of the word *wife*. But that hasn't happened. Rather than being eradicated, domestic violence has become entrenched in the cultural fabric.

The wife is no longer portrayed as a victim of the legal system but rather a hostage of love. So intense is this love that she's willing to put up with abuse to the point where she's rendered robotic, incapable of reasoned action. The abused wife has become the flip side of the bridal dream—not the fairy tale but the nightmare.

In the trial following her murder, Nicole Brown was presented as being as much a victim of love as of murder at the hands of the man who, eleven years after their fateful wedding day, was convicted of killing her in a civil suit. Such a portrayal of the wife as victim not only affects the perception of wives and women. It also paves the way for another new tradition in the depiction of wife—that of the heroic, avenging wife who acts as a social vigilante, righting centuries of repression and wrong. And her depiction, too, would have far-ranging social consequence.

Chapter 6

Hear Us Roar:
The Real First Wives' Club

With the abused wife firmly entrenched as a familiar icon, her battered form an indictment of the violent subtext seen to underlie modern marriage, wives who screw their husbands over but good have emerged as female role models. It is the perfect redemptive one-two punch: wife as victim, victim as victor. The most famous avenging wives, it must be noted, were not physically battered by their husbands. More grievously, more painfully, they were betrayed by that mythical promise of forever love that serves as the precarious foundation for modern marriage.

The jilted wife, particularly one replaced by a younger, beautiful woman, has become the ready object of sympathy, no questions asked. A "you go, girl" mentality reigns. For a glimpse into the mindset, we need only look to the phenomenal success of *The First Wives' Club*, by the late Olivia Goldsmith, published in 1992. The forty-two-year-old writer was seeking her own personal payback when she decided to write the fictional fantasy. She believed that she had received a raw deal when the assets were divided in her own divorce. Writing well, or well enough to appeal to the mass market, would be her revenge.

As a former marketing consultant, she knew women, married or not, would lap up her tale of three middle-aged ex-wives meting out clever, nonviolent vengeance on their rich, powerful, conniving husbands. The role of wife might be ambiguous, but the fury of the wronged ex-wife is readily understood. Feminism may have divided women along ideological grounds, but the wrath of the spurned wife is a unifying rallying point.

Goldsmith's inspiration for the book was a much-discussed 1989 cover story in *Fortune* titled "The CEO's Second Wife." The wife was presented as a commodity that could be rendered "new and improved," like laundry detergent. The article focused on the second, younger, more beautiful replacement wives of rich, powerful men whose first wives no longer met their needs. The trophy wife was regarded as one of the more visible symbols of the greed decade—a glossy, shiny testament to her husband's success and vitality. Although these women were usually accomplished—how else was she going to land her man?—the term became synonymous with *bimbo* because she was also a walking testament to her husband's virility.

According to *Fortune,* the trophy wife is not expected to have children—although she'll often have to cope with resentful children from the first marriage. Her tasks include adding new friends, new clothes, a new home, and new interior decoration to her husband's world. She will introduce modern fashion and art to his life and host exotic parties—she will know how to spend serious money on their fabulous life together. She will fuss about his health and get him on a fitness regimen. She understands her husband's business, probably because she did plenty of homework before she picked her target. Because trophy wives are usually successful career women themselves, they offer a contrast to their husbands' first wives, who spent years bringing up families and making sacrifices for their husbands' businesses. The first wife didn't have time to work out or to become a high flyer—she was too busy dutifully looking after children and home.

Goldsmith wanted to tell the story of the first wives these men left behind, women who helped them climb the ladder, only to be tossed down to the lowest rung. So she did, in an Upper East Side morality play disguised as a frothy frolic. One wife, Annie, suffers the indignity of being dumped by her husband, Aaron, for her sex therapist. A second, Brenda, is swindled out of her alimony by greedy, unscrupulous

Morty, a discount electronics magnate. "I want to see Morty broke, dead broke," she claims. "That would be the one thing in this life he couldn't bear." The third ex-wife, Elise, has quietly suffered for years at the hands of an adulterous ne'er-do-well and has retreated into alcoholic stupefaction. When a fourth friend commits suicide after learning of her husband's infidelity, the three decide to take action. They form a club, complete with cute satin warm-up jackets, to exact their revenge. And to tack an upbeat, socially relevant ending on it, they use their financial gains to open a women's crisis center for all the other beleaguered wives out there.

And they were out there, as a publicity stunt for the book made clear. Poseidon Press, a division of Simon & Schuster, advertised a "First Wives' Contest" on the book's jacket, offering prizes to the women who best described "just what a cad your ex-husband is." First prize was a $1,500 gift certificate at Cartier, the second a beauty makeover, and the third a black silk jacket sporting the First Wives' Club logo—a trophy crossed out with a big X.

Few of the hundred or so contestants were able to confine themselves to the thousand-word limit. Diane Kelson of Mounds View, Minnesota, carped, "For my nineteenth birthday, he gave me steak knives. For my twenty-first birthday, he went out and bought me the Sunday paper." Another woman pleaded that she deserved a bauble from Cartier because her former husband took back her wedding ring and gave the diamond to his second wife.

Though the contest was launched in a spirit of fun, both Goldsmith and her publisher were taken aback by the grimness of many entries. One woman who wrote from jail in Wisconsin began her letter saying that she found more enjoyment in her fourteen-month prison sentence than in her eighteen-year marriage. She claimed she had been trying to hire a private investigator to document her former husband's harassment but instead was tricked into hiring an undercover cop who believed she was looking for a hitman. Another woman claimed she was held captive at gunpoint for eighteen hours by her psychotic ex-husband and was hiding under a new name. The judges decided to take her out of the running because they felt, in her case, winning might prove fatal.

In the end, the panel of female judges, including the author, decided to base awards on "literary merit" rather than sheer horror. The first prize went to a woman in Colorado whose husband dumped her for his secretary while their son was being treated for cancer. Second prize went to a woman who had been married a year and was pregnant with her first child when her husband moved his girlfriend into their house and charged her rent, claiming she was a Bible instructor. "Almost all the women wished that their husbands were dead," Goldsmith claimed. She placed the blame on "our era's infatuation with divorce and social acceptance of 'wife shucking.'" "In the old days," she said in an interview, "men might have played around and had mistresses on the side. They didn't abandon their wives and children. They weren't allowed to. Society would not have accepted it." But those were the days before the wife had been untethered from her traditional moorings, when her emotional well-being was not a factor in the marital equation.

The term *wife shucking* summons the image of the old shell of the first wife cavalierly tossed, the young, glistening flesh of the second lovingly harvested. And it goes to the heart of the discarded wife's fury.

Decades earlier, the legal system took sides in marital dismantling, apportioning blame and moral censure when one party—usually the wife, though not always—appeared to be wronged. That changed with the implementation of no-fault divorce laws during the 1970s and '80s, much lobbied for by feminists because they permitted women to more easily get out of dangerous marriages. No longer were courts sympathetic when considering threats to marital union from without. No longer did they pass moral judgment when couples divorced. Under no-fault divorce, either spouse was able to dissolve the marriage contract and obtain a divorce by alleging that the marriage was irretrievably broken. Marital misconduct became a nonissue. The upshot was that the wronged party was left simmering, without any catharsis or social sympathy, unless he or she sought it personally.

The revenge fantasy assumed a husband's betrayal would completely unhinge a woman. In *She-Devil,* a 1989 movie based on the satirical Fay Weldon novel, for instance, a fat, middle-class housewife played by Roseanne Barr is transformed into a monster when her husband leaves her for a rich and beautiful romance novelist. In crazed response, she systematically sets about ruining everything dear to him. Female audiences also cheered as Bernadine, the heroine of Terry McMillan's 1992 best-selling novel, *Waiting to Exhale,* later a popular movie, takes her husband's possessions and sets them ablaze after he leaves her for a younger woman. They applauded her feistiness as she declares, "I tap danced for a man for eleven years. I'm not about to go out and get me a new owner."

Fictional and real wives blurred together in the revenge continuum. In 1993, Lady Sarah Graham-Moon briefly became the most popular woman in Britain when she lost her temper after discovering her husband was having an affair. She poured white paint over his BMW, cut four inches from the left arms of his Savile Row suits, and then anonymously distributed bottles of his best claret to neighbors. Lady Graham-Moon's actions were feted on television and in newspaper columns. Few bothered to question her gruesome need for such melodramatic vengeance. By her own admission, she and her husband had lived separate existences under the same roof, and she had no further use for him in bed. When he started having an affair with a woman in their village, he was the first to tell her. Granted, he hadn't asked for permission in advance, but that seemed to be the extent of his offense. Later, Lady Graham-Moon even confessed that she was having an affair with a married man, laying herself open to a white-paint attack outside her own front door.

Such details were technicalities in Britain, a country with a longstanding empathy for the wronged wife. Perhaps that was some kind of cosmic payback for Henry VIII, who treated his six wives, none of whom was able to strike back, with varying degrees of hatred. He beheaded Anne Boleyn and Catherine Howard. He divorced Catherine of Aragon and Anne of Cleves. Jane Seymour died shortly after giving birth to the male heir he so desperately wanted. Katherine Parr, the clever, religiously radical bluestocking, survived as his widow, which made her the dubious winner in terms of escaping mistreatment.

In the early nineteenth century, British women formed a petition against King George IV in support of his estranged wife, Caroline of Brunswick, when he attempted to put her on trial for adultery. The couple's 1795 arranged marriage had been doomed from the outset. The future monarch was then Prince of Wales, married to another woman, with a mistress or two hovering in the background. The Prince's wife was Roman Catholic, however, which meant that the Church of England didn't recognize the union. The German-born Caroline was enlisted for the job even though she was far from an acceptable royal wife. Accounts portrayed her as a crude, foul-smelling woman who possessed a huge sexual appetite. Her new husband reportedly was horrified by the sight of her. After only a few weeks of marriage, he declined her company and made her life intolerable. Still, they some-how managed to conceive a child. She left to live abroad. He kept her short of money and tried to deny her access to their daughter.

The Prince Regent maintained a string of mistresses, but his estranged wife was expected to remain chaste on pain of death, adultery being a capital offense for a mother of future heirs to the throne. She took lovers; her husband spied on her and did his best to sully her name. When her husband became king in 1820, she returned to England, inter-ested in restoring her place on the throne. He thought otherwise; the government brought in a Bill of Pains and Penalties, which sought to strip Caroline of her title of queen on the grounds of her scandalous conduct. The women of Britain rebelled, as it was seen as a "woman's cause" to protect a wife's position. A ballad of the day declaimed:

Attend ye virtuous British wives
Support your injured Queen,
Assert her rights; they are your own,
As plainly may be seen

Later historians would argue that the rebellion against the monarch was prompted as much by dislike for him as by support for his wife. In the end, Caroline was barred from Westminster Abbey when she tried to attend his coronation in July 1821. She became ill and died nineteen days later. The inscription on her coffin, which she wrote herself, bore the self-pitying message "Deposited, Caroline of Brunswick, the Injured Queen of England."

Caroline's injuries—many of which were self-inflicted—would later be compared to those of another thwarted Princess of Wales, Diana. When, in 1995, Diana murmured to the nation in a television interview that there had been "three in the marriage, so it was a bit crowded," a reference to her husband's mistress, Camilla Parker Bowles, the monarchy shuddered and wives everywhere stood a little taller.

Wives gleefully exposing their mistreatment by their husbands broke tradition with two longstanding wife rules: one, never betray the secrets of a marriage; two, defer to and respect your husband. That all changed as unleashed fury became a form of financial leverage. When the pop singer Phil Collins disported himself with a girl young enough to be his daughter in 1994, his wife, Jill, released to the press a copy of the fax he had sent to inform her their marriage was over. The headlines that followed were solidly for "loyal wife Jill," and her spoils in the divorce proceedings were swiftly secured.

American wives were showing their mettle too. As part of her ammunition during her divorce from the former General Electric chairman Jack Welch in 2002, Jane Beasley Welch made public her husband's extravagant retirement perks in her bid to go after more than half of Welch's assets, estimated to be worth as much as $800 million. Her court affidavits, which provided information about GE corporate practice far more detailed than the company's stock prospectus, revealed Welch to be not the disciplined tactician the world saw but an indulged man receiving some $2.5 million annually in cushy perks paid for by GE shareholders. She wreaked her revenge by outstrategizing the man once lionized as the most brilliant corporate strategist of the twentieth century, the man who earned his "Neutron Jack" nickname after nuking some 100,000 employees from the GE payroll. It quickly became apparent that if anyone deserved the Neutron sobriquet in this marriage, it was Jane. She was the perfect avenging trophy wife, Welch's second, who had left a career as a corporate lawyer to be Welch's full-time companion over a decade earlier. Her revelation was perceived as a reasonable tit for tat after Beasley Welch had discovered her husband having an affair with the then-editor of *The Harvard Business Review*, Suzy Wetlaufer. The allegations triggered a firestorm of bad publicity for both

Welch and GE and led him to voluntarily forfeit some of the benefits. The fact that Beasley Welch was willing to reveal details also lead to a hasty out-of-court divorce settlement in July 2003, in which she was believed to have secured far more than Welch had initially offered.

Famously wronged wives were not only spilling their stories to the media, they were publishing them in ex-wife memoirs, which emerged during the 1990s as a literary genre. Predictably, the onslaught of such books created the perception of the wife as a wronged, angry creature whose heart had gone cold with the fear of living forever alone. Of course, there is no market for the happy musings of satisfied wives, unless in the form of a how-to manual; the promise of conflict and drama is what prompts publishers to offer big-money book deals.

Even the mere threat of a tell-all ex-wife book can provide leverage. In her battle for a £30 million divorce settlement from Mick Jagger, Jerry Hall faxed to his lawyers a menu of the damaging personal recollections of their years together that she was prepared to publish in a book if her husband didn't agree to her demands. He did.

The fine line between fact and fiction was famously transgressed by Nora Ephron in her 1983 novel, *Heartburn,* a thinly veiled account of her marriage to the *Washington Post* columnist Carl Bernstein. It was a lovingly vicious account of a marriage that began in 1976; Ephron described the husband as a "a piece of work in the sack" who is nevertheless "capable of having sex with a Venetian blind." She held nothing back: his philandering; the fact that he left her for another woman when she was seven months pregnant. Through it all Ephron is a domestic paragon, punctuating her caustic tale with recipes, including one for an excellent key-lime pie.

Ephron had the commercial good sense to cast her former marriage as a comedy. By the late 1990s, the ex-wife memoir tended to treacly, weepy tragedy with the wife firmly in the role of victim. As with all genres, subcategories emerged. The largest was "Exposing the Bastard I Put Up with for Years." In this group, one could find *Leaving a Doll's House,* a scathing memoir published in 1996 by the actress Claire Bloom. In it, she accuses her ex-husband, the writer Philip Roth, with whom she had a seventeen-year relationship, of being a mean, miserly, paranoid philanderer. In *What Falls Away,* Mia Farrow chronicles Woody Allen's neuroses and shortcomings, not the least of which was running away with her adopted daughter. In *The Last Party: Scenes from My Life with Norman Mailer,* Adele Mailer recounts a marriage that came to an end when her husband attempted to murder her with a dirty pocket knife. The author was candid when explaining her rationale for exposing the foibles of a man who had gone on to marry another woman. "I want my book to make Norman suffer," she said.

Then there was the "What About Me?" subcategory, in which former wives lament the sacrifices they made to further their husbands' careers. In *Music to Move the Stars: A Life with Stephen,* Jane Hawking, the former wife of the disabled physicist Stephen Hawking, writes of abandoning her professional life to further his, and being pushed farther and farther into the background. As a stressed-out caregiver, she writes, she suffered bouts of depression. She describes herself as a "brittle, empty shell, alone and vulnerable, restrained only by the thought of my children from throwing myself into the river. Drowning in a slough of despond, I prayed for help with the desperate insistency of a potential suicide." She felt trapped, she writes. "I couldn't go off and leave Stephen. Coals of fire would have been heaped on my head if I had." In the end, though, Hawking was the one to leave when he fell in love with his nurse.

The "Refusing to Follow the Script" subcategory was exemplified by Sheila Rauch Kennedy's *Shattered Faith: A Woman's Struggle to Stop the Catholic Church from Annulling Her Marriage,* published in 1997. Rauch met Joseph P. Kennedy II, the eldest son of Robert Kennedy, in 1970. He was then seen as the heir to the Camelot legend. Nine years later, they married in the Catholic Church; she had been raised Episcopalian and insisted that an Episcopalian clergy also officiate. After their marriage, she worked as an urban planner. She quit her job in 1985, just before Joe Kennedy's first run for Congress. Unlike other Kennedy women, she refused to campaign. Her husband nonetheless won the seat. By 1991, the marriage was over. She did not ask for alimony. The following year, Joe Kennedy married his secretary in a civil ceremony. His wish was to be married in the Catholic Church, which required that his first marriage be annulled.

When Rauch Kennedy was informed of her husband's plans in 1993, she refused to roll over and pretend that her twelve-year marriage that had produced twin boys had never existed. When *Time* magazine published a story on her husband's plans, she wrote an angry letter to the editor. To her surprise, women responded, many of whom had been devastated by the annulment process. Some wrote about how divorce had been far easier to bear: at least divorce recognized there had been a marriage, whereas annulment left them feeling helpless and betrayed.

Joe Kennedy finally did obtain his annulment through the "lack of due discretion" ruling used in 98 percent of annulments, which holds that one or the other of the parties in the marriage was suffering a grave suspension of good judgment at the time of the wedding. Its issuance overlooked the fact that Kennedy had spent nine years courting his wife and had been an elected U.S. congressman with the power to affect millions of people's lives.

Rauch Kennedy's public laundering of her marriage defied the suffer-in-silence tradition of Kennedy women before her who had looked the other way in the face of their husbands' misbehavior. In her account of their marriage, Rauch Kennedy depicts her ex-husband as a narcissistic bully with a quick temper. He frequently told her she "was a nobody," she writes, and claimed he was "not exactly an advocate of equal rights." And, as the marriage fell apart, she writes that she "felt afraid" of her husband, although no harm came to her. On the publicity tour for her book, Rauch Kennedy told *The Irish Times* that "the church made them believe that their whole lives were in being wives and mothers. Then when they're too old to bear any more children and their marriages fall apart, the church tells them they were never really married in the first place. The man they thought was their husband often remarries a younger woman who is more likely to have children, and the church blesses the second union. In a religious sense, it's sort of like sending the brood mare to the glue factory when she can't have any more foals."

Women's solidarity with the wronged wife was made manifestly clear in one scene in the movie version of *The First Wives' Club*, which was released in 1996. In an inspired bit of casting, Ivana Trump was given a cameo. Women in the audience cheered when she uttered her trademark line: "Don't get mad, daaarlink, get everything." By then, Ivana had become a household name as the patron saint of avenging wives. Every newspaper in North America had recounted the story of how, in 1989, at age forty, after almost thirteen years of marriage and three children, she had been traded in by her wealthy developer husband, Donald, for a twenty-six-year-old former beauty pageant winner and aspiring actress. The Trumps had been celebrated as New York's ultimate power couple, fixtures on the social circuit. Years earlier Donald Trump had given his wife a job rehabilitating one of his properties, the then-tarnished Plaza Hotel. He mocked her input, saying he was paying her "$1 a year and all of the dresses she wants."

During her divorce, Ivana Trump contested to no avail the premarital agreement that entitled her to a mere $25 million of his fortune. She then embarked on what would become the famous-ex-wife trajectory—a medley of self-improvement and profitable revenge schemes. She had plastic surgery that made her look like her husband's new girlfriend, which she showed off on the cover of *Vogue*. She wrote *Free to Love*, a thinly disguised autobiography in the form of a romance novel. She designed ostentatious jewelry for the Shopping Channel. In 1995, she wrote a divorce guide, *The Best Is Yet to Come*, and took on a divorce advice column titled "Ask Ivana" for a supermarket tabloid.

The spectre of flocks of wronged wives, white paint and scissors by their sides, matches at the ready, doesn't square with the fact that women initiate divorce two times out of three. Of course, it's very possible that many of these women have been driven to the brink, like the employee subjected to constructive dismissal who believes she has no choice but to leave. Men, on the other hand, tend not to leave marriages unless they've got someone to leave for, a human safety net. Statistics also indicate that older women are more likely than younger women to initiate divorce, with more than 60 percent of divorced women in the United States over forty. (The National Center for Health Statistics reported that 61.5 percent of divorces acted on in the United States in 1986 were sought by women; 32.6 percent were sought by men, and the rest sought jointly. Women with children were more likely to initiate divorce 65.7 percent of the time, while 56.9 percent was the rate for childless women. Rarely was violence or abuse presented as a reason that women wanted to divorce. More often the explanations given included the vague "growing apart," not feeling loved or appreciated, or blaming the spouse for being unwilling or unable to meet "needs.") Wives, of course, have the historical home-field advantage when it comes to self-righteous anger. Decades earlier, an abandoned wife was seen to have lost her defining role, to have failed in her job. The wife by definition is the underdog.

The popularity of wife-revenge entertainment is an indicator that those historical associations linger. The fact that former wives who divulge marital secrets are cheered reflects that, despite social and economic progress, women continue to be viewed as the subordinate, vulnerable party in a marriage, and thus more readily wronged. Despite the flurry of studies that report men get more out of marriage than women, wives continue to be seen as losing more than men when their partner leaves the union—financially, emotionally, socially. Wife retribution is seen as sweet justice, whereas husbands who do the same thing are viewed as whiners, bullies, or criminals.

When men spill marital secrets in print, the response is rarely sympathetic. They're hailed not as heroes but as cads. Philip Roth's 1998 novel, *I Married a Communist,* seen as his partly settling the score with Claire Bloom's unkind words about him in her memoir, met with hostile reviews. Hanif Kureishi's *Intimacy,* published in 1998, told the story of betrayal from a man's point of view: the novella was a fictionalized account of how he walked out on his partner and two young sons for another woman. Critics pilloried it. *The Independent* newspaper engaged in a bit of amateur psychology, asking if it was "a crude exercise in self-help." Most men, however, don't sit around plotting revenge. Instead, they move on to second or third wives. The work of revenge, like so many other tasks associated with marriage, falls to women, who embrace it with zeal.

·   ·   ·

Compared to real first wives' clubs, however, fictional first wives' clubs pale. These real wives are not prancing about in Armani, worried about their next collagen injection as they bond over their mutual antipathy for their exes and their belief that the system has treated them unfairly. They are bent on righting the perceived wrongs done them and in redressing what they see as an unjust legal system.

The founder of one of the earliest first wives' clubs, Geraldine Jensen, was neither rich nor well connected. But Jensen shared with the fictional first wives' club a frustration that the system was not protecting her interests. When her five-year marriage to Stephen Gerharter, a factory worker, came to an end in 1977, Jensen was given custody of their two sons; her husband was ordered to pay $50 a week in support. He made payments for six months and then stopped.

When Jensen was unable to meet the house payments, she and her children moved back to her hometown of Toledo, Ohio, and she tried desperately to locate her ex-husband. For a time, she worked two jobs to make ends meet. Then she became ill. Finally, she ended up on welfare. The thirty-two-year-old had $12 in her pocket and half a pound of hamburger in her refrigerator when a prosecutor told her he could do nothing to collect more than $10,000 in overdue child support. If she wanted her money, he said dismissively, she should "get a bunch of women together and do something about it."

She did. In March 1984, she took $8.40 of her last $12 and placed a newspaper ad asking other women who had not received owed child support to contact her. The day the ad ran, she heard from nine women and one man. The Association for Children for Enforcement of Support, which would come to be known as ACES, was born. Jensen learned her legal rights. She figured out how to do a federal parent locator on the computer to track down a former spouse. She learned about bureaucratic bungling. She finally located her children's father, who was living in Iowa. Her ex-husband has never missed a payment since.

Jensen returned to school and became a nurse but later quit nursing to work for ACES full-time. Her attacks on the bureaucracy and determination to squeeze answers out of dry legalese made her the terror of courtrooms. In the process, she became a celebrity on daytime talk shows devoted to women in various forms of crisis. In 1995, a television movie about her crusade, *Abandoned and Deceived*, was aired. In 1998, Jensen flew to Washington to witness President Clinton sign the Dead-beat Parents Punishment Act, which made it a felony to cross state lines to avoid child support payments that have been unpaid for one year or total at least $5,000. By 2003, ACES, financed primarily by private foun-dations, counted among its members more than fifty thousand parents whose children are owed support.

But when it came time for *People* to pick its poster girl for child-support settlements in 1995, it chose not the middle-class Jensen but Marilyn Kane, a high-powered New York real estate agent who became an overnight celebrity when she recovered a record back payment of child support from Jeffrey Nichols, her wealthy ex-husband. Kane's story was filled with the kind of high-end nasty details that made Gold-smith's novel such a delicious read. There was the fact, for instance, that Kane once faced eviction while her ex-husband, who owed $580,000 in child support, went to Hawaii with his new wife. He sent her a postcard: "Having a ball. Glad you're not here." He went to jail until he could come up with a portion of what he owed. The federal case was the largest ever brought under the Child Support Recovery Act of 1992. Kane took to the speaking circuit and, in 1999, founded a group in New York best known in legal circles as the First Wives Club, which is now a chapter of the National Coalition for Family Justice.

The wifely showdown extended to second wives' clubs, which squared off against first wives' clubs like ACES for wife-on-wife battle. Second wives would prove energetic foot soldiers in the flourishing "fathers' rights" movement that has mushroomed to nearly three hun-dred groups throughout North America. It was an ironic loop: second wives were angry at first wives for siphoning off what they saw as right-fully their family funds, while first wives felt they were subordinate to the interests of the husband's next family. These second wives were the women at rallies brandishing signs that read "Second Family—Second Class" and accusing ex-wives of being "money grubbers" who use child-support money "to live high on the hog" and impoverish ex-husbands and their second families. These groups also went by acronyms, like

COPS, Coalition of Parent Support, California's largest fathers' rights group. Second wives' tearful testimony moved legislators in half a dozen states to pass laws that allow fathers to deduct second-marriage child-rearing costs before a court can calculate support to children from a first marriage. In California, second wives successfully pushed for legislation that prevents judges from including the new wives' income in court calculations of how much the husbands can pay. Second wives also helped defeat a proposed law to extend parents' child support obligations for educational purposes by three years, or until a son or daughter turns twenty-one.

Wifely mistrust of husbands translated into business opportunities that catered to the would-be avenging wife. Check A Mate, a New York City investigative agency that specializes in matrimonial cases, revealed that 80 percent of its clients are women, most of them white, educated, and middle class. Many are housewives who have given up jobs to care for children at home. Their marriages have changed, and they are unhappy, terrified of the financial insecurity awaiting them if the marriage ends.

The climate engendered a market for books such as the 1999 *How to Hide Money from Your Husband,* a manual advising wives to build their own nest egg even if it means lying, cheating, or rifling through their husbands' pockets. Under the dust jacket is a plain blue cover—no title—intended to allow women to read it without detection. Shrewdly, the book's marketing department enlisted Olivia Goldsmith to write an endorsement.

By then, *The First Wives' Club* had come to signify far more than a harmless, amusing novel. It was seen as a manifesto in the battle of the sexes, one that often included intentional harm, even violence, as reflected in the cover image on the book's British edition. Where the U.S. publisher of *The First Wives' Club* had chosen a discreet cover, its U.K. counterpart went for a more shocking image—that of a mani-cured hand crushing two golf balls. Clearly, it was intended as a visual witticism to amuse a female audience. But it also reflected the blithe attitude increasingly taken to violence toward men who wronged their wives. In this regard, crushing the bastard's manhood without a second thought was presented as just another female prerogative, like changing her mind.

When *People* published its "25 Most Intriguing People of 1993" issue in December 1993, few were surprised to see the name Lorena Bobbitt listed beside that of the put-upon Princess of Wales and the freakish Michael Jackson. Bobbitt, a twenty-four-year-old manicurist from Manassas, Virginia, who emigrated to the U.S. from South America when she was seventeen, had achieved overnight celebrity in June of that year when she cut off her husband's penis. Just what happened between the Bobbitts will always be a mystery. She said she was retaliating for being raped; he denied it. According to the courts, nothing illegal happened; both parties were acquitted.

The Bobbitt marriage had been troubled from its beginning in 1989. The couple had separated twice. In May 1993, they discussed divorce. According to Lorena Bobbitt's version of events, the night of June 23 was like many others in their miserable marriage. She said her husband forced himself on her sexually, then fell asleep. She went to get a glass of water and picked up a red-handled kitchen knife purchased at IKEA. She woke him, threatened him, then waited for him to fall asleep. Once he was asleep, she sliced off most of his penis and drove off with it in the family car, eventually tossing it in a neighbor's yard as if it were a flyer from a Thai restaurant. She then threw the knife in a trash can outside the beauty salon where she worked. After the police found her, they retrieved the penis, and John Bobbitt underwent a nine-and-a-half-hour operation to have it reattached.

Three weeks later, Lorena Bobbitt filed for divorce, citing repeated "marital sexual abuse." Her attorney, James M. Lowe, of Alexandria, announced that his client was "the classic battered wife." John Bobbitt was indicted, but for marital sexual assault rather than the more punitive spousal rape. (Virginia was one of the twenty-nine states with exceptions to the marital rape laws. In Virginia, the standards for proving spousal rape are tough: a spouse can be charged only if the couple is not living together and the victim shows serious physical injury. Marital sexual assault carries a maximum penalty of twenty years in prison, whereas conviction on spousal rape can bring a life sentence.) After

John Bobbitt was acquitted by a jury of nine women and three men, the prosecutor Paul Ebert said it was a "fair assumption" that the jury had been swayed by sympathy for the wounded twenty-six-year-old man.

Lorena Bobbitt faced prosecution for malicious wounding, which carried a twenty-year sentence. Originally, her lawyer intended to plead self-defense but later decided to plead temporary insanity. At trial, Lorena Bobbitt appeared demure and vulnerable. She wore a subdued button-front jacket with small checks and dark piping on the collar. Her hair was pulled back, with soft bangs framing her face. A cross hung from her neck. She claimed the marriage became violent just one month after the wedding, when her husband began driving erratically after drinking. She said she told him to stop, and when she tried to straighten the wheel he punched her. The prosecutor painted her as the aggressive party who got angry at her husband for wearing tennis shoes, which meant they couldn't get into a bar. When he was driving home, she started hitting him. She also admitted she knew she was still eligible for a permanent work permit when estranged from her American husband, thanks to a legal loophole enabling her to apply as a battered wife, which might have been seen to play a role in her motivation.

Lorena Bobbitt was found not guilty by reason of temporary insanity, subject to forty-five days of psychiatric examination. The judge conceded there had been many inconsistencies in evidence on both sides but expressed a view that the fact she was born in Ecuador and raised in Venezuela had given her problems in communicating.

By that time, the knife-wielding wife was a heroine in some quarters. Outside the court, brisk business was done selling $10 T-shirts carrying the words "Manassas—a cut above" and depicting a knife dripping blood. Even Lenore Walker, famous for defending the "battered wife," weighed in on the matter. "I am very pleased for Lorena Bobbitt," she told the press. "I think the verdict was fair and equitable, given the experiences she had.... But I'm saddened that she has to go off to a mental hospital. Once a woman is safe and has support, the psychological damage that we labeled 'battered woman's syndrome' disappears without any treatment."

The media treated her with sympathy. The news program *20/20* covered her version of the story. A profile in the November 1993 *Vanity Fair* titled "A Night to Dismember" featured provocative photographs of Lorena, wet in a bathing suit. The case sparked open season on penis jokes, including the slogan "Lorena Bobbitt for surgeon general." Outside the trial, free samples of hot dogs dubbed "Slice 'N Wieners" were handed out. Even President Clinton joked about the case. He claimed he asked his wife, Hillary, if penile reattachment surgery would be covered by her health-care plan.

Male genitalia in distress became an acceptable source of comedy. Ben Stiller, for example, had audiences howling with laughter over his depiction of the grotesque agony of getting a scrotum caught in a zipper in the movie *There's Something About Mary.* Tapping into the climate his story had helped to create, John Wayne Bobbitt took to the stand-up comedy circuit and then further capitalized on his misadventure with a book of penis-centric humor titled *Getting Cocky with John Wayne Bobbitt: A Book That Will Make You Laugh Your Balls Off.*

While the wife who maimed drew crowds and sympathy, the wife who killed drew record audiences, as was made clear by the March 2, 1992, episode of *The Oprah Winfrey Show.* The program garnered a 14.7 metered market rating, making it the second-highest combined market rating the show received in its near-six-year history in national syndication, according to A. C. Nielsen. (Only the November 15, 1988, "Diet Dreams Come True" show scored a higher average rating, with an 18.4.) Winfrey's guest that day was Betty Broderick, a woman whose name would have been familiar to the program's mostly female audience. They all would have known that three years previously, Broderick had killed her ex-husband and his new young wife in their bed. The story that emerged in the days and weeks after the murders followed a recognizable script: a beautiful young woman marries a handsome, ambitious young man. She supports him as he gets his degree. She raises children and keeps house while he attains professional success. In time, he tires of her and replaces her with a younger woman. With the center of her universe removed, she becomes unhinged. She cracks. She murders.

Or that was the predictable fictional script superimposed on the Betty Broderick story. Real-life narratives, as we know, are never as simple.

Elisabeth (Betsy) Anne Bisceglia met Daniel Broderick in 1965, just before her eighteenth birthday. She was tall, blond, and slender, the product of a sheltered, affluent Catholic upbringing in Connecticut. He was a student with big ambitions. Soon after they met, he told friends that this was the woman he would marry. They wed in April 1969.

Betty held a degree in early childhood education and supported her husband while he attended Harvard Law School. The early years of their marriage were difficult; they struggled, accumulating debt to pay for his education. As Dan's law practice grew, life became more comfortable. In 1973, the family—now with two children—moved into an oceanfront home in affluent La Jolla, California. They entered "American dream" territory with a monster home, multiple luxury cars, country club membership, private schools for the children, ski vacations, European holidays. Betty was a typical stay-at-home mom, a familiar sight in her sweats, ferrying her children around in her SUV with its LODEMUP license plates. The couple entertained lavishly. Dan became a pillar in San Diego's legal and social community.

In 1983, after fourteen years, the Brodericks' marriage came to an end. Betty accused Dan of having an affair with his new assistant, Linda Kolkena. In a fury, she piled his clothes in the backyard and burned them. Their messy divorce lasted two years. Dan obtained custody of their children and had their divorce records sealed. Betty sought more than $250,000 a year in support payments. She was eventually awarded nearly $10,000 a month.

"My career was that of a wife and mother," she said in a 1987 court declaration. "Being forced out of our marriage is like being thrown into a snake pit for me in terms of how I see my life and my happiness. . . ." After the divorce, Betty's weight ballooned. She devoted her life to making her former husband's life miserable. She placed obscene telephone calls, crashed her Chevy Blazer through his front door. Once she smeared his bed with Boston cream pies.

More than once, Betty told her children that she would kill their father. Dan countered by having Betty arrested, jailed, and briefly committed to a mental hospital. He tried to control her by withholding money from her support payments, docking her for behavior he deemed inappropriate. He obtained a temporary restraining order to keep her out of his house. When she threatened him, he wrote her curt letters in the coldest legalese. If she tried to kill him, the letters warned, he would make her regret it.

In March 1989, Betty Broderick attempted suicide. In April, Dan Broderick married twenty-eight-year-old Linda Kolkena. On November 5, 1989, at five-thirty in the morning, Betty Broderick shot the couple to death with a .38-calibre revolver while they slept in the upstairs master bedroom of their Georgian-style home. She surrendered later that day.

At trial, she pleaded not guilty. Predictably, the story drew the media—from tabloid TV shows to the made-for-TV-movie people to *Ladies' Home Journal,* which was focusing on the "trauma" of a middle-aged woman. The case became a lightning rod for the many women disgruntled with the divorce courts, who felt that their contributions to marriage had not been recognized. Many of the middle-aged to elderly women who came to watch her trial were there in support of Broderick, believing they could identify with what she went through.

Betty Broderick became a symbol of the rage and desire for revenge so familiar to divorcing couples. At one La Jolla cocktail party soon after the killings, a man who attended with his second, younger wife on his arm joked, "I guess this is 'be nice to the ex-wife' week." During the trial, it became evident that Betty was not the sad, abandoned woman she presented herself to be. It was discovered she had a thirty-six-year-old businessman boyfriend, Bradley T. Wright, whom she called immediately after the murders. Despite the incriminating evidence, the jury was unable to come to a verdict. At her second trial, Broderick was found guilty on two counts of murder and sentenced to two fifteen-year-to-life terms.

But that was not the end of Betty Broderick. She hired a public relations firm to help get her message out, one that cleaved to the traditional wife script. "We were both successful, very high-achieving people," Betty told the *Reader* newspaper. "I had all the skills he needed at home. He needed me to give him the legitimacy and normalcy of a wife who could entertain and have the kids and be a respectable family. And I needed him to bring home the bacon so that I could have all the kids and the car and the trips and the house. And it worked great! That was the deal."

Yet she also promoted herself according to a more modern narrative, one that presented the ceaselessly sacrificing wife as a victim. Even before their Caribbean honeymoon was over, Betty claimed, Dan stopped courting her, and she began to feel trapped in the role she'd chosen. "He had the idea that [the wedding] changed everything," she said. "He let the maids go at the honeymoon house. I was supposed to . . . cook and clean while he studied."

As her life went "from bliss to disaster," Betty says, she threatened to leave him. But she changed her mind when she discovered she was pregnant. ("With all my Catholic upbringing and education to be a 'wife,' never was sex or birth control one of the topics," she says.)

By the time the couple had been married four years, she says, "the balance of power between us had been totally reversed." Suddenly, Betty says, "I wasn't Mrs. Anything." But in fact she had a house, a car, a closet full of $8,000 ball gowns and $2,000 outfits. She was receiving $9,036 a month, tax-free, from Dan. She had teaching credentials, a real estate license, and plenty of friends. But from then on, Betty says, Dan held "all the cards. . . ."

At one point, Betty felt so distraught that she called a battered women's hot line and asked for help with what she described as emotional battery and verbal threats. She also poured energy into writing a book about her experience, an unpublished manuscript titled "What's a Nice Girl to Do? A Story of White Collar Domestic Violence in America." "I went from being accomplished, well connected and free to being isolated from family and friends . . . and trapped with two children for whom I was 100% responsible," she wrote. "Dan went from being a student on his own, with no possessions, no savings, no connections or contacts, to being an MD/JD, who had many, many contacts."

Broderick became a household name, a feminist folk hero. One women's magazine titled a story about her "In Hot Blood: Why Did Betty Broderick Wait So Long to Kill Her Husband?" There was the inevitable made-for-television movie, *A Woman Scorned: The Betty Broderick Story,* which aired in 1991 and was the highest-rated television movie of the year. A sequel, *Her Final Fury: Betty Broderick—The Last Chapter,* aired the following year. Broderick's story was also the subject of sympathetic portrayals in books with florid titles like *Until the Twelfth of Never: The Deadly Divorce of Dan & Betty Broderick* and *Forsaking All Others: The Real Betty Broderick Story.*

In her interview with Broderick from prison, Oprah Winfrey framed the story of bloody murder as a hijacked fairy tale. "How did this story-book marriage go so wrong?" the talk-show host asked. Broderick read-ily complied with the imagery. "Dan went out and slayed the dragons," she said. "He supported us.... I was home and hearth.... It was all I ever wanted to do." She portrayed the marriage in the terms of perfection associated with fairy tales. "I thought we had the perfect marriage," she told Oprah. "I was the perfect mom. Being a supermom was the only thing I wanted in life." She went so far as to say that "we had the best family in the whole world."

She presented herself as the victim. "Any woman married to a successful man—that's what you do in the young years. He was never there ... he never had time for me and the children. I want to warn women about what happens when we give too much of ourselves," she tearfully told the audience. "The law does not protect us." One could only wonder what kind of protection Broderick was talking about. What did she expect the law to protect her from? Heartbreak? Aban-donment? Herself?

There have always been women who kill their husbands, of course, though for centuries it wasn't a subject for polite company. In the nine-teenth century, incidences of poisoning believed to have been inten-tional murder were not uncommon. But city fathers just shook their collective heads over these "inhuman monsters" who killed "without motive." Assuming that women were passive creatures, the blame was usually placed on menstrual tension, hysterical disease, or that legal free-for-all, insanity.

Murderous wives have long been a theatrical staple, from Queen Gertrude in *Hamlet,* to Barbara Stanwyck in *Double Indemnity,* to Nicole Kidman's character in *To Die For,* which was based on the real-life case of Pam Smart, who seduced her teenage boyfriend into killing her husband. Thousands of years ago, the Greeks recognized the dramatic possibilities of the wronged wife, ignited by fury, hellbent on vengeance. The archetypal avenging first wife is to be found in the character of Medea. Greek theater-goers never meet the woman who tricked her father into stealing the mythical golden fleece or who killed her brother so she could elope with Jason to Corinth. Instead, they catch up with her as the brokenhearted wife spurned by the man for whom she willingly exiled herself from her Asian homeland.

Jason leaves Medea, after she bears his children, for Glauce, a classical trophy wife. Glauce is the daughter of Corinth's leader, Creon, who orders Medea into banishment, concerned that her jealousy may result in his daughter being harmed. Medea asks for one day's delay, which Creon grants. She uses the time to murder Glauce by giving her a wedding dress that erupts into flames. Depending on the version of the story, Medea also murders her children—either to protect them from being stoned by the people of Corinth or as a final act of vengeance on her husband. Medea disappears from Corinth. Jason becomes a wandering vagabond, crushed by the bow of his own rotting ship.

Over the centuries, Medea became a cultural touchstone, with her story being told and retold in plays, verse, musicals, and operas. The sympathy with which she was treated waxed and waned according to social mores. The Greek tragedian Euripedes offered a sympathetic version. Seneca played up the gory aspects of the story. *The Life and Death of Jason,* by the craftsman and poet William Morris, presented Medea as a fragile, weepy maiden, devastated by Jason's infidelity. When *Medea* was performed at the Shakespearean Festival in Stratford, Ontario, in the summer of 2000, the staging reflected empathy toward the wronged ex-wife. According to a review in *The Globe and Mail,* "*Medea* is a story of feminist suffering and power, its heroine made hugely sympathetic by actress Seana McKenna...."

By the 1990s the murderous wife was the source of blockbuster, rollicking entertainment. In 1996 came the revival of the hit Broadway musical *Chicago,* which starred six "merry murderesses" incarcerated for killing their husbands. Their lawyer gets the media to publicize their stories in the hope of garnering sympathy from the public—

which he does, as they become celebrities, even though it's clear the women did not kill in self-defense. In the song "Cell Block Tango," the women reveal how and why they killed their men; one woman describes cutting up a chicken for dinner when her husband enters the kitchen in a rage, accusing her of "screwin' the milkman." Then, she says, he "ran into" her knife—ten times.

The appetite for husbandicide fully registered with the unexpected success of *Double Jeopardy*, the sleeper movie of 1999. Even its producers at Paramount were taken by surprise. The film was intended to be light summer fare, a suspense-action flick that would draw a predominantly male audience. It stars Ashley Judd as Libby Parsons, a beautiful young wife who appears to have everything the "Housewife Wannabes" described by *Cosmopolitan* dreamed of—a devoted, successful husband, an adorable little boy, a beautiful waterfront house, and meaningful charity work to keep her busy. What she doesn't know is that her idyllic life is a facade. Her husband was in financial peril and conspiring against her to run away with her best friend.

To this end, he sets up an elaborate scheme that makes it look as if his wife has murdered him on their luxurious sailboat and then cast his body out to sea. Once in jail, Judd's character discovers his deception. With the help of her cellmates—most of them women with clichéd "hearts of gold" who are also serving time for killing their husbands— she plots her revenge. A former lawyer who is also incarcerated explains to her the double jeopardy ruling that precludes someone's being tried twice for the same crime. That, she advises Judd's character, means that she could track down her errant husband, kill him, and get off. Infused with a new righteous mission, the wronged wife embarks on a plan. She works out in the prison jail yard until she's highly buff. When released after serving what appears to be an extremely abbreviated sentence, she tracks down her husband with the help of her parole officer. After a series of cinematic thrills, she confronts him. But in the end it's her parole officer–protector, played by a macho Tommy Lee Jones, who fires the lethal bullet.

Reviews were mixed. Even so, audiences flocked to the movie, not bothered by its boilerplate script or by the fact that its underlying legal premise is illogical (if the husband isn't dead, no first crime was committed). In short order, the film took in over $100 million. What hadn't been anticipated was the high female turnout. Women accounted for more than 60 percent of the audience, an unusually high turnout for an action-adventure film. But it wasn't the action-adventure that women were lining up for: it was to experience the righteous catharsis of a wronged wife avenging her duplicitous husband. With typical marketing alacrity, Hollywood executives found a name for the phenomenon. "Hear me roar," they called the genre, a reference to Helen Reddy's "I Am Woman," a feminist anthem from the 1970s.

Fascination with the murderous wife resulted in a renewed interest in the lurid story of Evelyn Dick, a Hamilton, Ontario, woman accused in 1946 of murdering and dismembering her husband, a streetcar driver whose headless, armless, legless torso was found by children in the woods. He had been shot twice at close range. The trial focused on Dick's reputation as a party girl who "entertained" wealthy men. She was convicted of her husband's murder and sentenced to hang in January 1947, but was acquitted on appeal. She would later be convicted of manslaughter in a second murder case after her baby's body was found in a suitcase filled with cement. Dick was sentenced to life in prison. Her boyfriend was tried in both cases and acquitted. She served eleven years of a life sentence before being set free under a new name. In 2002, a made-for-television movie, *Torso: The Evelyn Dick Case*, aired on Canadian television, along with a companion documentary about the case. The movie, which rendered Dick's abusive childhood in a sympathetic manner, received huge media attention and was showered with awards.

The righteous embrace of imagery involving female violence against men had become so entrenched that it was even marketed as an antidote to the saccharine romanticism of that legislated day of love, Valentine's Day. On February 14, 2002, the British publisher Duckworth released *Valentine's Day: Women Against Men*, an anthology of female revenge tales. On its jacket was a reproduction of Artemisia Gentileschi's painting of Judith and Holofernes, a bloody tableau of two women decapitating a man.

The scene was inspired by the Book of Judith, an apocryphal text from the Old Testament. The story of Judith and Holofernes is set in Bethulia while it is under siege. Judith, a beautiful widow, is determined to save her people by assassinating the invading Assyrians' general, Holofernes. She pretends to flee the city with her maid but instead reaches his camp and encourages him to believe that victory will soon be his. Holofernes, with seduction in mind, invites her into his tent for a banquet; Judith waits until he falls into a drunken sleep, grabs his sword, and, with the assistance of her maid, cuts off his head, which she takes back with her to Bethulia. The Hebrew defenders mount the head on the town's ramparts and soon rout the leaderless Assyrian troops.

The murdering wife became the heroine of yet another twisted variation on the fairy tale, one that came to include husbandicide as an acceptable female fantasy. This too was not an exclusively modern theme. In the late nineteenth century, the American writer Kate Chopin took on the subject of the husband-death fantasy in her 1894 short story "The Story of an Hour," in which a young woman is told her husband has been killed in a railroad disaster. She weeps and takes to her room. Slowly, she becomes aware of her spirits lifting: "She said it over under her breath: 'free, free, free!' .... She saw beyond the bitter moment a long procession of years to come that would belong to her absolutely." Then, without warning, her husband, who had not been on the train after all, walks through the door. When she sees him, she suffers heart failure; everyone around her, of course, assumes she dies of joy. The reader knows differently.

Over one hundred years later, in Jane Shapiro's critically acclaimed black-comic 1999 novel, *The Dangerous Husband,* the fantasy is more explicit. The book's newly married heroine begins to fantasize about hiring a handsome hit man soon after becoming disenchanted with her bumbling, threatening husband. A "Chaplinesque and Hitchcockian little fairy tale," enthused the author Lorrie Moore in a review.

Indeed, the novel does begin as a middle-aged fairy tale. At first, the forty-year-old never-married heroine is captivated by the man who will become her husband. He appears perfect—charming, boasting inherited wealth, a Brooklyn brownstone, and a boyish ardor. During the dinner party where they first fall in love, the heroine tells him, "Here's something I know: I am not going to kill. I mean unless it was in some extreme self-defense situation, to save my own life, and that's just normal. Otherwise, even if I felt abused or victimized, believe me, I'm not murdering anybody."

She marries him, admitting, "I was tired and I was broke." Quickly, she becomes disenchanted. Her husband's goofy acts of clumsiness—tripping down stairs, breaking priceless antiques—begin to turn menacing and violent. A dropped skillet breaks her toe. She is tossed across the room. At the beginning she adopts "the attitude of the wise wife: implacable detached amusement commingled with dogged acceptance." But as the couple become increasingly isolated, she starts to fear for her life. Her fantasy of hiring a hit man begins. Shapiro writes of the diminishment that occurs in a bad marriage: "Is this what marriage is?" the narrator asks. "Discoveries and discoveries, and changes and changes, until everything you had was gone?"

Even women who claim to be happily married confess to thoughts of their husbands' dying. One woman I know in her mid-thirties who adores her older husband says she worries about his death, but also frets she will have lost her currency in the marriage market by the time he dies. "I do find myself looking in the mirror and wondering when my sell-by date is," she says, only half in jest. "And I say to myself, If he's going to kick, he should do it soon."

There is a logic, if perverse, to her thinking. Her husband is seven years older than she is; statistics tell her she'll spend some time as a widow. Her concern is that her four small children will not have a father at some point in their lives if she cannot snare a new husband. She's told her husband about these thoughts, and he's amused by them.

For happily married women, facing one's worst fear can be seen as an attempt to deal with it. For unhappily married women, it can be a pathetic survival mechanism. "I needed to see a life beyond him" is how another woman explained her frequent thoughts of her husband's dying. Though financially independent, she says she felt locked in her unhappy marriage. Thoughts of suicide crossed her mind. Focusing on his death, she realized, became a proxy for that. Theoretically, husbandicide is neat, the perfect exit strategy for women who believe themselves too weak to leave, who need a *deus ex machina* solution. It sidesteps the feelings of failure and guilt as well as the financial mess that accompany divorce. With divorce, if there are children, an ex-wife has to deal with her husband. Should he die, goes the fantasy, a woman is transformed into the heroic grieving widow, as well as the legal heir, entitled to insurance and the estate.

Of course, men who voice a desire to kill their wives would be issued restraining orders, not celebrated at the multiplex. But the husbandicide fantasy is regarded as benign, the by-product of being a modern wife, a role women supposedly dream about as a child, only to find it not to their liking in maturity. If one wanted to stretch it, the husbandicide fantasy could fit squarely into the continuum of being a fairy-tale bride: after Prince Charming sweeps her off her feet, the Grim Reaper enters to sweep the failed prince off his. And she lives happily ever after, liberated from the shackles of wifedom in the strange universe of the unwife.

Chapter 7

The Unwife

The confusion surrounding the meaning of wife in the first decade of the twenty-first century is most insidiously perpetuated in the depiction not of wives, but of women who are unattached. Let's call them *unwives,* given how often their representation hinges on the fact that they aren't married. For preliminary evidence, we need only look to the cover of *Time*'s August 28, 2000, issue, the one that asked "Who Needs a Husband?" Its subhead continued the inquiry: "More women are saying no to marriage and embracing the single life. Are they happy?" Illustrating these sweeping, unanswerable questions suggesting that all single women share a collective consciousness was an airbrushed photograph of the four perfectly coiffed, meticulously made up, and expensively outfitted actresses from the television program *Sex and the City.* Their iconic presence telegraphed the message that women with enough money, power, and Manolo Blahnik stilettos don't need husbands.

As a recruitment poster for the single life, the image needed some work. The lighting was lurid, the women appeared shellacked, the backdrop throbbed a garish fuchsia. More disturbing was its premise: once again single women were being reduced to fictional stereotypes that defined them primarily in terms of not being wives.

That "Who Needs a Husband?" was being asked in the year 2000, when a record number of women were unmarried in North America, Europe, and Japan should have raised its own fuchsia flag. The fact that women might not require husbands to lead fulfilling lives had been posited by mainstream media long before Gloria Steinem positioned herself as the single girl's champion. Certainly, legions of real women dating back a century could offer convincing testimony that a husband was not synonymous with personal happiness. In 1960, *The New York Mirror* magazine asked, "Who Needs A Man Around the House?" on its cover; inside was an article celebrating female self-sufficiency.

Forty years later, the never-married woman appeared, at least superficially, to have achieved the social approbation Steinem so desired for her. Samantha Stevens, the stay-at-home witch and mother in the 1960s sitcom *Bewitched,* had been replaced by the go-girl pyrotechnics of *Buffy the Vampire Slayer.* The "spinster" was replaced with the "cougar," the slightly sneering label given adventurous, sexual single women over age forty. The freedoms enjoyed by single women were cast in an idealized glow. The voluptuous and selfish pleasures of a life doing what one wanted, when one wanted, was constantly pitted against the tedium of married life, living in a "domestic gulag," as the writer Laura Kipnis refers to it in her 2003 book *Against Love.* "There's never been a better time for women to be single," *The Edmonton Journal* proclaimed in 2000. *Time* was equally effusive in its "Who Needs a Husband?" story: "More confident, more self-sufficient, and more choosy than ever, women no longer see marriage as a matter of survival and acceptance." And, as if to cap off the message, the week after *Time*'s "Who Needs A Husband?" issue hit newsstands, Steinem announced her marriage, as if to say, My work's been done. Single women no longer need me as their ambassador.

Yet during the 1990s, a countervailing message presented single women as neurotic, unhappy, and more desperate to marry than they had been in decades. For every magazine headline crowing about the fabulousness of single life, there was one questioning single women's emotional fragility and whether they were "too picky," too selfish, to make a commitment.

Chalk it up to the wife gap. Just as the wedding industrial complex and mystique chic provided commercialized templates for female behavior during the 1990s, a one-size-fits-all single-gal market emerged to sell single life as a condition best avoided. "Why Am I Still Single?" was the fretful headline of a feature in the April 2001 issue of *Marie Claire*. Books offering advice on how to snare "Mr. Right" topped best-seller lists. Movies presented single women as unhealthily obsessed with their careers or in a panic that they weren't married.

Women were constantly reminded that the ticking clock was a ticking time bomb. An "over-by-thirty" movie genre emerged in the late 1990s. In *If Lucy Fell*, released in 1997, two characters made plans to hurl themselves off the Brooklyn Bridge if they weren't married by thirty. *Wedding Bell Blues*, also released in 1997, featured three women—including the stunning model Paulina Porizkova—who run off to Las Vegas to get married before their thirtieth birthdays. In *My Best Friend's Wedding*, released in 1997, Julia Roberts plays a twenty-eight-year-old woman who flies into a panic and falls in love with her closest male friend when she discovers he is marrying.

Suddenly, being alone was questioned. The Canadian fashion magazine *Flare* ran a piece in April 1998 titled "The New Spinster," illustrated with a photograph of the television character Ally McBeal: "She's cool, she's attractive, she's thirtyish—and she's still single. Are we all right with that?" Of course we are "all right with that." Or are we? Reading the article gave one pause, particularly when it described single life as "a transitional stage, something to grow out of rather than embrace."

Even women who served as single-woman role models were questioned. "What money can't buy" was the cover line of *People* in August 2001 about unattached actresses. "They seem to have it all," read the underline, "but Julia Roberts, Meg Ryan and Nicole Kidman struggle to find the right script for romance." The accompanying article painted a bleak picture for the successful solo woman, claiming that "financially independent, well-educated women are statistically the most likely to find themselves alone watching *Xena: Warrior Princess* on a Saturday night." Where these statistics came from was never mentioned. But by then the statement sounded true. What did it matter whether it actually was?

Again, either-or, no-win fantasy scenarios were trotted out. The same *People* article went on to celebrate single life: "Given so many choices [single women] don't have to settle and are willing to give up the old-fashioned romantic fantasy of being with a man in favor of the fantasy of independence."

So abundant are the "fantasies" confronting single women that the reality is difficult to decipher. Where it did shine through, strangely enough, was in the article accompanying *Time*'s "Who Needs a Husband?" story. In it, Sarah Jessica Parker, one of the four *Sex and the City* actresses, revealed that she often feels guilty because she isn't being what she calls "a good traditional wife" to her husband, the actor Matthew Broderick. Her demanding job as the fictional, unrealistic role model for legions of single women paradoxically prevented her from following another script. "I know he doesn't have his laundry done, that he hasn't had a hot meal in days," she told *Time*. "That stuff weighs on my mind." Yet she also admitted that she regales single friends with tales of how boring married life is and how much luckier they are to have their freedom and fun. When asked if she really believed that, she said no. "It's just a fun thing to say to make single people feel better," she explained.

In the space of forty years, the time it took to create the wife gap, the depiction of single women has undergone a devolution in popular culture—from the sunny, naive optimism of Ann Marie in *That Girl* to the homicidal frustration of Alex Forrest in *Fatal Attraction* to the neurotic self-flagellation of Bridget Jones and Ally McBeal to the glossy consumers on *Sex and the City*. Indeed, the *Sex and the City* women personify millennial cultural priorities, at least as interpreted by the media. All live in fabulous apartments and wear off-the-runway clothes. Their lives are a hedonistic parade of shopping, restaurant openings, and jaunts to bars and spas. Conversations focus on consumption—of designer shoes, male sperm, the best vibrators, the best cosmetic surgeons. The message on the answering machine of the central character, Carrie, says it all: "I'm out buying shoes. Please leave a message."

Feminism had gone to the mall, co-opted by marketing that equated liberty with shopping. By the turn of the twenty-first century, single women were in a catch-22: on one hand, their social value was clearly tied to their economic clout; on the other, their consumer power allowed them to rewrite social rules in ways that threatened the status quo. And that, in turn, triggered a backlash in which single women were presented as needing husbands, or at least questioning whether they did.

To trace the emergence of this dilemma, one must track the creation of the single-gal market, one that appeared to be booming by the year 2000. The very month before the "Who Needs a Husband?" issue of *Time* hit newsstands, a report issued by the London-based Intelligence Factory, an arm of the advertising agency Young & Rubicam, proclaimed the single woman the "new yuppie." The study, titled "The Single Female Consumer," claimed that professional, well-educated single women who lived alone were the biggest consumer group in the Western world. "The results make it clear that women living alone had come to comprise the strongest consumer block in much the same way that yuppies did in the 1980s," said Marian Salzman, then principal of the Intelligence Factory.

And these "unapologetically independent" women, as the Intelligence Factory study called them (an adjective that quivered with the suggestion that maybe they did have something to apologize for), were not putting their lives on hold waiting for Mr. Right. The research was clearly at odds with the imagery pitched at women by the wedding industrial complex. As Salzman says, "Women are building their own picket fences; they're taking care of themselves. The ring is not the ideal anymore."

Other statistics bear out this point. In North America, single women are purchasing houses at a faster rate than single men. Three-quarters of never-married women own cars. They are also spending money on home renovation, entertainment, travel, even baby gear for the children they're having without husbands in increasing numbers. The old saw that husband equals security has been radically rewritten: now high income equals security.

Contrary to popular perception, the majority of single women are not twentysomethings waiting to get married. Rather, around the globe women are both delaying and avoiding marriage. In the U.S., the number of women living alone has increased more than 33 percent in the past fifteen years, to thirty million, and marriage rates are now at the lowest point in history. In the U.K., the number of first marriages is the lowest it has been for a century. One study, for the British Office for National Statistics, forecast that a quarter of all women will be single in Britain by the year 2020. Meanwhile, in Scandinavia, marriage rates have dropped by more than half since the 1950s. Australia's marriage rate is the lowest it has been in a hundred years, and it's estimated that as many as 45 percent of women now under thirty-five will never marry. The most dramatic increase in the number of unmarried women occurred in Japan, where the percentage of women who are single has risen by 50 percent over the last 15 years. Moreover, it is forecast that one in seven Japanese females born after 1980 will remain single throughout her life.

The steep decline in marriage rates in Japan is directly linked to the consumer ethic. Young women, known as "Parasite Singles," are unwilling to give up their careers and settle into life as subservient housewives, as remains the norm in that country. Instead, they continue to live with their parents while spending their salaries on Louis Vuitton bags, Eminem CDs, and dinners out with their girlfriends, just like the women on *Sex and the City*. As one Japanese woman told *The New York Times*, "'Mr. Right' can come later. I don't want to change my lifestyle or lower my standard of living."

The Intelligence Factory report capped a fifty-year trend in which consumerism was put forth as the "empowering" antidote to the confinements of marriage. For its origins we must return to the early 1950s, a time when men, not women, were encouraged to abandon their traditional, repressed gender roles. Husbands, not wives, were told to free themselves. The burgeoning husband liberation movement had as its bible *Playboy*, the revolutionary men's magazine that glorified bachelor life. From its first issue in December 1953, *Playboy* focused on the joys of material acquisition—owning a swank bachelor pad, the latest hi-fi system, a new sporty car, or dating a different woman every night.

The magazine preached an anti-marriage ideology long before the women's movement of the 1960s critiqued the role of the traditional wife. Its publisher, Hugh Hefner, who was twenty-seven when the first issue came out, was himself a disgruntled husband, married for four years and the father of a young daughter. The lead article, titled "Miss Gold Digger of 1953," complained about the unjust treatment of men in divorce courts, claiming that the "alimony deck is heavily stacked against any man in the game" and that "women married for profit."

Other pieces, such as "A Vote for Polygamy," reinforced the notion that marriage was undesirable for men. "What do we get out of monogamy?" the article asked. "Nerves, that's what we get. Anxiety states, manic depression, schizophrenia, hypertension, premature impotence, venereal diseases, and more than two million frigid, frustrated shrews."

Playboy reflected the dissent growing beneath the manicured green lawns of suburban life. Just as World War II had given both single and married women a taste of economic freedom, men who returned from the war found themselves under pressure to obtain government-sponsored home loans and start families. *Playboy* represented a flight from conventional obligation, an embrace of self-expression through material pleasure. Its publication also dovetailed with the decline of the sentiment that defined manhood as holding a job, being married, and supporting a wife. The new bachelor was linked to the social order not as a husband but as a consumer. The then-shocking prominence of naked women, or "Playmates," erased any doubt that the man who avoided marriage was anything but a red-blooded heterosexual.

The wife-free landscape was central to the idealized, air-brushed world *Playboy* presented. Like bridal magazines, the publication carried no advertising that conflicted with its artfully constructed fantasy. There were no ads for male balding products, obesity, or halitosis. A flip through now-archived early issues reveals that it was a harbinger of marital and social trends. A series of satirical articles titled "Selecting Your First Wife" foreshadowed the "trophy wife" phenomenon by decades, with its pronouncement: "The first wife, as opposed to the fiancée, must be practicable and serviceable. She is neither a toy nor an ornament nor a playmate. She will be your wife during the early, hard years before you can afford a staff of servants. She will serve as mother, cook, housemaid, chauffeur, nurse and charwoman." More than a decade before the women's movement, *Playboy* was griping that women were getting the upper hand in articles such as "The Womanization of America: An Embattled Male Takes a Look at What Was Once a Man's World."

Within months of its debut, the magazine's monthly circulation hit one million copies. In 1963, Gloria Steinem went undercover as a *Playboy* Bunny and published in *Show* magazine a scathing critique of the magazine's degradation of women. In response, thousands of women—many of whom made a living from various forms of male entertainment—responded with venom, not taking well to being told what they should do. What Steinem called degrading, they said, granted them a level of economic and sexual freedom that few women had previously experienced.

By then, single women were tapping into the consumer-based worldview propagated by the men's magazine. Their *Playboy* arrived in Helen Gurley Brown's book *Sex and the Single Girl,* published in 1962. Its very title was incendiary. Until the 1960s, single girls—"good" single girls, that is—saved themselves for marriage. The arrival of the Pill in 1960—which became fully available to single women by the end of the decade—forever changed that rule.

Previous books, Gurley Brown writes, "all treated the single girl like a scarlet-fever victim, a misfit." But *Sex and the Single Girl* fiercely defends her as "the newest glamour girl of our times." It claims a woman "is known by what she does rather than by whom she belongs to," urging her to "accept all the parts of your body as worthy and lovable," and to "reconsider the idea that sex without marriage is dirty."

The handbook's endorsement of perpetual female self-improvement set the template for the barrage of single-girl advice books and magazines to follow. It told women that no matter how poor or unattractive they might be, they must maximize their assets, from their physical appearances to their apartments. It advised women to build their own careers for both social status and money. A small stock portfolio, advised Gurley Brown, "is quite sexy."

Being sexy is the platonic ideal in the Gurley Brown universe, a place
where exclamation points are the preferred syntactical accessory. The
author has definite thoughts about what's sexy: "Clean hair is sexy. Lots
of hair is sexy, too. Skimpy little hair styles and hair under your arms,
on your legs and around your nipples, isn't sexy. Lovely lingerie is sexy.
And so is not wearing any!" She was equally sure about what is not sexy:
"food particles between your teeth, baggy stockings or pantyhose, bit-
ten fingernails, borrowing money (very unsexy), flesh not secured
firmly to the bone, and jitters (the dart-around, jerk-about kind that
makes people feel sand-papered)!"

Sex and the Single Girl presented marriage as a goal, though it also
made clear that if a woman didn't marry it wouldn't be the end of her
world. Gurley Brown told women that "most boyfriends don't want to
get married, so a fair amount of arm-twisting and ultimatum-giving is
necessary to close the deal." She provided living proof of her message,
rising above what she called her "mouseburger looks" and a hard-
scrabble childhood through a series of dead-end jobs to become a
successful advertising copywriter. In 1958, at age thirty-seven, she married David Brown, a successful movie producer.

By April 1963, *Sex and the Single Girl* had sold more than 150,000
copies, and Brown and her husband were busy drafting plans for a magazine aimed at the eighteen- to thirty-four-year-old single woman
with a career. In 1965, the Hearst Corporation bought the Browns' idea,
in hopes of reviving its flagging monthly *Cosmopolitan*. Helen Gurley
Brown was named editor in chief, and circulation soared. The magazine extolled the joys of single women's doing and having it all—
excelling at work, splurging on luxuries, beguiling men.

The single-woman market proved an advertisers' mecca that went far
beyond any specific magazine. Single women were eager to spend to
announce and celebrate their newfound independence. Reeling in a
man could be expensive, given the need for constant maintenance, new
clothes, fitness instruction, and the purchase of advice on how to catch
said man. Never mind that these spending patterns would by 2002
result in single women's constituting 40 percent of bankruptcy filings
in North America, the fastest-growing category of bankrupts.

Just as in the 1920s, advertisers appropriated the latest feminist demands for equality and freedom to make their wares appealing to women. In 1929, the American Tobacco Company attempted to induce women to smoke cigarettes in public places, a precursor of the "You've Come a Long Way, Baby" Virginia Slims campaign of the 1970s.

Here we shouldn't forget that unmarried women had been living alone, enjoying careers and relationships with men, since the nineteenth century, without the benefit of *Cosmopolitan* magazine. Female access to education and the workforce in the United States in the early to mid-nineteenth century even spawned a short-lived women's movement called "single blessedness," which celebrated single life. Among its advocates were Florence Nightingale, Louisa May Alcott, and Susan B. Anthony. Marriage continued to remain a female goal, but those who did not marry were seen as able to make a social contribution.

Even though women were breaking through education and career barriers, a woman without a husband in the late nineteenth and early twentieth centuries didn't fit neatly into the social jigsaw puzzle. She was seen to be unnatural, a man hater, even "afeminine," a term used to describe spinsters, many of whom were suspected to be lesbians. The unmarried woman was, as George Eliot described the unmarried Maggie Tulliver in *The Mill on the Floss,* "a small mistake of nature."

Well into the twentieth century, single women were treated by social science as "statistical deviants." In *The Second Sex,* published in 1949, Simone de Beauvoir wrote—in something of an exaggeration given the number of single women who then held jobs—that "for girls marriage is the only means of integration into the community, and if they remain unwanted, they are, socially viewed, so much wastage."

Unmarried women also presented a threat to the social order; they were playing outside the box, meaning that they didn't adhere to the rules governing wives. As Patricia O'Brien wrote in her 1974 study, *The Woman Alone,* the stigma experienced by single women stems in part from discomfort over the idea that an unmarried woman might feel complete without marriage and children: "Underlying all the criticisms and attacks on women along through history has been the uneasy fear that women who seek alternatives to marriage and motherhood might very well find them satisfying."

In the years following the publication of *Sex and the Single Girl,* the media depiction of the single woman experienced a 180-degree pendulum swing. Husbandless women were the ones having fun and leading fulfilling lives. Wives, on the other hand, were the new slaves, discussing their abusive husbands on television talk shows.

In 1966, the series *That Girl* introduced the first single woman on television who was not seeking a husband for self-definition, financial support, or social approbation. The comedy, which aired between 1966 and 1971, starred Marlo Thomas as an aspiring actress in her early twenties who leaves her parents' suburban home to find fame in New York. When Thomas proposed the idea to ABC-TV, male network executives wanted to give her character, Ann Marie, a surrogate family, to have her live with an aunt or a little brother. Thomas, whose production company owned the program and who herself was unmarried at the time, rejected that idea. She also made the radical announcement when the program began that her character would never get married. "If her story ended with marriage [young women] might think that that was the only way to have a happy ending," Thomas said years later.

Ann Marie, beautiful and fashionable, appealed to both men and women. She was ambitious, but never aggressive. Her constantly interfering father and devoted boyfriend, Donald, served as her protectors. Occasionally, the program dealt with the perils confronting single women (in one episode Ann Marie is mugged, in another she receives obscene telephone calls), but there was no mention of the sort of dangers that would later become prevalent in the depiction of single women. Ann Marie never met Mr. Goodbar. Nor were pregnancy scares an issue, given her seemingly chaste relationship with Donald.

Viewers also never witnessed Ann Marie in high anxiety over whether Donald would put an engagement ring on her finger. In the show's final season, the couple became engaged, though their wedding was never shown. To drive home the point that Ann Marie was foremost an emancipated woman, the program's last episode showed her taking Donald to a "women's lib" meeting.

That Girl was a huge ratings success, drawing a big female audience between the ages of eighteen and thirty-five. Young married women, in particular, tuned in to fantasize about the life they didn't have. Years after the show went off the air, Thomas commented on the viewer feedback: "It was amazing because we got so much mail. So much mail. Three thousand to five thousand letters a week! From young women saying, 'Oh, I know just how you feel. Don't get married to Donald! You just have to stay single. I'm married and I have two children and I'm twenty-three years old and I wish I was like you, in New York with a boyfriend....'"

The single girl as female role model was perpetuated by the character of Mary Richards on *The Mary Tyler Moore Show,* which went to air in September 1970. Audiences were familiar with Moore as the perky, capri-pant-wearing wife and mother Laura Petrie on *The Dick Van Dyke Show* between 1961 and 1966. Laura Petrie was the anti–Ann Marie, having given up a promising career as a dancer to marry and move to the suburbs. The single career woman on that program, comedy writer Sally Rogers, like Laura Petrie, was the product of a pre-feminist sensibility. Played by Rose Marie, Sally was a familiar single-woman cliché—a wisecracking career gal hardened by experience that made her sarcastic. She was desperate for a man but at the same time scared off suitors because she wasn't "feminine" enough. The depiction of the single working woman conformed to the post–World War II, back-to-the-house mentality that glorified the housewife and questioned the working woman. Before then, career women, like those played by Katharine Hepburn, Jean Arthur, and Rosalind Russell in the movies, were allowed to be feisty, content, and, yes, even attractive to men.

Mary Richards harked back to that tradition. The character, a single woman who moves to Minneapolis after ending an engagement, shared with Ann Marie an optimism about single life, reflected in the program's now-famous opening credits that show Moore throwing a beret in the air while the theme song proclaims: "You're going to make it after all." But Moore's character represented a subtle evolution from *That Girl.* She was in her thirties and unworried about snaring a husband. Though she had no shortage of male suitors, there was no steady boyfriend-protector. The program implied, though never expressly stated, that Mary Richards would have sex with a man she wasn't committed to. By the time the program went off the air in 1977, Mary showed no indication of heading to the altar.

Though Mary toiled in a male-dominated newsroom, her career didn't define her life, though her workmates came to form a surrogate family. Over the years, she was promoted, even though she always sat in the same desk and respectfully called her boss Mr. Grant while her male colleagues called him Lou. From time to time, gender inequity in the workforce made its way into story lines. In one episode, Mary confronts her boss after learning she earns $50 less a week than the man who held the job before her. In a matter-of-fact manner he explains that the inequity stemmed from the fact that she is a woman. Then, to reassure her, he says, "It has nothing to do with your work, Mary."

Moore, who in real life was married to Grant Tinker, the program's executive producer, also emerged as a role model for single women. So much so that Gloria Steinem invited Moore to accompany her to Washington in support of the ultimately unsuccessful Equal Rights Amendment in the early 1970s. Male politicians had expressed willingness to discuss the proposition provided that the television star be present.

That women could thrive, even perform superhuman acts, without husbands had become an entertainment staple by the late 1970s. Most lead female characters on television were "husband-free" or alpha wives like Maude Findlay, played by Bea Arthur on the program *Maude*. Many toiled in what were considered traditional male occupations—Angie Dickinson on *Police Woman*, the pinup "angels" of *Charlie's Angels*, and Lindsay Wagner in *The Bionic Woman*, a schoolteacher by day, undercover operative by night, outfitted with bionic legs, a bionic arm, and a bionic ear.

Divorce, unsurprisingly, was presented not as a shortcut to poverty but a shortcut to liberation, a phenomenon typified in *An Unmarried Woman*, Paul Mazursky's 1978 film. Jill Clayburgh plays Erica, a smart, stylish Upper East Side New Yorker and mother whose husband suddenly leaves her for another woman. When he announces his departure, she's so shattered that she vomits in the street. Of course, Erica eventually rises above her devastation, phoenixlike, with the assistance of therapy, a gaggle of supportive girlfriends, and the love of a sensitive, handsome, famous artist played by the British actor Alan Bates. But true to the ideal of self-sufficient womanhood vaunted in the '70s, Erica realizes that she needs to forge her own path, so she dumps the boyfriend. The movie's last scene shows the liberated heroine awkwardly navigating the cobbled streets of New York's SoHo carrying one of her former boyfriend's huge canvases against the wind. It's a memorable image, intended to convey her newly minted independence. Thirty years later, however, many women watching the movie would rightly ask, "What was she thinking? Why would she chuck a devoted man who loves her? What's wrong with having someone help you carry an unwieldy painting through the streets?"

Critics and audiences saw Erica as a bold new female prototype. Yet she wasn't when compared to the portrayal of divorcées in the 1920s and '30s, decades of female advancement. They were enlightened women, as depicted in the novel *Ex-Wife*, which was published anonymously in 1929 to great acclaim, selling more than 100,000 copies. Later printings revealed it to be the debut novel of Ursula Parrott, herself an ex-wife, who was then in between her first and second husbands (she'd end up having four).

The novel, set in a hedonistic New York during the Jazz Age, deals with a couple in a seemingly egalitarian marriage. Then the wife learns of her husband's infidelity. In retaliation, she sleeps with his best friend but learns a sexual double standard exists. When the husband discovers her infidelity, he can't accept it, and they divorce. She has fling after fling, and takes a glamorous, high-paying job. She even sleeps with her ex-husband on occasion, though she never contemplates reuniting with him. When she finally gets her divorce, she is philosophical: "It is so silly to mind. Just an incident in the career of a Modern Woman. What the hell!" She eventually marries a pal and sets off on a round-the-world cruise, hoping to run into her new true love, who is married, and stationed in Japan. (Predictably, Hollywood slapped a conventional happy ending on the story when the book was made into the movie *The Gay Divorcée,* starring Norma Schearer; in that version, the wife tracks down her husband in Paris and they reunite.)

Just as the portrayal of divorced women seemed more advanced in the early decades of the twentieth century, so too did the notion of the single-woman careerist. The sassy, smart single career women of the 1930s and '40s had been replaced by the hard-bitten, driven, and unbalanced professional unable to sustain a healthy personal life. We saw the prototype in the 1987 movie *Baby Boom,* in which Diane Keaton plays super-yuppie J. C. Wiatt. J. C., with her gender-ambiguous name, is an ambitious, competent executive whose life is thrown into turmoil when she inherits a baby from a distant relative. Her lack of maternal skill is played for laughs. She's so inept that she checks the baby with a coat-check clerk during a business meeting. The movie's happy resolution occurs only when J. C. quits her high-powered job, leaves the city, starts an organic baby food business, and takes up with a sensitive veterinarian.

J. C. was the warm-up act for Murphy Brown, the fictional star of the popular television comedy that began its ten-season run in 1988. Like *The Mary Tyler Moore Show, Murphy Brown* was set in a television newsroom. But Murphy, a veteran star reporter of a weekly magazine series, played by Candice Bergen, wasn't a sweet-tempered pleaser. She was aggressive, sarcastic, and driven. A reformed alcoholic, she had one marriage behind her as well as a stint at the Betty Ford Center. When the character gets pregnant at age forty-two, she rejects two proposals and chooses to raise the child alone, though, like J. C. Wiatt, her negligible maternal instinct became the source of humor.

Still, the character's refusal to conform to the conservative political agenda was disquieting to the conservative status quo. Dan Quayle, then the vice president to George Bush, was apoplectic over the prospect that the program might glamorize the unmarried mother. "It doesn't help matters when prime-time TV has Murphy Brown, a character who supposedly epitomizes today's intelligent, highly paid professional woman, mock the importance of fathers by bearing a child alone and calling it just another lifestyle choice," he said. (To that, the *Murphy Brown* producer Diane English quipped, "If he believes that a

woman cannot adequately raise a child without a father, then he'd better make sure abortion remains safe and legal.") Had Quayle watched
the program, he would have seen it, in fact, as an invective against single
parenting: Murphy was ludicrously inept, a sop to the notion perpetrated by Hollywood that a woman can't be both professionally and
domestically competent.

Having children out of wedlock was only one way the single woman
defied the social order. Increasingly, she was presented as a lawbreaking
predator. The first strains of this theme underlined television's most
celebrated prime-time cliffhanger—the "Who Shot J. R.?" episode of
the top-rated *Dallas*, which aired in 1980—which featured a wronged
single woman who gunned down her villainous brother-in-law
J. R. Ewing after he got her pregnant. She received her comeuppance,
though, when she was found murdered in a swimming pool.

By the end of 1980s, the demented, bunny-boiling Alex Forrest in
Fatal Attraction was routinely held up as a symbol of cultural backlash
against the single-woman careerist. There would be others to come,
such as the hard-bodied, ambitious Meredith Johnson played by Demi
Moore in the 1994 movie *Disclosure*, who sexually harasses a happy family man played by Michael Douglas, an actor increasingly cast as the
victim of predatory single female characters.

While television programs of the 1980s might seem like ancient history, keep in mind that the girls who watched them during their teenage
years would be the very ones targeted by the wedding industrial complex in the 1990s. As one woman who married briefly during the mid-
1990s complained to me, she had no wife role models growing up. She
knew she had no intention of being the housebound wife her mother
had been. But she also wanted the connection provided by marriage.
"When I was growing up, my role model was Murphy Brown," she says.
"And here I was, all of a sudden, married. There was not going to be
cooking and cleaning in my future. I mean, I kept my apartment neat
and I knew how to feed myself. But I wasn't going to be like my mother,
who kept the house, and had three kids and did everything for them."

By the 1990s, the depiction of single women on television had
descended into silly stereotyping. As one study pointed out, single

female characters were dichotomously depicted as "pathetic leftovers from the marriage market," unhappy and desperate, or "power-obsessed barracudas bent only on greedily acquiring the empty rewards of money and fame." The yuppie domestic drama *thirtysome-thing*, a harbinger of the divisive factions brewing in the culture, was famously emblematic of this dichotomy, as it presented a serene, idealized stay-at-home wife and mother, Hope, in stark contrast to striving, harsh, and frustrated single female characters. One, Ellen, was a driven yuppie with no personal life. Another, Melissa, was a struggling photographer who experienced surreal dreams about her biological clock, a trope that would reappear in *Ally McBeal* years later.

Single women whose lives did not revolve around their careers were similarly stigmatized. They were adrift and self-obsessed, like the central character in *The Days and Nights of Molly Dodd*, which aired during the 1987–88 season and was later revived by the Lifetime network. Molly was an attractive, divorced woman in her thirties living in New York who spent all of her time musing about herself, her love life, her goals, her ever-changing career. She had an unplanned pregnancy, not knowing who the father was.

The only single women able to escape the typecasting, ironically, were lesbians. And that was because they were finally socially acceptable, as "hot" marketable commodities. During the 1970s, lesbians were elevated by radical feminists as the ultimate fishes who didn't need bicycles. Occasionally, they were shown to lure women away from their husbands, as in Woody Allen's 1979 film *Manhattan*, in which Meryl Streep plays an angry feminist who leaves her inadequate husband for another woman. By the late 1980s, lesbianism within the culture was less an ideology than a gimmick to tantalize mass-market audiences. Madonna and Sandra Bernhard let it be known on network television that they were "an item." *L.A. Law* and *Roseanne* drew huge audiences with well-publicized kisses between female characters. In 1993, both *Newsweek* and *New York* heralded "lesbian chic" as a trend, not unlike the latest tapas bar or aerobics instructor. The cover of *Vanity Fair* served up Male Fantasy 101 as the lesbian singer k.d. lang sat in a barber's chair being shaved by the model Cindy Crawford in a skimpy bathing suit and stiletto boots.

That same year, *Rolling Stone*'s annual "Hot List" named lesbians "The Hot Subculture," gushing, "You're in if you're out." These "hot" lesbians conformed to socially acceptable standards of female desirability. They were "feminine," cast as "glamour dykes" or "lipstick lesbians." Universities were suddenly full of young women known as LUGs (lesbians until graduation), who toyed with their primal urges. Porn merchants picked up the idea and ran to the bank, selling male viewers on the idea that women left to themselves would fall on each other with a powerful lust.

In retrospect, the creation of lesbian chic was a harbinger of the way single women generally were integrated into the consumer infrastructure in the 1990s. In the case of heterosexual single women, however, their integration was even more insidious in that it asked them literally to buy into imagery that presented them as desperate to marry. The Cinderella myth, coupled with repeated messages that professional success did not bring happiness, had coalesced into what would become the clichéd form of the frustrated, lonely, incomplete single woman. By the mid-1990s, just when mystique chic was taking grip, the single-woman optimism exuded by Ann Marie was running on empty.

Replacing Ann Marie and Mary Richards was a fleet of fictional single women inspired by Bridget Jones, the protagonist of Helen Fielding's blockbuster *Bridget Jones's Diary*. Bridget, a neurotic, self-flagellating, thigh- and marriage-obsessed but oh-so-lovable mess, originated in Fielding's column in the British newspaper *The Independent*. Her story began as a send-up of that tired tale women had been fed for years by glossy magazines, television, and self-help tomes—the one about the single career woman who, rapidly approaching thirty, goes into a marriage frenzy. True to the women's magazine format that encourages constant self-improvement, Bridget routinely begins her diary with a to-do list, including "develop inner poise and authority and sense of self as woman of substance, complete, without boyfriend, as best way to obtain boyfriend." She methodically catalogs her intake of alcohol units, calories, and Silk Cut cigarettes.

But as frivolous as Bridget appeared, she resonated with women. She was real, her hopes often dashed as she so eagerly looked for love.

The book's dominant image—Bridget's fear of "dying alone and being found three weeks later half-eaten by an Alsatian"—is dire. But it was the movie version of the novel that contained the scene intended to summon up every single woman's worst nightmare. A pajama-clad Bridget, alone in her squalid flat, performs a drunken lip-synch to that mournful easy-listening ode "All by Myself." All the while, the television set flickering in the background plays the classic *Fatal Attraction* scene in which Alex attempts to murder the serene domestic goddess Beth.

Fielding deftly captures the mythic friction between the happily married woman and the miserable single woman exploited in *Fatal Attraction*. She revives the eighteenth-century term *singletons* to describe the lower caste of the unmarried and coins the expression *smug marrieds* to describe self-satisfied couples who treat their single friends with condescending sympathy. She also wisely ends the novel on a Cinderella note as Bridget finally snags her Prince Charming, Mark Darcy.

The American Bridget appeared soon after in the emaciated form of Ally McBeal. Ally was Bridget Jones with a law degree. The antithesis of the domineering Murphy Brown, she was a high-strung waif who wore micro-minis in court and saw hallucinations of a dancing baby. The character, played by the actress Calista Flockhart, consults the how-to-land-a-man guide *The Rules*. She complains to her roommate, after a chaste second date with a hot prospect, "I am a sexual object, for God's sake! He couldn't give me a little grope?" When a guy dumps her, she whines to a colleague, "All I wanted was to be rich and successful and to have three kids and a husband who would wait at home to tickle my feet, and look at me—I don't even like my hair!"

Critics praised her insecurity as adorable. One male *TV Guide* writer called *Ally McBeal* "everything that I want in a series (and that any man would want in a woman)...." A San Francisco newspaper critic declared, "Like Moore's Mary Richards, Flockhart's Ally McBeal beams an alluring blend of strength and delicacy." Joyce MacMillan, writing in *Salon*, was more critical: "*Ally McBeal* suggests that women today are so beyond feminism that we've come out the other side—it's strong to be self-diminishing, smart to be indecisive, brave to be a wimp."

Ally was ridiculous, sleeping in children's pajamas and dancing with an imaginary baby. But there was also a truth to her. She was a work in progress. Her aloneness had texture. She presented as the perfect antidote to the threatening single-woman careerist who had dominated movie and television screens. Yet she too was an extreme, perfect for prime time but not to be taken seriously. You wouldn't know that, however, given her constant deconstruction by media that treated her as if she were real.

The next totems of single-woman existence arrived in the form of the women from *Sex and the City*. The program, which went to air in 1998, was based on Candace Bushnell's long-running *New York Observer* column, a commentary on the sex lives of Manhattan's media elite that was turned into a best-selling novel. The women whose lives were detailed in the column, including Bushnell herself, didn't share Bridget's fondness for whining over personal deficiencies. They had it all figured out, or so they thought. "We all sat back smugly, sipping tea, like we were members of some special club," Bushnell writes. "We were hard and proud of it, and it hadn't been easy to get to this point, this place of complete independence where we had the luxury of treating men like sex objects. It had taken hard work, loneliness, and the realization that, since there might never be anyone there for you, you had to take care of yourself in every sense of the word."

Even though all the women are white and affluent—a recurring theme in the depiction of single women—they each have their own personalities and wants. Carrie Bradshaw, the program's narrator, writes a newspaper column about sexual mores and falls in and out of love affairs; Charlotte York, an art gallery manager when she does work, makes no bones about wanting to marry well (her first fairy-tale wedding is followed in short order by divorce; she converts to Judaism for her second marriage); Samantha Jones, a successful publicist with a sex life Hugh Hefner would envy, has no desire to marry; and Miranda Hobbes is a cynical attorney who ends up having a child out of wedlock, though she later marries the father. *Sex and the City* was an instant hit, serving up a female fantasy in a luxury landscape. It was Helen Gurley Brown's *Sex and the Single Girl* updated and brought to cable.

The pink Cosmopolitan cocktails regularly imbibed by the characters, in fact, pay homage to Gurley Brown's magazine. Indeed, Gurley Brown was herself the subject of a fashion renaissance when her original single-girl field guide was reissued in 2003.

The characters grappled with the inconsistencies surrounding the role of wife as reflected in the wedding industrial complex, Cinderella simplex, the allure of mystique chic, the desire to connect, and the stigmas surrounding dependence. On the 2000 season premiere, the pervasive female rescue fantasy was acknowledged. The scene takes place over brunch; the conversation turns to why firemen are so appealing to women. "It's because women just want to be rescued," suggests Charlotte. Immediately after uttering the line, she reacts with shame. "I'm sorry," she continues, "but I've been dating since I was fifteen. I'm exhausted. Where is he?" Sarah Jessica Parker, as the narrator, intones: "There it was. The sentence independent single women in their thirties are never supposed to think, let alone speak." But how "independent" were these women if they "were never supposed to think, let alone speak" of a given subject? Had we created a species of Stepford unwives, unable to express loneliness or vulnerability?

Antipathy toward becoming a wife was made clear during an episode in which Carrie finds an engagement ring in a boyfriend's gym bag. Her reaction? Not to squeal in excitement but rather to run to the sink to vomit. Whether her nausea is the result of the thought of becoming a wife or revulsion over the unfashionable pear-shaped diamond ring is never said, though it's suggested the ring is the culprit. In an exchange with her girlfriends, Carrie expresses doubts: "How can I marry a guy who doesn't know which ring is me?" To which Samantha responds, "Exactly, honey. Wrong ring, wrong guy." By the program's end, however, Carrie says yes after the boyfriend upgrades the ring to a Harry Winston emerald-cut three-carat diamond. But the wedding never does take place. Carrie ends up suffering a panic attack when trying on an elaborate wedding dress and calls the relationship off. It was ironic. More than twenty years after *An Unmarried Woman* depicted a wife losing a husband throwing up, a single woman facing the prospect of gaining a husband reacts the same way. Some might see this as progress. What it was, in fact, was the reverse side of the coin.

While the fictional *Sex and the City* women were prancing about a fairy-tale landscape, actual unmarried women were creating a new grid, one that is redefining family and motherhood. The Intelligence Factory report that gushed about single women being "the new yuppies" drew attention to this fact in its prognostication that "the term 'family' will cease to be limited to people tied to one another by blood or marriage and will be extended to include friends, pets, and even online virtual communities." This was not breaking news by the year 2000, when the study was released. We'd been watching non-blood-related "families" in life and on television for decades, from *Kate & Allie* to *The Golden Girls* to *Friends* and *Sex and the City*.

That said, most of the women on these programs were presented as in a holding pattern, waiting for Mr. Right. In reality, women were not waiting for husbands to make pivotal life decisions. The most dramatic example of this was the extreme rise in the number of unmarried mothers. The 2000 U.S. census indicated that the number of single mothers had grown 25 percent since 1990 to more than 7.5 million households. Almost one-third of babies were born to unmarried women, compared with less than 4 percent in 1940, when access to birth control was limited.

In the United Kingdom, 38 percent of all babies are born outside of marriage. British women are increasingly spurning the fathers of their children by refusing to put their names on birth certificates. Government statistics reveal that thousands of children are officially "fatherless" because mothers wish to bring them up alone and avoid possible claims for child custody. The number of women who have registered births without declaring paternity has doubled since the late 1970s, according to the Office of National Statistics. One in five women over age thirty who gives birth does not register the father's name. In the Scandinavian countries, almost half of single women are known as "free agent mothers," women who choose to have children outside the framework of marriage but are still in committed relationships.

Single parents in Europe—who are generally far better off economically than their counterparts in the United States—have become a potent political force. Policies enacted in the past two decades by many European governments include legislation ensuring that children born out of wedlock have the same inheritance rights as other children and providing financial grants to the children of single parents. In Britain, a special tax break for married couples has been removed and replaced by an increase in cash allowances for families with children.

The focus is on the children, not on the couple, which might be seen as a solution for the common specter of marital, and thus family, breakdown in North America. If the primary bond is between parent and child, dislocation between the parents should affect the children as deeply, at least in theory. As Kathleen Kiernan, a professor of social policy and demography at the London School of Economics, remarks, "They've taken the marital status out of it and focused on the children." In Scandinavia, highly complicated living and custodial arrangements between partners, children, and former couples are common. "We have little commitment to the institution of marriage, that's true, but we do have a commitment to parenthood," said Kari Moxnes, a professor of sociology at the University of Trondheim. "It's not socially acceptable anymore in Scandinavia to break the parental relationship."

The fact is that most single women don't conform to the either-or dualities that still dominate their depiction—that they either are marriage-hungry thirtysomethings or part of the 60 percent of single mothers who live in poverty, struggling to stay afloat.

A hunger for more realistic voices of single women exists, as was made apparent by the success of the Irish writer Nuala O'Faolain. As O'Faolain writes in her memoir, *Are You Somebody? The Accidental Memoir of a Dublin Woman*, she knew early on that marriage was not for her, though she couldn't see another path: "I'd spent my whole adult life on the errand that smoothed the way to being a woman in the home—a search for a man, for love, for the one man to love and be loved by and have babies with—without wanting to be a woman in the home." She won scholarships to University College Dublin and then Oxford. Her love life was both rich and varied. The art critic Clement Greenberg was a lover. Another was the esteemed literary critic Leslie Fiedler. She also had a long-term relationship with a leading Irish feminist.

O'Faolain never sugarcoats. She calls her thirties "a wasteland of misery and loss and mourning and drinking." She learned to drive a car at forty, and was given the op-ed column in *The Irish Times* that made her famous in her homeland at forty-seven. She took her first swimming lesson at fifty, wrote her memoir, a surprise best seller, at fifty-five, and published her first novel at sixty.

O'Faolain writes candidly of her fears of aging and loneliness, two cultural stigmas that confront single women with brutality. There is no Botox in this picture. The lesson she teaches is that every choice taken entails pain and sacrifice. In her memoir she speaks of being so lonely that her skin aches. "I can't wait to be an old lady," she told *The New York Times Magazine*. "I'm dying to wither up so I can stop hurting."

While single women are carving out their own reality, improvising their lives, they are routinely targeted by marketing intended to inspire them to conform, to marry, and to spend. In effect, single women are being asked to buy into imagery that reduces them to marriage-hungry stereotypes not seen since the 1950s. The success of *Bridget Jones's Diary* spawned the "chick lit" genre. It subscribed to the notion that all educated white women just under or over age thirty are restless in jobs for which they're overqualified or undermotivated, frantically hungry for the love of men, making continual muddles of their lives, but certain that marriage, motherhood, and slender thighs hold the answer.

Life imitated art as real women fretted that their currency on the marriage market diminished after thirty. "I wouldn't want to be 35 and looking for a husband," a young woman was quoted in "Early to Wed," a July 16, 1997, *New York* magazine piece that focused on the trend of wealthy, Ivy League–educated young women to marry straight out of college. These were women who had had sex by age fifteen, who had done their clubbing by twenty, and just wanted to settle down. The 2002 documentary *The Hamptons* presented Jacqueline Lipson, a matrimonial attorney, on a perpetual prowl for a husband: "I need to be engaged by twenty-nine—because otherwise I will not be married by 30," she announces. In the documentary *Always a Bridesmaid,* the wedding videographer Nina Davenport confesses that she feels jealous of the brides she photographs. Her big fear is becoming a "spinster." "I feel my time is running out," she says. "And I'm turning thirty."

Davenport's spinster reference was not isolated. By the late 1990s, the term was returning to the media, showing up in *Flare* magazine's "The New Spinster" story and in the headline for a review of the 2003 movie *Swimming Pool,* which starred a bookish fiftyish writer played by Charlotte Rampling sparring with a gorgeous young teenager played by Ludivine Sagnier: "Sex Kitten vs Spinster," it read.

The anxiety, predictably, was fueled and capitalized on by the sector that had the most to gain from it—the wedding industrial complex. A print advertisement for Manor Jewelers that ran in 2000 featured a beatific bride, praying. Above her, the copy read: "Luxury items: Princess cut diamond engagement ring. Never having to date again." Below the bride, in smaller print, the message read: "Which is the greater luxury—The fiery brilliance of a three-stone diamond engagement ring? Or packing your bags and moving out of singlehood? It's your luxury. We just help inspire it."

Also helping women on the journey out of "singlehood" was the emerging library of how-to-snare-a-husband guides that reverted to a post–World War II mentality. The prototype, of course, was the 1996 handbook *The Rules,* written by two Long Island housewives. Shrewdly, authors Ellen Fein and Sherrie Schneider recognized that dating had become confusing, shrouded in "who asks?"/"who pays?" dilemmas. Their solution was to reduce courtship rituals to easy-to-follow mathematical principles. Don't talk to him for more than ten minutes at a time on the telephone. Don't accept a date for Saturday after Wednesday. For every four e-mails he sends you, send him one. Let him pay for everything for the first three months. If he doesn't commit after two years of dating, ditch him. Women were instructed to employ Pavlovian conditioning techniques, even to get plastic surgery if necessary until they "closed the deal," also known as getting him down the aisle.

Critics lambasted the book's retrograde advice. But its man-is-by-nature-the-aggressor-who-must-be-trained mindset hit a nerve at a time of confused gender roles. *The Rules* sold more than two million copies in twenty-seven languages. It was followed in 1997 with *The Rules II: More Rules to Live and Love By*. The Princess of Wales, not a paragon in matters romantic, was said to have been a fan, which sent sales soaring. Carolyn Bessette Kennedy, too, was said to have employed *Rules*-style tactics to snare John F. Kennedy, Jr.

The Rules became a franchise. Its authors set up a $250-an-hour consulting service and cut a swath through the talk-show circuit, treating their advice as if it were science. "*The Rules* work," Schneider told a reporter. "It's the truth, like the laws of physics or gravity." As for their credentials, the former stay-at-home moms could offer only that they themselves were blissfully wed. "A *Rules* marriage is forever," they crowed, echoing De Beers' famous slogan.

Book number three, *The Rules III: Time-Tested Secrets for Making Your Marriage Work*, was scheduled for publication in spring 2001. The schedule hit a snag, however, when it became public that Ellen Fein was divorcing her husband of sixteen years on grounds of abandonment. Warner Books, anticipating another hit, had planned an initial print run of 100,000 copies. The publisher was forced to replace printed covers that crowed about the authors' marital track records: "Ellen and Sherrie, two long-time married women themselves, know that just because you've married the man of your dreams doesn't mean your work has ended; good marriages don't happen by accident."

A glimpse into how much drudgery may have been involved in Fein's alleged wedded bliss was foreshadowed in an interview she gave to *The Edmonton Sun* in 1997. She advised women to have sex with their husbands even if they didn't feel like it. "It doesn't take a lot of energy to have sex as a woman," she said. "I mean, what do you have to do?" She then counseled women to be stoic in the boudoir: "You have to look at it like things could be worse. I could have just gotten hit by a train."

One has to ask, What is the point? To snare Mr. Right, according to Fein and Schneider, women must downplay their cleverness, set an egg timer every time he calls, and submit to elective surgery until he forks over the Rock of Gibraltar and a marriage proposal. Thereafter, they must keep their complaints to themselves, tend to their long hair, and lie there, limp, during sex, reassuring themselves all the while that it's better than being mowed down by heavy machinery. And even then, there's no guarantee he won't abandon you. This is what *The Rules* gets you? Yet the market for snag-a-husband advice modeled on *The Rules* appears insatiable. The fall 2003 publishing season, for example, brought *Why Men Marry Some Women and Not Others,* which was billed as "just like *The Rules* but with research."

The return to the 1950s mentality that married women should "surrender" to their husbands is echoed in the recurring recommendation that single women "surrender" to their femininity. Successful professional women are told to mask their aggressiveness if they want to snag, and keep, a husband. In *Secrets of Relationship Success,* Vanessa Lloyd Platt, a London divorce lawyer, cites women's aggressive behavior as the chief reason behind the increase in British divorce rates. She reports that her evidence comes from her disgruntled male clients who "cannot cope with the way in which women are emasculating men today with their aggressive, demanding behaviour." According to Lloyd Platt, single women today don't want to be single. "To attract a man and keep him, women must develop their feminine side," she says. "When they leave the workplace and come home, they must switch into feminine mode. Otherwise, the men in their lives feel too threatened to stay in the relationship."

British women report reverting to Traditional Dating 101. Ursula Penn-Simkins, a single thirty-seven-year-old, admitted to *The Telegraph* newspaper that she would never telephone a man. "When I have done it in the past, it has been disastrous," she said. "Men don't like it if we take the initiative. I think it is an evolutionary thing: Men like demure women."

In such a climate, young women feel free to vent their sugar-daddy fantasies. Being "kept" is presented as a highly desirable female goal. "Of course, men have to pay and buy you presents. Men have to spoil you. You have to be spoiled," Mimi Valcin, who is twenty-six and works in public relations, told the *National Post.* "If you don't think you're a princess you're not going to be treated like one. It's the new feminism to say, 'I'm expensive. I need a lot of attention. I need men to bend over backwards for me.'" Another twenty-six-year-old woman quoted in the article claimed, "I love being taken care of. I love it when he takes control." After she got engaged, she said, and when she was still working, her fiancé took her paycheck from her and put her on a budget. "Of course, we all know, women can get any job they want and choose any career they want to pursue," she said. "Now, it seems, it's only a matter of if—if we want a job or if we want to be princesses."

A few women are so eager to depart from their single status that they willingly plonk down $9,600 for instruction on how to increase the odds of becoming a wife. That's the fee of a six-month seminar by the Manhattan psychotherapist Marilyn Graman titled "Marriage Works—A Step-by-Step Intensive Program Designed to Lead You Down the Aisle." Graman, a fifty-three-year-old widow who refers to herself as "a former angry feminist," shrewdly saw the market for such a course. She noticed that younger women were confusing softness and tenderness with weakness. Their tough demeanors, she concluded, were preventing them from becoming wives. It is only half-jokingly that she refers to the course as "The Marilyn Graman Finishing School for Feminists."

Graman says she's not asking women to change who they are but to recast how they present themselves. And this is accomplished via instruction styled like an army boot camp. The seminar is divided into study units—forty hours devoted to why participants might have a "relationship block"; twenty-six hours to talk with a "guidess," a relationship coach-cum-cheerleader who has already reaped the fruits of a Graman course; and eleven hours with an interior decorator who visits the women's homes to determine the "man readiness" of their living space in terms of color, furniture placement, even energy flow.

The hundreds of participants who have registered in the course also receive a consultation with an image consultant, attend a weekend workshop that teaches the women how to be "nicer" to be around, plus two question-and-answer sessions with a panel of men who field queries on what they find attractive. Nine hours are spent on teaching the women to move gracefully, eight on softening one's wardrobe, and three and a half on the art of gracious gift receiving. The women are also expected to attend two parties, which are treated as a laboratory of sorts for students to watch and learn about themselves. The finale is a field trip to a bridal shop, where women try on dresses and visualize their wedding day.

Women who have subjected themselves to Graman's drill talked about the stigma they felt being single. "Being older and single—there is so much shame associated with it," said Miriam Nelson-Gillett, a thirty-nine-year-old woman who met her future husband at one of Graman's seminars. "You think there's something wrong with you— there is a lot of humiliation about the whole thing."

Even the hoary joke from the 1950s that women attended college for their "MRS" degree was turned on its head as one inventive female Harvard MBA took the lessons of marketing and employed them in the marriage market. In *Find a Husband After 35: A Simple 15-Step Action Program Using What I Learned at Harvard Business School*, published in 2003, Rachel Greenwald tells women to create a brand for themselves as if they are products.

Older women looking for a husband are told to make the quest their number-one priority; those who can afford to do so are even advised to quit work for a year. Everything else in their lives—work, children, family, friends, pets—must come second. The program also dictates candidates' budgets—10 percent, optimally 20 percent, of their annual incomes on their marital campaigns—for grooming, dating services, parties, and the like. Borrow the money if necessary, the author implores: "Remember, after age 35, it's 'Marriage 911.' This is an emergency!"

A panic mentality reigns. In 2003, Barbara Dafoe Whitehead published *Why There Are No Good Men Left: The Romantic Plight of the New Single*. The title, clearly intended to inspire alarm, was misleading. Unmarried men outnumber unmarried women, if only slightly. Yet, as usual, single women are presented as being more desperate than men: "It is this pervasive anxiety on the part of unmarried women that explains the current popularity of such movies, television shows and books as *Bridget Jones's Diary, Sex and the City* and *Cowboys Are My*

Weakness," said Dafoe Whitehead, director of the National Marriage Project, in an interview. That the reverse might be the case—that media fuel the anxiety—was not considered.

In the 1990s, just as wives were being sold the romanticization of Victorian domesticity, the unwife was facing the romanticization of a Regency courtship ritual. The novelist Jane Austen was elevated to a dating arbiter, with a dash of Cinderella thrown in. (We must note here that the godmother of chick lit herself never married, despite having been asked.) The formula was writ large in *Bridget Jones's Diary,* a sly retelling of Austen's *Pride and Prejudice,* down to the fact that the hero is also called Mr. Darcy.

The message is clear. Single women are told they have to choose between "the glass ceiling and the glass slipper, the power limo and the pumpkin carriage," as Ruth Kemply put it in *The Washington Post* in 2002. This dichotomy was made explicit that year in the film *Kate and Leopold,* starring Meg Ryan and Hugh Jackman. Ryan plays Kate, an ambitious, never-married executive in a market research firm. Outside work, her life is barren. Close to forty, she's cynical about her prospects for love, having just broken up with her upstairs neighbor, Stuart, a boyish inventor. ("I wasted my best years on you," she accuses him. "Those were your best years?" is his caustic rejoinder.)

Stuart is presented as a genius who has discovered a portal below the Brooklyn Bridge that permits him to travel through time. On a journey back to 1876, he encounters Leopold, the 3rd Duke of Albany, a British aristocrat living in New York, who, in a fluke accident, returns with him to the twenty-first century. What ensues is a comedy of manners centered on how few manners exist in contemporary society. But the tall, dark, and dishy Victorian offers more than impeccable deportment; he's capable, cultured, kind, and strong—presumably the antidote to the modern man. He's a hero, literally sweeping Kate onto a white steed in order to foil a purse snatching. He prepares a rooftop dinner, which is serenaded by a violinist. He even makes breakfast for Kate, a gesture of male kindness so rare in her life that she weeps.

And all the while he remains the perfect gentleman. The pair waltz, kiss, and cuddle relentlessly. When, after making her dinner, he carries her off to bed, it's to tuck her in. When she murmurs for him to stay, he remains fully clothed and they snuggle off to sleep. The character was served up and received as the new female fantasy—a man who can cook, wash up, and slay metaphorical dragons.

Any attempts to distinguish modern women from Victorian women prove laughable. "Women are different now," Stuart warns Leopold. "They're dangerous." You wouldn't know it from watching this movie. Like Bridget Jones and Ally McBeal, Kate is a danger only to herself. She possesses little professional confidence and no domestic skills; the dinner she prepares is inedible. She is graceless, treating Leopold's civility with disdain, and clumsy, repeatedly stumbling, once in the middle of a major presentation at work. When Kate is finally awarded her long-anticipated promotion, she blows it off. In what appears to be a suicide attempt, she jumps off the Brooklyn Bridge; as the movie presents it, she's passing through the time portal to join Leopold in 1876 Victorian England, just in time to have him announce their marriage.

It's possible such a romanticized portrayal of the rescued single woman might have something to do with the fact that many of the women who write such scripts tend to be single themselves. As the Hollywood producer Lynda Obst points out in *Hello, He Lied,* many of the female screenwriters in Hollywood are unmarried and thus see marriage in fantasy terms. Obst presents Hollywood as mirroring middle America in terms of its conservatism: "underneath all of the pseudodecadence, Hollywood is really a very conventional place. Its daring pioneers, role models to many, those aggressive women in charge of their careers, are largely at home at night, in bed with a script, lamenting their loss of a picket fence. No matter how successful the woman, and often the more successful the woman, her dreams of a nuclear family die hard."

Most insidiously, marketers have fostered single-woman insecurity by repackaging it with a mantra of empowerment, independence, and well-being. According to the Intelligence Factory study, "targeting this demographic, advertisers are beginning to appeal to single women's aspirations of freedom and independence. Single women respond to advertising messages that respect their intelligence, honor a myriad of lifestyle choices, and affirm their self-esteem and independent spirit."

Pandering to the fantasy of independence was evident in a British television commercial for the Volkswagen Golf model that aired in 1993, a few months after Diana and Prince Charles separated. A radiant blond woman who could have been a Diana double leaves a town-house to the noise of a cheering crowd. She blows kisses, dodges confetti, then drives off with a smug little smile in a car with a "Just Divorced" sign affixed to the back. The symbolism is obvious. You don't have to put up with an unhappy marriage, ladies. And if you divorce, you will emerge looking terrific, twirling new car keys, and, best of all, finally in the driver's seat. The spot was a huge hit with both single and married women who saw it as celebrating single female independence and optimism.

The brokerage firm Charles Schwab played with the conflict between independence and fantasy when it hired its own former fairy-tale princess, Sarah Ferguson, to star in a series of print and television ads targeted at single women called "Financial security doesn't have to be a fairy tale." A 2002 television spot titled "One Day Your Knight Will ..." begins with a woman's voiceover telling a little girl a bedtime story. The little girl is told that when she grows up into a beautiful young lady, her "knight will come on a great white stallion" and sweep her off her feet. The knight will take her to his castle, marry her, and give her anything her "heart desires forever and ever." Viewers are shown the knight on the white stallion and the gigantic castle in the mist. The camera returns to the young girl's face, full of excitement and anticipation. Suddenly, though, the music stops and the beautiful woman, shrugging at us, pulls away from her wonderful knight. The viewer then sees that the story-teller is the former Duchess of York, who says, "Of course, if it doesn't work out, you'll need to understand the difference between a P/E ratio and a dividend yield...." Fast, upbeat music drowns out the dreamy romantic theme. The viewer is placed in front of a computer screen along with Ferguson, who appears suddenly to be much too busy to tell a silly fairy tale. A narrator has now assumed Ferguson's former role of financial guru. The message is that women want money, and that the most effective way of getting it is not hooking up with a knight but rather understanding the stock market.

Other ads play off the theme of insecurity and marriage lust advanced by single-girl lit. Even De Beers, the company that made the diamond engagement ring a romantic imperative, recognized the burgeoning single-gal market as a lucrative target. In a clever marketing twist, the company fashioned a campaign that transformed an entrenched symbol of wifedom into one of independence: "Who needs a husband when you can buy yourself two studs?" was the bold tagline of one of its ads. Another ad featured an image of a silhouetted woman wearing a diamond solitaire necklace with the copy "It beckons me as I pass the store window. A flash of light in the corner of my eye. I stop. I turn. We look at each other. And though I'm usually not that kind of girl, I take it home." The copy recasts diamond shopping as an illicit assignation, the single woman still protesting that she's "not usually that kind of girl." The point, of course, is that in buying a diamond for herself, flaunting her financial independence, she is "that kind of girl," one who doesn't conform to the wifely role. Most recently, De Beers has added another product to its roster of diamonds for the single gal: the right-hand ring. What it's meant to substitute for is all too clear.

These campaigns appear to affirm self-sufficiency. Yet both De Beers and the women who take in its advertisements are aware that the company has built its reputation and its fortunes by selling engagement rings. The underlying assumption for all these advertisements is that marriage is the norm. As a result, the single gal can't help being reminded of her marital status: she's the outsider. What's reinforced is not her independence but her singleness.

Ads that appear to celebrate young single women's happy confidence in fact often undermine it by suggesting that it hinges on self-improvement, the very transformation that women are told they need in order to snare a husband. A print advertisement for Mentor breast implants, for example, features a close-up of a smiling young woman and the message "Amber O'Brien, 25, is having the time of her life. Recently, she decided it was time to have breast augmentation." The ad then presents a fact file about Amber that lists, in *Playboy* magazine format, her "Pet Peeve" ("People who pressure you into doing things"), her "Proudest

Achievement" ("Buying a condo"), and her "Life Mission" ("Always be open to new ideas"). Again the message is clear: Amber is a "real" woman, successful and solvent enough to own her own condo. Purchasing fake breasts is simply another mark of her success and openmindedness.

Buy your own rock. Buy your own condo. Buy your own breasts. Positioning diamonds and breast implants—products that are generally assumed to be bought by or for a man—as choices made by women for their own pleasure validates the single woman while insidiously exploiting her fears and telling her that she's inadequate as is. Such marketing relies on a conception of singleness that still translates to "looking for a man" rather than "alone and fine with it, thank you."

Not only are single women being asked to buy imagery that reinforces their single status, thus engendering social insecurity, they're also fed the message that their single status is the result of being too "picky," the very quality honed by marketers. In other words, single women's consumer clout is presented as the reason they don't want to marry. As the Intelligence Factory study puts it, "These women feel entitled to have exactly what they want and won't settle for second best and that includes their intimate relationships." "Why am I still single?" reads the headline of a feature in the April 2001 issue of *Marie Claire*. "These women all want to be married. So why aren't they?" claims the subhead. Again, "high standards" are mostly to blame. But they are also seen to be influenced by the negative depictions of wife in the culture—that wives are controlled by their husbands, that being a wife means forfeiting ambition, that individuality is subsumed by marriage. Amy, a thirty-one-year-old financial analyst, is criticized for being too hard to get and too "picky." Shante, thirty, who works in the entertainment industry, is too afraid of being "controlled" by a man. An old boyfriend said her work ethic got in the way of becoming a wife: "she hasn't had the time to devote to a relationship." Debi, thirty-five, who owns a design store, is portrayed as too prudish. She has "an old-fashioned approach to sex," according to one friend.

"Picky, Picky, Picky: The dilemma of the new single woman," published in the September 2000 *Talk* magazine, had as its subtitle "The

American woman still wants to get married but is it really worth the trouble? Kristin Whiting is trying to decide." Whiting, a thirty-two-year-old on-air reporter for ABC Lifetime News, is portrayed in the article as a commitmentphobe. Statistically, the article suggests, she should be seen as an "aberration," in that the average woman marries at twenty-five.

Whiting has high standards when it comes to men. She doesn't want a boring investment banker. He must not be bald. Her mother is quoted as saying she doesn't understand her daughter, having come from a generation where "if you weren't married by 19 you were a loser." But for all Whiting's independence, she also wants a man who will take care of her. "I want to be taken for dinner, not for the economics but the principle."

Despite all the quibbling about her marital status, Kristen Whiting's life is a good one. She loves her job, she loves her home, and she has many friends. Indeed, even though the point of the article is to ask why Whiting hasn't settled down, it suggests marriage is in fact a fate worse than being alone: "Occasional moments of piercing loneliness and a lack of sex are drawbacks to being single, but they are nothing compared to the loneliness of a dead marriage, especially one that requires the inevitable sacrifices in throwing your lot in with another's."

Indeed, when successful single women choose to discard their unwife status, to throw their "lot in with another's," they too are questioned. The no-win situation was glaringly evident in the coverage of the marriages in 2002 of two single-girl icons: the *Sex and the City* author, Candace Bushnell, and the actress Julia Roberts. Both married on July 4. Bushnell, forty-three, married a ballet dancer ten years her junior, whom she had known a mere eight weeks. Roberts also wed a younger man. In its coverage, *The New York Times,* a newspaper that assiduously chronicles and stokes bridal fantasies, couldn't resist a pun, quoting a guest at Bushnell's wedding saying it was the "the end of independence day."

Even the woman who brought the world Bridget Jones expressed mixed emotions about the institution. In 2003, at age forty-five, Helen Fielding announced that she was both pregnant and engaged to be married for the first time. But, as she told *The Sunday Telegraph,* she might never wed because it "was so nice to be engaged." As she explains it: "My generation was caught up in the old-fashioned 1950s housewife thing to some extent. But at the same time they were a very different kind of woman, with the capacity to have a good life and their own friends and income. And, actually, you're not really lonely when you're single. You're more likely to be lonely when you're married and alone."

There it was. The woman who had birthed modern chick lit, an author worth millions, had figured out how to sidestep the antipathy many women harbored about marriage: get engaged and stay that way. It was genius. You have the beautiful ring. You have proof of your marital desirability. You live in eternal hope. Yet you avoid the confusion—and potential disappointment—that can accompany the role of wife. But Fielding's comment about the possible loneliness of the wife was freighted with another implication, one rarely discussed—that for all the talk of feminine "rescue" and being taken care of, it was the wife, not the single woman, who might have the more difficult social role.

For, like Helen Fielding, and beyond the media coverage, unmarried women are successfully breaking through stereotypes that reduce them to a one-size-fits-all market demographic, carving out meaningful lives that don't hinge on their ability to consume. Meanwhile, wives are facing the opposite challenge. And that is to take, at long last, their rightful place on the economic grid.

Chapter 8

What's a Wife Worth?

Say the following ad ran in your local newspaper. Would you answer it?

Employment opportunity: partnership opportunity in a venture known to have more than a 40 percent failure rate. You will fulfil a support role. Candidates must be attractive, cheerful, sociable, and organized. Responsibilities include domestic administration, entertaining, traveling, accompanying partner to professional events, and will often include reorganizing personal schedule at the last minute. Salary, vacation, sick leave, and pension to be determined by partner, and will be commensurate with the success or failure of venture. Performance to be evaluated at whim by partner. Position may require abandonment of education and/or career goals and is subject to termination at any time, without notice, by partner, even after thirty years of service. Severance to be determined by partner or the courts. No experience preferred.

The fact that millions of women have taken on, and continue to take on, precisely that position brings me to the Institute for Equality in Marriage in New York City. The first sight I see walking through the door is a framed *Playboy* magazine cover dating back to the 1970s. It's a discordant image, to say the least. *Playboy*, after all, advised husbands to ditch their wives, to abnegate their marital responsibility. So what's it doing on the wall of a nonprofit agency created to promote financial fairness in marriage? As it happens, the retro decorative touch is an ironic detail. It came with the rented and shared suite of offices in a down-at-the-heels building in midtown Manhattan.

The Institute for Equality in Marriage is a shoestring operation, founded in 1998 by Lorna Jorgenson Wendt and funded in part by the $20 million settlement she received from her 1997 divorce. Before her marriage unraveled, Wendt was the typical stay-at-home wife of a corporate executive, tending and supporting her successful husband, believing theirs was an equal partnership. That view changed after a bitter court battle, which left her with far less than half of the couple's assets. The awakening transformed the divorcée into an activist for equality in marriage, that theoretical principle she had assumed underlined her decades-long union.

Wendt is in her fifties but exudes a soft girlishness that doesn't mask a resolute will. Her short hair is a coppery gold. Her clothing is tasteful, punctuated with touches of flash. Her black skirt and stockings are paired with a silk leopard-spotted blouse and gold jewelry. Her black quilted bag is Prada. Documents from her divorce indicate that she requested a $10,000 monthly clothing allowance.

Wendt has nothing in common with the angry, avenging wives portrayed in *The First Wives' Club*. Rather, she views herself as an upper-class Norma Rae, fighting to increase the value accorded the work of millions of stay-at-home wives who are not in a position to request $10,000 monthly clothing allowances.

It's a role she never imagined she'd take on. When Lorna Jorgenson married Gary Wendt in 1965, she thought it would be forever. They were the proverbial high school sweethearts. She had been raised in a religious home. Her father was a Lutheran minister. Her mother, who raised six children, was her role model. "I wanted to be the best wife," she says. The couple moved to Cambridge so Gary could take his MBA at Harvard Business School. She supported them by giving music lessons. At night she typed his papers. Over the years, as Gary's career flourished, she sold and packed up five houses, drove carpools, and entertained his clients. Eight days after the birth of the first of their two daughters, her husband called to say twelve people were coming for dinner that night and that, as she remembers it, he told her "to make it happen."

As her husband rose in the ranks to chief executive officer of General Electric Capital Services, she never burdened him with household details such as asking him to call a plumber or look after a sick child. Her duties included removing any tension that would distract or annoy her husband. She often accompanied him on business trips, always briefing herself beforehand on corporate details. "I was representing the company even though I wasn't being paid," she says. "Gary was brilliant and made the business deals, but I was the social aspect. He couldn't remember people's names. I did. We had our roles."

In the world Lorna Wendt occupied, the stay-at-home wife was a business asset. Listening to her talk puts me in mind of the 1954 camp comedy *Woman's World*, starring Fred MacMurray and Lauren Bacall. The premise is simple. An auto executive searching for a general manager decides to make his final decision based on which one of their wives is best suited to the role of corporate wife. To decide, he invites the three top candidates and their wives to New York for a weekend. "A wife can make or break the step up the ladder if she's too outspoken, if she doesn't integrate," says Wendt. "If you have a husband in a high-profile position, there may be things you say at home but not publicly."

She watched the wives of her husband's colleagues focus on their own careers and turn into "Hillary Wives," as *The Wall Street Journal* derisively referred to women with demanding careers in 1994. "More women were going into the workforce," she says, "which meant they weren't available for corporate functions, and people would say, 'Oh, he's not going to advance very far.' Or they'd say, 'She didn't want to make the move because she's got a job; oh, that's going to hurt him.'"

After her daughters were grown, Wendt felt restless. She took several wilderness expeditions with Outward Bound and began singing in the Greenwich Chorale Society. She stopped accompanying her husband on business if the trip interfered with a concert. He began to complain that she wasn't there for him. In December 1995 he asked her for a divorce. Employing corporate-ese, Lorna Wendt would later refer to the request as a "unilateral decision" to end their marriage and "buy her out" in a "hostile takeover." Still, habits are hard to break. She hosted a black-tie Christmas party for his colleagues a week after he said he wanted to end the marriage.

When her husband offered her an $8 million settlement, Lorna Wendt balked. She had managed their finances and figured that their net worth was closer to $100 million, which meant her husband was offering less than 10 percent. In what is referred to as "an equal-distribution state" she would have been entitled to half, at least in theory. But the Wendts lived in Connecticut, which, like most other U.S. states, is a community-property state, which means that the judge decides what is fair.

And that usually means distributing half of the estate to each spouse, unless the assets are in excess of $10 million. That's when courts move away from the principle of equal distribution and revert to the old doctrine of "he who earns it owns it." We see this bias insinuated into media coverage of big-money divorces, with a couple's money often referred to as the "husband's fortune." The result is that wives of very rich men often have ended up with far less than half the marital assets—10 or maybe 20 percent. Diana, Princess of Wales, for instance, is believed to have wheedled a paltry £17 million out of Prince Charles.

Courts are also influenced by the "how much is enough" doctrine. In other words, wives being offered some $8 million are considered to be well taken care of. After all, $8 million is a lot of money. In such cases, the discussion focuses on what a husband "should" give a wife, a notion at odds with the lip service to the idea that marriage is an equal partnership, no matter who does what. But the fact remains that the person who literally earned the money is seen by the courts as having greater entitlement to it.

The Wendts divorced in 1997. In January 1999, after a strenuous appeal, Lorna Wendt was awarded $20 million, a sum she still views as far below her contribution as what she refers to as a "noneconomic partner." She also sought equal distribution of what are known as "soft assets" accrued during the marriage—stock options, restricted stock units, supplemental pensions that were earned during the marriage but that have payoff after divorce—a move that sent tremors through the financial community. Later, when she began to recognize her devalued role, she began referring to herself as "CEO of the Wendt household," again drawing on business jargon to buttress her status.

Wendt's case resonated with the public, particularly women in far less privileged circumstances who believed that despite the advances of the past thirty years, the wife is still given a raw deal in divorce, in that the standard of living of the ex-wife with children is seen to drop as much as 30 percent, according to some studies. Moreover, most women who re-enter the workforce after divorce remain the primary care-givers for children, even when custody is "shared." And this too can compromise their earning potential.

The fact that Lorna Wendt received far less than half the couple's net worth tends to be the norm, though there are signs of change, if only in the distribution of assets for longstanding marriages. In 1998, the sixty-three-year-old Vira Hladun-Goldmann made history when she walked away from a thirty-three-year marriage to a New York City banker with 50 percent of the couple's $86 million fortune. During her marriage she had cooked, cleaned, raised a child, entertained, redecorated and renovated his offices, accompanied her husband on trips, and even given him haircuts. She was the one who asked for the divorce in 1996. "We just didn't have anything in common anymore," she told *The Wall Street Journal*. "I remember saying: 'Robert, the first 25 years were yours, the next 25 will be mine.' He gave me his standard vague smile and seemed not to take any real notice."

This was his first big mistake. His second was failing to consult her about his will and not making her the executor. Goldmann describes it as being "treated like the upstairs maid." Finally, perhaps, she felt she had the excuse to walk out on the man she'd met when she was twenty-nine and stood by for more than thirty years—but had not loved from day one. The marriage was based on pragmatism, not passion, she later admitted. "I didn't feel I'd met the man of my dreams. He was just the best of the bunch," she once said in an interview. She maintains that there was no infidelity in the marriage. They simply grew apart.

His lawyer said that she did not make a direct contribution to their wealth by being a spouse. Even her lawyers counseled her to settle for less than 50 percent, which she refused to do. The Manhattan Supreme Court Justice Walter Tolub thought otherwise. He ruled that she receive half, though he qualified his judgment by saying that the length of the marriage was an overriding factor. "Married for thirty-three years, their fortunes are inseparable," he said. The statement reflected the fact that marriages that endure for decades, like the Goldmanns', and which begin with a couple owning few assets, are increasingly rare. The average duration of marriage in North America is now slightly longer than seven years. As such, for many, marriage has become a temporary assignment, or a series of temporary assignments, rather than a lifetime career, a trend that mirrors the wider job market.

In 2003, Goldmann published *Separate Ways: Relationships, Divorce & Independence of Mind,* inspired by the thousands of women who wrote to her after hearing of her record-breaking settlement. The book is reminiscent of *Sex and the Single Girl* in that it's packed with pithy advice and exclamation marks: "Don't be shy, you're getting a divorce not a murder rap"; "a good divorce is a quick divorce"; "the only person who can take care of you in a divorce is you yourself: so be methodical, start early, and think positive!" It suggests women preparing a case should draw up a road map of their marriage, describing in minute detail what they did for both their partner and their children: "Did you make breakfast? Write that down. Did your daughter get an A in the spelling bee? Write that down. Did you walk the children to the school bus? Write that down."

Robert Goldmann died shortly after their divorce. "I think he'd have lived longer if we'd stayed married," his former wife says. "Yes, I really do. I was his caretaker and I know my leaving was very difficult for him. But you know—we have to be selfish." Unlike Lorna Wendt, Goldmann does not call herself a feminist. "I support them in their work," she told the London *Observer.* "They have to be here for us because it's still a man's world out there. But back in the Sixties when Gloria Steinem and that other girl—I can't remember her name now—got this thing going, bra burning and all that kind of stuff, they lost sight of the importance of the wife and mother. Being a wife and mother is like a career. It's one of the most important jobs."

Slowly, courts are recognizing that being a stay-at-home-wife is a career option, one that deserves proper compensation should the employee be fired or wish to terminate employment. Precedents are being set that imply the breadwinner's role does not trump the homemaker's. In a landmark House of Lords judgment in 2000, Shan Lambert was awarded half of her ex-husband's £20 million fortune. Not only was it one of the largest divorce settlements in English history, but it was seen as radical in that it rated a wife's domestic contribution equally with her husband's work outside the home. It overturned the rule that the wives of rich men should be entitled to only enough for their "reasonable requirements."

In the past, the British Court of Appeal had ruled that husbands' and wives' contributions should be treated equally—but always found a reason for giving the wife less. Usually, judges said the husband's "genius" in making the money justified awarding him more. This effectively meant that it was difficult for wives ever to "clock up" enough contribution to justify as much as half.

The Lambert case changed that. The couple had been married years before Harry Lambert made his fortune as chairman of the Adscene group, a Kent-based free newspaper chain, which was eventually sold for more than £75 million. Shan Lambert ran the family home and also played a nonexecutive role on the Adscene board. After two decades the marriage foundered, and Lambert left his wife for another woman. During the court fight, Harry Lambert's lawyer argued that his client set up the company nine months before he met his wife, and its success was due to his initiative and drive alone. But three Court of Appeal judges increased Shan Lambert's lump sum to half the wealth created during the marriage. In his lead judgment, Lord Justice Thorpe said, "There must be an end to the sterile assertion that the breadwinner's contribution weighs heavier than the homemaker's." Nigel Shepherd, former national chairman of the Solicitors' Family Law Association, described it as a "sea change" in divorce law. "The courts have been looking at ways in which it would be right to say, 'You shouldn't get half'... but with equality the courts have now caught up with society—one can't argue with the logic of non-discrimination."

He argued that once the court had found that Harry Lambert's contribution to the business was special, but that he was not a genius, and the wife could not have done more, there was no reason to depart from equality of shares. Giving 50 percent to Mrs. Lambert has also presented a new dilemma. If a nonworking wife can get 50 percent, what happens to the wife who has raised the children and earned all the money? Does she get 60 percent?

In some cases, in fact, we are witnessing unequal distribution in favor of the wife. Jan Bobrow, whose husband of twenty-four years, Richard, was chief executive of the accounting firm Ernst & Young, was awarded 60 percent of the couple's $24.5 million fortune in an Indiana court in 2002. Jan Bobrow said that her husband concealed financial details from her and gave her a budget of $5,000 a month to raise their four children.

She said she decided to examine files in her husband's home office after he said he wanted a divorce and offered her a $1.2 million divorce settlement. She would have settled for $2 million, she said later. "I had no idea what he made or how much we had." In his ruling, the judge explained that he stepped past the customary fifty-fifty split because Jan Bobrow had been making $10 an hour working part-time for a church while her husband was paid $3.1 million in 2001.

The case made headlines less for the unusual split of assets than for the financial information it made public—information that Ernst & Young, a private company, would have preferred to stay within corporate walls. But increasingly, exposing corporate secrets has become a bargaining chip for wives in high-profile divorces. In her divorce from the former General Electric chairman Jack Welch, Jane Beasley Welch hired a lawyer who knew what her husband's stock options were worth. The strategy worked. After turning down a $130 million settlement deal, she settled out of court in 2003.

Beasley Welch had stepped down from a successful career as a corporate attorney when she married in 1999. In that respect, she was unlike women who tend to home and family for their entire marital lives, women who are dependent on the court settlement for redress. Conversely, a working spouse's earnings power and income are not curtailed by divorce. This was evident in the Wendt case, when, after the divorce, Gary Wendt landed at the helm of Conseco, a financial services firm. While the terms of his compensation package were not released, it was made public that he pocketed a $45 million signing bonus.

There's a nice irony in the fact that Lorna Wendt's first job after being "fired" from her position as wife was wife activist. Wendt's message is simple: monetary and "softer" nonmonetary contributions to a marriage should be assigned equal monetary value. She is careful to make the point that her mission is equality for men and women, but it is clear that women have the most to gain, though that surely will change as more men adopt the homemaker role.

After her settlement, Wendt became a fixture on the media circuit—showing up on the cover of *Fortune* magazine, on *Oprah*, and on *Nightline*. She speaks to financial groups and students, explaining that marriage is the most important social contract they'll ever make. She advises all who are getting married to discuss finances and to protect themselves with a marriage contract. The Institute for Equality in Marriage is at work creating a legally binding document for couples that acts as a living will and is revised every few years as circumstances change. That way the partner who does not make a "noneconomic" interest continues to be protected.

Wendt understands that such hard-headed planning is at odds with the romantic dream of "forever" on which many marriages are based. Signing a pre-nup forces couples to imagine the marriage's end. She admits that she too bought into a fairy-tale scenario during her marriage. "Yeah, I can see I was a little brought up on the Prince Charming story," she told me in her office. "I believed that if I did this and this and this, and if he did this and this and this, we'd live happily ever after. And a lot of that did happen. But there are no guarantees." Though she views marriage with a survivor's wariness, Lorna Wendt says she still believes in the institution and says she would become a wife again. Gary Wendt remarried in 1999. His ex-wife doesn't know if he made sure his new bride signed a pre-nuptial agreement. Wendt calls herself a feminist. "I've always supported feminism," she says. "I'm a child of God and I'm equal to anyone."

Lorna Jorgenson Wendt's story is part of a larger narrative. Hers is but one voice in the growing chorus of women who want to reassess the value of wife. Whether or not the full-time wife of a wealthy executive should be financially compensated may seem a frivolous subject at a time when more than 70 percent of married women work full-time outside the home. But it isn't, given that an increasing number of women are leaving careers midstream to have children or tend to family. Unlike Lorna Wendt, many of these women have professional degrees and marketable skills. They believe they can drop out of the workforce and re-enter it at their will.

The questions raised by Lorna Wendt's final marital paycheck have repercussions beyond the privileged strata of so-called professional wives. They speak to the relative values assigned to husbands and wives, men and women—arguably the great social issue of the post–World War II Western world. It's contentious ground that extends into a rethinking of what economists are now beginning to call "caring" labor, and even of basic economic precepts.

One of the fundamental purposes of the wife historically has been her role as an economic adjunct to her husband, the domestic backup required so a man could go out and make a living. Wife, not hooker, is the oldest profession. The first reference to a wife in the Bible is as "help-meet." In medieval Germany, having a wife was a requirement for full mastership in a guild, the assumption being that a workshop could not be properly run without a wife's presence. In seventeenth-century New England, keeping a tavern and selling spirits were so dependent on the cooperation of a wife that some authorities refused to give a license to a single man.

The benefits of a supportive wife in the corporate world have been well documented. In *The Organization Man*, published in 1956, William H. Whyte writes of the wife as an "island of tranquility" who would "liberate her husband's total energy for the job." In her 1977 book, *Men and Women of the Corporation,* the Harvard business professor Rosabeth Moss Kanter describes how companies were getting "two for the price of one" when a male executive had a supportive stay-at-home spouse. Although the wives were not paid directly by the corporation, they spent their lives promoting their husbands' careers and, thereby, the company's interests. Six years later, Kanter revisited the subject, suggesting that wives were also actively building networks outside the corporation that benefited their husbands.

The well-educated wife provides extra assistance that can lessen her mate's load and enhance his job performance, says the British sociologist Janet Finch, whose influential 1983 book, *Married to the Job,* offers numerous examples of two-for-the-price-of-one deals married men offer their employers. She mentions the academic wife, with similar qualifications to her husband's, who marks his students' essays; the politicians' wives roped into giving speeches; the wives expected to host diplomatic functions or answer nighttime calls for their obstetrician husbands.

Finch also concludes that women who remain secondary workers are making an economically sound decision. For most women, she argues, a higher standard of living can be gained over a lifetime by being a wife than most women could achieve in their own right. "In those circumstances it may well seem the most sensible economic option for a wife to invest her energies in her husband's work, thus promoting his earning potential, rather than to pursue her own." Such thinking continues today. One female lawyer quoted in an October 2003 *New York Times Magazine* story on women leaving the workforce admitted that before she became engaged to her future husband she turned down "fabulous offers" so she could follow him to Atlanta. "I knew the long-term career was going to be his," she said.

In turn, the presence of a stay-at-home wife is seen to bolster a husband's income potential, a phenomenon witnessed throughout the Western world. Historically, this registered in the "family wage" paid married men because they had a wife and family to support (recall that this provided the fodder for a memorable moment on *The Mary Tyler Moore Show* in the 1970s). Even after legislation was passed in the 1970s and '80s ruling such discrimination illegal, a mysterious "wage gap" prevailed between men and women. Theories abounded on what caused the wage gap, even on whether it existed. Annual reports announce that this gap continues to decline. Yet it persists, a legacy of the belief that men, husbands, deserve to earn more. By 2003, for instance, women were seen to earn 76 cents for every dollar earned by a man, compared with earning 63 cents for every dollar in 1979.

Sociologists refer to the "guardian effect" of wives to explain why married men thrive in corporations. Forty years of international research consistently supports the notion of a "marriage premium." Depending on the country, a married man earns between 10 and 40 percent more than an unmarried male, matched on age and other relevant characteristics such as qualifications and work experience. But whereas in some countries, such as the United States, the premium has recently been dropping, in Australia the economic benefits to a man of having a wife are holding up.

Dr. Jenny Chalmers, of the Social Policy Research Centre at the University of New South Wales in Australia, found that in 1989 the wages of married men in that country were on average 9.2 percent higher than matched unmarried men. By the mid-nineties this had risen to 9.6 percent, a figure that has since remained steady.

Her research shows a similar divide between couples in which the wife works full-time and those in which the wife works part-time or is a homemaker. The Australian marriage premium is dropping among full-timers (from 8.5 to 6.6 percent in the early '90s), while it has increased (from 9.5 to 11.4 percent) for the bulk of couples in which the women are employed part-time or not at all.

The finding is also quantified in a 1996 paper by Linda Stroh of Loyola University of Chicago and Jeanne Brett of Northwestern University in Evanston, Illinois. Titled "The Dual Earner Daddy Penalty in Salary Progression," it revealed that salaries of managers with stay-at-home wives increased by 79 percent over five years; for those with working wives, the average increase was only 59 percent. The researchers identified the wife as a resource that freed the manager to put in more time at work.

Why married men earn more is a question that has intrigued econo-mists in many countries. Is it a legacy of corporations taking greater responsiblity for men with families? Women, after all, have never been seen as having to provide for a family. Is it that women simply marry men who are more likely to be successful? No, say the economists, who conclude that although selection is part of the story, the evidence sug-gests that what happens after marriage may be even more important. The wage gap between married and unmarried men increases over time, the longer men stay married.

"Men's earnings begin to improve in the year before they marry, as grooms-to-be shrug off bachelor habits and begin to assume the out-look and priorities of married men," explains the Chicago University sociology professor Linda Waite, who, with her co-author, Maggie Gallagher, summarizes recent work on the marriage premium in their book, *The Case for Marriage.* Waite says the consensus is that married men with wives at home earn more because they are able to specialize in making money.

This theory holds that marriage makes men more productive because their wives usually perform the bulk of the housework and child care so they can concentrate on their jobs. Often women provide direct support for their husbands' careers—helping with the books, entertaining the boss, typing a thesis, helping him with vital career decisions. Married men's earnings also receive a boost from the increased work commitment that usually accompanies growing demands on the bank balance, such as a mortgage and children. "Mar-ried men make better workers than single guys do because they lead more settled lives," Waite says. "They have lower rates of absenteeism from work and are less likely to quit or be fired than are single men."

This contention is supported by the work of the economists Hyunbae Chun and Injae Lee, who analyzed 1999 survey data involving twenty-seven hundred men and found married men earned an average of 12.5 percent more than never-married men. The marriage premium still existed for men whose wives worked, though it dropped precipitously. Men whose wives weren't employed earned about 31 percent more, while men whose wives had a full-time job earned only 3.4 percent more.

No wonder *The Wall Street Journal* was so worked up about the "Hillary Wife" in 1994. The species was interfering with men's earning potential.

For women, marriage offers no such economic advantages in the workplace. Studies have gauged that married women earn less than single women, which is predictable. Married women—the majority of them, at any rate—don't have male wives. They're far more likely than single women to leave the workforce intermittently to give birth or to care for children. There's also the fact that being with a partner can have a negative influence on a woman's career trajectory, though it has the opposite effect on a man. Just look around. The most prominent women on both corporate and political landscapes are either single or have wifely support. Carly Fiorina, CEO of Hewlett-Packard, the most powerful woman in corporate America, has a husband who retired from his job to act as domestic backup. Condoleezza Rice, the most powerful woman in the Bush administration, is a single woman without children. Margaret Thatcher, the former British prime minister, had grown children and a supportive husband who had retired from a successful career. Kim Campbell, Canada's only female prime minister, who held office briefly in 1993, was single. The joke that working women didn't need a husband, they needed a wife, had been replaced in the late 1990s with the slogan on a T-shirt that did brisk business in Britain: "Behind every successful woman is a cat."

There is also evidence that married women play down their marital status during job interviews. One study revealed that some women take off their wedding rings because future employers might not want to hire a young married woman who may require maternity leave. Conversely, the same study found that young men often don wedding rings when applying for a job.

The transformation a woman experiences on turning into the coveted bride occurs for a man after the wedding. Suddenly he's a husband, thus seen, in an echo of coverture, to be capable of leadership. The playwright Wendy Wasserstein wrote of how John F. Kennedy, Jr., was imbued with a new maturity after he'd wed Carolyn Bessette: "the sanctity of marriage transforms the prince from just the most eligible hunk alive to a very responsible guy with a beautiful wife and political future."

A man in politics or the upper echelons of business without a wife was until very recently treated with suspicion, as if he were some kind of social anarchist. Within more conservative professions, a wife remains useful, providing the illusion of ballast. This is not always acknowledged, for fear of appearing discriminatory or politically incorrect. I conducted an informal poll among members of Toronto's financial community, asking whether high-profile businessmen needed wives. Most were quick to answer yes. As one businessman put it, "These guys need a strong woman, a womb, wrapped around them. All of the bank chairmen have wives like that."

The wife's role has been more rigidly typecast in the political realm, where she's a silent, supportive figure. She's a grace note, a reminder that her husband is an upright, responsible family man. That is changing, however. Canada has voted in several single prime ministers. In the United States, it is now not uncommon for a governor or mayor not to have a wife.

That said, every president of the United States elected in the twentieth century has had a wife who plays a crucial role in setting the image for the administration. The current first lady, Laura Bush, has been greeted as the anti-Hillary. She fulfills the traditional "ezer" role, described in Talmudic commentary as a "sustainer" or "help-meet" who provides a moral check on her husband: "When he is good, she supports him, when he is bad, she rises up against him." The *Houston Chronicle* columnist Julie Mason described Laura Bush's role as part disciplinarian: "She's the iron rod at her husband's back. She keeps him from going too far off the deep end when he gets all caught up in his cock-of-the-walk behavior."

The stoic wife is a definite asset to men facing sex scandal or refuting criminal charges. Early-morning television proved a popular platform on which teary wives defended charges against their husbands. Hillary Clinton used *Good Morning America* to deflect attacks against her husband after he had been discovered having an affair with a White House intern. Linda Lay, the wife of the disgraced Enron chairman, Kenneth Lay, released a flood of tears on the program a few years later, calling her beleaguered husband an "honest, decent, moral human being."

When the Los Angeles Laker Kobe Bryant was accused of sexual

assault in July 2003, his first move was to call a televised press conference to admit that he had committed adultery but was not guilty of
rape. By his side, a required prop, sat his wife, Vanessa, clutching his
hand. When Vanessa Bryant failed to show up at her husband's preliminary hearing, her absence was endlessly interpreted. Did it mean she
didn't believe in his innocence? Was it part of the defense strategy? The
latter option was unlikely. So crucial is the presence of a wife during a
criminal trial that defense lawyers have been known to hire actresses to
play the part in the courtroom in lower-profile cases.

The benefit of a wife's exuding wifely support was manifest in the election of Arnold Schwarzenegger as governor of California in October
2003. Without the backup of his wife, Maria Shriver, it is unlikely the
actor would have been given the nod. Shriver, referred to as
Schwarzenegger's "secret weapon," literally stood by her husband's side,
refuting repeated allegations that he had sexually humiliated some sixteen women. During his acceptance speech, he turned to her and said,
"I know how many votes I got because of you."

There's a corollary here. Husbands are mocked, even professionally
penalized, if their wives deviate from prescribed behavior. In 1997,
when Matthew Barrett, the chief executive of the Bank of Montreal,
married Anne-Marie Sten, a former model who once dated the arms
dealer Adnan Khashoggi, tongues wagged. Sten, the gossips said, was
too flamboyant to assume a buttoned-down role; some suggested she
was better suited for the role of mistress, not wife. The marriage didn't
last. When Barrett was named chief executive of Britain's Barclay's Plc
in 1999, the British tabloids had a feeding frenzy, printing pictures of his
ex-wife in her modeling days, wearing a fur bikini. The insinuation was
clear: how can a man who doesn't pick an "appropriate" wife have the
proper judgment to run a financial institution?

The wife who dares to step outside the boundaries of wifely propri-
ety can still compromise her husband's career. In 2002, the White
House speechwriter David Frum stepped down from his job shortly
after his wife, the writer Danielle Crittenden, boasted to friends and
family via e-mail that her husband had come up with the much-quoted
"axis of evil" phrase in President George W. Bush's 2002 State of the

Union address. In an e-mail to friends that was later widely circulated, she bragged that her husband's words could stand alongside such recognizable advertising slogans as "the pause that refreshes." Crittenden signed off with "So I'll hope you'll indulge my wifely pride in seeing this one repeated in headlines everywhere!!"

The admission was considered a breach of White House protocol, for which Frum was held accountable. He denied that his leaving his White House position had anything to do with the e-mail and that he had been planning to leave. Even so, the media interpretation was that his wife's indiscretion had done him in; there was even speculation over whether the couple might divorce. *The Washington Post* quoted Crittenden as saying, "I don't have anything more to say about this. I already feel too much like Lucy Ricardo."

As we saw in the treatment of Hillary Clinton, wives in the political realm—the very place laws are changed and social policies set—are expected to conform to a far more retrograde standard. This was glaringly apparent during the last U.S. presidential election. Teresa Heinz Kerry, who is older and far wealthier than her husband, John Kerry, was routinely subject to negative scrutiny in the press for being "outspoken" (read: "not subordinate"). Conversely, Laura Bush was presented as a wifely asset: in an echo of coverture she transferred to her husband her own qualities of literate, soft-spoken reason.

That a wife remains an extension of her husband is, in fact, institutionalized in the American political system. A spouse, for instance, can take over for a mate who cannot fulfill his or her duties in Congress. In November 2000, Jean Carnahan, the widow of Missouri's former governor Mel Carnahan, inherited the Democratic Senate position her husband won posthumously in the U.S. election. Governor Carnahan had died in a plane crash in October in which an aide and his son also perished. It was too late to remove his name from the ballot, so voters were told that his wife would take his place, should he win. In the United States, forty-four women have succeeded their spouses in Congress since 1923. One of the most high-profile was Mary Bono, whose career accomplishments include hostessing and being trophy wife to Sonny

Bono, who was elected to carry on his congressional mission in 1998; she was re-elected in November 2000.

Al Gore defended Jean Carnahan's appointment, saying that the woman who had been married to the politician for forty-six years, and who holds a degree in business administration, was "universally recognized as an equal partner with Mel in his career." Still, Katharine Meiszkowski, writing in *Salon,* was outraged at Jean Carnahan's posting: "the idea of a wife serving for her husband plays into our most dated notions of what a wife is—a legal pinch hitter who embodies her husband's ideals and views, who lives to carry out his will when he cannot."

Lorna's Wendt's post-divorce campaign is but one example of change in attitudes toward the valuation of wife. A budding trend in academic circles, for instance, sees professional wives like Lorna Wendt being directly compensated for their wife-related duties by their husbands' employers. One was Mary Catherine Birgeneau, the wife of the former University of Toronto president, Robert Birgeneau. In 1999, after Birgeneau left his post as dean of science at the Massachusetts Institute of Technology to become president of U. of T., Canada's largest university, it became known that his wife was being paid $60,000 annually to be a "university relations officer" during the seven years of his contract. It was a fancy title for the work involved—entertaining, traveling with her husband, serving as an unofficial ambassador to the business. Such roles have always been rewarded indirectly, through a husband's salary with its built-in wife premium.

Paying the president's spouse directly for work that wives used to do without remuneration was a first for the University of Toronto. When news of Mary Catherine Birgeneau's deal was made public in a university newspaper, the response was mixed. Some praised the decision, saying that it was a positive step in placing an economic value on the often invisible work of the "professional wife." More were critical. "Mary-ing for Money" was the snide headline in *The Independent,* a newspaper for the U. of T. community. "She's being paid to be a wife," sniffed an administrator at the university, a woman, not realizing that that was exactly the point. She was being paid for the kind of labor a wife has been expected to do for centuries in the recognition that it benefited her husband's employer. That in itself was shocking.

Mary Catherine Ware married Bob Birgeneau on June 20, 1964, at St. Monica's parish in Toronto. Both were born in the city. They met at a high school dance, though they didn't begin dating until they met again as students at the University of Toronto. After graduating with a BA in English in 1962, Mary Catherine was employed as a case worker for the Catholic Children's Aid Society in Toronto. She lived at home until her marriage. Her husband received his undergraduate degree a year after she did and headed to Yale on scholarship for graduate studies.

Their wedding day was picture perfect—hot, sunny, nothing but blue skies. After the reception at the Inn on the Park hotel, the couple got into their car, a secondhand Chevrolet Biscayne, he behind the wheel in the classic wedding-departure tableau as the guests waved goodbye. The twenty-two-year-old Birgeneau didn't yet have his license, only his learner's permit, but it would have been unseemly for a husband not to sit in the driver's seat, his bride by his side. When the car turned the corner, out of view, it came to a stop. The couple got out and traded places. Then the new Mrs. Birgeneau, who had a license to drive, got behind the wheel and drove away.

Mary Catherine Birgeneau sits demurely on a garish flowered couch in the "morning room" on the first floor of the rambling house in the heart of Toronto that came rent-free with her husband's appointment. The rooms on this floor are reserved for university functions, of which there are about sixty a year.

The Birgeneaus live upstairs, on the second and third floors. Like most official residences, this one has an institutional feel to it, the whiff of a mausoleum. Behind her, on the wall, hangs a black-and-white portrait taken on her wedding day. She's wearing a simple white satin gown with short sleeves. Her husband resembles the young Jimmy Stewart, dark-haired, smiling. They share that shocked, happy look commonly seen on newlyweds.

Nearly forty years later, Mary Catherine Birgeneau is a more worldly version of the fresh-faced young woman in the picture. Her dark hair is cut short. She is unfussy in her appearance, attired in a tailored black-and-white-checked jacket, black pants, black suede shoes, with a thin gold chain around her neck. Media attention is new to her. She says she prefers to be in the background, that she's not comfortable in the spotlight.

Mary Catherine has never read *The Feminine Mystique,* published a year before her marriage, but has a firsthand familiarity with its subject matter, having been a housewife most of her life, and having felt, from time to time, undervalued in the job. It was a role she also loved, and in which she raised four children, three girls and a boy.

The year Mary Catherine Birgeneau married, fewer than 40 percent of married women held jobs. "I was fortunate to stay at home," she says. "Yet I felt there were opportunities I had missed. I hope my daughters can have both."

After their wedding, Mary Catherine joined her husband in New Haven, where she worked until their son was born in 1966. Bob Birgeneau spent a year on the faculty at Yale, then the family moved to England for a year so he could complete a postdoctoral fellowship at Oxford. He then took a position on the technical staff at Bell Laboratories, a former research arm of AT&T, which brought the family to Plainfield, New Jersey.

In 1975, Birgeneau was offered a place in the physics department at MIT, and the family moved to Weston, an affluent suburb of Boston. Mary Catherine's life revolved around the children and their activities—Brownies, Girl Scouts, soccer—and she became active in the Parent Teacher Organization. As her children grew, her volunteer work took her into the community, where she tutored English as a second language and worked with welfare mothers.

Meanwhile, Bob Birgeneau's field research into the fundamental properties of condensed matter using neutron and X-ray spectroscopy was taking him to facilities across the U.S. and Europe. That meant

Mary Catherine did about 95 percent of the child-rearing when the children were young. Meanwhile, her husband won awards and academic acclaim. In 1988, he was named chair of the physics department at MIT. In 1991, he was appointed dean of science.

Bob Birgeneau admits that having a spouse at home enriched his life while he pursued his professional goals. "I think it's probably true for anybody who has had a successful, stable marriage where the spouse has chosen the traditional role. That probably makes life easier, more fulfilling. You have the advantage of a full family life and at the same time can focus on your work."

With his new administrative responsibilities at MIT, he says, his wife's training as a social worker and her people skills were invaluable, and he often sought her advice. Mary Catherine attended every social event at MIT that she was invited to. By the late 1980s, with her children entering university, Mary Catherine was beginning to question her own place in society. Her generation was the last to say that marriage was their career goal; it was also the first to have those aspirations questioned. She says she went to university not for training but to develop herself. What she had wanted most of all was a family. "Those were my priorities: I wanted to help my husband and his career." But all that came at a price. "Being at home and being a mother and wife is difficult," she says. "It was hard, selfless work, and I wasn't always rewarded."

Her husband was supportive; he even bought her *The Female Eunuch* by Germaine Greer. "Bob appreciated my being home," she says. "But I felt the conflict of wondering if I would be recognized and valued more if I were doing something else. Deep in my heart I felt I was a valuable person, but socially that wasn't the message."

As her children moved out into the world, their relationship with their father evolved. The girls, particularly, sought his recognition. "It was more important to them at that time than mine was," she says. In 1990, Mary Catherine enrolled in the master's program at Boston College's School of Social Work. She received her degree in 1993 but chose to stay in the volunteer realm rather than take a paying job. She worked part-time two to three days a week in Roxbury, a tough inner-city Boston neighborhood, where she helped run afterschool programs, and Weston, where she administered a work program that brought together high school and college students with senior citizens. "I wanted to stay involved in Bob's career, to share in his life," she explains. "I also wanted to be available to our children, who were going through changes in their own lives." The master's in social work didn't change her social identity, she says, but it did alter her perception of herself. "It was something I achieved for myself, and that was significant."

You might expect academia to be more enlightened than the old-school political and business ways. It isn't. The university model, while evolving, remains an ivory-tower version of the mythic *Leave It to Beaver* nuclear family. A solid marriage with a spouse willing to pack up and move is rewarded. Every president of the University of Toronto has been a man. All have had wives.

When Robert Birgeneau was considered for the U. of T. job, his admirable administrative record, particularly his work in fostering gender equity at MIT, often came up in discussions about him. So too did his marriage. People mentioned how lovely his wife was, what a strong marriage they had. The wife of the last president, a practicing lawyer with three young boys, had chosen not to be an active auxiliary spouse.

When hiring-committee members came to visit Birgeneau in Weston, a suburb of Boston, Mary Catherine prepared beef bourguignon. At the time, Mary Catherine made it clear that she was interested in contributing in any way she could if her husband took the job. Back in Toronto, after deciding on Birgeneau for the position, the senior salary committee began to talk about the appropriateness of paying Mary Catherine for her duties in fundraising, hosting, and accompanying her husband on behalf of the university, an idea that came from the committee, not the Birgeneaus.

The $60,000 figure came after much discussion. It is a safe amount, respectful but not excessive. To put a number on the job, they looked at the time and the labor involved—which made it equivalent to an event coordinator's role.

Mary Catherine Birgeneau is the first wife of the head of a Canadian university, all of which are funded mainly by the public sector, to receive a salary for this work, at least on the record. In the United

States, 4 percent of university presidents' spouses at major research institutions receive salaries, according to a study commissioned by the Association of American Universities. And a quarter of them receive indirect compensation in the form of office allowances, household budgets, car allowances, or even retirement annuities. This kind of indirect compensation for spouses is also common in the corporate world but rarely discussed. In the academic realm, the trend of paying the spouse of a senior administrator can be explained in part by harsh market reality: most married women have their own work; universities can no longer expect them to pick up and follow their partners without financial compensation. Dr. Alice Huang, wife of David Baltimore, the president of the California Institute of Technology, better known as Caltech, is a case in point.

Huang, a prominent biologist and former full professor at Harvard, gave up her position as dean of science at New York University to follow her husband to Caltech in 1997. While the search committee was recruiting her husband, she says, it also met with her to see what it would take to bring her there. She is now senior councillor for external relations, a position in which she finds research partners for Caltech. The work takes up one-third of her time, and she is paid roughly a third of the $200,000 she earned for her full-time work at NYU. She accompanies her husband to university functions, she says, when her schedule permits.

A woman who comes to the role without having a high-powered career tends to be paid less. Ann Shaw, wife of Syracuse University's chancellor, Kenneth Shaw, receives $65,000 in her full-time role as associate of the chancellor. Shaw was an unpaid spouse when her husband was president at two other universities. At one point, she quit her duties for a paid position with the United Way. To replace her, the university had to hire two three-quarter-time employees.

Offering a wife a salary as an incentive to a president isn't always the only factor at play. There's another kind of market reality: the growing need for university presidents to entertain for all-important fundraising purposes, where the so-called human touch of the right spouse is seen to be crucial. The social/fundraising aspect of the president's job has become so dominant—U. of T. has stated it plans to raise $1 billion in private funds by 2004—that having a spouse willing to pitch in is a huge asset, says Peter Smith, director of public affairs for the Association of American Universities. "Not having one is a definite negative. The work product you get with a spouse who's adept at fundraising is important."

That statement implies that wives offer soft skills of persuasion that men don't have, that they take care of the details, care more about entertaining, the duties traditionally associated with a wife. "I think it brings a human dimension to the university," says Bob Birgeneau, who in 2004 accepted the position of president of Berkeley. Mary Catherine concurs: "I see myself as having more time, I won't say interest, than my husband to deal with people in a more relaxed manner."

The two-for-one deal is irrelevant, of course, when the roles are reversed and the university president is a woman. One study indicated that while 90 percent of male university presidents are married, only 57 percent of female university presidents are.

When I talked to female presidents, their tone was defensive. Martha Piper, president of the University of British Columbia, is married to William Piper, a professor of psychiatry at the university. She fields questions about her marriage and her husband's role in her career politely, though with a slight edge in her voice. "I was hired to do the job," she says, with the emphasis on the word *I*. "One clearly needs a supportive partner to do any job. It's critical in life. But this is my job." Lorna Marsden, the president of Toronto's York University, doesn't even mention her husband, Ed Harvey—a lawyer who tends to the household responsibilites—in her official university biographical sketch.

Clearly, a double standard still exists in which husbands are not expected to play the same role, says Alice Huang of Caltech. She recalls visiting Nan Keohane for an official function when Keohane was the president of Wellesley College in Massachusetts. Keohane's husband, Robert, a professor who was lured to Duke University in Durham, North Carolina, from Harvard when she was appointed, was dashing out the door to play tennis.

. . .

With all seismic shifts, whether geological or social, ground tends to move in different directions before it settles. For every argument that paying Mary Catherine Birgeneau for her labor is progressive, another could be lodged that it is regressive, a throwback to a time when a wife was needed as professional accompaniment. Is paying the professional wife an enlightened move, or is it a sham that tries to make women's subordination to their husbands' careers more palatable? Or is it an attempt to sidestep another reality that might not play well culturally—that the wife who works only in the domestic realm is an employee of her husband without any of the protections typically granted workers?

Mary Catherine Birgeneau is being paid for her labor, but there is no pretense that she was hired for any other reason than that she is the wife of the president, even though she has many admirable qualities in her own right. No other candidates were considered. There was no checking of references. She would lose the job should they divorce, which makes the terms of her employment similar to those of the traditional wife. "It was Bob they wanted, and the decision [to take the job] was Bob's," Mary Catherine says.

Most of the trappings of an actual job are absent. Her only staff is a cleaning man who helps her around the house. Caterers are employed for university functions, and her activities are coordinated through her husband's office. She has no official office of her own. Even the people responsible for Mary Catherine's paycheck are not clear about the implications of the example they've set. I ask Rose Patten of U. of T.'s governing council, who is also an executive vice president at the Bank of Montreal, if one day the spouse of the chairman of the bank would be compensated as a professional wife. "I can't see that happening," she says. When pushed, she explains: "Because he's paid more money." What she means is that his salary compensates both.

The response reflects a common confusion over what the money represents. It's a variation of an old question, If the husband makes enough money, why should the wife work outside the home? Robert Birgeneau makes a similar leap in logic when asked if the wife of the president of MIT is paid. No, he says, because "the salaries are so high there," referring to the fact that some American university presidents are paid as much as $1 million a year. When it's suggested it's the wife's labor, her time, that's being recognized, Birgeneau is quick to see the point. "Of course, I agree 100 percent. You're absolutely correct—people should be compensated for the work they do." He believes his wife's official designation confers credibility. "It doesn't seem as if I'm saying I can't be bothered," he says, referring to the times that she fills in for him.

Whether what's happening at the university level will soon trickle into the political or corporate arenas seems a remote prospect. But, as Alice Huang remarks, the role of "lovely wife" is no longer the default. "Women are out in the workforce," she says. "They've been paid for their labor. It's not so easy to be put back inside the box."

Mary Catherine Birgeneau has received letters of support and praise. But the appointment has also been the subject of criticism in dinner-party conversation among other professional wives. "I have problems with her taking money," says one outspoken stay-at-home wife who is active in the Toronto charity scene. "If she wants money, she should go out and get a job." She says the role of president's wife should be seen as an "honor" in and of itself. Gossip around the university had it that his wife's salary was a way of topping up Bob Birgeneau's $350,000 annual salary or of sweetening it in terms of tax relief. Birgeneau is amused at the suggestion. His current salary is less than he was earning in the U.S. as a department head. "If Mary Catherine or I were interested in money," he says, "we would have stayed in the U.S." An article in the *Toronto Star* newspaper suggested Mary Catherine Birgeneau is being paid for "schmoozing," a word she dislikes. She was particularly stung by *The Independent*'s headline "Mary-ing for Money." "He was poorer than a churchmouse when we married," she says, shaking her head.

It was only six months since she had moved to Toronto when I interviewed her, but already Mary Catherine was putting her new role in context. "I see myself as a bridge between generations," she says. But her eyes well up when she discusses leaving her home of twenty-five years. Her children and grandchildren remain in the U.S., and because of university business, she wasn't able to be with her daughter when she defended her doctoral thesis.

Since returning to Toronto, the Birgeneaus have had less personal time together. The fact that he is under pressure has made her reluctant to share her concerns. "If I'm annoyed about something, I'm less likely to say so," Mary Catherine says. She also says she's becoming more comfortable in her new role. "I've never loved being at the center, but it's easier." She corrects herself. "But I'm not the center—my husband is."

Calculating the monetary value of a wife's work hasn't progressed much since the seventeenth century, when the Virginia Company imported to America 140 single women who were sold for between 120 and 150 pounds of tobacco each. Feminists, and feminist economists, have been trying to quantify the invisible work done by an unpaid spouse but have, for the most part, failed to reach anything resembling a consensus. It is treacherous territory where no standards exist. Central to the problem is the perception that this kind of work is done for love, not money—and that putting a financial value on it is unseemly. The housewife makes an economic contribution, of course, though it is one no one bothers to quantify. For centuries, the housewife has interacted directly with the economy as the "chief purchasing agent" for her family. Wives tending to the home also frequently contribute to the nonprofit sector as volunteers at, say, their children's schools or for charities or community organizations, work that again is unpaid and not included in economic measures. Since the homemaker is compensated by the family wage earner, the value assigned to keeping a home varies radically, commensurate with the wage earner's value in the marketplace.

Assigning a dollar figure to a wife's work usually happens only when it's over, as in divorce settlements or during litigation following a home-maker's accidental death in which the family is seeking damages. Usually the courts employ "market-replacement theory," which takes the various chores a homemaker engages in—cleaning, carpooling, cooking, hostessing, nursing—and assigns them the value an employment service would charge. In 2000, a study by Edelman Financial Services of Fairfax, Virginia, arrived at a figure of $674,700 a year, or more than $58,000 per month, based on an eight-hour workday. Who would pay housewives such a salary was a question left unanswered.

Some economists see paying professional wives like Mary Catherine Birgeneau as enlightened. "Otherwise," says Myra Strober, a labor economist and professor of education at Stanford University in California, "this work is taken for granted." Strober became a courtroom celebrity as an expert witness in the divorce trial of Lorna Wendt.

At the trial, Strober argued that the time a woman, or a man, spends nurturing a marriage ought to be seen in terms of traditional human-capital theory. What that means is that one spouse made a human-capital investment in the other spouse's career and made it at the inception of that career. And as Strober puts it, when you make an investment, you expect a return commensurate with the ultimate value of that career.

In a much quieter way, examples like Mary Catherine Birgeneau's raise important questions about the value of all kinds of invisible work, much of which is done by women. Domestic labor wasn't even mentioned in Canada's census until 1996. And that was only after the brave protestations of a Saskatchewan homemaker, Carol Lees, who refused to fill out the 1991 census form if it meant saying that as an unpaid homemaker she didn't work. The census now asks questions about household activity but refers to it as "unpaid labor."

Statistics shape political policy. Yet gross domestic product, which measures the sum of goods and services in the economy and is considered the key indicator of national economic health, doesn't include unpaid domestic labor such as housework—which in the United States has been assigned a value of more than $11 trillion by the Department of Commerce. As Robert Kennedy once said of the GDP, "It measures everything, in short, except that which makes life worthwhile."

Economists used to joke that if a bachelor hires a housekeeper and pays her for housekeeping, her work is counted as a contribution to the GDP. If, however, the housekeeper marries and continues doing the very same work—without pay—her work is no longer counted as part of the GDP.

Recalculating the worth of invisible, caring labor requires nothing less than the redefinition of basic economic precepts. The economists Marianne Ferber, professor emeritus at the University of Illinois, and Barbara Bergmann, professor at the University of Maryland, who sat on President Kennedy's Council of Economic Advisors, have devoted their careers to looking at women's pay, child care, and other economic policies that directly affect women. But while they've achieved a high profile in the economics community, they're little known publicly. (Never, curiously, has a female economist ever won the Nobel Prize.)

Part of the problem, ironically, is academia. There is a paucity of economics professors with tenure, particularly at the more influential research universities. As of 2003, not one woman was tenured in the economics faculty at Yale. At the University of Chicago, there is one tenured woman in the economics department. Likewise Stanford. At MIT two of twenty-five tenured economics professors are women. At Princeton, the number is three out of thirty-two. The University of Toronto has eight on the tenure track, versus forty-five men.

There are signs of change, as a new wave of economists, most of them women, are rethinking domestic economies. Most are in their forties and fifties and came of age during the rise of twentieth-century feminism. Old economic models with their mathematical rigidity don't leave space for addressing social issues that don't fit neatly into a market-driven economy. That said, these subjects are increasingly the focus of study. For example, Claudia Goldin, the first woman tenured in Harvard's economics department, has written of the birth control pill's effect on labor markets, as well as *Understanding the Gender Gap: An Economic History of American Women,* published in 1990, which is considered the definitive study of the integration of women in the economy.

Classic economics models are currently under scrutiny. Strober, for example, has studied the work of Adam Smith, the Scottish philosopher and economist best known for *The Wealth of Nations,* his pioneering 1776 book on division of labor and market economics. Smith is most famous for his notion of the "invisible hand" of the marketplace. But he also championed the lesser-known idea of "provisioning," which he defined as "the creation and distribution of the necessaries and conveniences of life." Strober argues that Smith's thinking about provisioning has been lost and that it would be a giant step for mainstream economics to consciously change its definition from a social science concerned with analyzing choices to one concerned with studying the provision of material well-being. She also questions the definition of accepted economics precepts like "efficiency," using the example of the woman who takes time off work to take a child to the doctor. "Everyone sees that as reduced productivity," Strober says. "We need to ask, whose productivity? We have to ask, as an economy as a whole, what are we trying to do? What are our values?"

Mainstream economics theory also cleaves to Smith's belief that each individual is a "rational man," pursuing his or her own self-interest, and that ultimately the aggregate pursuit of self-interest will yield the best possible outcome. But if markets work so well, the economist Nancy Folbre argues in her 2002 book, *The Invisible Heart: Economics and Reality*, why are wages for child-care workers so low that the profession is plagued with high turnover, which makes it difficult for these caregivers to form good relationships? As she presents it, caring labor simply does not fit standard economics models that divide work into paid and unpaid labor, because people who engage in this labor are often willing to work for low wages owing to the intrinsic, nonmonetary benefit of helping someone. Classical economics simply fails to capture the explicit reward of such value. But there is another question to be addressed. And that is the extent to which women's dominant role as unpaid domestic workers has carried into the workforce in terms of dragging down the perceived market value of both women's labor and also so-called caregiving jobs, be they in maintenance, teaching, or nursing.

In his judgment in the British landmark case of *Lambert* vs. *Lambert*, Lord Justice Thorpe employed language destined to strike a chord with all wives who choose to sacrifice their own career ambitions to raise a family: "The more driven the breadwinner, the less available he will be physically and emotionally both as a husband and a father." That sentence could have ramifications for the valuation of domestic or caring labor, implying as it does that the unpaid role of a husband and father—and by extension wife and mother—has value that remains unquantified. But as noble as the sentiment governing the ruling may have been, it remains moot. In 2002, Harry Lambert announced he was not giving his ex-wife an additional penny.

When asked whether she sees her marriage as an equal partnership, Mary Catherine Birgeneau pauses, then speaks carefully. "There are times in every marriage where balance shifts, which is not bad, but it shifts up and down." She pauses again. "I was equal to him when we married," she says. Then she thinks about it. "Actually that's not true. He brought dental bills into our marriage. He couldn't drive. I taught him to drive. And I supported us." She pauses again to reflect. "You know, in all of these years, I had forgotten about that."

Chapter 9

The Wife Axis

Diana, Princess of Wales. Vera Wang silk-faced organza gowns. Tiffany's classic six-prong engagement ring. Princess Bride Barbies. Idyllic scenes of Victorian domesticity. Betty Friedan. Cinderella. The Superwoman. Martha Stewart. Blow-job seminars. Hymen-replacement kits. Gloria Steinem. Isabella Beeton. Lemon-verbena dishwashing liquid. Female orgasm-enhancement medication. Kitchen knives smeared with husbands' blood. Bridget Jones. Photographs of battered women. The Superwife. *The Stepford Wives. The Rules.* Wife activists. Wives' clubs. Adam Smith. Manolo Blahnik stilettos.

This bizarre list is only a portion of the iconography that now fills the wife gap. It reminds us that in freeing the wife from her historical tethers without addressing the institutionalized wife construct, the role has been rendered an empty vessel, ready to be filled with new freight that will reinstate ballast. And as long as that remains the case, the role will serve as a useful female-control mechanism, a handy way of judging women, of telling them what they should do and who they should be.

The scolding has become increasingly shrill: play hard to get. Take regular sabbaticals from your marriage. Submit to sex when you don't want it. Have children early. Stifle your aggression. Grow your hair long. Take his name. Don't take his name. Embrace your femininity.

Stay single. Blame feminism. Drop out of the workforce and focus on family. Don't worry about economic independence: your prince will take care of you. If you don't marry, your life will be hollow. Consider all men bastards. Learn decoupage.

The invective reveals all is not well. This is most evident in the frequent presentation of the modern wife in a fugue state, as if medicated into submission. She's an anesthetized little-girl princess or a robotic twenty-first-century Stepford wife or a brutalized victim reduced to an automaton state. If she's not numbed in some sort of phenobarbital high, she's asserting her identity by bristling at a role that no longer fits. In this incarnation, she's a frustrated, avenging harridan. Or participating in the millennial wife-sex boycott. Or having an affair with an office mate. Or opting out as one of those "picky" unwives.

Is there any way out of this gap? Is it possible to approach the wife in a way that doesn't dead-end in either-or? Suggesting the position be detonated is pointless. For all the crowing that marriage is in crisis, the institution remains the preferred way to cement love. It appeals to that Noah's Ark instinct to pair up to face the flood together, whatever that flood might bring. A strong marriage is an advantageous incubator in which to raise children. It remains a source of varying degrees of economic support. And it continues to confer social approbation, one of the reasons why gays are agitating for the right to marry.

There's always the common-law option, one chosen by an increasing number of couples. Given the legal entitlements now accorded those who cohabit, however, the differences between it and the legal marital relation have blurred. That said, if we look to the Canadian province of Quebec, where civil law has led to common-law marriages being a norm, we can see women evidencing fewer "wifely" behaviors: the birth rate is declining and employment outside the home is more common.

Most women will be wives for some period, or various intervals, of their lives. The terrain they enter is far different from the landscape that made the wife a requirement for so many women decades ago. Not only has legislation recast the definition of wife, but so too have scientific breakthroughs, most notably the birth control pill. The doubling in lifespan in the Western world over the past century means that "till death do us part" can entail a sixty- or seventy-year commitment. That's a high-risk prospect in a society riddled by short attention spans and the belief that all can be "new and improved." There's also the fact that a modern preoccupation with individual satisfaction and personal expression runs contrary to the sacrifices required of marriage. (And the narcissism of "smug marrieds" who express their "we-ness" in idio-syncratic weddings and Saturday outings to IKEA—the retail chain where Lorena Bobbitt purchased her infamous knife—doesn't count.)

Becoming a wife means more than making a lifetime deal that may or may not pan out. The position has far greater implications than the inevitable blurring of identities destined to take place in a marriage. What a wife is reflects and reinforces the society that sanctions the role. It connects us to the social fabric, to the past and to the future. As the nineteenth-century philosopher John Stuart Mill noted, marriage is the first political institution most of us enter into as adults. As such, it offers both a mirror and a lens into what a society is and what it values.

If we look closely, we can see grassroots attempts being made to break through the institutionalized wife bulwark and recast the mean-ing of wife. It's apparent in popular culture, in academia, in the every-day lives of men and women. Wife has become the axis around which the next social revolution is fermenting. This isn't an organized move-ment; Procter & Gamble isn't funding it; there's no one circulating petitions or marching on government buildings brandishing "Wife Power" buttons, at least not yet.

The ferment reveals that a breaking point has been reached. A desire for a more civilized, less frenetic way of life is revealed in the current obsession with the surfaces of home and the romanticization of the housewife. And here we must tread carefully. For, contrary to popular belief, women can't be retrofitted like a tongue-and-groove backsplash in a pseudo-Victorian kitchen. Progress requires that we move ahead. The evolution in the definition of family and motherhood is one indi-cation of a shift. So is the attempt to rethink the value of invisible, caring labor. Other signs, too, point to a sea change.

Where the wife was once shunted to one side, derided in a manner that had consequences for all women, her contributions are being scrutinized and celebrated. The radical notion that wife could be connective tissue that binds women and men, for instance, fueled Lilith Fair, one of the most successful pop tours of the 1990s in terms of cultural influence. The performance kicked off on July 5, 1997, at the Gorge, an outdoor amphitheater outside Seattle. The thirty-five-city tour, organized by the thirty-year-old singer Sarah McLachlan, featured a rotating lineup of female performers. Despite big-name headliners, the industry viewed the venture as a commercial risk. Putting two female performers on the stage back to back wasn't done, according to the conventional wisdom of rock concert promotion. Women served as pretty punctuation. They weren't sufficiently alpha to be primary draws. McLachlan refused to heed this dictum, an instinct proven correct: Lilith Fair was a sold-out success repeated over three years.

The concert's name paid homage to the apocryphal figure said to be Adam's first wife; the reference to *fair*, according to McLachlan, was intended to represent the ideal of equality between the sexes. There are few more iconoclastic wife models than Lilith, whose story is found in the tenth-century manuscript "The Alphabet of Ben Sira." According to this rendering, Adam was lonely in the Garden of Eden, so God created Lilith using the same dust from which he created Adam. But Adam and Lilith quarreled over Adam's desire for domination. (One source of discord was Adam's insistence on the missionary position during sex. Even in the Garden of Eden, it seems, a wife couldn't bank on sexual satisfaction.)

Adam refused to accede to her wishes, and Lilith was exiled. God sent three angels in pursuit, who caught her and ordered her to return to Adam. She refused, vowing henceforth to kill babes in their cradles. After the scuffle with the angels, Lilith promised that if a child's mother hung an amulet over the baby bearing the names of the three angels, she would stay away from that home. So they let her go. Ever since, Lilith is said to fly around the world, howling her hatred of mankind through the night, having sex with demon lovers, propagating and vowing vengeance. Meanwhile, God created Eve from Adam's rib, which put the kibosh on any potential claim to equality she might dare make.

Lilith doesn't appear in the Bible. But the story of Lilith resisting domination and her subsequent punishment was embraced by twentieth-century feminists as a wife ideal—a woman whose quest for equality and independence causes her to reject the rules of marriage. Therein lies the dilemma: Lilith may be ideologically correct, the ultimate avenging wife, but she's unpalatable as an exemplar of a successful, shared marriage.

McLachlan's tribute to Lilith reveals the search by young women for alternative scripts, for unofficial versions of what a wife can be, versions that also include a husband. The singer herself was a newlywed when the tour kicked off; she had married Ashwin Sood, the drummer in her band, the previous February. They eloped to Jamaica, thereby avoiding the machinations of the wedding industrial complex. Even so, in an interview a year after the wedding, McLachlan admitted she couldn't escape the Cinderella fantasy. "I have a great sense of myself that I've never had before," she said. "A lot of things came together for me in the last year— getting married, finding somebody I really believe I'll spend the rest of my life with. Because I did have that Cinderella thing growing up. You think you deserve to find somebody who really, really loves you."

Cinderella-Lilith. Clearly it's time to replace that simplistic duality with the voices of actual wives who embody the complexities of the role. This we see happening with the emergent audience for the long-silenced voices of historical wives. Finally, their contributions, rather than only the hardships they faced, are being acknowledged. Witness the surprising amount of attention lavished on the posthumous publication of a minor memoir, *Some Memories of a Long Life,* by Malvina Shanklin Harlan in 2002. Shanklin Harlan, the wife of the U.S. Supreme Court Justice John Marshall Harlan, who served on the bench from 1877 until 1911, was unknown publicly. Her journal was filed away with Harlan's letters in the Library of Congress. It was unearthed by Justice Ruth Bader Ginsburg when she was researching a lecture on the wives of Supreme Court justices.

The diary was given prominent reviews in major newspapers and literary journals. That it would elicit any interest at all might be chalked up to the current romanticization of the Victorian helpmate. Certainly the judge's spouse follows the drill. When addressing public or political issues, she quotes from her husband's papers, mutes her voice, and defers to him even in death. As she puts it, the man was the "name-maker" for the family and the "ambitious wife" was ready to sacrifice her own identity to advance his "desired goal." But we can also view fascination with the document another way: as backlash to the romantic return to the home seen in the 1990s. It dispels the glossy nirvana seen in the pages of *Victoria* magazine. A letter written by Shanklin Harlan's mother to her daughter on the eve of her wedding in 1856, for instance, reminds the reader of how submerged a woman's identity used to become with marriage: "Remember, now, that his home is YOUR home; his people YOUR people; his interests YOUR interests—you must have no other," the letter read in part.

The journal also puts in context the fact that more than one hundred years ago women were not all playing happy homemaker. Many bridled at the constraints of matrimony. Even then, women were pushing for new definitions. In the "old days" of the mid-nineteenth century, Shanklin Harlan writes, the " 'helpmate' idea entered more universally into the marriage relation than is now the case." She laments that the supportive wife was being replaced by the "New Woman" who was more interested in independence from her husband than in her usefulness to him.

The fact that many Victorian women—the role models for mystique chic—were frustrated by marital limitations is also apparent in *A Rage to Live: A Biography of Richard and Isabel Burton,* by Mary S. Lowell, published in 1999. Isabel Burton, the wife of the famous scholar and explorer, is quoted: "I wish I were a man. If I were, I would be Richard Burton; but being only a woman I will be Richard Burton's wife."

Fascination with the noncompliant Victorian wife is evident too in the revival of interest in *The Awakening,* Kate Chopin's iconoclastic novel, published in 1899, which chronicles the experiences of a twenty-eight-year-old wife and mother, Edna Pontellier, who is locked in a stifling marriage. Edna aches for a fate different from the other wives, who, as she puts it, "idolized their children, worshiped their husbands, and esteemed it a holy privilege to efface themselves." Her view that "she has a position in the universe as a human being" propels her to breach social conventions. She wanders alone in public unescorted; she embarks on an adulterous affair without remorse; she slips off her crinoline to learn to swim; and she tells her lover that she is the possession of no man. In the end, she commits suicide rather than lead less than a fully human existence.

The Awakening created a scandal when it was published. America was not ready for its message, and the book was universally condemned. It was banned in Baltimore, Chopin's hometown. A relatively young widow and mother of six when she wrote the novel, Chopin was ostracized for transmitting the opinion that women's sexual and emotional needs might not be fulfilled by marriage. The criticism ended her career; she committed suicide in 1904, and her work would remain in obscurity for more than half a century.

A hundred years later, Jonathan Yardley, the book critic for *The Washington Post*, heralded *The Awakening* as "the first modern novel." Michael Berube, a professor at the University of Illinois at Urbana-Champaign, taught the novel to his American literature students. He twinned it with a clip from the 1991 female-escape movie *Thelma and Louise*, a combination that serves to remind us, as if we need the reminder, that the trapped-woman motif in popular culture continues a century later. That the either-or dilemma experienced by Edna Pontellier—a woman can make a home or be part of the wider world—remains the subject of social debate today should be read as a sign that alternating push-pull leverage exerted by the wife remains unresolved.

So intense is the desire to hear the voices of long-silenced wives that authors have invented them. In *Wide Sargasso Sea*, published in 1966, Jean Rhys imagined the early life of Bertha Rochester, the silent, attic-bound first wife in Charlotte Brontë's *Jane Eyre*. In 2001, Sally Beauman retold Daphne du Maurier's 1938 cult classic, *Rebecca*, in *Rebecca's Tale*. The original novel was narrated from the perspective of a sweet, pure, self-effacing "good wife" married to widower Maxim de Winter. She is known only as Mrs. de Winter. Beauman retold the story from the point of view of Rebecca, de Winter's first wife, a "bad" wife who was both promiscuous and vengeful, and who had been murdered by her husband. What particularly irked Beauman about du Maurier's novel was that Rebecca's narrative had been "handed to the voice of conformity," which is what the wife traditionally has represented. Likewise, Sandra Gulland's celebrated trilogy of fictional diaries composed by Napoleon's wife, Josephine (*The Many Lives and Secret Sorrows of Josephine B.; Tales of Passion, Tales of Woe*; and *The Last Great Dance on Earth*) recasts history through the eyes of a wife, here one who is presented as influencing history far more than official accounts allow.

The trend to parse long-hidden wifely contribution extends beyond fictional re-enactments to the lives of real women. History is being rewritten, homing in on wifely contributions. In *Six Wives: The Queens of Henry VIII*, published in 2003, the British historian David Starkey uncovers the heretofore unknown influence of England's most notoriously replaceable trophy wives. It was Anne Boleyn, Starkey reveals, not the monarch, who was intent on splitting the English Church away from Rome, a decision with far-reaching consequences that continue to reverberate today.

Similarly, the backstage power of American first ladies, those public paragons of wifely conformity, is also being mined. The huge appetite for first-lady imagery was apparent in the lineups for the hugely successful exhibit *Jacqueline Kennedy: The White House Years* at New York's Metropolitan Museum of Art in the summer of 2001. Record crowds endured ninety-minute waits to view eighty of the former first lady's outfits, along with personal mementos, all of which forcefully conveyed her influence as myth spinner. The most stunning example of this was the way she shrouded her husband's presidency in the fairy-tale imagery of Camelot. Only days after his death, she summoned the journalist Theodore White to tell him that her husband would play the title song by the musical from Alan Jay Lerner and Frederick Loewe as he fell asleep at night. Whether this is fact or fiction, no one really knows. (Even Lerner, a lifelong friend of Jack Kennedy's, doubted it.) Still, in a piece for *Life* magazine, White conveyed the former first lady's vision of the Kennedy White House as "a magic moment in American history, when gallant men danced with beautiful women, when great deeds were done, and when the White House became the center of the universe."

The interest in the show was consistent with the first wife–centric publishing trend of the late 1990s. This included titles such as Kati Marton's *Hidden Power: Presidential Marriages That Shaped Our Recent History,* Phyllis Lee Levin's *Edith and Woodrow: The Wilson White House,* and Jan Jarboe Russell's *Lady Bird: A Biography of Mrs. Johnson.* Nancy Reagan, reviled as out of touch and ostentatious when she was the first lady ("a Barbie doll with attitude," in the words of one journalist), was recast as one of the most powerful presidential spouses in the twentieth century and the devoted caretaker of both her husband and his legacy. Historians suggested détente between the U.S. and Russia might not have occurred without her behind-the-scenes involvement. Her influence was also registered in her compelling advocacy work for stem-cell research.

Laura Bush, too, has been credited with her husband's political success. *The Perfect Wife: The Life and Choices of Laura Bush,* by Ann Gerhart, published in 2004, posits that Laura Bush's now-famous ultimatum to her husband, "Me or Jim Beam," made her husband a credible political candidate: "If he hadn't stopped drinking, he never would have achieved that."

Interest in the wife biography extends beyond the desire to hear tales of furious women seeking revenge. Hillary Rodham Clinton's memoir, *Living History,* published in 2003, for which she was paid an $8 million advance, achieved record sales for an autobiography. Clinton waxed giddy about her attraction to her husband's hands and "Viking" demeanor when she met him. But there was more than that behind the fascination. Rodham Clinton, continuing in her role as Exhibit A for the modern wife, was forging new ground, showing that a formerly famous wife was capable of political power while remaining a wife. Still, many attributed her success not to her own strength but to the fact that she had won over the public as the stereotypical betrayed, victimized wife. Perhaps this is true. But more important is the fact that Rodham Clinton is taking traditional wife leverage beyond recognizable stereotype.

The abetting wife is gaining ground on the avenging wife as an audience draw. *The Model Wife,* a collection of the work of nine photographers, all of whom used their wives as primary subjects, toured the United States to great success in 2000 and 2001. The images reveal the multi-faceted possibilities of wife—subject and object, model and muse. Included were Baron Adolph de Meyer's highly stylized late-nineteenth-century portraits of his spouse, Olga; Alfred Stieglitz's famous photographs of the artist Georgia O'Keeffe; Edward Weston's topographical nudes of Charis Wilson; and Emmet Gowin's shockingly informal photograph of Edith, standing in a barn, backlit by sun, dressed only in a diaphanous blouse, peeing on the floor. The role of the literary-wife muse is also being explored—Bertha Georgie Hyde-Lees, the wife of W. B. Yeats; Nora Barnacle, the wife of James Joyce; and Vivienne Haigh-Wood, who was married to T. S. Eliot, being but a few such women subject to scrutiny.

The newfound, seemingly unconnected, focus on past wives reveals an unspoken truth: Popular culture has finally collectively snapped to the recognition that in rejecting the role of the wife, we reject not only her subservience and submission but also qualities such as loyalty, support, inspiration, and devotion. And that, in turn, has spawned another realization: that sacrifices made for a mate need not be synonymous with subjugation or the loss of self.

This message is telegraphed in the biography of Véra Nabokov as told by Stacy Schiff in *Véra (Mrs. Vladimir Nabokov)*, which was awarded the 2001 Pulitzer Prize. (One has to wonder whether the prize was also partially directed at the self-abnegating Véra, whose tombstone reads: "Wife, Muse and Agent.")

The Nabokov marriage was a symbiotic one; Véra was an indispensable adjunct to her husband's art. When the family lived in Berlin, Véra, who held a master's degree in modern languages from the Sorbonne, supported them. When her husband taught at Cornell, in Ithaca, New York, she attended his lectures and substituted for him when he was sick. She drove him from motel to motel in their Oldsmobile to trace the journey that would appear in his masterpiece, *Lolita*, while he wrote in the back seat. She plucked the manuscript of that novel from a burning fireplace after her husband threw it there in frustration. She corrected his stories in German, his memoir in French, his poetry in Italian, and translated *Pale Fire* into Russian when she was in her eighties.

Véra's ceaseless work was appreciated by her husband, who lovingly noted the "tender telepathy" he recognized with a woman who, like himself, enjoyed highly developed aesthetic tastes. The two would debate about "the color of Monday, the taste of E-flat." Small wonder Nabokov could write to her without exaggeration: "I need you, my fairy tale. For you are the only person I can talk to—about the hue of a cloud, about the singing of a thought, and about the fact that when I went out to work today and looked at each sunflower in the face, they all smiled back at me with their seeds."

Véra Nabokov's life, as presented by Schiff, defies the notion that being a devoted wife is a traitor to the cause of self-fulfillment, though it is difficult for the contemporary reader to understand why she would discard her own work, yet keep careful copies of her husband's. Nowhere in the biography is she portrayed as a frustrated wife. Hers is a life she chose—for her husband, for art, for herself. Which leads us to another perspective, one that recognizes that, for some, self-fulfillment can be realized by supporting and inspiring those whom we love.

The wife as a beacon of strength would become a recurrent theme following the terrorist attacks on America on September 11, 2001. Lisa Beamer was the first to emerge as a 9/11 icon. Her husband, Todd, was proclaimed a hero with others who stormed the cockpit of one of the hijacked airplanes, causing it to crash rather than hit its designated target in Washington, D.C. The young widow, five months pregnant, presented as a poignant symbol of stoic bereavement in her navy blue dress with a prim white collar when she was introduced by President Bush in his address to Congress a few weeks after the attack. In short order, she was a bona fide celebrity, a fixture on *Larry King Live* and other news shows. In October 2001, she boarded a flight from Newark to San Francisco, the same flight pattern her husband had been on, to complete his journey. Her book, *Let's Roll!*, sat on *The New York Times* best-seller list for months.

Tragedy also propelled Mariane Pearl, a journalist and widow of the *Wall Street Journal* reporter Daniel Pearl, into the spotlight. After her husband was kidnaped and savagely murdered in 2002, Mariane carried on his legacy in the memoir *A Mighty Heart: The Brave Life and Death of My Husband, Danny Pearl*, in which she writes of her "absolute love" for her husband.

Suddenly, supportive wives in popular culture received Hollywood's highest accolade, one that had been showered on abused wives on film for decades: portraying a long-suffering, supportive spouse became a sure-fire route to Oscar gold. In 2001, Marcia Gay Harden won a statuette for her portrayal of Lee Krasner, the common-law wife of Jackson Pollock who relinquished her own artistic ambitions to support her difficult and unfaithful mate's erratic genius. The following year, Jennifer Connelly received an Academy Award for her performance as Alicia Nash, a former academic who stood by her Nobel laureate husband, John Nash, during his battle with schizophrenia. (Tellingly, these actresses were nominated in the Best Supporting Actress category even though their roles were as dominant as those of the actors who played the husbands. But these men were nominated for Academy Awards in the Best Actor category.)

Of course, the celebration of behind-the-scenes backup can be written off as yet another example of the back-to-the-house message directed at women. Or as one intended to telegraph the point that supporting one's spouse is worthy of applause only if the spouse being supported is a best-selling novelist or a Nobel Prize winner. But before we dismiss the recognition of the supportive wife as yet another example of wife as a female-control mechanism, consider that the supportive wife role can extend to men, which would make *wife* a gender-neutral verb: *to wife*: to care for, to nurture, to support. We saw this in the awarding of the Best Supporting Actor Oscar in 2002 to Jim Broadbent for his portrayal of John Bayley in the movie *Iris*. A few years earlier, Bayley had gained accolades for *Elegy for Iris* and *Iris and Her Friends*, two memoirs that traversed his thirty-four-year marriage to the writer Iris Murdoch and her descent into the twilight fog of Alzheimer's. Bayley, a literary journalist and former Oxford don, was Murdoch's caregiver during her long illness. He cut and cleaned her fingernails, struggled to undress her at night, and laughed with her at Teletubbies to anesthetize his knowledge that they would never speak of Tolstoy or Piero della Francesca or Byron again. He would be roundly criticized in literary circles for writing of Murdoch's last painful years. Such revelations were seen to be a betrayal of the marital covenant; he had exploited private memories of his wife when she was at her most vulnerable.

Yet if there is a voyeuristic aspect to Bayley's accounts, it is not viewing Murdoch in a diminished form. Rather, it is the rare glimpses they provide of a husband's self-sacrifice for a female partner. Bayley, who would have been a literary footnote had he not written about his wife, cheerfully admitted he had the greater capacity for domesticity, even though the couple lived in legendary squalor. He appreciated in Murdoch what he referred to as her "complete indifference to the womanly image of a helpmate." He took huge pride in her work and success and in contributing to it in even the smallest of ways. Once, he reviewed a book for a newspaper under Murdoch's name, willing to submerge himself in her identity.

That is what modern marriage is, a give-and-take of strength and weakness, that unpredictable choreography of dependence and independence that the Australian poet A. D. Hope named in his poem "Man Friday" a love "to grow closer and closer apart." In such a fluid dance, movement depends on eliminating the idea that one partner is primary, the other secondary.

This isn't to say that men and women are the same. Obviously, they aren't. The very fact of men's superior physical strength, to name one accepted difference, means that men will continue to do most of society's risky heavy lifting, as construction workers, firemen, police officers, and soldiers. They'll continue to be called on to open the pickle jar. And until scientific breakthrough, women will bear children, give birth to children, and are more likely to engage in primary child-rearing than men. But just as men and women are different, so too are women different from other women, men from men. Some like to be on top—metaphorically, professionally, sexually. Others prefer a more submissive posture. One size does not fit all.

It's now fashionable to amplify the differences between the sexes, to adopt a "Men Are from Mars, Women Are from Venus" mentality. As cute as the maxim may be, it overlooks the point that we're all from Planet Earth and have to reside together on it. And that, at an elemental level, most earthlings, be they male or female, have similar goals—to survive; to feel safe, protected, and respected; to love and to be loved; to be remembered when we are gone.

The groundwork to eliminate male-alpha/female-beta is in place. The dominant male breadwinner/passive female homemaker model that formed the blueprint of "masculine" and "feminine" is being dismantled. Despite attempts to reinsert it, the line between the "feminine" homefront and the "masculine" office has blurred. The consumer imperative, once seen as a hardwired female prerogative, is now shared by men and women. So much so that the new joke is that men are the new women, busy shopping, moisturizing, and fretting over the thread count of bedding.

The shift in roles has been interpreted by many not as a positive challenge but rather as a pink-versus-blue showdown: if women gain power, goes the logic, men have to lose it. The outcome is all too predictable: a zero-sum game that pits women against men. We have seen this in panicked talk of a "masculinity crisis." What is now being dubbed the "feminization" of the culture has resulted in an 180-degree turn: men, not women, goes this new thinking, are subjugated and marginalized.

So drastic has been this reversal that men have been anointed the "second sex," the term Simone de Beauvoir used to describe women in the mid-twentieth century. In 2003, in a story about how boys were falling behind girls at school, *BusinessWeek* stated that "from kindergarten to grad school, boys are becoming the second sex." The British author and genetics professor Steve Jones's *Y: The Descent of Men* uses biology to explain the second-sex phenomenon: "Males are, in many ways, parasites upon their partners," Jones writes. "Their interests are to persuade the other party to invest in reproduction, while doing as little as they can themselves."

The status of the emasculated man has been attributed to a multiplicity of causes. In *Stiffed: The Betrayal of the American Male,* Susan Faludi laments that "social forces have destroyed men's very sense of what it means to be a man" and blames a lack of public father figures and a competitive "ornamental" culture fraught with economic dislocation, corporate venality, and sexual confusion for the problem. *The Trouble with Boys,* by Angela Phillips, argues that men have been rendered ineffectual by a feminist-dominated status quo. In *Blood Rites: Origins and History of the Passion of War*, Barbara Ehrenreich suggests that male identity has been dislocated by the fact that men, no longer hunters and providers, are less central to women's and children's survival. That message is echoed by the social anthropologist Lionel Tiger in *The Decline of Males*, which posits that men are so discriminated against by public policy that families are returning to "mammalian default mode," in which mothers alone live with offspring. But while all of these arguments can credibly be made, we might also want to look at the "crisis" in terms of the inevitable reordering that took place but was not accounted for when the wife was untethered.

The fallout was reflected on the cover of the June 1999 issue of *Harper's*, which asked "Who Needs Men?" The "redundant" male trope has become routine fodder for comedians. As Dennis Miller put it: "Between reasonably priced landscaping services, Jiffy-Lube, and sperm banks, men are pretty much optional these days." The most amusing aspect of that joke is that men are anything but "optional" when one is looking at the top of Fortune 500 companies, most world governments, the military, or *Forbes* magazine's list of the "most wealthy." Nor are they extraneous when looking for recruits for high-risk, physically demanding jobs.

Again, we're back in that tired chorus of "Who Needs Men?" "Who Needs a Husband?" "Who Needs a Man Around the House?" Clearly women need men, just as men need women. What's the alternative? Women going off to live in Utopian "feminaries" that have been written about since the nineteenth century?

And here we come to the crux of the matter: the meaning of wife hinges on the meaning of husband, just as the meaning of woman hinges on the meaning of man. Until the late twentieth century, this was dictated by the alpha-beta construct reinforced by marital roles. But this too is slowly changing. Public displays of men such as John Bayley, providing support to more prominent wives, remind us that the nominal "wife" doesn't have to be the actual "wife." Only a decade ago, the male wife was a member of an exclusive, eccentric club. There was Leonard Woolf, the emotional nursemaid to the brilliant, manic-depressive Virginia. And

Denis Thatcher, the devoted consort of Margaret Thatcher, the first female prime minister of the United Kingdom, who held office between 1979 and 1990. Theirs was an intriguing partnership. He was a successful businessman before he became known primarily as her husband; he believed that the ideal political spouse was "always present, never there." In his case, this adage was doubly wise: his visibility was a reminder that even though he was the "wife," Margaret Thatcher was also literally a "wife," which ran the risk of shifting her power from alpha to beta. That it never did was a testament to her governance. Yet the fact that the culture didn't know how to frame her aberrant power was reflected in her nickname of "Iron Lady." Her husband, however, viewed her as a remarkable, nonmetallic human. As he once praised her, "For forty years I have been married to one of the greatest women the world has ever produced. All I could produce, small as it may be, was love and loyalty."

During the 1990s, derision of the male wife abated. In fact, the species began emerging as a fashionable accessory. Andrew Tilberis, widower of former *Harper's Bazaar* editor Liz Tilberis, was a full-time househusband until his wife's death and now carries on her commitment to ovarian cancer research. Andy Spade, the husband of the famed handbag designer Kate Spade, quit his job in advertising to work with her. Donna Karan's late husband, Stephan, was instrumental behind the scenes building the empire that made his wife a household name. Thierry Boué, husband and business partner of Marcia Kilgore, the founder of Bliss spas, sounded like a clichéd traditional wife in an interview in which he discussed his spouse's onerous workload: "If we weren't working together, I would see her only for a few hours a day," he said. Even the ultimate alpha husband, Bill Clinton, was recast as the supportive spouse, as he campaigned for his wife during her successful run for the U.S. Senate in 2000.

The househusband, too, has been identified as a big trend, even though men who stay at home with their children remain a tiny minority. Many take on homemaking duties owing to a temporary layoff, or they use the time at home to engage in home-based employment. Still, a growing number of couples are deciding the husband should sacrifice his career advancement for a few years or even until children are grown to permit his wife to devote more time to her career. Yet stigma exists. Staying home is not mannish, a perception revealed in an article on Canada's top female lawyers that ran in the *National Post* newspaper in September 2003. One female lawyer with two children admitted that if her husband, also a lawyer, was honest, he would say that staying home would be easier for him than it would be for her. That he isn't able to do so reveals the female prerogative that continues to govern the home sphere.

Replacing female wives with male wives only shifts systemic wife problems to another gender. Men staying home experience the same marginalization felt by women who stay home. This point shone through in an October 2002 *Fortune* cover story titled "Trophy Husbands," which enthused about the new breed of stay-at-home man. Only months previously, the business magazine had profiled women who dropped out of the workforce to stay home in "Goodbye Boss Lady, Hello Soccer Mom." The apparent double standard was disheartening. When women step off the fast track to return home, it is assumed they can't cope. When men do it, they're welcomed as heroes. This message was conveyed in the subtitle to "Trophy Husbands": "Arm candy? Are you kidding? While their fast-track wives go to work, stay-at-home husbands mind the kids. They deserve a trophy for trading places."

As the magazine explained, the trophy wife's only job was to "lunch, party, conspicuously consume, and keep their husbands off Viagra," whereas the trophy husband is busy with a long list of practical tasks: "carpool the kids, coach the soccer team, pay the bills, pick up the dry cleaning, and fix dinner." Their sacrifices were lauded in a way those of stay-at-home wives rarely are. As the magazine gushed, "credit him with setting aside his own career by dropping out, retiring early, or going part-time so that his wife's career might flourish and their family might thrive. Behind a great woman at work, there is often a great man at home."

Yet the article made clear that the small number of men who are primary caregivers face similar no-win polarities as women who do the same. They were seen to be opportunists: "If they have nannies—a few of the men we interviewed did; most did not—they are presumed to be freeloaders, members of the leisure class, even when the nanny is enabling them to sneak in some part-time work." Or they were depicted as experiencing the same problems Betty Friedan has been accused of exaggerating in *The Feminine Mystique*: "isolation, lack of intellectual stimulation, lack of appreciation." Many felt the additional social taint of no longer being the family breadwinner. Frank Fiorina, the husband of the Hewlett-Packard CEO, Carly Fiorina, who retired from his job so that the couple could focus on her career, refused to comment on the *Fortune* article. "To describe him as a stay-at-home husband is not fair to him," Carly Fiorina told the magazine.

Yet ground is shifting. Five years earlier, when the magazine wanted to proclaim the "trophy-husband" trend, it had been unable to find enough people willing to talk on the record. Even so, there's still stigma associated with the wife being the greater wage-earner. Now, however, it's often masked with self-deprecating humor. In a television commercial for a discount telephone service, the actor John Stamos joked that he needed to save money because his wife, the actress-model Rebecca Romijn Stamos, earned more. (The couple divorced soon after, though their economic disparity was not cited as the reason.)

Bringing men onto the wife team is crucial if the wife gap is to be closed. And team building is necessary both in the home and in the workplace. It's particularly necessary for stay-at-home parents who require the kind of social interaction available in the market economy. We tend to see that househusbands gravitate more readily into social networks such as Stay at Home Dad (whose morose acronym SAHD definitely needs an update), which stages conventions, organizes a Web site, and sends out newsletters.

The most radical redefinition of the gender dynamic underlying marriage is witnessed in the attempts to legalize homosexual unions. As I write, the Netherlands, Belgium, and two Canadian provinces confer equal marital rights on gay couples. The Supreme Court of Massachussets has just approved gay marriages. Many other jurisdictions grant some legal privileges to same-sex couples. As gays marry, the institution will lose its status as an exclusively male-female domain, a prospect that inflames many. But as gays are given the right to wed, the gender biases that continue to dictate roles in modern marriages are destined to disintegrate further.

Most married couples don't toil at top levels of Fortune 500 companies or run fashion empires. They are not quoted in *Forbes* magazine. In most marriages, both partners hold jobs, some out of choice, more out of necessity. In single-adult households—the dominant and fastest-growing demographic—one income has to cover all the bases. It is for these people, not the privileged men and women extolling the benefits of stay-at-home wives in the pages of *The New York Times*, that the entrenched-wife model causes the greatest hardship.

Solutions do exist. To find them, however, we need to return to models created during World War II, the last time wives' efforts in the workplace were solicited and celebrated by government and corporations. Recognizing that women were no longer playing the traditional role, companies in the United States provided backup for them in the form of on-site round-the-clock centers for children between eighteen months and six years. The British government provided working wives with daycare, home help, prepared meals, and one free afternoon a week for shopping. To encourage women to join the labor force, the Canadian government provided childcare centers and tax incentives.

The "glass ceiling" must also be recognized for what it is. And that is not as an impenetrable abstraction but rather as a blockade, representing the bias against wives and mothers toiling outside the home, built into corporations and professions. Joan C. Williams, the director of the Program on WorkLife Law at American University in Washington, D.C., spelled this out in an article in *The Harvard Law Journal* in 2003. As she put it, the reason many women never get near the glass ceiling is that they are "stopped long before by the maternal wall." We are finally arriving at the perception that the careers of women—and men—who drop out of the workforce to care for children for extended periods of time must be viewed as "non-linear," a concept foreign to the corporate lexicon. It's no surprise that companies seen to be leaders in terms of flexible work practices have more women in prominent positions. Over the past decade, the accounting firm Deloitte & Touche has more than doubled the number of employees choosing to work on a flexible schedule. During that period the number of female partners and directors rose to 567 from 97. But men, too, benefit from less rigid scheduling. Since Deloitte & Touche offered extended paternity leave for fathers, for example, nearly half of eligible men have taken it.

Such examples, routinely trotted out, remain the exception, showing up on *Working Woman*'s annual "Top 100 Companies for Mothers to Work," which lists businesses that excel in providing childcare, before- and afterschool care, family childcare homes and summer programs, and flexible work schedules. It won't be until *Fortune* gives up on proclaiming the latest flavor of "trophy wife" and focuses on "Top 100 Companies for Fathers to Work" that we will know substantial progress is being made. Not that *Fortune*'s foray into the trophy-husband arena wasn't instructive. It revealed yet again that househusbands do not perform nearly as much housework as housewives do. That still remains women's work, wife work. And it will continue to be so until women let go of the power premium that comes from controlling the home. Until then, expect to see women in advertising and on television pushing mops and separating whites with the zealous intensity of a Stepford wife. That this imagery remains entrenched can be chalked up to yet another of those circular chicken-egg equations: when they are questioned by advertising focus groups, women say they don't buy into imagery of men doing housework because it doesn't reflect reality. And it doesn't reflect reality because of the entrenched stereotype, one perpetuated by the mass media, that men don't do household chores (or that when they do them, it's usually grudgingly or incompetently).

Ground is shifting here also. Women are showing signs of negotiating this domestic imperative. Nori Starck, the wife of the designer Philippe Starck, confessed in an interview in *Vogue* magazine in October 2003 that she fought with her husband in the early days of their marriage over who would rule the domestic front, even though they both maintained thriving careers. The modern twist? They both wanted the job. As she says: "One of the reasons he kept asking me for a divorce is that we couldn't decide who would be the woman of the house. Finally, I gave in and said, 'OK, I'm married to a wife.'"

The wife in the home extends to the workplace as the alpha and beta of married life is etched large in the professional and political realms. In 1931, Virginia Woolf addressed young professional women about the phantom who threatened to ruin her writing. This creature she referred to as the "utterly unselfish Angel of the House," that idealized version of Victorian womanliness as expressed by the Victorian poet Coventry Patmore in "The Angel in the House," a work dedicated to his wife, Emily. Woolf said such a compliant creature "must be killed" if women are going to be truly creative in their work. Later, in an essay titled "Angel in the House," Woolf writes, "Had I not killed her she would have killed me." As the writer saw it, women had been programmed by this ideal: "they must charm, they must conciliate, they must—to put it bluntly—tell lies if they are to succeed." More than sixty years later, that "angel" remains fortified by commercial forces that tell women their homes must be showplaces, boasting handmade table centerpieces, lavender-scented laundry, and elaborate dinner parties on a Tuscan theme.

Signs exist that women are trying to break free of this martyr complex. In *The Bitch in the House: 26 Women Tell the Truth About Sex, Solitude, Work, Motherhood and Marriage*, published in 2002, essayists vent about their lot in life, channeling what the book's editor, Cathi Hanauer, refers to as their "inner bitch." Reading these tales of discontent from middle-class successful women trying to juggle family and work, one can't help being astonished at the ferocity of their rage. They have achieved what women a century earlier could only dream of—citizens' rights, access to education, employment prospects, reproductive freedom. But they are angry, a fury that stems from the fact that they can't "have it all," that commercial construct presented to women in media and popular culture. The essays reveal the extent to which social expectations have been shaped by aggressive late-twentieth-century capitalism—by romance novels, Hollywood movies, and women's magazines. The women writing these accounts register a constant desire for more, the perpetual state of yearning cultivated by the marketplace. The book's title also reflects the entrenched polarities that continue to apply to women: the "angel in the house" had been replaced by the "bitch in the house." Women expressing anger can't simply be women. Rather, they have to be cast as the bitch, that term frequently used as a put-down for the assertive woman, so much so that some women regard being called a bitch a badge of honor.

Within the culture, the powerful wife remains an aberration. Like the househusband, she's treated like a novelty item, a showpiece trotted out to demonstrate how far we have come, despite the fact that she's singled out suggests otherwise. In the spring of 2003, *The New York Observer* made the grand declaration that the trophy wife had been replaced by "middle-aged babes with power dowries." These women were dubbed the "new breed of fortysomething Superdames who have been around the block—sex bombs who can do a balance sheet and set the dinner table—and they're retiring the old-fashioned Bimbettes from the forefront of New York society."

Superwoman. Superwife. Supermom. Superdame. One stereotype replaces another. Yet in their daily lives women and men are defying such glib categorization. More and more we see wives who are older and more prominent than their husbands. We see couples negotiating their domestic lives in unorthodox—or traditional—patterns that work for them. We see both women and men sacrifice their own personal ambitions for the benefit of their families, to give their homes the order, the ritual, and the attention central to a civilized life and society. But we also see men and women opting out of the marital arrangement, choosing to create new forms of family and connection with their community.

Finally, then, we will be able to see the wife is never the lesser. In an interview published in the October 12, 2003, *New York Times Magazine,* the singer-songwriter Edie Brickell, who is married to Paul Simon, was asked, "Does it irritate you that people often refer to you as Paul Simon's wife?" The question was burdened with the entrenched assumption that a woman with a more publicly dominant spouse would automatically view it as a blow to her identity. But Brickell's confident response deflected any suggestion that this is so. "No," she said, "because I am his wife and proud of it."

The wife Edie Brickell represents is far different than that of Mary Catherine Birgeneau. Just as Melissa Schuloff, who organized the fellatio seminar in Edmonton, is not the wife Hillary Clinton is.

There is no singular meaning of wife. That is the point. That is its meaning. To see the wife fully through a multi-faceted lens is one of the central challenges facing society in the twenty-first century. To do this, new scripts are required that employ wife as a verb and as a gender-neutral concept. These are essential if we are to create necessary new narratives, new ways of living as women and men together.

I think back to July 29, 1981, that day of magical veneer. We know it now to be a fraudulent pageant, a business deal disguised as a fairy tale. The characters no longer exist. Diana is dead, though fascination with her life continues unabated. Prince Charles lives with Camilla Parker Bowles, the divorced woman with whom he was famously involved during his marriage. They have never wed. Whether they will remains a subject of much speculation, even censure. Church of England rules allow Charles to marry, but he needs permission from his mother, who is influenced by public sentiment. And the majority of that public does not want to see Camilla as his wife. Many don't want her to be granted the status the role confers. But there's also an unspoken subtext—the knowledge that their wedding would only remind the world of that long-ago shattered fairy tale so many wanted to be true.

More than twenty years after watching the Wedding of the Century, I have never married, never been a wife. Did its imagery and its aftermath affect my decision? I don't know. Maybe. Maybe not. I do know, however, that the choice has played a part in defining me. And that it's a decision I neither regret nor view as permanent.

Looking back, knowing all that is known about that day, I remember it with awe—partly for the hope it was capable of unleashing, partly for its still-poignant wonder. And while it contributed to the fractured imagery surrounding the wife in the culture, it also paved the way to where we are now. And that is to the understanding that the meaning of wife within a society is an elemental cultural indicator. While Western women fret about who does the dishes and gripe about being too tired to have sex, the role of wife for millions of women continues to be not one of choice but of subjugation.

In 1997, before I began writing this book, I clipped a story that ran in *The Times* of London reporting that bride prices in the United Arab Emirates had risen to £18,000. As a result, some 40 percent of men in the region were looking to source cheaper foreign brides. This in turn was a source of concern for Arab women, who are considered to be "on the shelf" if they are not married by age twenty-five. How quaint, smug Western readers scanning the piece might have thought. How much more enlightened are we.

Since then, the plight of women in conservative Muslim countries has become a flash point in discussions of political, social, and religious repression. Once again, the lesson gleaned from the history of marriage in the Western is borne out—that marital rights echo citizen rights and reconfirm social values. Which is why the meaning of wife is so important. For better or worse, the new meaning of wife will provide a new axis, a pivot around which we can arrive at a new understanding of what it means not only to be wife, but to be woman, to be man, to be human.

Acknowledgments

It took a cast of thousands to bring this book into existence, not only those who helped me directly but so many others whose inspirational ideas, work, expertise, and personal experiences are integral to its substance.

Bruce Westwood, my remarkable agent, must be credited for bringing my idea to life and for staying in my corner. I must also thank Natasha Daneman and Nicole Winstanley of Westwood Creative Artists in Toronto for their skilled work on my behalf. Thanks also to Gary Ross for coming up with such a clever title.

It was an honor to work with Denise Oswald at Farrar, Straus and Giroux. Thank you, Denise, for your support, keen editorial suggestions, and boundless generosity. Thanks also to Sarah Almond, Liz Calamari, JoAnna Kremer, and Charlotte Strick.

I am also indebted to Iris Tupholme at HarperCollins Canada for her unflagging trust and patience, without which *The Meaning of Wife* could never have been written. Iris also introduced me to the talented editor Jennifer Glossop, whose guidance and suggestions were invaluable. Nicole Langlois also offered wonderful editorial input, and Barney Gilmore must be thanked for preparing the index.

Moira Daly provided excellent research assistance, as did Theresa Butcher, Scott Maniquet, and Selma Davidson of the National Post library.

To my amazing family and friends, thanks for putting up with me during what seemed an endless ordeal, with added gratitude to my brother Robert Kingston for creating a brilliant cover concept and design.

Beppi Crosariol supported this book from day one, and was always there to offer his moral support and to make astute editorial suggestions. Many others contributed in so many ways. Thank you Sarah Murdoch, Peter Cundill, Gwen Kingston, David Kingston, Beth Kingston, Suzanne Depoe, Dianna Symonds, Sara Angel, Rob Firing, Noelle Zitzer, Siobhan Blessing, Heather Mallick, Ken Whyte, Dianne de Fenoyl, Sarmishta Subramanian, Natasha Hassan, Lorna Wendt Jorgansen, Mary Catherine Birgeneau, Nan Talese, Gail Singer, Sarah Hampson, Theresa Shecter, Myra Strober, Holly Maguigan, Lou Paget, Melissa Schuloff, Frank Addario, Tycho Manson, Richard Siklos, Patricia Best, Tassie Cameron, Eleanore Rosenstein, and Carol Rosenstein. I owe you all.

ANNE KINGSTON
September 2004

Notes

Epigraph

Page vii: Carolyn G. Heilbrun, *Writing a Woman's Life* (New York: W. W. Norton & Company, 1988).

Chapter 1: The Wife Gap

Page 1: Changes in Teen Attitudes Toward Marriage, Cohabitation and Children, 1975–1999, National Marriage Project Staff, 1999; see also Barbara Dafoe Whitehead and David Popenoe, "The State of Our Union 2001," The National Marriage Project 2001.

Page 2: Tamal M. Edwards, "Who Needs A Husband?" ("Single By Choice: Flying Solo"), *Time*, August 28, 2000.

Page 2: Susan Maushart, *Wifework: What Marriage Really Means for Women* (London: Bloomsbury, 2003), p. 6.

Page 3: Elizabeth Hurley quoted in William Cash, "The Split-up: Liz and Let Liz," *The Straits Times* (Singapore), April 27, 2000.

Page 3: Lara Flynn Boyle quoted in Kevin Sessums, "Call of the Wild," *Vanity Fair*, February 2001, p. 140.

Page 4: Henrik Ibsen, *A Doll's House* (new version by Frank McGuinness, from a translation by Charlotte Barslund), London: Faber and Faber, 1996, p. 100.

Page 5: John T. Molloy, *Why Men Marry Some Women and Not Others* (New York: Warner Books, 2003), p. 37.

Page 6: Deirdre Kelly, "Glamour Jobs," *Elle Canada*, September 2001, p. 101.

Page 6: "As one female social commentator wrote": Meghan Cox Gurdon, "She's Back," *The Women's Quarterly*, Spring 1998.

Page 6: "contemporary status symbol": Amy Finnerty, "What We Look Up to Now" (issue) *New York Times Magazine*, November 15, 1998, p. 81.

Page 6: "housewife wannabes": Judy Dutton, "Meet the New Housewife Wannabes," *Cosmopolitan*, June 2000, p. 164.

Page 6: Helen Fielding, *Bridget Jones's Diary* (London: Picador, 1998).

Page 6: Barbara Dafoe Whitehead, *Why There Are No Good Men Left: The Romantic Plight of the New Single Woman* (New York: Broadway Books, 2002).

Page 7: "female Rorschach test": interviews with author.

Page 10: Sir William Blackstone, Book the First: Chapter 15: "Of Husband and Wife," *Commentaries on the Laws of England*, from the Avalon Project, Yale Law School.

Page 11: Lawrence Stone, *Family, Sex and Marriage in England* (New York: HarperCollins, 1983), pp. 217–253.

Page 11: Alexis de Tocqueville, *Democracy in America* (New York: Schocken Books, 1974), Book 2, p. 241.

Page 11: Ellen duBois, ed., *The Elizabeth Cady Stanton–Susan B. Anthony Reader: Correspondence, Writing, Speeches* (Boston Northeastern University Press, 1992), pp. 55–56.

Page 12: Simone de Beauvoir, *The Second Sex* (New York: Vintage Books, 1989), p. 456.

Page 12: Norman Mailer's first wife: Deirdre Bair, *Simone de Beauvoir: A Biography* (New York: Simon & Schuster, 1990).

Page 12: Betty Friedan, *The Feminine Mystique* (New York: A Laurel Book, Dell Publishing, 1983), pp. 243–46.

Page 13: Interview with Gloria Steinem, *Good Morning America*, September 6, 2000.

Page 13: "It didn't take courage not to want": *New York*, April 6, 1998, p. 89.

Page 14: Germaine Greer, *The Female Eunuch* (New York: Farrar, Straus & Giroux, 2002).

Page 15: U.S. Supreme Court cited in Nancy Cott, *Public Vows: A History of Marriage and the Nation* (Cambridge: Harvard University Press, 2000).

Page 16: Simone de Beauvoir, *A Transatlantic Love Affair: Letters to Nelson Algren* (New York: The New Press, 1999), p. 20.

Page 16: Raymond Carver, *A New Path to the Waterfall* (New York: The Atlantic Monthly Press, 1989), p. 117.

Page 17: Philip Delves Broughton, "How the Fish Found Her Bicycle," *The Daily Telegraph* (London), November 7, 2001, p. 17.

Page 17: Dave Tianen, "Steinem at 66: a new bride with an old cause," *Milwaukee Journal*, March 22, 2001, p. E1.

Page 18: "America's Ur-wife": Lucinda Franks, "The Intimate Hillary," *Talk*, September 1999, p. 167; and James Bennett, "The Next Clinton," *The New York Times Magazine*, May 30, 1999, p. 23.

Page 20: David Lister, "Greer Says PM's Wife Appears Like His Concubine," *The Independent* (London), January 18, 2001, p. 9.

Pages 20–21: George Bush on "the best wife" quoted in Susan Schindehette, "The First Lady Next Door," *People*, January 29, 2001, p. 50.

Page 21: Erica Jong, "Sometimes a Beard Changes Everything," *New York Times*, August 18, 2001, p. A15.

Page 21: Lynda Rosen Obst, *Hello, He Lied: And Other Truths from the Hollywood Trenches* (New York: Broadway Books, 1996), p. 167.

Pages 21–22: Eisenhower and Hoover on Communist wives: "Closet-Case Studies," *New York Times Magazine*, December 16, 2001, p. 23.

Page 23: "... even women's choice of career": See M.V. Lee Badgett and Nancy Folbre, "Job Gendering: Occupational Choice and the Marriage Market," *Industrial Relations*, vol. 42, no. 2 (April 2003), p. 270, which argues women tend to select traditional careers, which often pay lower wages, to avoid being penalized in the marriage market.

Page 24: Jill Bialosky, "How We Became Strangers," in Hanauer, Cathi, ed., *The Bitch in the House: 26 Women Tell the Truth About Sex, Solitude, Work, Motherhood and Marriage* (New York: William Morrow, 2002), p. 119.

Page 24: Peggy Orenstein, *Flux: Women on Sex, Work, Love, Kids and Life in a Half-Changed World* (New York: Doubleday, 2000), p. 103.

Page 24: "young women expect their husbands to be the primary breadwinners," cited in Anne Machung, "Talking Career; Thinking Job: Gender Differences in Career and Family Expectations of Berkeley Seniors," *Feminist Studies*, 15:1 (Spring 1989), pp. 35–38.

Page 25: Ginia Bellefante, "Is Feminism Dead?" ("It's All About Me!"), *Time*, June 29, 1998, p. 49.

Page 26: Susan B. Anthony quoted in *Not for Ourselves Alone: The Story of Elizabeth Cady Stanton and Susan B. Anthony*, a documentary by Ken Burns and Paul Barnes, a production of Florentine Films and WETA, Washington, D.C. (1999).

Page 26: Betty Friedan, *Life So Far: A Memoir* (New York: First Touchstone Edition, Simon & Schuster, 2000), p. 132.

Chapter 2: The Heart of Whiteness

Page 27: Robin Ward quoted in Nina Munk, "Why Women Find Lauder Mesmerizing," *Fortune*, May 25, 1998, p. 96.

Page 29: Margaret Visser, *The Way We Are* (Toronto: HarperPerennial, 1994), p. 135; and Jeffrey Steingarten, "Tiers and Laughter," *Vogue*, June 1998, p. 142.

Page 30: Garry Marshall quoted in Amy M. Spindler, "The Wedding Dress That Ate Hollywood," *The New York Times*, August 30, 1998, section 9, p. 1.

Page 31: "one compulsive mother of the bride": Anna Jane Grossman, "Countdown to Bliss," *New York Observer*, August 14, 2002.

Page 33: Patricia Ireland, "Fox's Arranged Marriage Draws Viewer Protest," Reuters, February 17, 2000.

Page 37: Vera Wang on bridal fantasy: Barbara Thomas, "Getting Married: What to Wear Profile: Vera Wang, Visionary in White," *Los Angeles Times*, February 3, 1999, p. S1.

Page 38: Elizabeth Wurtzel, *Bitch: In Praise of Difficult Women* (New York: Anchor Books, 1998), p. 385.

Page 38: Amanda Beesley, *Something New: Reflections on the Beginning of a Marriage* (New York: Doubleday, 2000), p. 4.

Page 38: Deborah Fine quoted in Wendy Bounds, "Online: Here Comes the Bride, Clicking a Mouse," *The Wall Street Journal*, January 16, 1999, p. B1.

Page 38: Nina Lawrence quoted in Marci McDonald, "Not-so-rosy times for women's mags?," *U.S. News and World Report*, June 18, 2001, p. 35.

Page 39: Alexandra Wentworth, "Dressed-Down Gown," *Vogue*, July 1998, p. 108.

Page 40: Jerry Shiner, letter to the editor, *The Globe and Mail*, September 12, 2000, p. A16.

Page 40: Vera Wang, *Vera Wang on Weddings* (New York: HarperResource/HarperCollins, 2001), p. 137.

Page 40: Vera Wang quoted in Amy Spindler, "The Wedding Dress That Ate Hollywood," *The New York Times*, August 30, 1998, section 9, p. 1.

Page 41: Patricia Leigh Brown, "The Perfect Wedding: Only Tears of Joy," *The New York Times Book Review*, April 4, 1987, p. 52.

Page 41: Martha Stewart, with text by Elizabeth B. Hawes, *Martha Stewart Weddings* (New York: Clarkson Potter, 1987), p. xii.

Pages 41–42: For more on tradition in the modern wedding ceremony, see Dawn H. Currie, "Here Comes the Bride: The Making of a 'Modern Traditional Wedding' in Western Culture," *Journal of Comparative Family Studies*, vol. XXIV, no. 3 (Autumn 1993), p. 403.

Page 42: Study on religion as part of ceremony, by Peter D. Hart Research Associates, July 2003.

Page 42: "… a man asking his future wife's father for his daughter's hand": Samantha Grice, "Step One: Get In-Laws On Side," *National Post*, January 11, 2003, p. SR1.

Page 43: Articles on the increase of women taking their husbands' names: Stephanie Nolen, "Name Change Revival," *Globe and Mail*, September 3, 1998, p. C5; Claudia Goldin and Maria Shin, "Making a Name," *American Demographics* (Boston: Harvard University), September 1, 2001; and Ellen Goodman, "The Feminist Formerly Known as … Ellen Goodman," *Boston Globe*, September 6, 2001.

Page 45: "couples who create a new name": Paula Span, "Taking a Wife, and Her Name," *The Washington Post*, January 4, 1998, F01.

Page 48: Lori Weil quoted in Samantha Critchell, "Bridal Aisle Looking More like a Runway," AP Newswires, May 28, 2001.

Page 48: Gloria Steinem, *Revolution from Within: A Book of Self-Esteem* (New York: Little, Brown & Company, 1993).

Page 49: Colette Dowling, *The Cinderella Complex: Women's Hidden Fear of Independence* (New York: Summit Books, 1991).

Page 50: Clemente Lisi and Adam Miller, "Tears for Aaliyah: Cinderella Funeral for Music Princess," *New York Post*, September 1, 2001, p. 4.

Page 51: Hilary Davidson, "Mirror, Mirror," *Wedding Bells*, Spring/Summer 2001, p. 99.

Page 51: Gilda Carle, *Don't Bet on the Prince! How to Have the Man You Want by Betting on Yourself* (New York: Golden Books, 1999).

Page 54: N.W. Ayre quoted in Edward Jay Epstein, "Have You Ever Tried to Sell a Diamond?," *The Atlantic Monthly*, February 1982, vol. 249, no. 2; pp. 23–34. For more on De Beers and the diamond industry, see Edward Jay Epstein, *The Rise and Fall of Diamonds: The Shattering of a Beautiful Illusion*

(New York: Simon & Schuster, 1982); Stefan Kanfer, *The Last Empire: De Beers, Diamonds, and the World* (New York: Farrar, Straus & Giroux, 1993); Greg Campbell, *Blood Diamonds: Tracing the Path of the World's Most Precious Stones* (Boulder, Col.: Westview Press, 2002); and Matthew Hart, *Diamond: A Journey to the Heart of an Obsession* (Toronto: Viking, 2001).

Page 55: "84 percent of all U.S. brides had celebrated their engagement with a diamond engagement ring," study cited in Hilary E. MacGregor, "Leave No Stone Unturned," *Chicago Tribune*, May 8, 2002, p. C4.

Page 55: "adjacencies to hard news or anti-love-romance theme," cited in Gloria Steinem, "Sex, Lies and Advertising," *Ms.*, July/August 1990.

Page 56: Nicky Oppenheimer quoted in Alex Duval Smith, "The Gem Trail—Diamonds from Angolan mine to third finger left hand," *The Independent* (London), February 13, 1999.

Page 57: "Susan Emerling, writing for *Salon*, greeted the news of De Beers' strategy with a cynical eye": Susan Emerling, "Not Forever: The death of South African diamond magnate Harry Oppenheimer last month might mark the end of global domination for one of the world's most infamous cartels," Salon.com, September 27, 2000.

Page 57: Molly Jong-Fast quoted in Anna Jane Grossman, "Countdown to Bliss," *The New York Observer*, February 26, 2003.

Page 58: Kate Cohen, *A Walk Down the Aisle: Notes on a Modern Wedding* (New York: W. W. Norton & Company, 2001), p. 95.

Page 58: Helen, a twenty-one-year-old student, quoted in Dawn H. Currie, "Here Comes the Bride," p. 401.

Page 58: Shawna Snukst quoted in Barbara Brotman, "Nuptial Planning Thrusts Brides into a Strange and Expensive Realm," *Chicago Tribune*, March 28, 2001, p. S1.

Pages 58–59: Jennifer Tung, "Attack of the Bridezilla: Demanding Perfection Before 'I Do,'" *The New York Times*, May 20, 2001, section 9, p. 1.

Page 59: Dorian Solot and Marshall Miller, *Unmarried to Each Other* (New York: Marlow & Company, 2002).

Page 60: Kirsti Karina Scutt quoted in Lois Smith Brady, "Vows," *The New York Times*, March 10, 2002.

Page 60: Lynn Darling, "For Better or Worse," *Esquire*, May 1996, p. 58.

Page 60: Jennifer Aniston quoted in Leslie Bennett, "Deconstructing Jennifer," *Vanity Fair*, May 2001, p. 162.

Pages 61–62: For more on the historical depiction of bridal imagery in advertising, see Ellen Lupton, *Mechanical Brides: Women and Machines from Home to Office* (New York: Princeton Architectural Press, 1996).

Page 62: Allison Glock, "Remembrance of Flings Past," *Elle*, February 2000, p. 96.

Page 62: Vera Wang quoted in Janet Carlson Freed, "Designer of Dreams," *Town & Country*, February 2002, p. 144.

Pages 62–63: Jessie Bernard, *The Future of Marriage* (New York: World Publishing, 1972), p. 37.

Page 63: Dalma Heyn, *Marriage Shock: The Transformation of Women into Wives* (New York: Villard, 1997).

Page 63: Marg Stark, *What No One Tells the Bride: Surviving the Wedding, Sex After the Honeymoon, Second Thoughts, Wedding Cake Freezer Burn, Becoming Your Mother* (New York: Hyperion, 1998).

Page 64: Martha Stewart quoted in "Remembering: Alexis Stewart to John Cuti," *Martha Stewart Living*, November 1999, p. 376.

Chapter 3: Mystique Chic

Page 65: "the luxe laundry room": *Canadian House & Home*, January 2003.

Page 65: Nordstrom selling detergent: Ruth La Perla, "On the Shelf of a Goddess, Gathering Dust," *The New York Times*, April 7, 2002, section 8, p. 1.

Page 66: Cheryl Mendelson, *Home Comforts: The Art & Science of Keeping House* (New York: Scribner, 1999), p. 7.

Page 66: Rita Konig, *Domestic Bliss: How to Live* (London: Vintage/Ebury, 2002).

Page 69: Cheryl Mendelson, *Home Comforts*, p. 10.

Page 70: Isabella Beeton, *Mrs. Beeton's Book of Household Management* (facsimile of the original 1861 edition), (London: Cassell & Co., 2000), from the introduction.

Page 71: Margarette Driscoll and Stephen McGinty, "Superwoman's Mission Impossible," *The Sunday Times* (London), December 1, 1996. Focus front.

Page 71: Amy Finnerty, "What We Look Up to Now," *The New York Times Magazine*, November 15, 1998.

Page 72: "very Stepford wife": Ginia Bellafante, "Stepping Out in Stepford Style," *The New York Times*, October 20, 2002, section 9, p. 8.

Pages 72–73: Judy Dutton, "Meet the New Housewife Wannabes," *Cosmopolitan*, June 2000, p. 164.

Page 73: Maureen Dowd, "Rescue Me Please!," *The New York Times*, June 7, 2000, p. A31.

Pages 74–75: Allison Pearson, *I Don't Know How She Does It: The Life of Kate Reddy, Working Mother* (New York: Alfred A. Knopf, 2002), p. 95, p. 183.

Page 75: Mary A. Hill, *Charlotte Perkins Gilman: The Making of a Radical Feminist 1860–1896* (Philadelphia: Temple University Press, 1980), p. 149.

Page 76: Marriage and birth rates obtained from the U.S. Bureau of the Census: "Historical Statistics of the United States."

Page 76: "firm push back into the house": See Claudia Goldin, "Marriage Bias: Discrimination Against Married Women Workers 1920 to 1950," in *Favorites or Fortune: Technology, Growth and Economic Development Since the Industrial Revolution* (H. Rosovsky, D. Landes, P. Higgonet, eds.), (Cambridge: Harvard University Press, 1991).

Page 76: "Where the mother works, the baby dies": Alison Prentice, Paula Bourne, Gail Cuthbert Brandt, Beth Light, Wendy Michinson, and Naomi Black, *Canadian Women: A History* (Toronto: Harcourt Brace Jovanovich, 1980).

Page 76: "We shall hear less of breakdowns and neurasthenia ...": Lilly Grove Fraser, *First Aid to the Servantless* (Cambridge: W. Heffer, 1913), p. 23.

Page 77: "wives as the 'chief purchasing agents'": Kathy L. Peiss, "American Women and the Making of Modern Consumer Culture," *The Journal for MultiMedia History*, vol. 1, no. 1, 1998.

Page 77: "a U.S. government survey of women...": C. Hartley Grattan, "No More Excursions! The Defense of Democracy Begins at Home," *Harper's Magazine*, 1943; reprinted in *The World War II Era: Perspectives from All Fronts* (New York: Franklin Square Press, 1994), pp. 21–22.

Page 78: "... restrictions on married women in the Canadian federal public service ...": Status of Women Canada, Canadian Committee on Women's History and Department of the Secretary of State of Canada, "Towards Equality for Women: A Canadian Chronology," October 1992.

Page 78: Truman's address cited in Betsy Israel, *Bachelor Girl: The Secret History of Single Women in the Twentieth Century* (New York: William Morrow, 2002), p. 175.

Page 79: Jesse Birnbaum, "The Roots of Home" (cover story), *Time*, June 20, 1960, p. 24.

Page 80: For more on the history of the birth control pill, see Andrea Tone, *Devices and Desires: A History of Contraceptives in America* (New York: Hill and Wang, 2001); Marilyn Yalom, *A History of the Wife* (New York: HarperCollins, 2001), pp. 294–307; and Carl Djerassi, *This Man's Pill: Reflections on the 50th Birthday of the Pill* (Oxford: Oxford University Press, 2001).

Pages 80–81: Claudia Goldin and Lawrence F. Katz, "The Power of the Pill: Oral Contraceptives and Women's Career and Marriage Decisions," NBER working paper 7527, February 2000.

Page 81: Ann Oakley, *The Sociology of Housework* (New York: Alfred A. Knopf, 1976), p. 43.

Page 81: Penney Kome, *Somebody Has to Do It: Whose Work Is Housework?* (Toronto: McClelland & Stewart, 1982).

Pages 81–82: Shirley Conran, *Superwoman* (Middlesex, UK: Penguin, 1975), epigraph and p. 20.

Pages 82–83: Arlie Russell Hochschild with Anne Machung, *Second Shift: Working Parents and the Revolution at Home* (New York: Penguin USA, reissue edition, 2003).

Page 83: Randall Collins and Scott Coltrane, *Sociology of Marriage & the Family: Gender, Love and Property* (Chicago: Wadworth/Thomson Learning, 5th edition, 2001).

Page 83: "Wives also contribute more 'emotional labor'": Coltrane quoted in Karen S. Peterson, "Both Sexes Enjoy Feast of Marriage: Wedded Bliss Is Just as Good for Women," *USA Today*, October 3, 2000, p. D1.

Page 84: Susan Maushart, *Wifework*, pp. 10–11. See also Lena Corner, "A Woman's Work Is Never Done," *The Independent* (London), January 14, 2002, p. 7.

Page 84: Anne and Bill Moir, *Why Men Don't Iron: The Fascinating and Unalterable Differences Between Men and Women* (London: HarperCollins, 1998).

Page 84: "Husbandly avoidance of housekeeping": Boris Palameta, "Who pays for domestic help?" from "Perspectives on Labour and Income," Autumn 2003 (vol. 15, no. 3), Statistics Canada.

Pages 84–85: "The media looking for real-life examples . . .": Julie Smyth, "Breadwinner Decides Who Cleans House," *National Post*, August 27, 2001, p. A16.

Page 85: "Women expressed anger anywhere they could over the double duty": Ken Dempsey, "Women's Perceptions of Fairness and the Persistence of an Unequal Distribution of Housework," *Family Matters*, Spring–Summer 1997, p. 13.

Pages 85–86: Cynthia Pugh quoted in Erin Anderssen, "Women Do Lion's Share at Home," *Globe and Mail* (Toronto), February 12, 2003, page A7.

Page 86: Joanne S. Lublin, "A Career Wife Complicates the CEO's Life," *The Wall Street Journal*, December 15, 1994, p. B1.

Page 87: Reed Abelson, "When Waaa Turns to Why: Mom and Dad Both Work? Sure, But What to Tell the Children," *The New York Times*, November 11, 1997, p. 1.

Page 87: Felice N. Schwartz, "Management Women and the New Facts of Life," *The Harvard Business Review*, January/February 1989.

Page 88: Nicola Horlick: Linda Grant, "The Curse of Superwoman," *The Guardian* (Manchester), January 16, 1997, p. 4.

Page 88: Rachel Cooke, "The Office Wife," *The Sunday Times* (London), April 15, 2001.

Page 89: "Of the chief executives of Fortune 500 companies...": 2002 Catalyst Census of Women Corporate Officers and Top Earners, "Women corporate officers in US top 500 companies almost doubled since 1995," May 5, 2002.

Page 89: Sandra Rubin, "At the Top of Their Game," *National Post* (Toronto), September 10, 2003, p. FP 9.

Page 90: Rhonda Richards, "More Women Poised for Role as CEO," *USA Today*, March 26, 1996, p. B2.

Page 92: "Her identity was so wrapped up in her professional persona ...": Judith Timson, "Movie a Peek into Dilemma of Women," *Toronto Star*, February 14, 2002, p. E11.

Page 92: Patrick McGeehan, "From High-Flyer to Outcast: Ex–Wall Streeter Says Firm Held Women Back," *New York Times* News Service, *Chicago Tribune*, February 13, 2002.

Pages 93–94: "the impossible demands of home and career": Driscoll and McGinty, "Superwoman's Mission Impossible."

Page 94: Canadian government study: "Wives, Mothers and Wages: Does Timing Matter?" *The Daily*, May 1, 2002, Statistics Canada.

Page 94: Sylvia Ann Hewlett, *Creating a Life: Professional Women and the Quest for Children* (New York: Miramax, 2002), p. 34.

Page 95: Caryl Rivers quoted in Nancy Gibbs and Christine Gorman, "Making Time for a Baby," *Time* (Canadian Edition), April 15, 2002, p. 48.

Page 95: Arabella Kenealy quoted in Jane Cafarella, "Couples Without Children—Why Do We Still Judge?," *The Age* (Australia), October 23, 1992, p. 20.

Page 95: Christopher Byron, "Pack It in, Babe. You Stink," *New York Observer*, May 28, 2001.

Page 95: "Working in Britain," London School of Economics and the Policy Studies Institute, 2000.

Page 96: Alex Kuczynski, "They Conquered, They Left: Are powerful women more likely to be quitters than men?," *The New York Times*, March 24, 2002, section 9, p. 1.

Page 96: Jane Swift, "In Her Own Words: Derided while in office by a largely hostile media, the state's first woman governor now tells her side of the story," *Boston Magazine*, January 2003.

Page 96: Michelle Conlin and Diane Brady, "Goodbye Boss Lady, Hello Soccer Mom," *Business Week*, p. 79.

Page 97: Candice Olson described as "born-again evangelist of power domesticity" and quoted in Alex Witchel, "Trading Places: CEO does Mrs. Mom," *New York Times*, July 2, 2002, section F, p. 1.

Page 97: Brian Swette quoted in Nick Wingfield, "Operating Chief of eBay Will Be Stepping Down to Be with His Family," *The Wall Street Journal*, December 18, 2001, p. B9.

Page 98: Monique P. Yazigi, "The Glamour Girl's Guide to Life," *The New York Times*, April 5, 1998, section 9, p. 1.

Page 99: Birth rates obtained from the U.S. Census Bureau, U.S. National Center for Health Statistics, March 2002.

Page 100: "The Feminine Satisfaction Survey 2001," redirect.com.uk, online version of *Red* magazine.

Page 100: Update: Women survey: Suzanne Hiller, "You Worked Too Much, Mom: The daughters of exhausted, workaholic Boomer mothers are showing signs of rebellion," *National Post* (Toronto), March 7, 2001, p. B1.

Page 100: Daniel Horowitz, *Betty Friedan and the Making of The Feminine Mystique: The American Left, the Cold War, and Modern Feminism* (Amherst: University of Massachusetts, 1999). See also Daphne Merkin, "Sister Act: Did Betty Friedan go wrong, or did feminism?," *The New Yorker*, June 14, 1999, p. 77.

Page 100: Betty Friedan, *The Feminine Mystique*, p. 386.

Page 101: Melissa Hill, *The Smart Woman's Guide to Staying at Home* (London: Vermillion, 2001), introduction.

Page 101: "... Canadian women's magazine *HQ* chose to revise the *Homemaker's* title . . .": Rebecca Eckler, "The Housewife Experiment in Progress," *National Post* (Toronto), March 12, 2003, p. AL1.

Page 101: Bonnie Fuller story in Maureen Littlejohn, "Working Moms ... Can they have it all?," *Homemaker's Magazine*, April 2003, p. 50.

Page 102: Danielle Crittenden, *What Our Mothers Didn't Tell Us: Why Happiness Eludes the Modern Woman* (New York: Touchstone, 1999), p. 108.

Page 102: Meghan Cox Gurdon, "She's Back," *The Women's Quarterly.*

Page 103: "Nigella syndrome": Bel Littlejohn, "The magic of the N-word," *The Guardian*, November 3, 2000, p. 21.

Page 103: Amy Bookman, "My New Client: Thinking of bagging that big career to spend more time with family? Be careful what you wish for," *Talk*, August 2001, p. 50.

Chapter 4: Sex and the Married Woman

Page 107: *The Journal of the American Medical Association* (1999), 281, pp. 537–544.

Page 108: Barbara Pocock, "Having a Life: Work, Family, Fairness and Community in 2000," Centre for Labour Research, Department of Social Inquiry, Adelaide University.

Page 108: Barbara Pocock quoted in Adele Horin, "Sex, What's That? Say Stressed and Fed-up Working Mothers," *Sydney Morning Herald*, May 12, 2001, p. 1.

Page 108: Michele Weiner-Davis, *The Sex-Starved Marriage: A Couple's Guide to Boosting Their Marriage Libido* (New York: Simon & Schuster, 2003), p. 15.

Page 108: Kathleen Deven, "We're Not in the Mood," *Newsweek*, June 30, 2003, p. 41.

Page 110: Jill Elaine Hasday, "Contest and Consent: A Legal History of Marital Rape," *California Law Review*, vol. 88, no. 5 (October 2000), p. 1402.

Page 113: Allison Glock, "How'd Ya Do in Your Oral?," *GQ*, March 2000, p. 187.

Page 113: Krista Smith, "Lips Together, Teeth Apart," *Vanity Fair*, March 2000, p. 146.

Page 115: Ellen Fein and Sherrie Schneider, *The Rules: Time-Tested Secrets for Capturing the Heart of Mr. Right* (New York: Warner Books, 1996).

Page 115: Melissa Schulhof: author interview.

Page 118: Sinclair Lewis, *Babbitt* (New York: Bantam, 1998), p. 11 and p. 23.

Page 118: Philip Slater, "What Hath Spock Wrought?" *The Washington Post*, March 1, 1970.

Page 119: Nancy Friday, *Women on Top* (New York: Pocket Books, 1993), introduction.

Page 119: Marlen Cowpland quoted in Rod Laver, *Random Excess* (Toronto: Viking, 1998), p. 209.

Pages 119–120: Dalma Heyn, *Marriage Shock*, p. 8 and pp. 8–9.

Page 121: Carol Botwin, *Tempted Women: The Passions, Perils, and Agonies of Female Infidelity* (New York: William Morrow & Company, 1994), p. 75.

Page 121: Jed Kaminetsky quoted in Hillary Rosner, "The Silence of O," *New York,* April 30, 2001.

Page 121: Celia Duel Mosher, *The Mosher Survey: Sexual Attitudes of 45 Victorian Women* (James MaHood & Kristine Weinburg, eds., 1980).

Page 122: Katharine Bement Davis and her 1929 study are discussed in Jill Elaine Hasday, "Contest and Consent," p. 1408.

Page 123: Rachel P. Maines, *The Technology of Orgasm: Hysteria, the Vibrator and Women's Sexual Satisfaction* (Baltimore: Johns Hopkins University Press, 2001), p. 43.

Page 124: Jane Wagner, *Signs of Intelligent Life in the Universe* (New York: Perennial Library; Harper & Row, 1986), pp. 33–34.

Page 124: Theodoor H. van de Velde, *Ideal Marriage: Its Physiology and Technique* (New York: Random House, 1968), p. 15.

Page 125: Natalie Angier, *Woman: An Intimate Geography* (New York: Anchor Books, 1999), p. 63.

Page 125: Barbara Smuts quoted in Natalie Angier, *Woman: An Intimate Geography,* p. 366.

Page 125: "Attending to the new female maladies of 'sexual dysfunction …'": Roy Moynihan, "The Making of a Disease: Female sexual dysfuction," *British Medical Journal,* vol. 326, issue 7379 (January 2003).

Page 126: "As one doctor remarked …": Hillary Rosner, "The Silence of O," *New York,* April 30, 2001, p. 26.

Page 127: *The Hite Report* is quoted in John Heindry, *What Wild Ecstasy: The Rise and Fall of the Sexual Revolution* (New York: Simon & Schuster, 1997), p. 186.

Page 127: John Bancroft quoted in the Associated Press, "Women's sexual problems debunked—Research was from male view," *Toronto Star,* January 20, 2003, p. E6.

Page 128: The virginity movement is described in Susan Dominus, "Abstinence Minded," *New York Times Magazine,* January 21, 2001, p. 9.

Page 129: Wendy Shalit, *A Return to Modesty: Rediscovering the Lost Virtue* (New York: The Free Press, 1999).

Page 129: Danielle Crittenden, *What Our Mothers Didn't Tell Us: Why Happiness Eludes the Modern Woman* (New York: Touchstone, 1999), p. 35.

Page 129: Naomi Wolf, *Promiscuities: The Secret Struggle for Womanhood* (Toronto: Vintage Canada, 1998), p. 223.

Pages 129–130: Information about hymenoplasty and "revirgining" was taken from "Maidenhead Revisited," *Harper's,* May 2003; Susan Oh, "Just like a virgin?: Surgeons restore hymens for cultural reasons and tighten vagina walls for better sex," *Maclean's*, June 12, 2000; and Elizabeth Hayt, "It's Never Too Late to Be a Virgin," *New York Times*, August 4, 2002.

Page 132: Laura Doyle, *The Surrendered Wife: A Practical Guide to Finding Intimacy, Passion, and Peace with Your Man* (New York: Fireside, 2001), p. 59.

Page 132: Michele Weiner-Davis quoted in Sarah Baxter and Jane Mulkerrins, "Marriage Was Hotter in the 1950s," *The Sunday Times* (London), January 19, 2003, Focus, p. 18.

Page 132: Lana L. Holstein, *How to Have Magnificent Sex: Improve Your Relationships and Start to Have the Best Sex of Your Life* (New York: Three Rivers Press, 2003).

Page 132: Linda J. Waite and Maggie Gallagher, *The Case For Marriage: Why Married People Are Happier, Healthier, and Better Off Financially* (New York: Doubleday, 2000).

Page 134: Gayle MacDonald, "Actress's sex tips a hot commodity," *The Globe and Mail* (Toronto), January 23, 2002, p. A3.

Pages 134–135: "Sarah" quoted in Ralph Gardner, Jr., "Widows on the World," *New York*, June 15, 1998, p. 24.

Page 135: Margaret Trudeau Kemper quoted in Knight-Ridder News Service, "Trudeau's Ex Reported to Be in Psych Ward," *Winnipeg Free Press*, April 15, 1998, p. D9.

Page 135: Robert A. Wilson, *Feminine Forever: Menopause—The Loss of Womanhood and the Loss of Good Health* (New York: Evans [with Lippincott], 1966), p. 21 and p. 56.

Page 137: Brad Holmes quoted in Sharon Krum, "Private Investigation," *The Guardian* (Manchester), November 15, 2001, p. 8.

Page 138: Lois Rogers, "One in seven fathers 'not the real parent,'" *The Sunday Times* (London), January 23, 2000.

Page 138: Shirley Glass and Helen Fisher quoted in Hara Estroff Marano, "The New Sex Scorecard," *Psychology Today*, July/August 2003.

Page 139: David Buss, *The Dangerous Passion: Why Jealousy Is as Necessary as Love and Sex* (London: Bloomsbury, 2000).

Page 140: Katie Roiphe, "Adultery's Double Standard," *New York Times Magazine*, October 12, 1997, p. 54.

Page 140: Janet Reibstein and Martin Richards, *Sexual Arrangements: Marriage and the Temptation of Infidelity* (London: Heinemann, 1992), p. 37.

Page 141: *Elle* and *Harper's Bazaar* references from Katie Roiphe, "Adultery's Double Standard," *New York Times Magazine*, October 12, 1997, p. 54.

Page 141: Candace Bushnell, *Trading Up* (New York: Hyperion, 2003), p. 224.

Chapter 5: Love Hurts: The Abused Wife as Icon

Page 144: "so in love with him": Sara Rimmer, "A Celebrity to Her Friends, Nicole Brown Was Escaping Her Husband's Shadow," *New York Times* News Service, reprinted in *Los Angeles Daily News,* June 23, 1994, p. N1.

Page 147: Murray Straus, Richard J. Gelles, and S. K. Steinmetz, *Behind Closed Doors: Violence in the American Family* (Garden City, N.Y.: Anchor Books, 1980).

Page 147: Faith McNulty, *The Burning Bed: The True Story of Francine Hughes—A Beaten Wife Who Rebelled* (New York: Harcourt Brace Jovanovich, 1980).

Page 147: "woman beaten every eighteen minutes": *The Progress of Nations 1995,* UNICEF; "beaten every twelve seconds": Radio address by President Bill Clinton on October 28, 2000; "one of four women will be beaten" from Lieberman Research Inc., Tracking Survey conducted for the Advertising Council and the Family Violence Prevention Fund, July–October 1996; "two-thirds of all marriages experience abuse" from U.S. Department of Justice, *Prevalence, Incidence, and Consequences of Violence Against Women: Findings from the National Violence Against Women Survey,* November 1998; "one in every three" from *Report of the American Psychological Association Presidential Task Force on Violence and the Family,* 1996; Diana Russell, *Rape in Marriage,* (Bloomington: Indiana University Press, 1990).

Page 148: "feminist orthodoxy": Joan Smith, "Repenting at Leisure," *The Guardian,* July 8, 1995, p. 14.

Page 150: Paul Burrell, *A Royal Duty* (London: Putnam Pub Group, 2003), p. 191.

Page 151: statistics on abuse: Deborah Sontag, "Fiery Entanglement," *New York Times Magazine,* November 17, 2002, p., 57; see also Elizabeth M. Schneider, *Battered Women: Feminist Lawmaking* (New Haven: Yale University Press, 2000).

Page 152: Patricia Pearson, *When She Was Bad: How and Why Women Get Away with Murder* (Toronto: Random House of Canada, 1997), p. 7. See also pp. 136–145.

Page 153: Lenore E. Walker, *The Battered Woman* (New York: Harper & Row, 1977), pp. 49, 87, and 194.

Page 154: "Walker became an influential force...": Ronnie Green, "From Broward Trial to the O. J. Spotlight: Abuse Expert Saved Wife Killer's Life," *Miami Herald,* February 2, 1995, p. 1.

Page 155: The story of Lillian and Maury Getkate is told in the following: Peter Hum, "This Abuse Thing Is a Crock," *Ottawa Citizen,* October 5, 1998, p. B1; and Peter Hum, "Getkate Convicted on a Lesser Charge," *Ottawa Citizen.*

Pages 157–158: Elizabeth Schneider quoted in "Fiery Entanglement," *New York Times Magazine,* November 17, 2002, p. 57.

Page 158: The notion of the "good wife": James Ptacek, "Why Do Men Batter Their Wives?," *Feminist Perspectives on Wife Abuse*, p. 133, supra note 48.

Page 158: The story of Sara and Malcolm Thornton is told in Clare Dyer, "Husband Killer Freed on Bail Pending Appeal," *The Guardian*, July 29, 1995, p. 1.

Pages 158–159: Rachel Cooke, "A man kills his unfaithful wife and gets two years," *The Guardian*, October 30, 2001, p. 8; Sally Weale, "Carrying the can for men," *The Guardian*, March 31, 1998, p. 8; Sue Lees, "If a man kills his wife for having an affair, is it a crime of passion? Or is it murder?," *Scotland on Sunday*, July 13, 1997, p. 17; Richard Ford, "Woman who killed husband challenges law of provocation," *The Times* (London), July 20, 1992; Yvonne Roberts, "Mad as a desperate woman," *The Observer*, May 18, 2003, p. 29.

Page 160: Statistics Canada, *Family Violence in Canada: A Statistical Profile* (Cat. No. 85-224-xie).

Page 160: Robert Butterworth quoted in Sharon Krum, "Has Feminism Killed the American Marriage?," *The Guardian* (Manchester), February 24, 2000.

Page 160: Denise Brown quoted in Sara Rimmer, "A Celebrity to Her Friends, Nicole Brown Was Escaping Her Husband's Shadow."

Page 161: "this belongs to me": Kenneth B. Noble, "Simpson Threw Wife into Wall, Her Sister Tells Jury," *The New York Times*, February 4, 1995, section 1, p. 7.

Page 161: Margaret Mitchell, *Gone With the Wind* (New York: Warner Books, 1999), pp. 938–941.

Page 163: Richard Pryor, *Pryor Convictions—And Other Life Sentences* (New York: Pantheon, 1995), p. 128.

Page 164: Associated Press, "Reconciled after rape trial Rideouts' marriage is not 'peachy keen,'" *The Globe and Mail* (Toronto), March 6, 1979, p. 12.

Page 164: Alanna Mitchell, "Joudrie hoping to get on with life now that she's free," *The Globe and Mail*, October 23, 1998, p. A4.

Page 165: Jill Murray, *But I Love Him: Protecting Your Teenage Daughter from Controlling, Abusive Dating Relationships* (New York: Regan Books, 2001), p. 15.

Page 165: Susan Weitzman, *Not to People Like Us: Hidden Abuse in Upscale Marriage* (New York: Basic Books, 2000); and Susan Weitzman, "Painfully Privileged," *People*, July 2, 2001, p. 139.

Page 166: Steve Delsohn quoted in Aurora Mackey, "Catharsis for a Victim of Incest, Rape Fiction," *Los Angeles Times*, February 16, 1993, p. 1.

Page 167: Donna Ferrato passage: Jan Wong, "Photographing domestic abuse takes a lot out of Donna Ferrato, whose stark work has helped raise awareness of the issue. Sex is much easier," *The Globe and Mail*, June 3, 2000, p. R11.

Page 168: Lee Grant quoted in *Chicago Tribune* wire services, "Battered women in spotlight for two upcoming TV projects," *Chicago Tribune*, August 28, 1989, p. C10.

Page 168: Gail Singer: author interview.

Page 170: Salma Hayek quoted in Jessica Callan, Eva Simpson, Suzanne Kerins, "Hay, Here Comes the Protester," *Daily Mirror*, June 25, 2002, p. 12.

Chapter 6: Hear Us Roar: The Real First Wives' Club

Page 173: Julie Connelly, "The CEO's Second Wife," *Fortune*, August 28, 1989, p. 52.

Page 174: Olivia Goldsmith, *The First Wives' Club* (New York: Poseidon Press, 1992), p. 132.

Page 174: First wives' contest: Meg Cox, "The Woman Scorned Now Has a Contest to Vent Hostilities—First Wives Seek Revenge More Than Big Prizes; Novel Touches a Nerve," *The Wall Street Journal*, May 14, 1992, p. 1.

Page 175: Interview with Olivia Goldsmith in Lynn Smith, "Revenge of the Firsts Means Taking Action: Divorce: For women of a certain age, the end of a marriage can be an emotional and financial free fall," *Los Angeles Times*, October 4, 1996, p. E1.

Page 177: The story of Caroline of Brunswick told in Roger Fulford, *Trial of Queen Caroline* (London: Stein and Day, 1968).

Page 179: Nora Ephron, *Heartburn* (New York: Vintage Books reissue edition, 1996).

Page 180: Jane Hawking, *Music to Move the Stars: A Life with Stephen* (London: Pan Books/Macmillan, 2000), p. 13.

Pages 180–181: Sheila Rauch Kennedy, *Shattered Faith: A Woman's Struggle to Stop the Catholic Church from Annulling Her Marriage* (New York: Pantheon Books, 1997).

Page 181: Sheila Rauch Kennedy quoted in Kathy Sheridan, *The Irish Times* (Dublin), "Mrs. Kennedy, I Presume?," September 25, 1997, p. 13.

Page 182: Donald Trump quoted in James R. Norman, "Donald Trump: What's Behind the Hype?," *BusinessWeek*, July 20, 1987, p. 93.

Page 183: Domenic Cavendish, "Making a Novella Out of Crisis," *The Independent* (London), May 2, 1998, p. 65.

Page 185: "The wifely showdown extended to second wives' clubs": Sonia Nazario, "The Second Wives' Crusade: Those Men. They Get Married and Start a Family. Then There's That Messy Divorce. They Get Married

Again, and the Second Wife Wants What the First Wife Had. See Where We're Headed Here?," *Los Angeles Times Magazine*, December 3, 1995, p. 20.

Page 186: Heidi Evans and Judi Sheindlin, *How to Hide Money from Your Husband ... and other Time-Honored Ways to Build a Nest Egg: The Best-Kept Secret of a Marriage* (New York: Simon & Schuster, 1999).

Page 187: James M. Lowe quoted in Carlos Sanchez and Maria E. Odum, "Wife Who Cut Husband Is Suing For Divorce: Va. Woman Alleges 'Marital Sexual Abuse,'" *The Washington Post*, July 13, 1993, p. B1.

Page 188: Lenore Walker comment on Lorena Bobbitt: Marie E. Odum, "Irreconcilable Differences Revealed: Women's Groups Hail a Verdict That Makes Some Grown Men Wail," *The Washington Post*, January 22, 1994, p. A1.

Pages 190–191: Betty Broderick's story from Bella Stumbo, *Until the Twelfth of Never: The Deadly Divorce of Dan & Betty Broderick* (New York: Pocket Star, 1993); Loretta Schwartz-Nobel, *Forsaking All Others: The Real Betty Broderick Story* (New York: Villard, 1993); Amy Wallace, "Till Murder Does Us Part," *Los Angeles Times Magazine*, June 3, 1990, p. 12; Alan Abrahamson, "Broderick Has No Regrets in Slaying Crimes," *Los Angeles Times*, February 11, 1992, Section B, p. 1.

Page 191: "I guess this is 'be nice to the ex-wife' week": John Glionna, "Broderick Trial Was an Ordeal for La Jolla Divorcees," *Los Angeles Times*, December 12, 1991, part 3, p. 1.

Page 192: "I went from being accomplished ...": Amy Wallace, "Till Murder Does Us Part."

Page 194: Kate Taylor, "Stratford takes sympathetic view of Medea," *The Globe and Mail* (Toronto), June 30, 2000, p. R7.

Page 197: Kate Chopin, "The Story of an Hour," *The Awakening and Selected Short Stories of Kate Chopin*, Barbara H. Soloman, ed. (New York: Signet, 1976), p. 61.

Page 197: Lorrie Moore quoted in "Praise for Jane Shapiro," found in front matter of Jane Shapiro, *The Dangerous Husband* (Boston: Little, Brown and Co., 1999).

Page 198: Jane Shapiro, *The Dangerous Husband*, pp. 8, 11, 30, and 58.

Chapter 7: The Unwife

Page 201: Chris Zdeb, "The growing power of single women: It's never been better to be unattached—women today are reinventing the single life," *The Edmonton Journal*, November 17, 2000, p. C1.

Page 202: Catherine Keri, "The New Spinster," *Flare*, April 1998, p. 104.

Pages 202–203: "What money can't buy": Karen S. Schneider, *People*, August 27, 2001, p. 77.

Page 203: Sarah Jessica Parker quoted in Tamara M. Edwards, "Single by Choice: Flying Solo," *Time*, August 28, 2000.

Page 204: Young & Rubicam's Intelligence Factory, "The Single Female Consumer," July 2000, Futurescope 2000 series.

Page 204: Marian Salzman: author interview.

Page 205: Hiroyuki Takahashi and Jeanette Voss, "Parasite Singles—A Uniquely Japanese Phenomenon," U.S.-Japan Links (www.us-japan.org).

Page 205: "'Mr. Right' can come later": quoted in Peggy Orenstein, "Parasites in Prêt-à-Porter," *The New York Times Magazine*, July 1, 2001, p. 31.

Pages 205–206: For more on the history and the cultural significance of *Playboy* and male identity, see Barbara Ehrenreich, *The Hearts of Men: American Dreams and the Flight from Commitment* (New York: An Anchor Book/ Doubleday, 1983), and Gay Talese, *Thy Neighbor's Wife* (New York: An Ivy Book, 1993).

Page 206: Jay Smith, "A Vote for Polygamy," *Playboy*, July 1955, p. 15.

Pages 206–207: Shepherd Mead, "Selecting Your First Wife," *Playboy*, April 1956, p. 28; Shepherd Mead, "Selecting Your Second Wife," *Playboy*, November 1956, p. 68.

Page 207: P. Wylie, "The Womanization of America," *Playboy*, September 1958, p. 52.

Pages 207–208: Helen Gurley Brown, *Sex and the Single Girl* (New York: Barricade Books, 2003), pp. 2, 5, 15, 22, 78.

Page 209: For more on single blessedness, see Betsy Israel, *Bachelor Girl*, p. 25.

Page 209: Beauvoir, *The Second Sex*, p. 655.

Pages 209–210: Patricia O'Brien, *The Woman Alone* (New York: Time Books, 1974), p. 68.

Page 210: Marlo Thomas quoted in Steven Cole, *That Book About That Girl* (Los Angeles: Renaissance Books, 1999), p. 142.

Page 211: Marlo Thomas quoted in Steven Cole, p. 88.

Page 213: Ursula Parrott, *Ex-Wife* (New York: American Library, 1989), p. 89.

Page 214: Dan Quayle quoted in Christopher Connell, "Quayle Blames Riots on 'Poverty of Values,' Rips Murphy Brown," The Associated Press Wire, May 19, 1992.

Pages 217–218: Helen Fielding, *Bridget Jones's Diary*, p. 33.

Page 219: Candace Bushnell, *Sex and the City* (New York: The Atlantic Monthly Press, 1996), p. 41.

Page 221: "British women are increasingly spurning the fathers of their children ...": Cherry Norton, "Go-It-Alone Mums Refuse to Name Dads," *Sunday Times* (London), October 26, 1997.

Page 222: Kathleen Kiernan and Kari Moxnes quoted by Sarah Lyall, "Marriage in Europe Becomes Passé," *The New York Times* News Service, March 24, 2002, reprinted in *The Seattle Times*, p. A18.

Page 222: Nuala O'Faolain, *Are You Somebody?: The Accidental Memoirs of a Dublin Woman* (New York: Henry Holt & Co. Inc, 1996), p. 131.

Page 223: Nuala O'Faolain quoted in Daphne Merkin, "A Thorny Irish Rose," *New York Times Magazine*, February 18, 2001, p. 22.

Page 223: Sarah Bernard, "Early to Wed," *New York*, June 16, 1997, p. 38.

Page 224: "Sex Kitten vs Spinster": *The Globe and Mail* (Toronto), July 11, 2003, p. 1.

Page 225: Sherrie Schneider quoted in Mark McClusky, "The Ruling Class: One man's night out with a pack of Manhattan mantrappers," Salon.com, October 10, 1996.

Page 225: Ellen Fein quoted in Shelley Decker, "Rules to Wed By," *The Edmonton Sun*, Sunday, November 30, 1997.

Page 226: Vanessa Lloyd Platt, *Secrets of Relationship Success* (London: Random House UK, 2001).

Page 226: Ursula Penn-Simkins quoted in Olga Craig, "First came the Surrendered Wife, now prepare to meet her docile daughter," *The Sunday Telegraph* (London), July 8, 2001, p. 18.

Pages 226–227: Mimi Valcin quoted in Rebecca Eckler, "Material Girls Have More Fun," *National Post* (Toronto), August 26, 2000, p. B01.

Page 227: Marilyn Graman quoted in Abby Ellin, "A Class Feminists Might Abhor," *The New York Times*, March 5, 2000, section 3, p. 12.

Page 228: Rachel Greenwald, *Find a Husband After 35: A Simple 15-Step Action Program Using What I Learned at Harvard Business School* (New York: Ballantine Books, 2003), p. 23.

Page 228: Barbara Dafoe Whitehead quoted in "In Search of Mr. Right," Atlantic Unbound (online version of *The Atlantic Monthly*), December 18, 2002.

Page 230: Obst, *Hello, He Lied*, p. 178.

Page 233: Sally Schultheiss, "Why am I still single? These women all want to be married—so why aren't they?," *Marie Claire*, April 2001, p. 138.

Pages 233–234: Rebecca Johnson, "Picky, Picky, Picky: The dilemma of the new single woman," *Talk*, September 2000, p. 104.

Page 234: "the end of independence day": Bob Morris, "Wedding Vows: Candace Bushnell, Charles Askegard," *The New York Times*, July 7, 2002, section 9, p. 1.

Page 234–35: Helen Fielding quoted in Marianne Macdonald, "Life after Bridget: Helen Fielding has achieved the hat trick that eluded her for so long," *The Sunday Telegraph* (London), reprinted in the *National Post* (Toronto) November 8, 2003, p. SP 3.

Chapter 8: What's a Wife Worth?

Pages 237–238: Lorna Jorgenson Wendt: author interview.

Page 238: "Hillary wives": Joanne S. Lublin, "A Career Wife Complicates the CEO's Life," *The Wall Street Journal*.

Page 240: Vira Hladu-Goldmann quoted in Louise France, "First, Marry a Banker…," *The Observer* (London), July 13, 2003, p. 3.

Page 241: Vira Hladun-Goldmann, *Separate Ways: Relationships, Divorce & Independence of Mind* (New York: Sweetpea Press, 2003).

Page 241: Goldmann quoted in Louise France, "First, Marry a Banker…"

Page 242: The Lambert story is told in Clare Dyer, "Divorce court history as wife wins half of £20m fortune," *The Guardian*, November 15, 2002, p. 3.

Page 243: Jan Bobrow quoted in Philip Aldrick, "Ernst & Young chief has some explaining to do," *The Daily Telegraph* (London), October 16, 2002.

Page 245: "In seventeenth-century New England …": Melville Cobbledick, "The Status of Women in Puritan New England, 1630–1660: A Demographic Study," doctoral dissertation, Yale University, 1936.

Page 245: William Hollingsworth Whyte, *The Organization Man* (New York: Simon & Schuster, 1972), p. 102.

Page 245–46: Rosabeth Moss Kanter, *Men and Women of the Corporation* (New York: Basic Books, 1994).

Page 246: Janet Finch, *Married to the Job: Wives' Incorporation in Men's Work* (London, Boston: Allen & Unwin, 1983).

Page 246: "One female lawyer" quoted in Lisa Belkin, "The Opt-Out Revolution," *The New York Times Magazine*, October 26, 2003, p. 42.

Page 247: Wage statistics are taken from the United States Bureau of Labor Statistics.

Page 247: Jenny Chalmers quoted in Bettina Arndt, "For Richer, Not Poorer," *Sydney Morning Herald*, March 29, 2002.

Page 248: "specialize in making money": Linda J. Waite and Maggie Gallagher, *The Case For Marriage: Why Married People Are Happier, Healthier, and Better Off Financially*, pp. 25–31.

Page 248: Hyunbae Chun and Injae Lee, "Why Do Married Men Earn More: Productivity or Marriage Selection?," *Economic Inquiry*, vol. 39, no. 2 (April 2001), pp. 307–319. See also Christopher Cornell and Peter Rupert, "Unobserved Individual Effects, Marriage, and the Earnings of Young Men," *Economic Inquiry*, vol. 35, no. 2 (April 1999), pp. 285–294; and Joni Hersch and Leslie S. Stratton, "Household Specialization and the Male Marriage Wage Premium," *Industrial and Labor Review*, October 2000, pp. 78–94.

Page 249: "There is also evidence that married women play down their marital status …": Felice N. Schwartz, *Breaking with Tradition: Women and Work, the New Facts of Life* (New York: Warner Books, 1992), p. 10.

Page 249: Wendy Wasserstein, "The Princess Brides," *The New York Times Magazine*, November 24, 1996, p. 92.

Page 250: Julie Mason, "First lady a capital asset in Bush's re-election bid," *Houston Chronicle*, June 29, 2003.

Page 252: Danielle Crittenden quoted in Lloyd Grove, "The Reliable Source," *The Washington Post*, February 7, 2002, p. C3.

Page 253: Al Gore quoted in Katharine Mieszkowski, "Behind every dead candidate …," Salon.com, November 9, 2000.

Page 253: Robert and Mary Catherine Birgeneau: author interview.

Page 253: Nicholas Keung, "Mary-ing for Money: U of T Creates a $60,000 Job for Spouse," *Toronto Star*, August 12, 2000, p. 1.

Page 258: Alice Huang: author interview.

Page 259: Peter Smith: author interview.

Page 259: Martha Piper: author interview.

Page 259: Lorna Marsden: author interview.

Page 260: Rose Patten: author interview.

Page 262: "… the seventeenth century, when the Virginia Company imported 140 single women to America …": Marilyn Yalom, *A History of the Wife* (New York: HarperCollins, 2001), p. 141.

Page 262: For more on wife's work, see Kathy L. Peiss, *American Women and the Making of Modern Consumer Culture*.

Page 263: Study by Edelman Financial Services Inc., Fairfax, Va., "Mother's Day Index," May 1, 2003.

Page 263: Myra Strober: author interview.

Page 264: Claudia Goldin, *Understanding the Gender Gap: An Economic History of*

American Women (Oxford: Oxford University Press, reprint edition 1992). See also Claudia Goldin, "Labor Markets in the Twentieth Century," National Bureau of Economic Research, April 21, 1998.

Page 265: Lord Justice Thorpe quoted in Clare Dyer, "Divorce court history as wife wins half of £20m fortune," *The Guardian.*

Chapter 9: The Wife Axis

Page 270: "... the industry viewed the venture as a commercial risk": David M. Deal, "A Fair to Remember: McLachlan 'Surfacing' for All-Female Lineup," *USA Today,* June 5, 1997, p. D4.

Page 271: Sarah McLachlan quoted in Laurie Lynch, "This Summer's Singing Sensation 30-year-old Lilith Fair Leader Sarah McLachlan Plugs into the Issues of Her Generation," *USA Today,* August 16, 1998.

Page 272: Malvina Shanklin Harlan, *Some Memories of a Long Life* (New York: Modern Paperback Library, 2003), p. 11.

Page 272: Isabel Burton quoted in Mary S. Lowell, *A Rage to Live: A Biography of Richard and Isabel Burton* (New York: W. W. Norton, 1999), p. 12.

Page 273: Jonathan Yardley, "Thoroughly Modern Edna," *The Washington Post,* March 29, 1999, p. C2.

Page 273: Sally Beauman, "The Dead Wife Rises Up," *National Post,* August 18, 2001, p. B10.

Page 274: David Starkey, *Six Wives: The Queens of Henry VIII* (New York: HarperCollins, 2003), pp. 368–375.

Page 274: Theodore White, "For President Kennedy: An Epilogue," *Life,* December 6, 1963.

Page 275: Nancy Reagan as "a Barbie doll with attitude": Julia Reed, "The Quiet Crusader," *Vogue,* December 2002, p. 280.

Page 275: Ann Gerhart, *The Perfect Wife: The Life and Choices of Laura Bush* (New York: Simon & Schuster, 2004), p. 75.

Page 275: Arthur Ollman, *The Model Wife* (Boston: Little, Brown & Co., 1999).

Page 277: Stacy Schiff, *Véra (Mrs. Vladimir Nabokov),* (New York: Picador, 2000).

Page 277: Mariane Pearl, *A Mighty Heart: The Brave Life and Death of My Husband, Danny Pearl* (New York: Simon & Schuster, 2003).

Pages 278–279: John Bayley, *Elegy for Iris* (New York: Picador, 1999); John Bayley, *Iris and Her Friends: A Memoir of Memory and Desire* (W. W. Norton & Company, 2000).

Page 280: Michelle Conlin, "The New Gender Gap: From kindergarten to grad school, boys are becoming the second sex," *BusinessWeek*, May 26, 2003.

Page 280: Steve Jones, *Y: The Descent of Men* (London: Little, Brown and Co., 2003).

Page 280: Susan Faludi, *Stiffed: The Betrayal of the American Man* (New York: William Morrow Co., 1999).

Page 281: Lionel Tiger, *The Decline of Males: The First Look at an Unexpected New World for Men and Women* (New York: Golden Books, 2000).

Page 282: Denis Thatcher quoted on BBC News, World Edition, June 26, 2003, http://news.bbc.co.uk/2/hi/uk_news/politics/2669923.stm.

Page 283: Betsy Morris, Lisa Munoz, Patricia Neering, "Trophy Husbands," *Fortune*, October 14, 2002, p. 78.

Page 285: Joan C. Williams and Nancy Segal, "Beyond the Maternal Wall: Relief for Family Caregivers Who Are Discriminated Against on the Job," *The Harvard Law Journal*, vol. 26, Spring 2003.

Pages 286–287: Nori Starck quoted in Ashley Brittingham McDermott, "Keys to the World," *Vogue*, October, 2003, p. 376.

Page 287: Virginia Woolf's essay "Professions For Women" was read to the Women's Service League in 1931. "Angel in the House," Woolf's essay, appears in *Virginia Woolf*, Monique Nathan, ed. (New York: Grove Press, 1961).

Page 288: Rebecca Traister, Alexandra Wolfe, and Anne Jane Grossman, "Hot Flash! Trophy Wife Models Are Passé," *The New York Observer*, June 2, 2003, p. 1.

Page 289: Edie Brickell quoted in Amy Barrett, "Doing It Her Way," *The New York Times Magazine*, October 12, 2003, p. 51.

Page 290: Michael Dynes, "Gulf suitors forced to look abroad as bride prices rocket," *The Times* (London), February 10, 1997, p. 13.

Selected Bibliography

Abbott, Elizabeth. *A History of Celibacy* (Toronto: HarperPerennial Canada, 1999).

Angier, Natalie. *Woman: An Intimate Geography* (New York: Anchor Books/ Random House, 1999).

Apter, Terri. *Why Women Don't Have Wives* (London: Macmillan, 1985).

Bair, Deirdre. *Simone de Beauvoir: A Biography* (New York: Summit Books, 1990).

Bayley, John. *Elegy for Iris* (New York: Picador, 1999).

———. *Iris and Her Friends: A Memoir of Memory and Desire* (New York: W. W. Norton & Company, 2000).

Beauvoir, Simone de. *The Second Sex* (New York: Vintage Books reissue edition, 1989).

Beesley, Amanda. *Something New: Reflections on the Beginnings of a Marriage* (New York: Doubleday, 2000).

Beeton, Isabella. *Mrs. Beeton's Book of Household Management (Facsimile of the original 1861 edition)* (London: Cassell & Co., 2000).

Bernard, Jessie. *The Future of Marriage* (New York: World Publishing, 1972).

Bloom, Claire. *Leaving a Doll's House* (Boston: Back Bay Books, 1998).

Brooks, Geraldine. *Nine Parts of Desire: The Hidden World of Islamic Women* (New York: Anchor Books, 1995).

Bushnell, Candace. *Sex and the City* (New York: The Atlantic Monthly Press, 1996).

———. *Trading Up* (New York: Hyperion, 2003).

Byron, Christopher. *Martha Stewart Inc.: The Incredible Story of Martha Stewart Omnimedia* (New York: John Wiley & Sons, 2003).

Cattrall, Kim, and Mark Levinson. *Satisfaction: The Art of the Female Orgasm* (New York: Warner Books, 2002).

Chandler, Joan. *Women Without Husbands* (London: Macmillan Education, 1992).

Chopin, Kate. *The Awakening and Selected Short Stories of Kate Chopin*, Barbara H. Soloman, ed. (New York: Signet, 1976).

Cohen, Kate. *A Walk Down the Aisle: Notes on a Modern Wedding* (New York: W. W. Norton & Company, 2001).

Conran, Shirley. *Superwoman* (Middlesex: Penguin UK, 1975).

Coontz, Stephanie. *The Way We Never Were: American Families and the Nostalgia Trap* (New York: Basic Books, 1992).

Cott, Nancy. *Public Vows: A History of Marriage and the Nation* (Cambridge: Harvard University Press, 2000).

Crittenden, Danielle. *What Our Mothers Didn't Tell Us: Why Happiness Eludes the Modern Woman* (New York: Touchstone, 1999).

Delphy, Christine and Diana Leonard. *Familiar Exploitation: A New Analysis of Marriage in Western Society* (Cambridge: Polity, 1992).

Djerassi, Carl. *This Man's Pill: Reflections on the 50th Birthday of the Pill* (Oxford: Oxford University Press, 2001).

Dowling, Colette. *The Cinderella Complex: Women's Hidden Fear of Independence* (New York: Summit Books, 1991).

Doyle, Laura. *The Surrendered Wife: A Practical Guide to Finding Intimacy, Passion and Peace with Your Man* (New York: Fireside Books, 2001).

DuBois, Ellen, ed. *The Elizabeth Cady Stanton–Susan B. Anthony Reader: Correspondence, Writing, Speeches* (Boston Northeastern University Press, 1992).

Ehrenreich, Barbara. *The Hearts of Men: American Dreams and the Flight from Commitment* (New York: Anchor Books/ Doubleday, 1983).

Ephron, Nora. *Heartburn* (New York: Vintage Books reissue edition, 1996).

Epstein, Edward Jay. *The Rise and Fall of Diamonds: The Shattering of a Beautiful Illusion* (New York: Simon & Schuster, 1982).

Faludi, Susan. *Backlash: The Undeclared War Against American Women* (New York: Anchor reprint edition, 1992).

———. *Stiffed: The Betrayal of the American Man* (New York: William Morrow, 1999).

Farrow, Mia. *What Falls Away* (New York: Random House, 1997).

Fielding, Helen. *Bridget Jones's Diary* (London: Picador, 1998).

Folbre, Nancy. *The Invisible Heart: Economics and Reality* (New York: New Press, 2002).

Fraser, Antonia. *The Weaker Vessel: Women's Lot in Seventeenth-Century England* (London: Methuen, 1985).

Friedan, Betty. *The Feminine Mystique* (New York: A Laurel Book, Dell Publishing, 1983).

———. *Life So Far: A Memoir* (New York: Touchstone, Simon & Schuster, 2000).

Gerhart, Ann. *The Perfect Wife: The Life and Choices of Laura Bush* (New York: Simon & Schuster, 2004).

Goldin, Claudia. *Understanding the Gender Gap: An Economic History of American Women* (Oxford: Oxford University Press, 1992).

Goldsmith, Olivia. *The First Wives' Club* (New York: Poseidon Press, 1992).

Greenwald, Rachel. *Find a Husband After 35: A Simple 15-Step Action Program Using What I Learned at Harvard Business School* (New York: Ballantine Books, Random House, 2003).

Gurley Brown, Helen. *Sex and the Single Girl* (New York: Barricade Books, 2003).

Hanauer, Cathi, ed. *The Bitch in the House: 26 Women Tell the Truth About Sex, Solitude, Work, Motherhood and Marriage* (New York: William Morrow, 2002).

Harlan, Malvina Shanklin. *Some Memories of a Long Life* (New York: Modern Library, 2003).

Hart, Matthew. *Diamond: A Journey to the Heart of an Obsession* (Toronto: Viking, the Penguin Group, 2001).

Hawking, Jane. *Music to Move the Stars: A Life with Stephen* (London: Pan Books/Macmillan UK [updated edition]), 2000.

Heilbrun, Carolyn G. *Writing a Woman's Life* (New York: W. W. Norton & Company, 1988).

Heindry, John. *What Wild Ecstasy: The Rise and Fall of the Sexual Revolution* (New York: Simon & Schuster, 1997).

Hewlett, Sylvia Ann. *Creating a Life: Professional Women and the Quest for Children* (New York: Miramax, 2002).

Heyn, Dalma. *Marriage Shock: The Transformation of Women into Wives* (New York: Villard Books, 1997).

———. *The Erotic Silence of the American Wife* (New York: Plume, 1997).

Hite, Shere. *The Hite Report* (New York: Macmillan, 1976).

Horowitz, Daniel. *Betty Friedan and the Making of The Feminine Mystique: The American Left, the Cold War, and Modern Feminism* (Amherst: University of Massachusetts, 1999).

Ibsen, Henrik. *A Doll's House* (in a new version by Frank McGuinness, from a translation by Charlotte Barslund) (London: Faber and Faber, 1996).

Israel, Betsy. *Bachelor Girl: The Secret History of Single Women in the Twentieth Century* (New York: William Morrow, 2002).

Jong, Erica. *Fear of Flying* (New York: Signet, Penguin, 1995).

Kamen, Paula. *Her Way: Young Women Remake the Sexual Revolution* (New York: Broadway Books, 2000).

Kanfer, Stephan. *The Last Empire: De Beers, Diamonds, and the World* (New York: Farrar, Straus & Giroux, 1993).

Karbo, Karen. *Generation Ex: Tales From the Second Wives' Club* (New York: Bloomsbury, 2001).

Kipnis, Laura. *Against Love: A Polemic* (New York: Pantheon, 2003).

Konig, Rita. *Domestic Bliss: How to Live* (London: Vintage/Ebury, 2002).

Lasch, Christopher. *Women and the Common Life: Love, Marriage and Feminism*, Elizabeth Lasch-Quinn, ed. (New York: W. W. Norton & Co., 1997).

Leach, William. *Land of Desire: Merchants, Power, and the Rise of a New American Culture* (New York: Pantheon, 1993).

Leff, Mark. "The Politics of Sacrifice on the American Home Front in World War II," *Journal of American History*, March 1991.

Mailer, Adele. *The Last Party: Scenes from My Life with Norman Mailer* (New York: Barricade Books, 1997).

Maines, Rachel P. *The Technology of Orgasm: "Hysteria," the Vibrator and Women's Sexual Satisfaction* (Baltimore: Johns Hopkins University Press, 2001).

Mason, Mary Ann. *The Equality Trap: Why Working Women Shouldn't Be Treated Like Men* (New York: Touchstone, 1988).

Matthews, Glenna. *"Just a Housewife": The Rise and Fall of Domesticity in America* (Oxford: Oxford University Press, 1987).

Maushart, Susan. *Wifework: What Marriage Really Means for Women* (London: Bloomsbury, 2003).

McNulty, Faith. *The Burning Bed: The True Story of Francine Hughes—A Beaten Wife Who Rebelled* (New York: Harcourt Brace Jovanovich, 1980).

Mendelson, Cheryl. *Home Comforts: The Art & Science of Keeping House* (New York: Scribner, 1999).

Mitchell, Margaret. *Gone With the Wind* (New York: Warner Books, 1999).

Oakley, Ann. *The Sociology of Housework* (New York: Alfred A. Knopf, 1976).

O'Brien, Patricia. *The Woman Alone* (New York: Time Books, 1974).

Obst, Lynda. *Hello, He Lied: And Other Half Truths from the Hollywood Trenches* (New York: Broadway Books, 1996).

Orenstein, Peggy. *Flux: Women on Sex, Work, Love, Kids, and Life in a Half-Changed World* (New York: Doubleday, 2000).

Parrott, Ursula. *Ex-Wife* (New York: American Library, 1989).

Pearson, Allison. *I Don't Know How She Does It: The Life of Kate Reddy, Working Mother* (New York: Alfred A. Knopf, 2002).

Pearson, Patricia. *When She Was Bad: How and Why Women Get Away with Murder* (Toronto: Random House of Canada, 1997).

Rauch Kennedy, Sheila. *Shattered Faith: A Woman's Struggle to Stop the Catholic Church from Annulling Her Marriage* (New York: Pantheon Books, 1997).

Sanger, Joan. *Regulating Girls and Women: Sexuality, Family, and the Law in Ontario, 1920–1960* (Oxford: Oxford University Press, 2001).

Schiff, Stacy. *Véra (Mrs. Vladimir Nabokov)* (New York: Picador, 2000).

Schneider, Sherrie, and Ellen Fein. *The Rules: Time-Tested Secrets for Capturing the Heart of Mr. Right* (New York: Warner Books, 1996).

Scott, Joan. "Rewriting History" in *Behind the Lines: Gender and the Two World Wars*, from Margaret Higgonet et al., eds. (New Haven: Yale University Press, 1988).

Shalit, Wendy. *A Return to Modesty: Rediscovering the Lost Virtue* (New York: Free Press, 1999).

Shapiro, Jane. *The Dangerous Husband* (Boston: Little, Brown and Co., 1999).

Shapiro, Laura. *Perfection Salad: Women and Cooking at the Turn of the Century* (New York: Modern Library, 2001).

Shorter, Edward. *The Making of the Modern Family* (New York: Basic Books, 1975).

Simons, Margaret A., ed. *Feminist Interpretations of Simone de Beauvoir* (University Park: Pennsylvania State University Press, 1995).

Spain, Daphne, and Suzanne Bianchi. *Balancing Act: Motherhood, Marriage and Employment Among American Women* (New York: Russell Sage Foundation, 1996).

Stark, Marg. *What No One Tells the Bride: Surviving the Wedding, Sex After the Honeymoon, Second Thoughts, Wedding Cake, Freezer Burn, Becoming Your Mother* (New York: Hyperion, 1998).

Starkey, David. *Six Wives: The Queens of Henry VIII* (New York: HarperCollins, 2003).

Steinem, Gloria. *Revolution from Within: A Book of Self-Esteem* (New York: Little, Brown and Co., 1993).

Stewart, Martha, Christopher Baker, and Elizabeth B. Hawes. *Martha Stewart Weddings* (New York: Clarkson Potter, 1987).

Stone, Lawrence. *Family, Sex and Marriage in England* (New York: HarperCollins, 1983).

Swallow, Wendy. *Breaking Apart: Dreaming of Divorce* (New York: Hyperion, 2001).

Talese, Gay. *Thy Neighbor's Wife* (New York: Ivy, 1993).

Tocqueville, Alexis de. *Democracy in America* (New York: Schocken Books, 1974).

Tone, Andrea. *Devices and Desires: A History of Contraceptives in America* (New York: Hill and Wang, 2001).

Visser, Margaret. *The Way We Are* (Toronto: HarperPerennial, 1994).

Waite, Linda J., and Maggie Gallagher. *The Case for Marriage: Why Married People Are Happier, Healthier, and Better Off Financially* (New York: Doubleday, 2000).

Walker, Lenore. *The Battered Woman* (New York: Harper & Row, 1977).

Wang, Vera. *Vera Wang on Weddings* (New York: HarperResource, 2001).

Weiner-Davis, Michele. *The Sex-Starved Marriage: A Couple's Guide to Boosting Their Marriage Libido* (New York: Simon & Schuster, 2003).

Whyte, William Hollingsworth. *The Organization Man* (New York: Simon & Schuster, 1972).

Wolf, Naomi. *Promiscuities: The Secret Struggle for Womanhood* (Toronto: Vintage Canada Edition, 1998).

Wurtzel, Elizabeth. *Bitch: In Praise of Difficult Women* (New York: Anchor Books, Doubleday, 1998).

Yalom, Marilyn. *A History of the Wife* (New York: HarperCollins, 2001).

Index

as independent and happy, 231–32
the perceived advantages of, 2
perceived flaws in, 201–3, 233–34
surrogate "families" and, 221
as unwed mothers, 215, 221–22
Until the Twelfth of Never (book), 193
Up the Sandbox (film), 81

Valcin, Mimi, 226
Valentine's Day: Women Against Men (book), 196
van de Velde, Theodoor, 124–25
Véra (book), 276
Viagra, 124, 126
vibrators (mechanical), 122–24
Victoria (magazine), 68
violence, domestic. *See* abuse (wife)
Virgin Bride Superstores, 35
virginity, ascribed importance to, xii, 5,
    128–31

wages
    advantages in due to having a wife,
        247–49
    gender gaps in, 247
Wagner, Jane, 124
Wagner, Lindsay, 212
Waite, Linda J., 132, 248
Waiting to Exhale (book, film), 176
Walker, Leonore E., 153–55, 162, 188
Walters, Barbara, 17
Wang, Vera, 35–37, 39–40, 52, 62
Ward, Robin, 27
The Wealth of Nations (book), 264
Wedding Bell Blues (film), 202
wedding gowns, as the main focus at
    weddings, 39–40
the "wedding industrial complex," 27, 33–
    35, 37, 42, 45, 47, 50, 52–54, 56, 64, 73, 98,
    202, 204, 215, 220, 224, 271
The Wedding Planner (film), 167
wedding(s). *See also* Disney World; doves;
    fireworks; marriage(s), 45
    ambivalence over "traditional," 42
    commercial industry and, 27–64
    as eclipsing the marriage, 59

irrational nature of, 59–60
religious, 42
rings and, xii
as TV ratings boosters, 30
Weddings (book), 41–42
Weil, Lori, 48
Weiner-Davis, Michele, 108, 132
Weitzman, Susan, 165
Welch, Jack, 178–79, 243
Welch, Jane Beasley, 178–79, 243–44
Weldon, Fay, 175
Wendt, Gary, 237, 244
Wendt, Lorna Jorgenson, 237–41, 244–45,
    253, 263
Wentworth, Alexandra, 39
Weston, Edward, 276
Wetlaufer, Suzy, 178
Wharton, Edith, 98
Whateley, William, 117
What Falls Away (book), 180
What Men Want (book), 115
What No One Tells the Bride (book), 63
What Our Mothers Didn't Tell Us (book),
    102, 129
What's Love Got to Do with It (film), 166
When She Was Bad (book), 152
White, Theodore, 274
Whitehead, Dafoe, 228
Whiting, Kristin, 234
Who's Afraid of Virginia Woolf? (film), 81
Who Wants to Marry a Millionaire
    (TV show), 32–33
Why Men Don't Iron (book; TV series), 84
Why Men Marry Some Women and Not Others
    (book), 5, 226
Whyte, William H., 245
Why There Are No Good Men Left (book), 6, 228
Wide Sargasso Sea (book), 273
Widow's Delight (film), 123
wife. *See also* marriage(s); rescue; schools;
    wives
    the avenging, 171–83, 189–99
    the career of, xii
    changing cultural expectations of a, 10–
        11, 24–25, 77–79, 105